MARXISM

One Hundred Years
in the Life of a Doctrine

BY BERTRAM D. WOLFE

Marxism: One Hundred Years in the Life of a Doctrine

Three Who Made a Revolution

Communist Totalitarianism

Strange Communists I Have Known

Khrushchev and Stalin's Ghost

MARXISM

One Hundred Years in the Life of a Doctrine

by Bertram D. Wolfe

THE DIAL PRESS · NEW YORK 1965

To the cartographers and travelers
—and those who have lost their way—
on the journey to Utopia

CONTENTS

Part V. The Flaw in the Foundation

Part VI. Problems of Utopia

INTRODUCTION

The two key works of Marx are the *Communist Manifesto* and *Das Kapital*. The first became a hundred years old in 1948; in 1967 the world will observe the hundredth anniversary of the publication of the second. For a world in flux, a century is a long time. To examine the fate of these two polar works of Marxism, and the passions and deeds that sprang from them, is to get a deeper insight into the history of that century.

In the beginning, neither book seemed influential. The *Manifesto*, despite its popular form, programmatic character, brilliant rhetorical flourishes, and sweeping and confident generalizations, had so little influence on the risings of 1848 for which it was intended, that the authors themselves, returning to their native Rhineland to engage in combative journalism and political action, found it expedient to dissolve the tiny League of Communists that had formed around the *Manifesto* (Marx did this by use of a dictatorial power invested in him, much to the indignation of the handful of Communists), and to conceal the *Manifesto*'s principles and proposals. The journal which some well-to-do Rhinelanders entrusted to Marx's editorship was run not as an organ of Communism but—or so its masthead proclaimed—an "Organ of Democracy." Later Marx and Engels were to offer a number of not always concordant explanations of this subterfuge. Several years after Marx's death, Engels wrote to Florence Kelley in America:

> We joined the democratic party as the only possible means of getting the ear of the working class.

And in a retrospective historical sketch on the *Neue Rheinische Zeitung*, he wrote:

> The banner under which we had to take our stand . . . could only be the banner of democracy. . . . Had we been unwilling . . . we should have had no choice but to teach communism in some little hole-in-the-corner sheet, and, instead of a large party of action, to found a little sect.

In their private letters to each other during 1848, the two friends were more explicit. Thus, while Engels was in the nearby Rhenish town of Barmen, trying to get additional shareholders for the new journal, he wrote to Marx:

If a single copy of our seventeen-point program were to be distributed here, then we would be finished.[1]

If the doctrines of the *Manifesto* could not be publicly advanced by its own authors in 1848, the more ponderous *Das Kapital* got no notice at all upon publication—except, to Marx's astonishment, in a land which seemed to him quite unsuitable for its application: "precapitalist," nonindustrial Russia.[2]

In Western Europe, Engels had to write virtually all the reviews and get them published as best he could under his own name and various pseudonyms. He even proposed to stir up some interest in the work by attacking it "from a bourgeois standpoint" under yet another pseudonym, and for this got Marx's approval as well as formulations for certain passages.[3]

---

[1] The letter to Florence Kelley is in Marx-Engels, *Ausgewaehlte Briefe*, Berlin, 1935, p. 477; the historical sketch of the *Neue Rheinische Zeitung* is in Marx-Engels, *Werke* (hereafter referred to as *Werke*), Berlin, 1962, Vol. XXI, p. 18; the letter of Engels to Marx is dated April 25, 1848, *Marx-Engels Gesamtausgabe* (hereafter referred to as *MEGA*), III, 1, p. 100. The "seventeen-point manifesto" was drawn up by Marx in Paris in March 1848. It is less sweeping and more moderate than the *Communist Manifesto*, making as its first demand the conversion of "all Germany" into "a single indivisible republic." The seventeenth demand is "universal free elementary education." Its best demands are all realizable without revolution in a democratic society, and the modern "welfare state" has gone far beyond them. The document in full is in *MEGA*, I/7, pp. 3–4. It is discussed more fully in Chapter IX.

[2] One year after his book appeared, Marx wrote to Kugelmann: "A few days ago a Petersburg bookseller surprised me with the news that *Das Kapital* is now in print in a Russian translation. . . . It is an irony of fate that the Russians, whom I have fought unceasingly for twenty-five years and not only in Germany but in France and England, too, have always been my 'patrons.' In 1843 and 1844 in Paris, the Russian aristocrats treated me with the greatest consideration. My attack on Proudhon (1847), and the one on Duncker (1859) sold nowhere as well as in Russia. And the first foreign nation to translate *Das Kapital* is the Russian. But one must not take it too seriously. . . . They always snatch at the most extreme things the West offers. It is pure gluttony (*gourmandise*), as with a part of the French aristocracy during the eighteenth century. *Ce n'est pas pour les tailleurs et les bottiers,* said Voltaire at that time of his own enlightenment. This doesn't prevent the same Russians from becoming scoundrels as soon as they have entered into the service of the State." (*Briefe an Kugelmann* 2d edition, Berlin, 1924, pp. 56–57.) Now that *Das Kapital* is rounding out a hundred years of existence, it is no longer possible to accept Marx's simple explanation of Russian "gourmandise" and Western Europe's satiety as adequate to the startling fact that in Russia the rulers claim to chart their course by a book which no Western European land accepts. As we look at the British, German, and American labor movements we are tempted to think that Marx might have come closer by paraphrasing Voltaire: *Ce n'est pas pour les travailleurs et les ouvriers.*

[3] The letters of Marx and Engels on these various reviews are in *MEGA*, III/3, pp. 422, 423, 432, 440, 442, 443. The nine reviews written by Engels are republished in *Werke*, Vol. XVI, pp. 207–309. Eventually there was a review by

Yet these two books, the slender *Manifesto* with its ringing slogans and confident generalizations, and the ponderous *Das Kapital*, left their deep impress upon the succeeding century. Merely to hear the call to battle in the war cries of the *Manifesto*, and to know that, in his unread and for many unreadable, masterpiece, *Das Kapital*, Marx had "proved" that "with the necessity of a natural process" a socialist society was developing within the existing order and that the day must "inevitably" come when the expropriators would be expropriated—these certitudes have had a powerful influence in many lands and on many generations. Certain aspects of the history of our own time cannot be understood without taking account of their influence.

The books themselves have had a strange and various fate. Many intellectual Marxists of the Western World are today uncomfortable about both of them and seek to take refuge in the quite different spirit of the work of a still younger Marx: his notebooks of 1844. This is the more surprising for they were but notebooks embodying a transitory stage in the development of Marx's thought, and some of the points of view in which these latter-day Marxists take refuge were soon sloughed off by Marx himself, even mocked at many times in his later writings.

Many of the slogans and rhetorical formulations of the *Communist Manifesto*, drastically simplified, passed into the common coin of socialist speeches and writings, then into the pronouncements of rulers of various types of "socialist" nations. The rest has been quietly consigned to oblivion.

Das Kapital, because it offered itself as the more serious work, indeed, Marx's *chef d'oeuvre*, the scientific underpinning and moral foundation of his doctrine, has had tougher going. History, which was its chosen court of last resort, has ruled against its dynamic schemata and its apocalyptic prophecies. The term *capitalism*, which Marx popularized, has passed into journalese virtually unexamined. The questions he asked so powerfully and insistently have had a stimulating effect on economic theory. The passion with which he expounded his views is moving, the social history and criticism illuminating, the sardonic examination of rival schools of thought remain models of ponderous and deadly satirical writing. But of *Das Kapital's* basic intellectual structure nothing now stands up. Its very approach to the economy of modern industrial society has been

Schweitzer in Lassalle's *Sozial-demokrat*, one by Professor Duehring in Meyer's *Encyclopedia*, and one by Josef Dietzgen which Marx helped to place in Liebknecht's *Demokratisches Wochenblatt*.

bypassed by contemporary economics, which concerns itself not with abstract definitions of the nature of value but with the problems of the optimal employment of scarce resources for competing ends.

Even in Russia, the self-proclaimed land of Marxism, economists and planners have had to ignore the labor theory of value as a useful unit of measure in their planning. To a greater extent than in the Western World, where the market performs many of the functions of determining the optimal allocation of scarce resources, in the centralized, statized, command-economy of Russia the central problem has become the mathematical determination of the marginal or differential yield in alternative uses of scarce resources—capital, skills, labor, materials—among competing ends. Every rational directive of the total planners involves a theory and a mathematical computation in units that cannot be derived from Marx's economic doctrines.[4]

Though refuted by history and abandoned for the practical purposes of economic calculation and planning in the land where men

---

[4] On the embarrassing and reluctant abandonment of Marxian economics for modern Western economic theory and econometric calculation, see Robert W. Campbell, "Marx, Kantorovich, and Novozhilov: *Stoimost* versus Reality," in *The Slavic Review*, Seattle, October 1961, pp. 402–18; and Leon Smolinski, "What Next in Soviet Planning?" in *Foreign Affairs*, July 1964, pp. 602–13. Mr. Smolinski quotes leading Soviet economists concerning the blind alley into which Soviet planning is visibly heading; Glushkov's warning that with present methods the planning bureaucracy would grow thirty-six-fold by 1980 and require the services of the entire population for paper work; Kantorovich's estimate that the introduction of the reforms he proposes would raise Soviet industrial output by as much as 50 per cent without additional inputs; reports in *Izvestia* of April 20, 1963, and *Ekonomicheskaya Gazeta* of Nov. 10, 1962, to the effect that the project for the Novo-Lipetsk steel mill comprises 91 volumes totaling 70,000 pages and "blueprints the emplacement of each nail, lamp or washstand . . . everything except one thing: its economic effectiveness"; and other warnings to the effect that Soviet planning is drowning in a paper sea. The article then quotes and analyzes reform proposals of Professor Birman, Professor Liberman, mathematician V. A. Volkonskii, Professor A. Arzumanian, and others; and discusses the possibilities and the dangers involved in "the current transition from charismatics to mathematics in Soviet economic planning." The political bosses are proving to be recalcitrant to the reform suggestions, but then so is the economy. In any case, all three factors, the new theories, the technical experts, and the political bosses—not to mention the plant managers who are doggedly violating one directive to make a semblance of complying with another—are all making mincemeat of Marxian economic theory.

Of the "Marxist planning" of a Mao or a Castro or an Nkrumah it is best not to speak at all.

claim to steer their course by Marx, *Das Kapital* remains one of history's most influential books. No other economic treatise, from Adam Smith's *Inquiry into the Nature and Causes of the Wealth of Nations*, published in 1776, to John Maynard Keynes's *General Theory of Employment, Interest and Money*, published in 1936, can be said to have so deeply moved so many men in so many lands as this book, unread by most of them. Engels called it "the Bible of the Working Class"—other disciples have termed it "the Bible of Socialism." Both terms suggest the quasi-religious nature of its influence.[5]

Nowhere in the writings of Marx is there a clear definition of what he meant by socialism, or, for that matter, by feudalism or capitalism. But he was sure that each of these represented a system, the parts of which had an inner coherence, and that each system— except for that of socialism itself, in which history was to come to its predestined end—was fated by the laws of its inner development to become pregnant in time with the next, "higher" system. He did not, as do his simplistic descendants, see "feudalism" wherever there was latifundian land ownership and agricultural servitude. He recognized that there were many despotic states and self-contained village and tribal regimes where there was neither feudalism nor capitalism. But with great dedication he studied the land of most advanced industry in his time, convinced that, wherever modern industry advanced, there it begot capitalism and a proletariat, thereby becoming ripe for a new system which he called as a matter of political convenience now socialism and now communism.

If it is startling to see the Russian "planners," who swear by Marx, forced to ignore his labor theory of value in their actual planning, it is no less thought-provoking to find that the Marxian doctrine has been quite generally rejected by the labor movements of the industrially advanced lands to which he was so sure it did apply, while his name has become a household word in some of the far ends of the earth where modern industry and proletariat are virtually nonexistent, and where Marx was explicit in his statement that his theories did not apply.

In our country there is a kind of journalistic Marxist jargon which causes the correspondents of the *New York Times* for ex-

---

[5] *Cf.* the constant reference in Soviet literature to the *Communist Manifesto* as "the song of songs of Marxism." The liturgical phrase presumably originated with Stalin but continued to be used under Khrushchev, as, for example, in E. D. Modrzhinskaya, *Protiv Burzhuaznykh Falsifikatorov Marksizma: Kritika Nashikh Kritikov,* Moscow, 1958, p. 3.

ample to wire news of a "socialist Zanzibar," proclaim that "Algeria Chooses a Socialist Path," that "Ghana Is Viewed as Going Marxist," that "Uganda will restrict the growth of political parties and develop as a one-party Socialist State," and that "whereas Algeria's professed socialist model is Cuba, Tunisia's might be said to be Sweden," and so, bewilderingly around the nonindustrialized, nonbourgeois, non-proletarian, nondemocratic, and frequently tribal, portions of the globe.[6]

We can imagine how ironical Karl Marx would have been about the "Marxism" of North Vietnam, Algeria, Egypt, Burma, Ghana, Senegal, Uganda or Zanzibar, or Mao's China, Castro's Cuba, and Cheddi Jagan's Guiana! Yet in each of these preindustrial and "pre-proletarian" lands, some of them congeries of tribes ruled over by tribal chieftains or Western-trained intellectuals equipped with modern arms, the rulers invoke Marx's name to justify or to label euphemistically varying degrees of personal dictatorship, persecution of rival leaders or chieftains or opposition nationalist groups, and varying degrees of despotic, autocratic, or totalitarian rule. That invocation is part of the climate of our time, demanding of us that we re-examine and reassess Socialism and Marxism, and find out more about Marx's doctrines and deeds than most Americans have wanted to know.

As if to make our task more difficult, the great anthill society being run by the fusion of its ancient heritage of "oriental despotism" with the instruments and techniques of modern communist totalitarianism, the "People's Republic of China," has its own niceties concerning the application of the terms Marxist and socialist to

---

[6] All these quotations have been taken from the *New York Times* during January 1964, all but one appearing in the financial section of the single issue of January 20, 1964, which carried a special annual "African Business Review." But it must not be imagined that the *Times* has a monopoly among newspapers on this sort of thing, or that the month of January has a monopoly either. Any other month, indeed any other week of the last few years, has brought us at least one such analysis, of sometimes skeptical—the skepticism being shown by the use of quotation marks—and sometimes uncritical dicta concerning some such "Marxist" revolution. In serious publishers' catalogs have begun to appear books by African rulers on their "socialist" regimes. Thus the Spring catalog for the year 1964 of Frederick S. Praeger has a book by Kwame Nkrumah which "presents the outlines of ethical and moral precepts based on certain socialist and materialistic theories," and another by the President of Senegal, Leopold Sedar Senghor, entitled *African Socialism*. And in February 1965 President Achmed Ben Bella of Algeria compounded the confusion by telling Algerian union leaders that Algeria had adopted "Marxist economic analysis" but not "Marxist Ideology."

other, still less industrialized peoples. From the middle of December 1963 until near the middle of February 1964, the Chinese Premier, Chou En-lai with a suite of sixty, toured ten states of North, West, and East Africa to see what he could pick up or stir up, and to speak in the names of Marxism and Leninism. Aid (large principles and small deeds), subsidy, bribery, flattery, agitation against Western Imperialism and Soviet Marxism, offers of arms, guerrilla training, and support for various ventures and adventures, and impressive assurances that "the 650,000,000 people of China are with you!"— these and other open and secret goods were all part of his stock-in-trade on the journey. Many of the countries he visited call themselves Marxist and Socialist. Yet for reasons either doctrinal or more directly political, Chou En-lai gave the accolade that he was "leading his country on the path of socialism" only to Ben Bella in Algeria. To the governments of Ghana, Guinea, and Mali, he stubbornly refused to apply the term socialist. The decoration *Marxist* was not even pinned on Ben Bella![7]

The writings of Marx, and of his chief collaborator and popularizer, Engels, have been interpreted in startlingly different and opposing ways by differing and contentious adherents. Despite the claim to systematic unity and continuity, Marx himself went through various transformations in his own lifetime. His original writings, thoughts, and deeds have since then been buried under successive layers of commentary and interpretation, popularization, oversimplification, and specious rationalization, to produce warring creeds, each invoking his name. There is Orthodox Marxism (with how many orthodoxies?); Revisionism (with what varied revisions!); Marxism-Leninism; Stalinism; Trotskyism; Khrushchevism; Titoism; Maoism; and such Marxisms of Asia, Africa and Latin America as Baathism, Nasserism, and Castroism, which, for intellectual purposes, we need not take too seriously yet whose influence on political acts and political passions may be serious indeed.

Politically, the last hundred years have not dealt kindly with Marxism in Western Europe, which was Marx's theoretical model and intellectual home.

In England, the land on which Marx based his analytical studies, the Labour Movement has all along rejected him.

---

[7] On this tour and its selling devices and objectives, see Robert A. Scalapino, "Sino-Soviet Competition in Africa," in *Foreign Affairs*, July 1964, pp. 640–54, and the same author's *The Sino-Soviet Conflict in Perspective*, Institute of International Studies, Chinese Series, Reprint No. 133, Berkeley, 1964.

In France, the war between what Marx himself called "our German theory" and French Socialism, was a hundred years' war with no real truces. Now there has arisen in Paris a strange mélange of Roman Catholic theology, warmed-over Kierkegaard and Hegel, intellectual fellow-travelerism, bits of the young Marx of the notebooks of 1844, a dash of eighteenth-century rationalism and anti-clericalism, flavored with sauces from Blanqui, Proudhon and Saint-Simon, all heated in the same pot by the warmth of power: the fact that the Communist Party is the largest party in France and the Soviet Union the greatest power on the Continent. In any case, the French Communist Party is not Marxist in any sense that Marx would have recognized, nor is the French Socialist Party.

In his native Germany, it was Lassalle, whom he detested and envied, who founded and led the first real German labor movement.[8] In its latest program, adopted at Bad Godesberg in 1959, German Social Democracy declared that "the SPD traces its origin back to the General Workers' Union, which Ferdinand Lassalle founded in Leipzig in 1863, and not to the Social Democratic Workers' Party [formed as a counterforce by some of Marx's disciples], which was brought into being in Eisenach six years later." Thus another hundred-year anniversary of Marxism is remembered, and rejected. The new program of the German Social Democracy, moreover, comes out flatly against total nationalization ("socialization") and for a "mixed economy." The Party defines itself not in terms of class or class struggle but as "a community of people of various trends of faith and thought, whose unity rests on a common sense of moral values and a unity of political purpose."

The Dutch, the Swedes, the Swiss, even the Austrian Socialists, once so noted for their Marxist orthodoxy that it gave rise to the term "Austro-Marxism," have all adopted programs closely similar to

---

[8] The letters of Marx and Engels to each other are full of bitter, niggling and denigrating expressions concerning Lassalle, in which Marx uses such epithets as *Baron Izzy, little Jew Braun, Jewish Nigger,* etc. Many of these passages are so unpleasant that they have been little quoted by commentators, who feel uneasy when they make use of them. Publicly they carried on a war against Lassalle's organization and his programmatic writings, and after his death tried to prevent the unity of their own disciples with the Lassalleans, and to discredit and refute the formulations of the joint program drawn up at the unifying congress. The reader can get a fair sampling of Marx's attitude toward Lassalle in Chapter XI, entitled "The 'Jewish Nigger,'" in Edward Hallett Carr's *Karl Marx: A Study in Fanaticism,* London, 1938. Marx's disquisition to Engels on the evidence and evil effect of the supposed mixture of Jew and Negro in Lassalle is in *MEGA,* III/3, p. 84.

that of the German Socialists. The Dutch program makes clear what is behind the abandonment of total nationalization and other sacrosanct Marxist dogmas by including a specific warning against "State Socialism and the bureaucratic assumption of power." Both the course of development in Western Europe and the abhorrence of what Lenin and his disciples have made of their Marxism, have taught compelling lessons to these parties.[9]

In the United States Marx's doctrines have not been taken seriously enough to be seriously studied. Only after world leadership was thrust upon us did we become aware of the fact that many of our allies in the struggle against totalitarian communism regard themselves as democratic socialists: two successive embattled mayors of West Berlin, Ernst Reuter and Willi Brandt; England with its Labour Party government; two successive Indian premiers; leaders of the Scandinavian peoples, and of Belgium, and other countries run by social democratic coalition-governments; Italy, with first one and then two socialist parties in its predominantly Christian Democratic government, and Austria, which has had three consecutive socialist presidents spanning the two decades from 1945 to 1965. At the same time we have heard the name of Marx invoked in the most unexpected places on the Asian and African continents. It is no longer sufficient for Americans simply to be against a doctrine which they have not taken the trouble to study or understand.

Beginning with Marx and Engels themselves, a great many Marxians have sought to give learned explanations of America's neglect of their theory, and to predict just when and how America would overcome this "theoretical" or "cultural" lag. To German Marxists like Sorge, who had emigrated to America, Engels wrote to explain that as soon as the frontier with its free land had disappeared, or as soon as chattel slavery had been abolished, or as soon as a nationwide labor movement had been formed and had acquired some experience in action, then "things will move faster, just like everything else in America."

But eight or nine decades later, with the frontier gone, slavery abolished, and a permanent labor movement formed, the lag, if lag it was, still continued. America remained as indifferent to the the-

---

[9] *Basic Program of the Social Democratic Party,* adopted at Bad Godesberg, 1959; *News from Germany,* Bulletin of the German Social Democracy, April–July 1963. The programs of the other parties were also adopted in 1959, except that of Austria (1958) and of Sweden (1944).

ories of the founders of "scientific socialism" as it had been in their lifetime. Perhaps more so, for the age of Greeley and Dana, and of American utopias like New Harmony and Brook Farm, were far in the past.

Now suddenly, with the "giant strides," the "seven-league boots" and "speed of a prairie fire," to which Engels referred as so characteristically American, all at once the colleges and universities of the United States are taking to the study of latter-day Marxism, Marxism-Leninism, or communism. Rejection and denunciation no longer seem enough to the nation which finds itself thrust into a place of world leadership with socialist leaders among its allies and communist governments as its opponents. Nor is uninformed rejection sufficient for a land which finds the soldiers and officers of its far-flung armies unable to defend themselves with understanding and rational argument against the clichés of indoctrinators and brainwashing jailers.

But where shall we turn for knowledge and understanding? How enter into a fruitful and self-confident dialogue with those who assail us in this unwonted language? Teachers, texts, concepts, real knowledge of the subject matter, all the essential tools are lacking. The news columns of our great journals are confusing, their editorials incompetent to handle these issues. On our campuses we hear such formulations as the "Marxist theory of the State" when what is meant is the Leninist theory; the "Marxist concept of the Party" when Lenin's organization doctrines are intended. Even in the special area studies on East Europe, Russia, and China, there are a surprising number of graduate students and, for that matter, instructors, who know Marx only as he has been filtered through the prism of Leninism or Stalinism, or the still more poverty-stricken "theoretical" dicta of Tito, Khrushchev, and Mao Tse-tung.

As in high places in Asia and Africa, so in our journals and on our campuses one hears of the "Marxist" theory of imperialism. Properly speaking there is no theory of imperialism in Marx and Engels. If one combs the writings of Marx from end to end, one finds the word *imperialism* used only to refer to the imperial structure and domestic policy of the Second French Empire under Napoleon III. When Marx thought of the policy of territorial conquest in Europe itself, he wrote of such conquest in moral and historical terms as something anachronistic and long outlived, something which it was disgraceful and criminal of Bismarck to have "revived in the second half of the nineteenth century" in the conquest of Alsace and Lorraine. When he wrote of the colonialism of European powers in Asia, Marx wrote of it as a cruel and brutal force but one making for "progress" in the backward regions of the earth. Harsh to be sure, as for Marx all progress is likely to be, yet salutary as well, as it breaks its way into the millennial slumber of the patriarchal villages and despotic regimes of the Orient; and moves these stagnant peoples at last into "the main course of historical development."[10]

Indeed, there is no Leninist theory of imperialism either. The great age of Europe's expansion overseas and the formation of the Spanish, Portuguese, French, Dutch, and British Empires was over when, at the end of the nineteenth century, there came one more flare-up, a belated final imperialist spree amidst the unrewarding lands of Africa. Then the anti-imperialist response came first from Little Englanders, next from liberals and Christian Socialists like Hobson and Morel, then from Marxists like Hilferding and Rosa Luxemburg. Lenin did not even concern himself with these theories until he had to explain the difference in his attitude toward "capitalist" wars from that of Marx and Engels, and justify his program of "defeatism" for all countries in World War One, including his own. This was so unlike the attitude of Marx and Engels toward all the wars of their day that he had to invent a new "era" requiring new tactics. From shreds and patches of Hobson, Hilferding, and Luxemburg he put together his little brochure on "imperialism." In retrospect it is interesting to note that the hero-people of Hobson's anti-imperialist crusade were the Dutch Boers of South Africa, today the incarnation of the imperialist race supremacy theory in the African continent.[11] And the government which Lenin founded and

---

[10] Marx's attitude toward "imperialism" and its contrast with the theories of Hobson, Hilferding, Luxemburg, and Lenin are not treated in the present work, since I plan to write a separate study of Lenin's "Imperialism."

[11] Lenin, too, when he got around to discovering his "new era of imperialism" often made the Boer War the starting point. In the book he set Zinoviev to writing under his editorship, we read: "The Boers were the aggressors, the English troops formally on the defensive. . . . And yet, the Boer War was a just war on the part of the Boers, and the world proletariat took their side." So, too, did Tsar Nicholas II! (See the comments at the appropriate point in the Tsar's diary, and Sinowjew, *Der Krieg und die Krise des Sozialismus*, 1924, p. 196.) The original work was written in 1915–16, and this section, like the entire first part, "was read through by V. I. Lenin, whose view had a decisive influence on it." By 1924 Zinoviev felt called upon to add a footnote explaining that though "the Boer people were fighting for their independence against imperialism, this did not hinder the Boers from exploiting a part of the native population."

which supposedly incorporated in its very foundations his anti-imperialist doctrines, has today become the last aggressive empire in Europe, ruling now over areas as great as England ruled, areas more advanced and more used to independent nationhood than those which once made up the British Empire. The only serious rival for the distinction thus enjoyed by the Soviet Empire is that empire in Asia ruled over by another avowed Marxist-Leninist, Mao Tse-tung.

In dealing with Marxism we are not dealing merely with theoretical formulations but with the thoughts and deeds of a man whose proudest boast was that his work represented "a unity of theory and practice." "The philosophers," he wrote at the beginning of his career, "have only *interpreted* the world in different ways, but the point is to *make it different.*" This effort to "change the world" involved a steady stream of articles, letters, instructions to disciples, polemics against rival tinkerers with the social order, manifestoes, tactical and programmatic pronouncements, prophecies based upon assumed scientific insight, efforts at organization and struggle. Marx, and with him Engels, who continued these activities for another twelve years after Marx's death, made constant attempts to intervene in the life of the German, French, and British labor and socialist movements, and in the foundation and guidance of an international socialist movement. They engaged in political pamphleteering and journalism. They sought to persuade already existing organizations to accept their directives, their manifestoes, programs, and tactical proposals. These multiform activities form the core of both the Marxism-in-theory and the Marxism-in-action which are the objects of the present study. If one would know what Marx's theories meant to Marx himself, one must study attentively these, his own applications of his doctrines, his attempts to intervene actively in the history of his own time, to shape the course of future history, and to accelerate what he took to be history's ineluctable fulfillment. His predictions were intended as self-fulfilling predictions, predictions which he was determined to make come true.

Closely related to this study of Marxism-in-action is another problem which gives to this present work its focus.

Marxism was a nineteenth-century product, perhaps the most influential social, economic, and political theory which the nineteenth century engendered. But in 1914, when a general crisis in Western civilization manifested itself in the first total war of our time, all the grand theories of the preceding century broke down. Like the existing institutions, all the existing theories proved inadequate to the Time of Troubles then beginning. The Marxian Socialist International and Marxian theory and practice, though they had claimed to foresee the future of mankind and indeed to embody the future in themselves, proved as vulnerable as all the other theories and institutions. One day of war and the great Socialist International was in ruins. Its parties entered into the war, and the war entered into its parties and its doctrine. First came shocked silence, and afterward mutual recriminations among yesterday's confident preachers of international solidarity.

Lenin charged then that all the other leaders of the socialist parties of other lands, and all the leaders of other socialist parties in his own land, had betrayed the heritage of Marx. He bombarded the "traitors" with a hail of quotations from Marx and Engels. They answered that it was he who was the betrayer of the heritage. For every quotation of his, they offered a dozen by way of rebuttal. So badly did he fare in the battle of quotations (though not of course in the fusillade of abusive epithets in which no man was a better marksman), that he set his lieutenant, Gregory Zinoviev, to writing the extraordinarily fat book entitled *War and the Crisis of Socialism* to which we have already referred, with the intention of explaining away most of the writings of Marx and Engels on the wars of their own day. Since by temperament Lenin was an orthodox believer to whom the writings of Marx and Engels were all "scientific," i.e. sacred, texts, he made the claim that all these writings were correct and appropriate to their day, but not applicable to "the changed historical conditions." (This was perilously like the words which Lenin had found an abomination when they had been uttered by the "revisionist" Bernstein.)

It was the need to hold that Marx and Engels were in their day infallible and at the same time to prove that he operated in a new epoch requiring new tactics, which caused Lenin, after considerable wavering as to the appropriate date, to set "the era of imperialism" as something new in principle which had begun only after 1895, the last year of Engels' life. This was the more necessary because one of Engels' activities in his very last years was impressively to depict the outlines of a war in which Germany would be on one side and France and Russia on the other, and to predict, for once with startling rightness, the probable line-up of a number of other countries and the course of the war, a war in which Engels declared that the

German Social Democrats would rally to the defense of their country.

The running battle of quotations among the broken remnants of the old Socialist or Marxian International and the new Third International continued right up to the Second World War, growing constantly more complicated by virtue of the appearance of new combatants, new meanings given to old terms, and new conditions of which indeed Marx had never dreamed. Civil war, purge, and assassination have been used to reinforce one interpretation as against another. Always the central issue was declared to be: Who is the true guardian of the heritage of Marx and its "creative developer," who the unfaithful heir and "revisionist," the heretic, the betrayer?

But what is the heritage? Who has been faithful and who traitor to what? What words of Marx and what deeds, and what spirit, can the combatants point to? What Marxism-in-theory and what Marxism-in-action is the subject of their contention?

Having found it necessary to examine this question in the course of my studies in the intellectual history of the Russian Revolution, I have quarried from those studies the sections dealing with the Marxist heritage to which the contesting heirs lay claim, and which they denounce each other for having betrayed. It is my hope that this little work will throw some fresh light on the controversies, verbal and physical, that form so large a part of the history of the socialist movement in 1914, of the Russian Revolution of 1917, and of many subsequent events to the present moment.

As once men slew and were slain in disputes which appeared to turn around such questions as infant or adult baptism, so men have died for one interpretation of this heritage as against another. But the heritage is complex and varied, unified by a single person and a temperament rather than by any systemic logic or consistency. Much of its appeal has lain precisely in the fact that for its adepts it is at once science and faith. In its vast, emotion-charged, constantly changing and internally contradictory exposition and application (constantly changing even in the day of its founder and in his deeds), there are to be found the most contrary propositions, moods, attitudes, approaches, the most varied relations to reality. The very combination of often logically incompatible things has facilitated Marxism's acceptance, in whole or in part, in spirit or in letter, by the most varied temperaments. Sometimes its contradictory propositions are held by one and the same mind, in tandem fashion, or in separate, logic-tight compartments.

Who then was the traitor who in 1914 betrayed the heritage? Who in 1917? Who guards it faithfully, and who betrays it now? The answer lies, as I shall try to demonstrate in a multiple ambiguity in Marxism: ambiguity in the spirit of Marx himself, ambiguity in the heritage he left, and ambiguity in those who claimed to be his heirs. But with the demonstration that Marxism is an ambiguous heritage, our problem is not ended, as well it might be if we were dealing with a mere exercise in logic. Indeed, with that verdict, our problem begins. . . .

ACKNOWLEDGMENTS

I owe a debt of gratitude to the Relm Foundation for making this study of Marxian writings possible; the Hoover Institution on War, Revolution, and Peace for granting facilities for my work; to the Staff and Librarians of the Hoover, Columbia, and Tamiment Institute Libraries for their friendly and generous help in research; to my wife for her editorial labors on the manuscript; and finally, to my publishers for their patience.

BERTRAM D. WOLFE
Spring 1965

PART I

Nationalism
or Internationalism?

For romanticism, in its rebellion against rationalism and skepticism, proceeded to create strange gods. In truth, the mighty idols of today, the idols of nation, and race, and class, all owe much to the romanticists. The latter did their work well: even now it takes an effort to realize that once upon a time, for instance in the Gospels, all these things were not believed.
—Nicholas V. Riasanovsky

To Marx, self-enrichment seemed the natural aim of man's political actions. But modern psychology has dived deeper into the ocean of insanity upon which the little barque of human reason insecurely floats.
—Bertrand Russell

In short, one may say anything about the history of the world, anything that might enter into the most disordered imagination. The one thing one cannot say is that it is rational.
—Fyodor Dostoevsky

Chapter 1

WAR AND THE UNIFICATION
OF GERMANY

The Russians want to utilize quickly the diplomatic union
with France. Bebel and I have been carrying on correspondence concerning this, and we are of the opinion that if the
Russians begin a war with us, we should be attacking the
Russians and their allies à l'outrance, no matter who these
allies may be. If Germany is beaten, we will be beaten with
her. Even in the best case the war will be so great that
Germany will be able to defend herself only by revolutionary means, and it is quite possible that we will have to be
in power and repeat the year 1793. . . . Though I would
consider it a great misfortune if it should come to war and
if this should at the same time put us in power, all the same
we ought to be ready for it. . . .

—Engels to Sorge,
October 24, 1891

Patriotism may be more ardent or less in each of us; its
nature is the same, its absence a monstrosity.

—Proudhon

Prussia needs to arm the entire population so that it can
withstand the two giants that will always threaten it from
East and West. Should the state fear its own people more?

—Clausewitz

"PEACE IS the first and indispensable condition of any emancipation
of the working class," said a unanimous resolution of the founding
Congress of the Socialist International in 1889. "The international

3

socialist party," resolved the Second Congress (1891), "is the true and only *party of peace*—the only means of preventing general war." The Third Congress (1893) began a debate on what the Socialist Parties could do to make good these boasts, a debate which continued in Congress after Congress, until the guns took up the argument in August 1914.

The Third Congress in 1893 resolved that socialists in parliament were obligated "to reject all military credits . . . demand *disarmament* . . . support all associations aiming at universal peace." Who doubted then, as the aging Engels said after the Congress, that "we [the International] are a great power . . . more depends on us than on the other Great Powers"?

In addresses to the multitudes in all the tongues of Europe, the proportions in which the watchwords of the International were mixed might vary, but the ingredients were always the same. For half a century, socialist, syndicalist, and anarchist speakers kept repeating: *The worker has no country to defend . . . he knows no frontier . . . he will not shoot at his class brothers across the border . . . he finds his main enemy at home . . . he regards the class war as the only holy war in which he is willing to shed his blood . . . the age of national wars between the great powers is now over,*[1] *for such a war would now surely bring social revolution . . ."*

Leon Trotsky, doctrinaire Marxist internationalist, was in Vienna in 1914 on the midsummer day when Austria declared war on Serbia. In a dispatch to *Kievskaya Mysl,* for which he was foreign correspondent, he wrote:

I wandered through the streets watching the multitudes demonstrate on the Ring. . . . Not "the public" but the real people, with scuffed shoes and calloused hands . . . black and yellow flags . . . patriotic songs, cries of *Alle Serben muessen sterben!*

What made these people demonstrate? . . . A national idea? But what national idea? Austria-Hungary is the negation of the national idea . . . where have the centrifugal tendencies hidden themselves? . . . The press, basing itself on these street demonstrations and

---

[1] Let not the reader, wise after the fact, laugh at this naïve expectation. Did not the economic wizard, Andrew Carnegie, when he set up the Carnegie Foundation for International Peace in 1910, wonder what role the Foundation could play after it had succeeded in abolishing war? He left it to the judgment of the trustees to decide what evil they would tackle next with what was left of the $10,000,000 with which he endowed them.

pathos-filled meetings . . . has proclaimed the complete reconcilia-
tion, of . . . Germans with Czechs, Poles with Ruthenians, oppres-
sors with oppressed, wolves with sheep—the complete triumph of the
state principle over the principle of nationalities. . . .

The mobilization and declaration of war have, as it were, swept
from the face of the earth all national and social contradictions in the
country. But that is only a historical postponement, a sort of political
moratorium. The notes have been extended to a new date, but they
will have to be paid. . . .

Trotsky was using Aesopian language to suggest that Russia too
was backward, bureaucratic, multinational, devoid of a national
idea; that in Russia, too, a promissory note was only being extended
as to due date, but in the end would have to be paid.

But above and beyond the Aesopian language, he was reporting
a bewildering, unpalatable, indigestible fact—a spectacle, moreover,
which in one or two more days would be repeating itself in all the
warring countries.

Sixteen years later, when Trotsky was writing *My Life* in exile on
the Island of Prinkipo, where he no longer needed Aesopian language for his description of this scene, he was still unable to come to
terms with it. Still he strove to grasp what he had stared at with
incredulous eyes on August 2, 1914. No, the force that had taken
possession of these internationalist workingmen and centrifugally
nationalist Czechs, South Slavs, and Poles of old Austria-Hungary,
he thought, could not have been the "national idea." It was "something different." But what?

The lives of the people pass in a monotony of hopelessness. . . .
The alarm of mobilization breaks in like a promise; the familiar and
long hated is overthrown, and the new and unusual reigns. . . . Still
more incredible changes are in store. . . . For better or for worse?
For better of course—what can seem worse . . . than "normal" conditions?

. . . A most amazing crowd fills the fashionable Ring, a crowd in
which hopes have been awakened. But wasn't a small part of these
hopes already being realized? At any other time would it have been
possible for porters, laundresses, shoemakers' apprentices, and young-
sters from the suburbs, to feel themselves masters of the Ring? War
affects everybody. Those who are oppressed . . . feel that they are
on an equal footing with the rich and the powerful.

It may seem a paradox, but in the moods of the Viennese crowd demonstrating to the glory of Hapsburg arms I detected something familiar to me from October days of 1905 in St. Petersburg . . .[2]

The "materialist interpretation of history," once its monistic, reductivist claims are rejected, can contribute some useful insights to historical thought. But here it is clear that historical materialism has failed an adept. In his bewilderment Trotsky has gone beyond his dogmas. His analysis has much in common with such anti-Marxist analysts of the psychology of war as Roepke and Bergson. Thus Roepke says:

War gives to the man of the masses, who suffers from an "insufficient social integration," a chance to satisfy his thirst for community and self-sacrifice.

Roepke, too, speaks of the pent-up emotion favorable alike "to war and revolution," which accumulates "when a great part of the people is subjected to an occupational servitude, a monotonous labor, a severe discipline in workshop and office, economic fluctuations of the market and the wages of labor."[3]

Karl Popper writes: "Nationalism appeals to our nostalgic desire to be relieved from the strain of individual responsibility." Aldous Huxley says of wartime:

For the average individual, that which renders life worthy of being lived is emotion. Boredom is an infinite source of moral misery. Now, in time of war, it is almost impossible to be bored.[4]

Bergson adds a touch of the sacred, an element absent in Roepke, and of course, in Trotsky. To Bergson love of country is:

. . . the only principle capable of neutralizing the tendencies of societies to disintegration . . . a warlike virtue, which may be tinged with mysticism, which mingles no calculations with its religion, which overspreads a great country, which is slowly and reverently evolved out of memories and hopes, out of poetry and love, with a faint perfume of every moral beauty under heaven. . . .[5]

Bergson's apostrophe is profoundly French. It can be matched

---

[2] Trotsky's dispatch to *Kievskaya Mysl* is in his *Collected Works*, Vol. IX, *Evropa v voine*, 1927, pp. 3–6. The quotation from *My Life*, New York, 1930, is on pp. 233–35.

[3] Roepke, *La Communauté internationale*, Geneva, 1947, p. 33.

[4] Popper, *The Open Society and Its Enemies*, Princeton, 1950, pp. 244–45. To Aldous Huxley's remark it should be added that there was an incredible boredom in trench life in World War One, but it was a boredom which, in Huxley's words, was "lived in emotion."

[5] Bergson, *The Two Sources of Morality and Religion*, Garden City, N.Y., 1954, p. 277.

by many luminous passages in the speeches and writings of France's greatest socialist, Jean Jaurès. Though the older German Marxists were by no means as negative and doctrinaire about patriotism as a Trotsky or a Luxemburg, one would look in vain for this touch of poetry in Engels or Bebel, though both were patriots enough to offer, in their old age, to "mount a horse" or "shoulder a rifle," if Russia, or Russia and France, should attack their country.[6]

Even in the richer and more flexible doctrine of Marx himself Marxism is ardently reductivist, striving to reduce the driving forces or war and nationalism to "material forces." But with the epigoni who called themselves Marxists or Marxist-Leninists, the driving forces that lead to war are further simplified to the point of naïve cynicism, in the employment of the explanatory principle of economic interest or material calculation.

The Marxists treat as mere epiphenomena, as distorted and deceptive reflections of economic interests in consciousness, such powerful emotions as pride, envy, hatred, xenophobia, thirst for national prestige, detestation of foreign rule, the sense of community, love of country. In a still more simplistic variant, these emotions are treated as the product of cunning deception, deliberately worked up by a crafty, unfeeling ruling class to camouflage its own interests, to excite the (of course) "backward" masses of one country against those of another, to distract them from their "real class interests" and draw them into the service of the calculating aims of their rulers. So it was that Lenin explained these emotions, and so the latest *History of the Communist Party of the Soviet Union* explains them too. The most serious cause of the First World War that *History* finds was "the striving of the imperialists to check the mighty revolutionary movement that had been growing in all lands during the preceding decades."[7]

---

[6] When Engels was sixty-two he wrote a letter to Bebel, in December 1882, in which he concluded: "But if it must come, I shall only hope that my old fracture does not keep me from mounting my horse again." Gustav Mayer, *Friedrich Engels, a Biography,* New York, 1936, p. 289. Bebel made many such statements, the first noted by his biographer, Kluehs, in 1880 (two years prior to the letters from Engels) and the last in 1907, at the age of sixty-seven: "Still ready, old boy that I am, to shoulder a rifle." See Kluehs, *August Bebel,* Berlin, 1923, pp. 68–78.

[7] *History of the Communist Party of the Soviet Union,* English, Moscow, 1960, pp. 185–87. The section on "Causes of the First World War" performs the feat of omitting altogether the assassination of the Austrian heir-apparent, Austria's attack on Serbia, and the conflicts of the Balkan powers with each other. In the

Another variant of pre-1914 Marxism, duly giving rise to a unanimous resolution in each Congress of the Socialist International, maintained that "the cause of war is capitalism," hence wars are "inevitable" as long as capitalism continues, but will vanish automatically and forever as soon as socialism prevails. In view of this, many held—Lenin foremost among them—that the very struggle against war was at best misguided pacifism: a struggle against a symptom rather than the cause. The core of Lenin's writings during World War One is a savage denunciation of all socialists who longed for and worked for a speedy peace without victory, in place of striving for "the defeat of their own ruling class" and the "transforming of the imperialist war into a civil war."

In all its variants, sophisticated as well as vulgar, Marxism tends to overlook the age-old nature of war itself: its occurrence throughout recorded history, and the indelible marks it has left upon the ruins of cultures that existed before recorded history began, and its occurrence under all "systems" and all "social orders." Marxism fails to take account of the deep-rooted power of nonmaterial passions, the reality of emotions not "called forth" by material structures, economic arrangements, or calculations not evoked by a "master class," or indeed, by any class.

In this shallow picture of man there is no place for the deeper and more terrible passions capable of taking complete possession of human beings, overpowering all calculation of personal safety or individual or class interest. For better or worse, man's psyche eludes this curious conception of a shopkeeper, in the midst of life's passionate turmoil, reckoning up the potential profit or loss in each venture and adventure.

Lenin himself would one day be impelled to contemplate with wonder the fact that the deeper passions of war had so overpowered all calculation on the part of the "international imperialists" concerning their "real interests" that "they" had already permitted his revolutionary government to exist for an entire year, and had not yet had the sense to bury their differences in order to unite and crush him. So too Stalin would be astonished to behold in 1941, when Hitler attacked the Soviet Union, that England and the United States did not join Hitler, as his doctrine taught him to expect. Rather, Eng-

---

early years of our century, muted and vulgarized echoes of Marx's "economic explanation" seeped into journalism and popular, "debunking historiography" as "the new craft of translating all *chansons de geste* into horse-trading." (For this apt formulation I am indebted to G. A. Borghese.)

land offered loyal, even uncritical alliance, while the United States—which had not yet suffered the attack on Pearl Harbor and was not even at war—proffered unstinting support without conditions of any kind.[8]

The failure of the Entente and the Central Powers in 1918 to unite against "the government of World Revolution" was the more incomprehensible to Lenin, as he told the Sixth Congress of the Soviets, because he had "openly declared war on the imperialists of all lands, taken away from them their capital invested in foreign loans, smashed them in the face, struck openly at their robber pockets." Struggling aloud with this strange phenomenon, Lenin told the Congress: "War's bloody fog has blinded their eyes!" It was the least Marxist statement he was ever to make on war . . . and the soundest.[9]

The *Communist Manifesto* treated nationalism as a dwindling survival from an earlier day, about to disappear for good. Yet it was nationalism that would set its seal upon the rest of the nineteenth century and dominate the twentieth to the present moment, and is spreading now from Europe, its home, to Asia and Africa, which hitherto had not known the nation.

The *Communist Manifesto* was printed in German in London, and mailed to the branches of the Communist League in Germany some time late in February 1848. On February 24, Paris rose; on March 13, Vienna; on March 15, Hungary declared its autonomy in the Hapsburg Empire, and the populace of Prague took possession of the streets of their city to demand Bohemian (Czech) autonomy, civil liberties and the abolition of serfdom; on March 18, barricades were set up in Berlin. Only the uprising in Paris, in its June aftermath, involved any special working-class questions: those of unemployment and "National Workshops."

If the *Manifesto* came too late to have any influence upon these risings, the risings themselves tested its resounding formulas as in a great social laboratory. This cosmopolitan and internationalist document which treated nationalism as dying or already dead, had

---

[8] With not one word about a just peace or the freeing of the nations seized in league with Hitler, Hopkins committed us to "all possible aid to Stalin in tanks, planes, and whatever was needed." (See Robert Sherwood, *Roosevelt and Hopkins*, New York, 1948, pp. 327–28, 333.)

[9] Lenin, *Sochineniya*, Vol. XXVIII, pp. 135–36. Except where otherwise indicated all quotations from Lenin are translated by me from the Fourth Russian Edition.

proposed itself as the program for what turned out to be the greatest explosion of nationalism Europe had ever known.

How was Marxism to comprehend this explosion? How come to terms with the fact that, far from marking the end, or a last flare-up, the year 1848 opened up a new epoch of nationalism for countries which scarcely had existed as nations, such as Marx's own native Germany with its three dozen independent princedoms and Mazzini's Italy with its splintered and alien sovereignties? How was Marxism to comprehend that in the following century national feeling would become a successful rival to socialism and even fuse with it in all sorts of startling and explosive combinations? How could Marxism accept the fact that, both in its everyday form and in its extreme manifestations in war, nationalism would give the fragmented and lonely crowd a sense of integration into a superindividual aggregate, a sense of collective destiny, a chance to satisfy the thirst for community and self-sacrifice? Or someday even set avowed Marxist and Communist states into conflict with each other?

Marx and Engels assumed that with them and their *Manifesto* the age of internationalism was beginning. But actually the great ages of internationalism were to be sought in the past: the Roman Empire with its *Pax Romana;* the feudal world with its localism, on the foundation of which arose those two ghosts of ancient Rome, the Holy Roman Empire and the Roman Catholic Church; the Age of the Enlightenment, with its "citizens of the world" and its cosmopolitan rationalism. In the nineteenth century the French Revolution, the romantic reaction, and the risings of 1848, all combined to create the strange gods of which this chapter's epigraph speaks: the idols of race and nation and class.

What the nineteenth century was gestating, then, was a new age of nationalism. The historic dates of its growth are 1793, 1848, 1870, 1914, 1939, 1948, 1956 to the present,[10] plus a veritable explosion of

---

[10] The year 1948 marks the open break between Tito and Stalin and the rise of Titoism in the Cominform and Communist Empire. The years 1956 to the present mark the break between Mao and Khrushchev as leaders of two Communist superpowers. Thus the development from the "internationalism" of the *Communist Manifesto* to the nationalism of the nations forming part of the International Communist Movement has taken place in a little over a century. But the ambiguities of national communism or "nationalistic internationalism" were already present in the *Communist Manifesto* and the historical situation in which its authors found themselves when they launched their famous declaration. All that was necessary to the development of non-Euclidean geometry was a set of circumstances which would prompt some thinker to challenge the axioms and postulates of Euclid. But in the case of the *Manifesto,* the very

new nations in Asia, Africa, and the Pacific Archipelago from 1945 to the time of this writing and beyond.

In 1913 Sir Norman Angell wrote that nationalism was now to "become for the European of our age the most important thing in the world, more important than civilization, human decency, kindness, pity; more important than life itself."

Nationalism was to be the religion at whose altar modern man would be most prone to worship, the cause for which millions would show themselves most ready to fight, suffer, and die. In the name of nationalism, Hitler would lead a whole nation into temporary madness. When Hitler attacked Communist Russia, Stalin would find that nationalism was a far better banner than communism with which to rally the Russian people. In the French underground, though the communists had all the experience and the disciplined organization, it was not the banner of Communism but of national resistance that would rally France to resume its struggle to exist, and would create the Fourth and the Fifth Republics.

Even as we watch, and think we have a firm hold on the phenomenon of nationalism, it is assuming yet another of its protean forms.

The two great power blocs that issued from World War Two disintegrate under our gaze at unequal rates and with unequal consequences for the respective blocs. The free world takes nationalism in its stride never having pretended nor desired to be a monolith, hence the pursuit of narrower national interests by a De Gaulle is no more than a complication of a picture that has been loosely confederal in its nature. But the would-be monolith of international communism has been shattered on the rock of nationalism. Both Communist Russia and Communist China have learned that national feeling and national interest do not disappear when a "camp" of Communist nations has been formed. Their quarrels have given even puppet rulers some elbow room for national maneuver. The Warsaw Pact and the Comecon were never more than shadows, by-products of the dogma that the economy, the polity, and the planning, of a "socialist world" would be international. They were reflexes of Moscow's long period of absolute hegemony, and an in-

---

history of the year in which it was launched and the psychic make-up of its authors themselves, called its axioms and postulates into question. The ambiguities have deepened in the heirs but they were already present and deep in the heritage, a sort of non-Marxian dialectic to match non-Euclidean geometry.

tended counterweight to the Atlantic Community. Today the phoe-
nix of nationalism revives inside the international communist bloc,
while Russia and China contend with each other as rival great-
power imperialisms rooted in their respective great-nation interests
as well as in their dogmas. These latter compel them to clothe
national contentions and imperialist rivalries in the raiment of
"orthodoxy" and "heresy" and of "communist internationalism," even
as they use the banner of nationalism in all lands where their power
or their influence reaches, to advance their own great-power interests, their ideological-hegemony aspirations, and their imperial
power. Meanwhile men of good will who yesterday regarded nationalism as an outlived survival of an earlier day, accept in puzzle-
ment and wonder the gift of the growing disintegration of the aggressive Communist Bloc from the hands of yesterday's bête noire,
the national spirit.

In Africa, vast geographical regions along the 2900-mile long
Congo River and its tributaries, in whose jungles and savannahs live
congeries of disparate warring tribes, were first grouped together
into larger units by colonizing powers merely for administrative
convenience—grouped together often by a line drawn across a map
by men who had never so much as seen the lands they thus divided
and put together without regard for the realities of geography and
social life. Then from these divisions, in the age of decolonization,
two or three "Congo Republics" have issued, proclaiming themselves
to be nations, seeking to turn the old tribal struggles into "political"
contests, to enlarge each "nation" at the expense of its neighbor, to
overcome the fragmentation of economically, ideologically, and
often geographically unconnected areas, in order to find for each
"new land" a voice, a common ideological framework, a political and
institutional structure, a "modern industrialized" economy, a life as a
nation.

The *Communist Manifesto* explained nationalism as an ideological "superstructure" which grew up on the "foundations" of the
need of the merchant-manufacturer class for a nationwide market
and a nationwide economy. Nationalism's function, Marx explained,
was to serve as a banner for a crusade to sweep away all medieval
localisms which hindered the development of such a national economy.

Yet the same *Manifesto* supported the struggle of the Poles for
national independence, although the reconstitution of an indepen-

dent and unitary Poland could be accomplished only by tearing Poland's fragments out of three already integrated great-nation economies. Thus Polish nationalism is somehow recognized as a passion independent of the "real economic foundation," a demiurge, growing great and powerful only after its nationwide economic foundation, if one ever existed at all, had already disappeared, and the three parts of Poland had been geared into the German, the Austrian, and the Russian economies. How was the "materialistic" conception of history to explain the tenacious national memory of the Poles living underground without an economic foundation for over one hundred and fifty years? During the period when Poland was an independent nation, culturally, linguistically, religiously, if not institutionally and economically, the Poles seemed scarcely aware of their national existence. But when the "economic foundation" disappeared, Polish nationalism, like Irish nationalism, waxed mighty until it possessed heart and head, crowding out all else. No calculated interest, no unity of market or economy, no love of the lost institution of independent fiefdoms whose nobles possessed the *liberum veto*, but a quixotic disregard for practical calculation and individual fate drove the notoriously "romantic" Poles to rise again and again—to tear themselves free from the "higher" economies and polities into which they had been integrated, whether these were the "higher bourgeois economies" of the nineteenth century, or the "higher proletarian economies" of the Soviet Union and her satellite empire into which the Poles have now been uneasily integrated.

If Marx and Engels were unable to explain by their schemata the inextinguishable nationalism of the extinguished Polish nation, which they supported, how much less able were they to come to terms with the nascent nationalist feelings of Czechs and South Slavs and other "historyless peoples" (as Marx and Engels called them), who were not yet born to independent economic and political life, and whose aspiration to be born they condemned?

The minuscule trading class that these peoples did possess was indifferent to the national feelings articulated by a handful of intellectuals, and dumbly cherished by millions of inarticulate peasants. Yet in the wake of World War One, whose immediate outbreak was triggered by the struggles of the Southern Slavs, these "historyless peoples" would be born into nationhood. In the wake of World War Two they would lose this independence—but already we have Tito's break with Stalin, the 1953 risings in Prague and East Berlin, the all-embracing Hungarian Revolution, and the Polish "October" of 1956, to remind us that Comecon or no Comecon, the national aspirations of the peoples of the Soviet Empire are not dead. "Polycentrism" may be an exaggerated term or a misleading one, but at the very least, it bespeaks the presence of national feeling and national difference inside the Communist Parties and the countries over which they rule.

War fits even less than nationalism into the materialist interpretation of history. Monstrous and terrible, rather than sordid and calculating, kindled by feelings deeper and more powerful than computation of loss and gain, reckless of all except victory, the driving forces of modern war are fierce untamable mass passions—pride, anger, xenophobia, fear, jealousy, camaraderie, exaltation, savagery—almost anything but calculations of gain or petty market interests.

Nineteen-fourteen burst upon the world after a century of comparative peace punctuated by limited wars. It erupted as an explosion of pent-up emotions not knowingly entertained the day before by the "civilized" peoples of Europe. These warlike emotions were closer to the surface and fiercer in the tiny nations and sub-nations of the Balkans, whose feuds finally involved the great powers, than they were in the great powers themselves. Yet civilized, cosmopolitan intellectuals, socialist workingmen whose spirits had been formed by endless repetition of the formulas of their creed, and socialist leaders who had constantly reassured themselves as they reassured their listeners, were as overpoweringly possessed by these feelings as the rest of society.

The "war aims," the material motives and calculations, had hastily to be improvised after war erupted—to give the irrational explosion and sacrifices an ostensibly rational explanation, a "meaning," a "justification."[11]

---

[11] Florinsky writes in his *Russia* (Vol. II, p. 1347): "Having stumbled into the war unprepared and more or less by accident, Russia was caught short not only of guns and munitions but also of that all-important prerequisite of modern warfare—war aims." Far from going to war to get the Dardanelles as has so often been loosely asserted, Russia exerted herself to keep Turkey neutral and made all kinds of offers to that end. Only after Turkey joined the Central Powers on October 31, 1914, did it occur to Russia to raise the question of Constantinople and the Straits with her traditionally reluctant ally, England. And only in March 1915 was a formal agreement signed. The biggest auctioning of anticipated spoils of war began when both sides were making rival offers to Rumania, Bulgaria, and Italy, none of whom entered the war in its first year. (Michael T. Florinsky, *Russia: A History and an Interpretation*, two volumes, New York, 1953.)

Actually the "meaning" of the war was in the passions themselves that the war unleashed. Nothing was so unpopular during it as proposals, made by what to inflamed feelings seemed a "treasonable" or "disloyal" handful in each country who ventured to urge that "reasonable limits" be set on the war and its aims, and that peace be concluded as speedily as possible without victory for either side. "In my heart reigns a truly paschal peace," the Tsar wrote to his wife when he learned that Count Witte, who had opposed war with Germany and was now urging an early peace, died at the beginning of 1915. In France they put the patriot Caillaux in jail as a traitor, though he was subsequently rehabilitated in a saner period and made Premier of France. Other warring lands behaved in like manner toward those who ventured to speak of reasonable limits to unlimited war. The unwholesome, manifestly unfulfillable terms of the Treaty of Versailles—pregnant as a few lonely prophets foretold with yet another war—were the product of this limitless irrationality. As Clausewitz had written of the wars of the French Revolution and the wars of Napoleon, so now, a century later it had come to pass again:

> War . . . became a matter for the people as a whole, took on an entirely different nature, or rather, approached more nearly to its true nature, its absolute perfection. The resources that were mobilized had no apparent limits—these were swallowed up by the energy and enthusiasm of governments and peoples . . . war, freed from every bond of convention . . . broke loose in all its elemental fury.

And every event from Versailles to the Berlin Wall has confirmed Clausewitz's further remark: "Once the barriers are torn down, they are not easily set up again."

It is not the "bourgeois" era, with its entrance of the masses upon the stage of history, but the era before the "democratization of war" to which the historian must look for some signs of "rational calculation" in regard to war's irrational way of settling differences between nations or rulers. Then wars were often fought "rationally" for limited objectives. Then monarchs and ministers sometimes attempted to set forth their objectives and assay potential gains against mounting costs and losses. Then soldiers themselves were drilled to suppress all emotion and initiative, so that they resembled, in Clausewitz's words, clockwork figures and mechanical puppets.[12]

---

12 For the ideas of Clausewitz I am indebted to Peter Paret's paper presented to the Annual Meeting of the American Historical Association, Chicago, Dec. 29, 1962.

But the *levée en masse* and the release of the energies of the people through the French Revolution opened a new era in warfare which the first half of the twentieth century brought to "absolute perfection"; making the well-drilled mechanical soldier who fought for a few cents a day into an anachronism, and substituting the volatile popular soldier, who might fight for principle or passion or because he was conscripted, might make the cause of his state or nation his own, might more easily yield to panic or the temptation to desert, or display more astonishing and uncalculating valor. But he was as far away from the professional soldier of the seventeenth and eighteenth centuries as limited war is from total.

It is this harking back to eighteenth-century modes of thought that gives Marxist explanations their oddly old-fashioned air, for with the coming of the French Revolution the age of rationalism and enlightened calculation in war—insofar as they ever prevailed— was completely over. (Or at least until the development by absolute war of the absolute weapon which has, let us hope, introduced a new element of rational calculation.)

When the long peace after the Napoleonic Wars drew toward its end, war was to embrace ever more completely the entire population. It was to assume terrible dynamic, defying limited aims, not to be contained in careful balance sheets nor measured by the petty calculus of gain and loss. With mass audiences and mass sounding board, foreign policy suffered a megalophonous enlargement. Its issues underwent a terrible simplification. When a whole people must be set in motion it is well-nigh impossible to mobilize them with limited and realistic aims. Where is the accountant to draw the balance sheet, or the mathematician to make the equation, between human lives and territory in total war? or among the incommensurable magnitudes of national feeling, honor, prestige, population, surface, treasure? Civilization itself, as Bergson put it, "conceals a profound instinct for war."

It was a neat and satisfying cynicism on the part of Marxism to reduce the beast, the brute, the warrior, the passion-ruled, the irrationalist in man, to the rational, and calculating economic man. This reduction began as an "abstract model" in the economic theorists of the "nation of shopkeepers" but it remained for the philosophic German studying their work in the British Museum to reduce it to absurdity by making this abstract model into the key to the soul and actions of the whole man. When war actually struck, as Henri de Man records, "my Marxism received a mortal blow, for it could not explain the behavior of the masses." And the sometime socialist, sometime communist leader, Frossard, wrote: "war devastated socialism as it devastated the world."[13]

The source of the half-century of socialist oratory referred to earlier lies in the following sentences from the *Communist Manifesto:*

Through its exploitation of the world market, the bourgeoisie had given to the production and consumption of all lands a cosmopolitan form . . . taken the national ground out from under the feet of industry . . . created a universal interdependence of the nations. As in material production, so also in intellectual production. . . .

Modern industrial labor, modern subjection to capital . . . has stripped the worker of all national character. . . .

The workers have no country to defend, you cannot take from them what they have not got. . . .

Even under the bourgeoisie, national divisions and antagonisms between peoples are disappearing. . . . The rule of the proletariat will make them disappear yet further. United action of at least the civilized lands is one of the first conditions for its emancipation. . . .

Communists have been accused of wanting to do away with country, with nationality. The workers have no country. . . . Since the proletariat must first of all win political power, make itself the ruling class, raise itself to the position of a national class, establish itself as the nation—to that extent it is still national, but not in the bourgeois sense of the term. . . . The proletarians have nothing to lose but their chains. They have a world to win. *Proletarians of all lands unite!*[14]

From these statements, more distinguished for their sweep and resonance than their freedom from ambiguities, socialists culled in particular two slogans: *no country to defend* and *proletarians of all lands unite.* It was these, ripped rather crudely out of their context, that the orators had been endlessly glossing.

In fact, Marx and Engels were themselves neither antiwar, nor, as they were to prove as soon as the great nationalist explosion of

13 Henri de Man, *Audelà du Marxisme*, Brussels, 1927, p. 69; L.–O. Frossard, *De Jaurès à Lénine*, Paris, 1930, p. 5. For more on this point see: Milorad Dratchkovitch, *Les socialismes français et allemand et le problème de la guerre*, and *De Karl Marx à Léon Blum*, Geneva, 1953 and Geneva, 1954 respectively.
14 *MEGA*, I/6, pp. 529, 536, 543, 557.

1848 had actually begun, were they devoid of German national feeling. To the *Rights of Man,* proclaimed in 1789, their *Manifesto* had added the *Rights of Labor.* Unexpectedly to them the risings of 1848 brought to the fore a third set of claims: the *Rights of Nations.*

Except in the case of Poland, the *Communist Manifesto* had had nothing to say on the rights of nations. Once the uprisings of 1848 had raised the banner of nationhood, Marx and Engels hastened to advance the slogan of the unification of Germany—in the name of the class which a month earlier they had said "had no country." Writing in March from revolutionary Paris, Marx issued a leaflet giving "The Demands of the Communist Party of Germany." At the head of the list, we find: "(1) All Germany is declared a single, indivisible republic."[15]

The other demands in the leaflet are a mélange of recipes of the various Paris schools of socialism with an unmistakable authoritarian, centralist, and statist trend added by Marx himself. From Paris he presumably derived his proposal for "national workshops" for the unemployed, the complete separation of church and state, equal pay for all officials with higher compensation for those with families, universal suffrage, salaried parliamentary representatives. These demands were in the air in Chartist England, in revolutionary Paris, and among the democrats of Germany. The same is true of a "general arming of the people" to take the place of the standing armies.

But what was peculiar to the Marxian statism of the period emerged in other demands which today have a terrifying sound. The "armed people" was to serve not only for defense, but also in "labor armies" and "as a means for the organization of work." Feudal estates, mines, etc. were to become state property; mortgages were to be taken over by the state and the state was to receive the interest payments on the mortgages. Leased lands, too, were to be taken over by the state and rents for them paid to the state. Agriculture was to be conducted by the state on a large scale with modern "scientific methods" by armies of agricultural laborers directly responsible to the state, which would receive the product and devote it to the public welfare. There was none of the spirit so common in French socialism of the autonomous commune, the independent co-operative, "mutual aid," the encouragement of small producers or

---

[15] This is the "seventeen-point program" referred to earlier in Engels's letter to Marx.

private peasants. Centralized state capitalism with state organization of labor appeared alike in the armed people, the national workshops, the state organization of industry and agriculture.[16] Stalin could have made these proposals his sacred text, as Lenin and Trotsky attempted to do under war communism until massive peasant resistance and general economic collapse forced Lenin to abandon these aspects of his Marxism and introduce the NEP ("New Economic Policy").

Two years later, in the last proclamation which Marx wrote before they admitted to themselves that the storms of '48 had blown over, the same spirit appears, still more strongly marked. The proclamation is in the form of a *Circular of the Central Committee to the League of Communists.* It was doubtless written by Marx, as both style and cast of thought suggest, but in consultation with Engels.

The *Circular* is noteworthy both for the extremism of the methods advocated to secure its aims and the highly statist and centralist formulation of those aims. It is doubtful if there is any other document from the hands of Marx in which Lenin, Stalin, Khrushchev, and Mao Tse-tung could find so much evidence for their claim to be the faithful heirs and so large a heritage to claim.

Marx almost appears here to be guided by Lenin's celebrated dictum that the key to all politics is the question *Kto kogo—Who whom?*—in this case who uses whom? For the *Circular* instructs the members of the Bund to use the "petty bourgeois democrats," to "march together with them against the faction which they aim to overthrow, and to oppose them in everything whereby they seek to consolidate their position." Marx pictures the petty bourgeois democrats as "needing a democratic state structure" in which, as a matter of course since Germany is a predominantly petty bourgeois and peasant country, the latter classes will have a majority. He further conceives that they will aim at a "democratic communal structure," and an end to the revolution as soon as their aims are achieved.

Against these proposals the *Circular* urges that "it is our interest and our task to make the revolution permanent." Every demand made by the petty bourgeois democrats should be pushed to an extreme by the proletariat. When the "bourgeois democrats" win, the workingmen must form alongside of the official government "their own revolutionary workers' governments, whether in the form

---

[16] *MEGA,* I/7, pp. 3–4.

of municipal committees or municipal councils or in the form of workers' clubs and workers' committees." These should act as overseers and threats to the new regime, sow lack of confidence in it, drive it to extremes, arouse the workingmen, who must be armed, against their yesterday's ally. "Far from opposing the so-called popular excesses, the examples of popular revenge on hated individuals or public buildings . . . we must not merely tolerate these examples, but ourselves take over the leadership of them." (Marx and Engels might think better of this in later periods. While Lenin, to whose "orthodox" mind every word of Marx was a sacred canon, would find ample occasion to cite these utterances, yet never their later modification.)

The extreme statism of the *Circular* is no less made to order for Lenin's temperament. The democrats will want, as in the first French Revolution, "to give the land to the peasants as free property. . . . The workers . . . must demand that the confiscated feudal property remain state property and be transformed into labor colonies.

"The democrats will . . . work for a federal republic, or, if they cannot avoid a single and indivisible republic, will seek to cripple the central government by the greatest possible autonomy and independence of the communal [municipal] governments and provinces." Against this the *Circular* proposes that the workers must fight for "a single and indivisible German republic . . . with the most determined centralization of power in the hands of the State." The *Circular* ends with the words: "The battle cry [of the party of the proletariat] must be: The revolution in permanence."[17] It was this battle cry which Parvus and Trotsky were to make the starting point of their own conception of the Russian Revolution, a conception which Lenin ambivalently opposed, but finally, in the course of the year 1917, took over.

Many forces combined to develop this strong streak of statism and centralism in Marx and Engels. The natural authoritarianism of Marx's temperament was reinforced by the deep admiration he and Engels conceived for the Jacobins in the first French Revolution, who had striven to make Paris the ruler of all France. To this must be added their conception of "socialization" as the nationalization of

---

[17] *Werke*, Vol. VII, pp. 244–54. English translation in Marx-Engels, *Selected Works*, Moscow, 1951, Vol. I, pp. 98–108.

both industry and agriculture, along with banking, mortgaging, and money lending and other financial functions, by the State. Of the various schools of socialism in Paris, Marx quite clearly at this moment conceived the greatest admiration for that of Blanqui, a belated Jacobin in a land where most socialist schools tended to be cooperative, mutualist and antistatist.

Underlying and reinforcing all these influences was the bitter nature of Germany's own history. In the centuries when Spain and France and England were building their unifying monarchies, the Germans formed a variegated congeries of innumerable petty and particularist states, kingdoms, dukedoms, free cities, and principalities under the aegis of the cosmopolitan, personalist, antinational, Holy Roman Empire of the Hapsburgs. The history of Germany's attempts at building a nation was a history of defeats and frustrations. The Hanseatic cities had lost their hold on the northern trade and the Rhenish towns on that of the Mediterranean when the center of trade and navigation shifted westward to the Atlantic. The Protestant Reformation, far from producing a single national church and national state as it did in England, Spain and France, tore the Germans into a Protestant North, and a Catholic South and East, unleashing the furies of the Peasant Wars and the Thirty Years' War, then made Germany the playground of the intervention of her powerful unified neighbors, Sweden, France, and Russia. By a trick of fate, the South was by inclination democratic, the Rhineland liberal, while partly Slavic and Junker Prussia, chief counterweight to the Hapsburgs, was hopelessly archaic in its institutions, its monarchy and its landed nobility. The Rhineland, birthplace of Marx and Engels, belonged to Prussia, so that they had no choice in the end but to work within the Prussian framework and support Prussia against Austria at the moment of the showdown between them.

Culturally, however, the Germans had long been one nation. In her little principalities and rival kingdoms had appeared such spokesmen for all Germans as Lessing, Goethe, Schiller, Bach, Handel, Hayden, Mozart, Beethoven, Kant, Herder, Schelling, Fichte and Hegel. Yet German intellectuals saw with frustrating bitterness that politically, economically, militarily, Germany remained fragmented as before, hemmed in by petty, small-town courts, local tariff walls, multiplicity of laws, customs, circumstances, and local vested interests. To Marx and Engels, seeking a unified national economy, a unified national working class, and a national

socialist party, federalism was not seen as it might be, as a democratic device to allow for pluralism and difference, or to reconcile
Catholic with Protestant, and industrial region with agrarian, but as
a frustrating perpetuation of all they found most detestable in Germany's history. The "Democrats" thought otherwise of autonomy
and federalism, therefore, though the Communists must work with
the Democrats at this stage, they must sharpen the workers' distrust
for them, so that working with them, they might still be working
against them.

The *Circular* from which we have been quoting put the matter in
these words:

> The workers must not let themselves be seduced by the democratic
> talk of freedom for the communes [municipalities], of self-govern-
> ment, etc. In a land like Germany, where there are still so many
> vestiges of the middle ages to eliminate, where so much local and
> provincial obstinacy has to be broken, it must in no case be tolerated
> that every village, every town, every province, should put an addi-
> tional obstacle in the way of that revolutionary activity which can
> only issue in all its strength from the center.

True this left unclear where "*the* center" should be, in Berlin, in
Vienna, in Munich, or in the Rhineland, and what might happen to
Germany and democracy in the course of a centralized elimination
or "smashing" of all the traditional barriers of religion and custom.
Such questions did not cross the minds of Marx and Engels, or,
insofar as they involved democratic self-government and free federation, they rejected the very idea when they urged that "the workers
must work against these plans not only for the one and indivisible
German republic, but also within it for the most determined centralization of power in the hands of the state."[18]

This demand for a unified Germany with the most decisive centralization of power in the hands of the state, Marx and Engels
continued to make throughout their lifetime—until Bismarck, in fulfilling his own "mission," completed the unifying and centralizing of
"our revolution" by his own "revolution from above." For this reason
their attitude toward Bismarck was strikingly ambivalent. In "The
Role of Force in History," an unpublished fragment written by
Engels after Marx's death, he said:

> Bismarck recognized the German civil war of 1866 for what it is,

---

[18] *Ibid.*

namely a *revolution,* and he was prepared to carry out this revolution by revolutionary methods.

The "civil war" Engels was alluding to was the war Bismarck provoked with Austria and her South German allies, to secure the unification of Germany.

In his reissue of Marx's *Class Struggles in France* after the latter's death, Engels explained the relationship between the Bismarckian and the Marxian efforts to unify Germany:

The period of revolution from below was [after 1848], for the time being, closed. Followed a period of revolution from above. . . . After the war of 1870–1871 Bonaparte disappears from the scene, and Bismarck's mission is completed, so that he can now sink to an ordinary Junker once more.

To Bebel Engels wrote on November 18, 1884:

The German-Prussian Empire . . . is a thoroughly revolutionary creation. . . . What I reproach the people who made it for is that they were only miserable revolutionaries; they failed to go much farther and to annex all Germany to Prussia.

Engels was angry that Bismarck had not fought the war with Austria to an overwhelming conclusion in which he should have annexed to Greater Germany all of German Austria, and all the Slavic lands (except the Polish provinces) ruled over by the Austro-Germans. But Engels approved of the methods Bismarck had used as far as they went. His letter to Bebel ends:

He who operates with blood and iron, who swallows up entire states, overthrows thrones, and confiscates property, should not condemn other people for being revolutionaries. If our party should have the right to be neither more nor less revolutionary than the government of the Reich has been, it would have all it needs.

Marx, for his part, shared Engels's views on Bismarck. During the Franco-Prussian War, he wrote to his comrade-in-arms of the "strange way" in which history was realizing "our own national aims" of 1848:

L'Empire est fait, I mean the German Empire. By hook or crook, neither on the road we intended nor in the way we imagined, it seems that all the trickery since the Second Empire [i.e. the trickery of Napoleon III] has led in the end to the carrying out of the "national" aims of 1848—Hungary, Italy, Germany! This kind of development, it seems to me, will not come to an end until it comes to a clash between *Prussians and Russians.*

Engels replied: "If we were paying the Old Boy, he couldn't be doing better work for us."[19]

Neither in 1848, nor in 1870, nor at any time in their lives, were Marx and Engels antinationalist or "defeatist" for their native land, as Lenin was to be for his in 1905, in 1914, and for the democratic Russia of 1917. On the contrary, during 1848–49, these two intellectuals, Marx being then 30 and Engels 28, were among the most warlike men in Europe. The newspaper Marx set up in the Rhineland in 1848 was Germany's, and probably Europe's, most bellicose journal. Perhaps "set up" is not the right word, for, although Marx invested in it what little money he had, the paper was set up, owned, and financed by Rhenish "bourgeois" shareholders. Marx was, in Engels's words, "the Dictator" of the editorial board. Engels and other disciples were contributing editors. Karl Marx had left his native Rhineland five years earlier still a democrat and an antisocialist, and, in the eyes of the German democrats, a martyr to Prussian censorship in the *Rheinische Zeitung*. Hence, when he returned, the new paper given to him to edit was called *Die Neue Rheinische Zeitung* (henceforth to be referred to as NRZ), with the subtitle "Organ of Democracy."

Since the resounding *Communist Manifesto* had no echo in Germany, "we joined the democratic party as the only means of getting the ear of the working class," Engels explained forty years later. In short, the two young Communists secured the bourgeois shareholders for their journal by sailing under false colors. The paper's program, as Engels summed it up later, "consisted of two main points: a single, indivisible, democratic German Republic, and war with Russia."[20]

The democratic part of this two-pronged program, as we have seen, was strongly circumscribed by their rejection of federalism for such diverse states as the Rhineland, Bavaria, and Austria, and their penchant for a strong centralized state. But it was through the second half of the paper's program, i.e., "war with Russia," that they hoped to implement their secret communist aims.

The importance they attached to war in general and war with

<hr>

[19] *MELS*, II/2, pp. 1160, 1305; *MEGA*, III/4, p. 358; Gustav Mayer, *Friedrich Engels*, New York, 1936, p. 246.
[20] Letter to Florence Kelley Wischnewetzky, January 27, 1887, in Marx-Engels, *Ausgewaehlte Briefe*, Berlin, 1953, p. 477; letter to Karl Marx, April 25, 1848, in *MEGA*, III/1, p. 100; *MELS*, II, p. 218. See also *Introduction*, pp. ix-x.

Russia in particular requires further examination. Some biographers of Marx and Engels have suggested that they became enamored of war with Russia only *after* the "gendarme of Europe" had intervened in Hungary to crush the Hungarian revolution, and restore the Hapsburg Empire, and had offered aid to the Prussian King. But the two young warriors demanded war with Russia before any of these things occurred.

They viewed the turbulent events of the stormy year 1848 through the distorting vision of a dream. They were convinced that they were living through a second "Great French Revolution," this time destined to embrace not only France but also Germany and all of Europe. "The tradition of all the dead generations weighed like an incubus," to use Marx's own language, "upon their brains." Recalling how the French Revolution had led to general European war, they dreamed that now a general European war would lead to a new version of the French Revolution—as if in history cause and effect sequences were interchangeable.

Remembering that the French Revolution had led to the total mobilization of the French nation, the dictatorship of the Jacobins, the Terror, and the march of the French armies of Carnot against the "old regimes" of Europe, they dreamed that war against Russia, and then against all and sundry, would put the fatherland in danger, sweep aside with an iron broom all of Germany's petty principalities, and call them, as latter-day Jacobins, to power, to save the fatherland, to unify and revolutionize Germany, and thereafter Europe. So on any and all pretexts, and often with no pretext at all, they called for war!

The first issue of NRZ appeared on June 1, 1848. When the paper was six days old, Marx wrote that German unification and democratization could "only arise as a result of a movement which will push to a decision both the internal conflicts, and war with the East." On June 25, he declared:

> The Germans, allied with the French . . . will wage a war of the West against the East.

On July 12:

> Only a *war with Russia* is a war of a revolutionary Germany, a war which can wash away the sins of the past, in which Germany can become virile, in which it can defeat its own autocrats, in which as befits a people shaking off the chains of a long, ignoble slavery, it will purchase the propaganda of civilization with the sacrifice of its sons and free itself at home while it liberates abroad.

On August 12, Marx urged war with Russia to free Poland and "bring about an open and genuine break with our quite shameful past."

War with Russia did not exhaust the calls of these two young warriors of the pen (*warmongers* in the language of their latter-day heirs) for war. On the fourth day of its existence, NRZ denounced the half-hearted quadrille (*Gegentanz*) which Germany was performing in its war with Denmark over Schleswig-Holstein. The modest restraint with which this war of brother peoples was being waged, Marx found "shameful." The armistice which brought it to a halt more shameful still. Without restraint Marx began to adopt the epithets concerning Denmark which can only be characterized as German professorial beer-hall nationalism. Here are a few samples:

With the same right with which France has taken Flanders, Lorraine and Alsace, and, sooner or later, will take Belgium, with that same right Germany takes Silesia: with the right of civilization against barbarism, of progress against stability . . . this right is worth more than all treaties, for it is the right of historical development.

Scandinavianism [to which Denmark was appealing for protection] consists of enthusiasm for the brutal, dirty, piratical, old-Nordic nationality, for that deep inwardness which cannot bring its over-pregnant feelings out in words, but can in deeds, namely in brutality toward women, permanent drunkenness, and a tearful sentimentality that alternates with berserk fury.

It is hard to believe that such writing is the work of men who have just written the *Communist Manifesto*, proclaiming the imminent demise of nationalism. The connection lies in the fact that Marx and Engels, having espoused the cause of German "bourgeois" democracy, were convinced that war was the road to the victory of the German Revolution. By September 10, Marx had worked himself into a state where he believed that "the Danish war is the first *revolutionary war* that Germany has waged." Yet the only "revolutionary" meaning a war with Denmark could have was to wrest from her Schleswig and Holstein, both inhabited confusedly partly by Danes, partly by Germans. (Many years later, Engels was to promise that a socialist victory in Germany would result in the return of the more northern of the two provinces.)* When Denmark appealed to Germany and Russia, Marx called in the NRZ for a breaking of the armistice with Denmark, and the taking on simul-

---

* See below, page 78.

taneously of England, Russia, Prussia, and Denmark. A large order!
But so much the better:

> Just such a war is what the somnolent German movement needs: a
> war against the Great Powers of the Counterrevolution . . . which
> will put the "fatherland in danger" and, just by that fact, save
> it—making the victory of Germany dependent on the victory of de-
> mocracy.[21]

Though Marx and Engels would grow less warlike as they grew
older, finally becoming fearful of the incalculable consequences for
Germany and for European civilization of a general war, they never
gave up one part of their youthful dream: if the fatherland were in
danger, "men of greater energy and decisiveness," i.e. their party,
would be "called to the helm" to save the fatherland by waging
"revolutionary war," as once the Jacobins had saved France. Much
of their patent misunderstanding of the Europe of their own day
was due to this habit of "conjuring into their service the spirits, the
battle cries, the scenes" of the French Revolution.

In the twentieth century Russian Marxists of all varieties would
derive their own errors from the same mirage. Much was the to-do
in the Russian underground, in exile, and in the press, to determine
whether Russia was on the eve of her 1789, her 1793, or her 1848! In
the end, the strategical and tactical formulas implied by these debates led socialists to two sides of the barricades. Later blood was
shed by the Bolshevik leaders in their own debate: was the Soviet
Union threatened with a "Restoration" or "Bonapartism" or "Thermidor"? Trotsky in his last miserable, lonely exile from the land of
his birth, ordered by the government he had helped to bring into

---

[21] The excerpts given from agitation for the Danish War and war with all the
great powers at once are in *MEGA*, I/7, pp. 352, 353, 355. The principal calls
for war by Marx and Engels in NRZ (mostly written by Marx, who in any case
as "the dictator" determined the form and content of everything in the paper),
are in *MEGA*, I/7, pp. 24, 30, 92, 181, 204, 303–04, 354–55, and 376. Many
another passage is strewn with dragon's teeth or breathes dragon fire. In part
this is attributable to the nationalistic mood in Germany and Europe during the
turbulent year 1848, so different from the anticipation of the early end of
nationalism with which the *Communist Manifesto* greeted the year's beginning.
In part it was due to the notion that since the Great French Revolution was
linked with war in all Europe, so war in Europe was necessary to a new edition
of the French Revolution. On March 5, 1852, Engels published over Marx's
signature in the *New York Tribune* the explanation: "The radical party in
Germany . . . regarded a war with Russia in the interest of the movement on
the continent and believed . . . that it would bring men of greater energy and
decisiveness to the helm." (*Revolution and Counterrevolution in Germany*, in
Werke, Vol. VIII, p. 51.)

being, could still excommunicate some of his own little handful of followers because of differences as to how far Stalinist Russia had gone on the road to "Thermidor," and whether "Thermidor" would come through Stalin and the bureaucracy or by an upheaval against them.

When the hopes of 1848 were extinguished, and their war and barricade fury had died down, Marx and Engels, from their refuge in England, continued to urge upon their native land—as well as the land of their refuge—war with Russia. The English press, for all its Russophobia, was not anti-Russian enough to suit them. Two prime ministers, the Marquis of Salisbury and Lord Palmerston, because they hesitated before the prospect of such a war, were branded by Marx "Russian agents" and declared to be "in Russia's pay." On June 4, 1853 when tension was building up in Europe and the Near East, soon to culminate in the Crimean War, Marx wrote for the *New York Tribune* the most powerful indictment of Russian expansion that has ever been written. He called on all parties "in this country and in Europe" to help defend Turkey and the Christian peoples of the Balkans from Russia's pretense that she would become their protector:

> Mankind will not forget that Russia was the *protector* of Poland, the *protector* of the Crimea, the *protector* of Courland, the *protector* of Georgia, Mingrelia, the Circassian and Caucasian tribes. And now Russia, the *protector* of Turkey! As to Russia's antipathy against aggrandizement:
>
> The Russian frontier (since Peter the Great) has advanced:
>
> Toward Berlin, Dresden and Vienna about . . . .　700 miles
> Toward Constantinople . . . .　500 miles
> Toward Stockholm . . . .　600 miles
> Toward Teheran . . . .　1000 miles
>
> Russia's acquisitions from Sweden are greater than what remains of that kingdom; from Poland nearly equal to the Austrian Empire; from Turkey in Europe, greater than Prussia . . . from Turkey in Asia, as large as the whole dominion of Germany proper; from Persia, equal to England; from Tartary, to an extent as large as European Turkey, Greece, Italy and Spain taken together. The total acquisitions of Russia during the last sixty years are equal in extent and importance to the whole Empire she had in Europe before that time.

When the Crimean War began, Marx and Engels were so excited that they forgot to berate Russia, directing their wrath instead against the Concert of Western Powers for the "halfhearted" way in which they waged the war.

It is interesting to see how differently Lassalle, leading the workingmen inside Germany, and Marx, looking at foreign policy from abroad, viewed the question of war with Russia. To make propaganda against Russia in Germany, Lassalle wrote to Marx, is like "bringing owls to Athens" or "carrying water to the sea." "The bitterness of our people toward Russia" simply could not be any greater. Precisely because *"war against Russia* would be the most popular of all the battle cries in Germany's history," it was dangerous to call upon the Hohenzollerns to wage such a war. Far from revolutionizing Germany, as Marx expected, war and victory under such a banner would serve to make the monarchy secure in the affections of the German people. But Marx was so blinded by the image of the French Revolution floating before his eyes that he was incapable of seeing the soundness of Lassalle's warning.[22]

---

[22] Marx's *Tribune* article of June 14, 1853, is in *The Russian Menace to Europe*, by Karl Marx and Friedrich Engels, Paul W. Blackstock and Bert F. Hoselitz, eds., Glencoe, Illinois, 1952, pp. 140–142, and in German translation in *Werke*, Vol. IX, pp. 114–116. The letters exchanged by Marx and Lassalle on war with Russia are quoted in Karl Kautsky, *Sozializten und Krieg*, Prague, 1937, pp. 131–33.

Chapter 2

SELF-DETERMINATION

FOR WHOM?

The first free word uttered after centuries of silence by the
representatives of Germany seeking her emancipation, was in
opposition to the oppressed and weak nationalities.

—Alexander Herzen on the Revolution of 1848 in Germany

I am no advocate of nationalities on principle. . . . I attribute the right of nationality only to the *great culture
nations*.

—Lassalle to Rodbertus in 1863

There is not a land in Europe without . . . one or more
ruins of peoples . . . driven back and subjected by the nation which later became the bearer of historical development.
These cast-offs of nations, mercilessly trampled down by the
course of history, will remain until their complete denational-
ization and extermination, fanatical bearers of counterrevolution, as their continuing existence is itself a protest against
a great historical revolution.

—Friedrich Engels in the *Neue Rheinische Zeitung,*
January 13, 1849

ONCE THEY had raised the issue of German unification, it was from
the standpoint of their hopes for a unified Greater Germany that
Marx and Engels judged the rights of all other nations and all the
national movements in Europe.

They supported Italy's struggle for unification and for the annexation of her "unredeemed" lands from Austria-Hungary because

30

they thought that this would end the antagonism of the Italians toward the Eastern Germans and turn Italy from enemy to ally in the struggles of Germany with France and Russia.

When in the Italian kingdom's war with Austria, Napoleon III allied himself with Sardinia in 1859, Marx and Engels were in a dilemma. To this dilemma Engels addressed himself in two pamphlets, published anonymously in Berlin: *Po und Rhein* (1859) and *Savoyen, Nizza und der Rhein* (1860). No one suspected his authorship, and with good reason, for not a line in them speaks of, or so much as suggests, socialism or internationalism. "It is absolutely impossible," Engels explained to Marx by way of justification, "to come forward openly in Germany itself, either politically or polemically, in the interests of our party." However, "we have the advantage that we represent the popular, national side."[1]

He spoke of the hatred with which Italians pronounced the word *Tedeschi* (Germans). He urged that it was in the best interests of the German nation (which they always envisaged as including Western and Eastern Germans, Germany and Austria) to relinquish Italy's northern provinces. He concluded the first of the two pamphlets with these words:

> Whether we have Lombardy or not, we will have an important influence on Italy as long as we are strong at home. . . . We Germans could make an excellent deal by exchanging the Po, the Mincio and the Adige for unity. . . . Then the defensive can come to an end [for Germany-Austria] . . . then our genius will again be "to attack"; and there still are a few rotten spots [on the map of Europe] where this will be necessary enough.

His pamphlet of the following year was even more successful with the German public. He warned that France and Russia might form an alliance against Germany—a thought that would obsess him henceforward all the days of his life and form the setting for the truest of his many prophecies, indeed the only true ones.

Though the starting point of *Savoy, Nice and the Rhine* is once more the course of Italian events, the pamphlet soon forgets both Italy and France, the former being referred to with passing interest, the latter with passing contempt. The heart of the pamphlet is one more clarion call for war with Russia. Unlike the war cries of '48 and '49, this one makes no mention of either defending or unleashing a

---

[1] *Karl Marx*, by Franz Mehring, New York, 1935, p. 301; *MEGA*, III/2, p. 462.

revolution, whether in Germany or Europe generally. The war is spoken of entirely from a national standpoint as a war to defend certain German provinces (the Rhineland) which Engels conceives to be coveted by France, aided and abetted by Russia. It is to be a war to free Germany once and for all from the nightmare of a Franco-Russian alliance. The tone may be gathered from the rhetorical question and answer with which the pamphlet closes:

> Shall we any longer tolerate this? . . . Shall we forty-five millions suffer it any longer that one of our most beautiful and industrial provinces should continue to serve as a lure dangled by Russia before the praetorian rule in France? . . . That is the question. We hope that Germany will answer it soon, sword in hand. If we stick together, then we shall manage to send the French praetorians and the Russian *kapuschtchiks* packing.[2]

So nationalistic in tone were Engels's two pamphlets, and so devoid of any trace of socialist feeling, that it was widely believed that they had both been written by a Prussian general! This conjecture did not displease the man who delighted all his life to write on military matters, and received from his intimates the nickname *Der General*. (The Lafargues frequently called him "Dear General" in their letters to him, and he often signed himself "General.")[3]

That Engels's views did not altogether represent a mere personal idiosyncrasy or a "Deviation" from the "Marxism" of Marx, is testified to by a letter Marx wrote him after reading the first of the two pamphlets:

---

[2] *Po und Rhein*, pp. 50–52; *Savoyen, Nizza und der Rhein*, pp. 46–47, Stuttgart, 1915, an edition in which the two pamphlets are bound together. *Kapuschtschiks* is a term of contempt for the Russian soldier; *praetorian guard* for the French. I could not find the German slang word in any etymological dictionary, nor could the philologists I consulted determine its origin. It is probably derived from the Russian word for cabbage (*kapusta*), in which case it would mean "cabbage-eaters," as sometimes the French are called "frogs" or "frog-eaters." Thus Marx writes in letters to Engels "these *crapauds*" for the French socialists who are fighting him in the First International (*MEGA*, III/3, p. 422, *inter alia*). But here Engels was using the contemptuous term in a public work.

[3] In October 1841, Engels was called up for military service. He spent a year in the artillery barracks in Berlin. In the spring of 1848, he spent almost a month on the revolutionary military committee that tried to prepare the defense of the Rhenish town of Elberfeld. He wrote a good deal on military matters, both from a technical and from a political point of view. The articles on such matters signed by Marx for the *New York Tribune* were all written by Engels, and, whenever Marx had to include military considerations in a manifesto, he consulted Engels and accepted his expertise. Hence the nickname.

Exceedingly clever: the political side, too, is handled marvelously, which was damned hard. The pamphlet will have a great success.[4]

Marx too wrote articles on the Italian question, for the *New York Tribune* and *Das Volk* of London.[5] They are among the more badly thought through of his writings on foreign affairs. Their central theme is a call to Prussia to join Austria in a war against France, a strange proposal since at that moment France was allied with Italy against Austria. Marx reconciles his advocacy of Italian liberation with his proposal for an Austro-German war on Italy's ally by contending that such a war would require a general arming of the German people, which would lead to revolution and unification in Germany. Then a unified Germany would liberate Italy—the old mirage of the sanative and revolutionizing effect of a general war.

Far more ardent than his championing of the Italians was the backing Marx gave the Hungarians and the Poles. The Hungarians, Marx held, were brave, noble, civilized and civilizing, a freedom-loving, and a "historic" people, with the natural right of historic peoples to rule over and civilize the "inferior" and "historyless" (*geschichtslose*) lesser Slav peoples, and with the right themselves to be free of German, i.e. Austro-German, rule. Moreover, every patriotic German must want to see Hungary freed from the Hapsburgs, since a unification of East (Austrian) and West Germany into a single German land was unthinkable without the prior breakup of the multinational Hapsburg Empire.

As for the Poles, they were the hero-people *par excellence*, one of the "necessary peoples" of Europe, whose liberation had been put on the order of the day by all the movements for liberation, unification, democracy, and socialism of the nineteenth century. Germany should demand Polish freedom "sword in hand," force Prussia and Austria to give up what they had taken in the partition of Poland, and force Russia to give up her share. Of course, that would mean a war of the German people against Russia, perhaps against Austria and Prussia, too, but what was that but the longed-for war that was to unify, make democratic, and revolutionize Germany,

---

4 The letter is in German, but the italicized words were written by Marx in English. *MEGA*, III/2, p. 371.,

5 *MELS*, Vol. II, Part 1 pp. 771–94. For some reason these articles are not included in the corresponding volume of Marx-Engels, *Werke* (Vol. XIV), being published in East Berlin. For Lenin's attempt to defend Marx's position of 1859, see *Sochineniya* Vol. XXI, pp. 119–22, "Pod chuzhim flagom," which is also in *MELS*, pp. 795–99.

and bring Germany's "most energetic elements" to power? It would free Germany from servile dependence on the Russian autocrat. It would kindle agrarian revolution in Poland—a revolution which must surely spread to all of Eastern Europe. It would push Russia's frontiers back toward the East, from which they had advanced too far into the freer West. It would set up a brave and free Poland as a shield of the West against Russia's millennial expansion.

Most astonishing to latter-day Marxists, if they trouble to go from the Wilsonian-Leninist slogans on self-determination of the twentieth century to the writings of Marx and Engels, is the fact that the two fighters resolutely set their faces against the very slogan itself. Neither a greater Germany, nor a restored Poland, nor a liberated Hungary, should permit self-determination to the "lesser" peoples over whom they ruled.

A restored Poland, Marx held, must not be a "sham Poland," but a "viable Poland, with at least the area it had possessed in 1772. It must not only have the watersheds, but also the mouths of the great rivers, and a considerable stretch of the coast of the Baltic Sea." Its borders should include all of Prussian Poland, regardless of the degree of Germanization of some parts; all of Austrian Poland; and all of the old Lithuanian, White Russian (Belo-Russian) and Ukrainian areas that Russia was trying to Russianize and that had formed an integral part of "the Poland of 1772." Marx and Engels would not settle for the truncated Poland of any later date. "A Poland without Galicia," Engels wrote in Marx's name and with Marx's approval, "one that does not extend from the Baltic to the Carpathians, is no Poland."[6]

---

[6] It would be worse than impolitic to quote such utterances in the "Marxist" Russia, Poland, or East Germany of the present day. Yet there is one respect in which Marx and Stalin showed a resemblance in their methods of calculating the interests of their countries. In an article signed by Marx, but written by Engels, for the *New York Tribune* (March 5, 1852), we read: "The Poles, by receiving extended territories in the East, would become more tractable in the West." And Stalin, for his part, when he annexed the eastern half of Poland with its largely Ukrainian and Belo-Russian population, "compensated" Poland with additional territory to the west, thus increasing its fear of Germany and its dependence on Russia, and making it "more tractable in the East." Is it any wonder that in Polish Party circles a common jest explains that "the Polish idea of utopia would be to have the geographical situation of Chile"?

The articles from which the above quotations have been taken, as well as a number to be cited below, are available in English (the language in which they were written for the *Tribune*) in the compilation of most of the articles of Marx and Engels that are taboo to Marxists behind the Iron Curtain, made by Blackstock and Hoselitz. The articles on the Polish question occupy pages 91–120.

In the national unification of Greater Germany, and the restoration of an independent Hungary, Marx and Engels left no room for self-determination for any of the various Slavic peoples, with the exception of the Poles, that had come under German or Hungarian sway. Some, they held, had been "civilized" by the Magyars (Hungarians) and some by the Eastern (Austro) Germans, or by those of Germany proper. As early as 1848, in the NRZ Marx and Engels categorically denied to these lesser breeds outside of history any significant past, any possible future, or any right of self-determination against "the culturally and historically" viable great peoples who had conquered them.

> If the eight million Slavs [they wrote of those under Magyar rule] have had to be satisfied to let four million Magyars keep them under the yoke, then this alone is enough to show which is more capable of living and more energetic, the many Slavs or the few Magyars. It turns out that this "crime" of the Germans and the Magyars against the questionable Slavs belongs to the best and most worthy deeds of which our people and the Hungarian people can boast.[7]

Did the doctrine of imperialist conquest and civilizing mission ever find a more ardent statement?

The first attack on "the Slavic riff-raff" (*Lumpengesindel*) was published by Marx in his new year's roundup of the year 1848 on January 1, 1849. But Engels soon enlarged and improved upon the theme, and the vocabulary of contempt. It has taken a century of literary detective work to determine who wrote which article. Many articles in NRZ were unsigned, but Marx as "Dictator," in Engels's fond language, determined what went in, and sometimes even how it was expressed. In many cases, the articles of Marx for the *New York Tribune*, whose foreign correspondent he was, were written by Engels, though Marx, of course, signed them and of necessity collected the modest fee. Marx's own daughter, Eleanor, actually published an entire book of articles as Marx's which subsequent research has proved to be all from the pen of Engels.[8]

---

[7] NRZ, February 15, 1849. The NRZ articles are in *Aus dem literarischen Nachlass von Karl Marx und Friedrich Engels* (hereafter referred to as *Nachlass*), fourth edition, Berlin-Stuttgart, 1923, Vol. III, p. 255. They can also be found by date in the new East German edition of "Karl Marx/Friedrich Engels," *Werke*, Vol. 6, Berlin, 1959. So far as "class" is concerned the leaders of Hungary were landed gentry, the "historyless Slavs," peasants.

[8] *Revolution and Counter-Revolution in Germany in 1848*, London, 1896. Edited by Eleanor Marx Aveling in English; the French translation was done by another of Marx's daughters, Laura Lafargue, Paris, 1900. Ryazanov showed after a study of the Marx-Engels letters that Engels wrote this series and Marx sent them to the *Tribune* over his signature.

In any case, the two friends had no difference in their views on Poland, the "lesser Slavs," Hungary, Italy, German unity, or war with Russia—beyond differences of focus of interest and differences in those aspects of style which come from temperament. Now that the disentanglement of their writings is virtually completed and certain, it is clear that most of the calls for war came from Marx's pen while most of the scornful utterances concerning the "historyless Slavs" came from Engels.

When they came out for the right of the Poles to rule over the Ukrainians and Belo-Russians of Old Poland, the two comrades-in-arms deepened their feelings and casual judgments on the non-Polish Slavs into a theoretical system. In 1866, urged on by Marx, Engels gave to their joint views their most finished expression in three long letters in successive issues of the English magazine, *Commonwealth*.[9] The purpose of these letters was to influence British public opinion and British foreign policy with regard to the Continent, and to influence the constituent parties of the newly-formed International. It is this systematic statement that the Marxists of today must examine if they would understand that part of the heritage of the Marxism-in-action of the founding fathers, and would compare it with the views on self-determination that have become prevalent in the present age of decolonization, an age which got its ringing slogans from the Democrat, Woodrow Wilson, and the Revolutionist, Lenin, during World War One.

In his *Commonwealth* articles, Engels wrote:

It has been said that to claim independence for Poland is to acknowledge the "principle of nationalities."

There could, indeed be no two opinions as to the right of every one of the great national subdivisions of Europe to dispose of itself . . . [However] there is no country in Europe where there are not different nationalities under the same government. . . . The Highland Gaels . . . the Welsh . . . the Celtic inhabitants of Brittany. . . . No state boundary corresponds with the natural bond of nationality, that of language. There are plenty of people out of France whose natural tongue is French, same as there are plenty of

---

[9] Marx and several other members of the General Council of the International Workingmen's Association were on the editorial board of *Commonwealth*. Two Marx-followers, Eccarius and Odger, were successively the editors. Its owners and financial backers were "bourgeois" nonconformist radicals. (Carr, *op. cit.*, p. 195.)

people of German language out of Germany; and in all probability will ever remain so. . . . The Germans in Switzerland and Alsace do not wish to be reunited to Germany, any more than the French in Belgium and Switzerland wish to become politically attached to France. . . .

Here then we perceive the difference between the "principle of nationalities" and the old democratic and working-class tenet as to the right of the European *nations* to separate and independent existence. The "principle of nationalities" leaves entirely untouched the great question of the right to national existence for the historic peoples of Europe; nay, if it touches it, it is merely to disturb it.

The principle of nationalities raises two sorts of questions; first of all, questions of boundary between these great historic peoples; and secondly, questions as to the right to independent national existence of those numerous small relics of peoples which, after having figured for a longer or shorter period on the stage of history, were finally absorbed as integral portions into one or the other of those more powerful nations whose greater vitality enabled them to overcome greater obstacles. The European importance, the vitality of a people, is as nothing in the eyes of the principle of nationalities. Before it, the Roumanians of Wallachia, who never had a history nor the energy required to have one, are of equal importance to the Italians who have a history of two thousand years, and an unimpaired national vitality. . . . The whole thing is an absurdity got up in popular dress in order to throw dust in shallow people's eyes, and to be used as a convenient phrase, or to be laid aside if the occasion requires it.

. . . The principle of nationalities is nothing but a *Russian invention concocted to destroy Poland.* Russia has absorbed the greater part of Poland on the plea of the principle of nationalities. . . .

Engels then analyzes Russia's use of the "principle of nationalities" as a pretext for adding the Ukrainians of Old Poland to the other Ukrainians over whom the Russians rule and the Belo-Russians of Old Poland to the Belo-Russians already under Great Russian rule (all of which has a peculiar timeliness today.)[10]

Therefore [Engels concludes] if people say that to demand the restoration of Poland is to appeal to the principle of nationalities, they

---

[10] The partition of Poland under Catherine the Great, and its partition along the "Curzon line" after both world wars, is based on the same principle, advanced in the nineteenth century by the Tsars, and in the twentieth by Lenin, Stalin, and Khrushchev.

merely prove that they do not know what they are talking about, for the restoration of Poland means the re-establishment of a state composed of at least four different nationalities. . . . Talk about a war of class against class as something extremely revolutionary—why, Russia set such a war on foot in Poland nearly one hundred years ago, and a fine specimen of a class-war it was when Russian soldiers and Little Russian [i.e. Ukrainian] serfs went in company to burn down the castles of Polish lords, merely to prepare Russian annexation, which being once accomplished, the same Russian soldiers put the serfs back again under the yoke of their lords. . . . So much for the principle of nationalities in Polish affairs.[11]

With what assurance Engels spoke on "History's irreversible judgments" against the lesser Slavic peoples of the central plain! He was as sure of East Prussia and Koenigsburg (now Kaliningrad) as of Breslau (ten centuries earlier called Breslavl and today Wroclaw); as sure of Bohemia (today Czechoslovakia) as of the South Slavs (yesterday Serbia, today Yugoslavia)—all of whom he relegated to the "ruins of peoples, leftovers . . . pushed back and made subject to the nation which had become the bearer of historical development," namely the Germans. Though Slav and Teuton had contended over the central plain for ten centuries, so far as Marx and Engels are concerned:

The affair has been settled and cannot be changed. . . . This conquest was in the interest of civilization. . . . At a time when . . . great monarchies were a "historical necessity" what a "crime" it was that the Germans and the Magyars should have bound these tiny, crippled, powerless little nations together in a great empire, and thereby enabled them to take part in an historical development which . . . would have remained alien to them! To be sure, such things are not accomplished without forcibly crushing many a delicate little national flower. But without force and iron ruthlessness nothing is accomplished in history. And if Alexander, Caesar, and Napoleon had had the capacity for compassion to which Panslavism now appeals in favor of its rotten clients, what would have become of History![12]

---

[11] "What have the working classes to do with Poland?" Three letters in English to Commonwealth, Blackstock and Hoselitz, pp. 95–104.
[12] This and the two succeeding quotations are from articles by Engels in NRZ, January 13 and February 15 and 16, 1849; Werke, Vol. VI, pp. 165–76, 270–86.

If Marx and Engels—or History—needed any further proof of the finality of these judgments, it had been supplied by the behavior of the respective peoples during 1848. Germans, Hungarians, and Poles alone had proved revolutionary and *lebensfaehig*, while the other peoples—particularly the Croats—had flocked into the armies of the reactionary Hapsburg emperor. (Marx and Engels soon forgot the Prague uprising which, on its occurrence, they had hailed; by the year-end they were assimilating Czechs to Croats and both to the Slavic *Lumpengesindel*.) To cap the climax, in 1849 the Muscovite Tsar added 100,000 Russian Slavs to the imperial forces of reaction, to crush the Hungarian revolution. That settled it! Now, Engels declared, all these great and small "retrograde" races and peoples had nothing left for them by fate except "the immediate task of perishing in the revolutionary world storm." Germans, Poles, and Magyars would

> . . . take frightful revenge on Slavic barbarism. The general war that will then begin will blow up this separatist Slavic League (*Sonderbund*), and *destroy* all these little, bull-headed nations so that *their very name will vanish*. The coming world war will cause not only reactionary classes and dynasties but entire reactionary peoples, too, to disappear from the face of the earth. And that will also be progress.

For the sake of the argument—at the moment he was arguing with Bakunin—Engels was willing to admit that if any of these peoples were to show a spark of progressive or revolutionary spirit, he and History might still spare them, for that would "renew their vitality." But he hastened to close the escape:

> The so-called democrats among the Austrian Slavs are either scoundrels or visionaries, and the visionaries . . . are constantly being led by the nose by the scoundrels. To the sentimental slogans offered us in the name of the counterrevolutionary peoples of Europe we reply that the hatred of Russia was, and still is, the first revolutionary passion of the Germans; and that since the revolution, hatred of the Czechs and Croats has been added. . . . We and the Poles and the Magyars will only be able to safeguard the revolution through the most determined terror against these Slavic peoples.

There was yet one other way in which historical necessity doomed these peoples: Marx and Engels insisted on the right of Germans, Magyars, and Poles to continuous terrain without enclaves, to "historic borders," "strategic frontiers," and "necessary outlets to the seas." These "vital peoples" could never tolerate the coming into existence of a Czech, a Slovak, or a Serb or South Slav nation, which by its existence would cut the vital peoples off from the Baltic or Mediterranean, or riddle their lands with bits and pieces of Slavic sovereignty. Would Eastern Germany (i.e. Austria) "permit itself to be torn to pieces like a loaf of bread that has been gnawed by rats"? Was this "the thanks the Germans got for taking the trouble to civilize the stubborn Czechs and Slovenes"?[13]

In the light of such pronouncements, it is obvious that Marx and Engels were what Lenin would call "great power chauvinists," opponents on principle of Lenin's slogan of "self-determination for all nationalities to the point of separation." And they supported the Hungarian and Polish gentry against their "historyless" Slavic peasants regardless of class. How Lenin, following his masters, was able to reconcile his own worship of great-power economic unity and political centralism with his subversive use of the slogan of self-determination we shall have to examine elsewhere in this book.

Historical realities and deep irrational emotions are interwoven in this obsession of Marx and Engels with war against Russia and the unworthiness of all Slavs except the Poles. One of the sources of these emotions is the unexamined acceptance of many views of the educated Germans of their day. A second is the teaching of their chosen master, Hegel, who held the Slavs unworthy to figure in his grand historical scheme, since to him they were a race that had played an insufficient role in the development of the Human Spirit. Hegel's description of the Balkan Slavs as "the scattered dregs of barbarism" reappears again and again in the writings of his two disciples.[14]

Both reason and emotion were stirred by the terrifying secular expansion of Muscovy, which no one has described more eloquently than Marx and Engels. Here their feelings as democrats and revolutionists and Western men reinforced their feelings as Germans. Russia's role in crushing Napoleon I, whom they admired, partitioning Poland, which they idealized, and maintaining the partition of Germany, made them anti-Russian even before Russia's armies crushed the Hungarian revolution. On Russia and the Slav peoples of Austria-Hungary they vented all their bitter disappointment when their dreams of 1848 were reduced to naught. In England their feelings

---

13 *Ibid.*, pp. 276–77.
14 Mayer, *op. cit.*, p. 107.

were further intensified by the contagion of British fear of Muscovite expansion. Marx was ever ready to urge upon the country of his refuge yet greater distrust, yet stronger measures. His articles on the Crimean Question, on the Near East, on Lord Palmerston, are a blend of Russophobia with revolutionary and democratic hatred of Russia as the "bulwark of reaction." His Russophobia made him prone to see Russian machinations and Russian agents everywhere.

In 1848 he accused Bakunin of being a tsarist agent, though he soon apologized; in 1870 he revived the charge, adding Herzen as well! Even after Lassalle gave him confidential information on Lord Palmerston's real attitude ("I won't say that I want to ruin Russia [Palmerston said] but I do want to deal her a blow that will last a lifetime"), Marx still contended that he had "proved Palmerston's relations with the Russian government."

> Curious as it may seem to you [he wrote Engels] I have come to the same conclusions as the monomaniac, Urquhart, that Palmerston sold out to the Russians several decades ago.[15]

Of the many warnings and exhortations of Marx and Engels to England, the most striking foreshadows the outlines of a future Russia, Stalin's Soviet Empire after World War Two:

> Having come thus far on the way to universal empire, is it probable that this gigantic and swollen power will pause? . . . With the Albanian coast she is in the very center of the Adriatic. . . . The "natural frontier" of Russia runs from Danzig or perhaps Stettin to Trieste. . . . The conquest of Turkey would be only a prelude for the annexation of Hungary, Prussia, Galicia, and the ultimate realization of the Slavonic Empire. . . . In this instance, the interests of democracy and of England go hand in hand.[16]

In the eighties, after Marx's death, Engels went over the whole argument against self-determination for the lesser Slav peoples once more, in a letter to Eduard Bernstein.[17] In 1890 he wrote for the Russian journal, *Sozial Demokrat* (published in Geneva by Plekhanov and Axelrod) so blistering an indictment of "The Foreign Policy of Russian Tsarism" that Stalin forbade its publication by *Bolshevik* in 1934, when that journal wanted to give a festive Marx-

---

[15] Blackstock and Hoselitz, p. 269; *MEGA*, III/1, p. 511.
[16] Article in *New York Tribune*, April 12, 1853, written by Engels, signed by Marx; *Werke*, Vol. IX, pp. 16–17.
[17] *Die Briefe von F. Engels an E. Bernstein*, Berlin, 1925, pp. 54 ff; also in Kautsky, *op. cit.*, pp. 245 ff.

ist dress to its issue commemorating the twentieth anniversary of the outbreak of the war of 1914.[18]

In 1892, when the French *Parti Ouvrier* invited Engels to contribute to its *Almanac,* he chose to make his article a warning to the French people that their newly formed alliance with Russia might lead to a war with Germany in which they would find *every German Socialist* ready to fight in his country's defense. Engels was then nearing seventy-three and had only two more years to live. This was his valedictory article on war with Russia, a theme which had preoccupied "The General" all his life.

---

[18] Stalin's suppression of Engels's article was kept secret from 1934 to 1941. It was revealed in *Bolshevik,* No. 9, 1941. The article itself is in German in *Neue Zeit,* 8th Year (1890), pp. 145–54, 193–203; in English in Blackstock and Hoselitz, pp. 25–55.

PART II

Defensism, Defeatism,
or Pacifism?

To reject the defeat slogan means to turn one's revolutionism into an empty phrase or sheer hypocrisy. . . . Whoever is in favor of the slogan, *neither victory nor defeat,* is a conscious or an unconscious chauvinist, at best a pacifistic petty bourgeois, and in any case an *enemy* of proletarian policy, a supporter of the existing governments and present ruling classes.
　　—Lenin in "On the Defeat of One's Own Government"

Chapter 3

FROM WAR FOR THE

REVOLUTION TO PEACE

FOR THE REVOLUTION

> World events seem to want to take a very satisfactory turn.
> A better basis for a thoroughgoing German revolution can
> hardly be imagined than is provided by a French-Russian
> alliance. For us Germans the water has to come up to our
> necks before we are thrown en masse into a furor teutonicus;
> and this time the danger of drowning seems to want to come
> close enough for us. Tant mieux. In such a crisis all existing
> powers must be ruined, and all parties, one after another,
> wear themselves out. . . . In such a struggle, the moment
> must come when only the most determined, the boldest
> party is in a position to save the nation. . . .
> —from a letter of Friedrich Engels to
> Ferdinand Lassalle, May 18, 1859

> But he who thinks that socialism can be built in a peaceful,
> quiet time is deeply mistaken: everywhere it will be built in
> time of ruin, in time of famine, and thus it must be.
> —Lenin to the All-Russian Congress
> of Soviets, July 5, 1918

THE FRANCO-PRUSSIAN WAR marked a turning point in the history of
Europe. And, though it took a decade for them to realize all its
implications, it marked a turning point in the attitude of Marx and
Engels toward war.

From 1864 to 1870 Bismarck waged the unifying wars that Marx

45

and Engels had been calling for. To be sure, he did not take on so many countries at once, and he wooed Russia to avoid tangling with her in the East while engaged in war with Austria or France in the West. Not the least of his wisdom was his awareness that Germany, as a central European power, was vulnerable if it waged war with East and West at the same time.

"We have the advantage," Engels had written complacently to Marx in 1859, "that we represent the popular, national side." But before long it was Otto von Bismarck, Chancellor of Prussia from 1862 to 1890, who contrived to make himself, his native Prussia, his king, and the Hohenzollern dynasty, into the representatives in German eyes of "the popular, national side." Somehow, everything turned out differently from what the two masters of historical science and prophecy had expected.

The Liberal opposition to Bismarck did not understand the situation either. When the Iron Chancellor laid plans to conquer German unity by strengthening the Prussian Army, the Liberals, with a majority in the Prussian legislature, refused to vote the appropriations lest the army "stifle democracy." It was Bismarck's celebrated answer that earned him the title of the "Iron Chancellor." Defying the legislature, he levied, collected, and spent taxes without legislative approval, and built up his army for war.

> Germany does not look to Prussia's Liberalism [he declared] but to her might. . . . The great questions of the day are not to be decided by speeches . . . therein lay the failure of 1848 and 1849 . . . but by blood and iron.

Bismarck's words were closer to the hearts of the two exiles than they cared to admit. So Lenin, too, would one day write, and repeat again and again: "Great questions in the life of nations are settled only by force."[1]

In the space of six years Bismarck plunged Prussia into three wars. The superiority of Prussian arms and preparations made them localized lightning wars, whence the fateful legend of the *blitzkrieg,* a war over before it had well begun and before others could get in.

The first was waged in 1864 by a league of Prussia, Austria, and the states and principalities of the German Confederation against Denmark over Schleswig-Holstein. The Danish provinces that were won in that war were administered jointly by Prussia and Austria. But in 1866, Bismarck provoked Austria into declaring war by seiz-

---

[1] Lenin, *Selected Works,* Vol. III, pp. 126, 305, 313, *inter alia.*

ing the part of Holstein which Austria was administering, and proposing the exclusion of Austria from the German Confederation.

The South German states rallied to Austria's side. As a military expert, Engels predicted Prussia's humiliating defeat. As a political expert, Marx foresaw a revolt of Berlin and of the Prussian *Landwehr*. But the Prussian railway network proved superior; Prussian organization and preparation proved superior, too. The breech-loading rifle with which Bismarck's army was newly equipped enabled its user to lie prone, firing three shots for each Austrian soldier's one, while the Austrian's muzzle-loader required him to remain a standing target. Within three weeks Engels was writing to Marx with unconcealed admiration:

> What do you think of the Prussians? They followed up their success [at Koeniggraetz] with enormous energy. Such a decisive battle all over in eight hours is unparalleled; under other circumstances it would have lasted two days, but the needle gun [breech-loader] is a deadly weapon, and then the boys fought with a bravery I have never seen in peace-time recruits . . .[2]

From this moment begins a change in the attitude of both friends toward Bismarck, a change from contemptuous antipathy to ambivalent admiration. (The same change, in varying degrees and at varying speeds, was observable among Prussian Liberals, and among the other states of the German Confederation.) Another three weeks and Engels wrote:

> The story in Germany now seems quite clear to me. Now that Bismarck has carried out [his] plan by means of the Prussian army with such colossal success . . . we, like everybody else, must recognize the *fait accompli, we may like it or not*.[3]

Though Engels still hoped for a greater Germany than Bismarck cared to contemplate, since Engels wanted Austria in the Reich while Bismarck wanted undisputed hegemony for Prussia, with Austria an ally, the letter to Marx continued complacently:

> This business has its good side in that it simplifies the situation, makes a revolution easier by eliminating the brawling of petty capitals and speeding up development. . . . The whole petty state particularism will be drawn into the movement . . . parties will at last become really national instead of only local.[4]

---

[2] Letter of July 4, 1866, *MEGA*, III/3, p. 342.
[3] Letter of July 25, *MEGA*, III/3, p. 349. The italicized words are in French and English respectively in the original.
[4] *Ibid.*, p. 350.

Bismarck needed one more war to complete his plans for the unification of Germany under Prussian leadership, and for German hegemony on the continent—a war with France. Until now, France had been the dominant power in Europe thanks to the fragmentation of Germany and the rivalry of Austria and Prussia. To get the support of the South German Confederation, Bismarck had to make France appear to attack him. His problem was more one of diplomatic maneuver than of military preparation. Bismarck did both well.

At the head of the French state was the enigmatic, vacillating adventurer, Louis Napoleon III ("Napoleon the Little," a pallid imitator of his uncle, "Napoleon the Great"). Because Louis Napoleon had made himself Emperor on the ruins of the Revolution of 1848, and because he coveted their native Rhineland, Marx and Engels detested him even more cordially than they did the Tsar of All the Russias. Marx's passionate dislike of the Emperor made "The Eighteenth Brumaire of Louis Napoleon" the most brilliant and mordant of Marx's historical-polemical works.

Napoleon III was a likely subject for Bismarck to provoke. Already in his pursuit of glory he had engaged France's armies in a number of colonial wars, conquering Algeria, New Caledonia, and Cochin China half a century before Lenin's "era of imperialism" began. He had joined England in the Crimean War, from which no one gained any credit, and had lost a long fruitless struggle to make Maximilian of Austria the Emperor of Mexico. His intervention in Italy had ended indecisively. With none of his famous uncle's generalship or love for the battlefield, he was haunted by the need of victorious wars to consolidate his imperial prestige as his uncle had done before him. History was indeed repeating itself, as Marx acerbly remarked, "the first time as tragedy, the second time as farce."

In 1866, when Bismarck struck at Austria, Napoleon weighed the advantages of joining Austria to check Prussia's growing might, or waiting instead until the two wore each other out so that he could be arbiter between them. Bismarck cannily hinted at "compensation" if he would remain neutral, which gave the Emperor something else to think about: should he ask for the Rhineland? Belgium? Luxembourg? While he was still pondering these alternatives, in seven short weeks the war was fought and won, and Bismarck was ready to mock at Napoleon's request for "compensation," taking care to shock England by letting her know that the French Emperor had asked for support in annexing neutral Belgium. Thus Bismarck began the isolation and provocation of Louis Napoleon.

When the latter played the liberal by giving the Poles empty verbal support in their insurrection against Russia, Bismarck offered help to the Tsar. Defeated Austria Bismarck treated generously. He returned Venice to the Italians, and encouraged Italy to hope that a defeat of France would free Rome of French troops. These chess moves left France without an ally.

At this moment came one more of the dozen or so insurrections which kept Spain in turmoil from the restoration of Ferdinand in 1814 to the flight of Queen Isabella in 1868. For some incomprehensible reason, both Marx and Engels wrote each other congratulatory letters to the effect that the latest Spanish insurrection had "cut the Gordian knot of a repugnant German-Franco War," but it was just this squabble about the succession to Queen Isabella which gave Bismarck the opportunity he was waiting for.[5]

Bismarck proposed a member of the House of Hohenzollern for the Spanish throne. His candidate, Prince Leopold, first accepted, then, under Napoleon's pressure, withdrew. Not content with this quiet diplomatic victory, Napoleon sent his ambassador to Ems, where King William of Prussia was taking a cure, to demand an apology and a solemn promise that no Hohenzollern would in the future accept the throne of Spain. King William refused to discuss these demands with the French emissary. Bismarck's editing of his monarch's telegram to him, before releasing it to the press (the famous Ems dispatch), was calculated to give the impression that the two countries had broken off all relations. This was indeed, as Marx had written to Engels and Kugelmann, "the deus ex machina to cut the Gordian knot," but in a fashion quite contrary to Marx's expectations. Crowds paraded the streets of Paris and Berlin, crying for war, and Napoleon declared the war which Bismarck had been working for.

France was isolated from her possible allies, Russia, Austria, Italy, and England; Bismarck's military plans were all ready; in seven weeks the French army was cut to pieces and the Emperor himself a

---

[5] The letter of Engels is in *MEGA*, III/4, p. 97, that of Marx on p. 98. At the same time, Marx wrote to Kugelmann, "The Spanish Revolution has come like a *deus ex machina* to prevent an otherwise inevitable and disastrous Prussian-French war." (*Letters to Kugelmann*, Berlin, 1927, p. 57) Presumably Marx expected the Spanish insurrection to be contagious and cause a revolution against Napoleon, whom he thought of as the only source of the danger of a Franco-Prussian war.

prisoner at Sedan. Bismarck's third lightning war had once more brought Prussia an easy victory. This time, Prussia won the support of all Germany, North and South, and all classes of the German people. The German Empire was promulgated with symbolic pomp on French soil, in the Hall of Mirrors of the Palace of Versailles, with William I of Prussia as Emperor of the Germans.

Like most of their countrymen, and Europeans in general, Marx and Engels were taken in by Bismarck's diplomatic maneuvers and his doctored Ems dispatch. "The French need a thrashing," Marx wrote to Engels one day after war was declared. Prussian victory would "move the center of gravity of the West European Labor Movement from France to Germany" and would guarantee "the predominance of *our* theory over those of the Proudhons, etc."[6]

The two exiles were proud of the progress of their country's arms. "What do you say to our soldiers," Engels wrote to Marx on August 5, "who take a fortified position with the bayonet against machine guns and breechloaders? *Molodets!*"[7]

And on August 10, when her husband and oldest daughter were in Ramsgate looking for a house, Mrs. Marx wrote to Engels:

You have no idea how disgusting the insults [toward the Germans] are in *Figaro*. They want to tear the Vandals limb from limb for having the impudence . . . to set foot on the *sol sacré de la patrie* [the sacred soil of the fatherland]. How they all deserve the beating the Prussians are giving them; for all Frenchmen, even the tiny handful of the better ones, all of them have chauvinism hidden in the deepest corner of their hearts. That will yet be knocked out of them. Here at home too, where we have also been a bit chauvinistic in mood, we are indignant at these gentlemen with their civilis–a– a–ation and their ideas, which they were so kind as to want to bring to Germany, which is no *sol sacré*.[8]

Besides being a German intellectual, Marx was by now the leading figure in the General Council of the International Workingmen's Association, founded at a meeting of French and British workingmen in London in 1864. For this body, which has since come to be known as the First International, Marx drafted three documents that have played a notable role in socialist and communist history. The

---

[6] *MEGA*, III/4, p. 340.
[7] *Ibid.*, p. 357. The exclamation, *molodets!*, is Russian for *Good boy!* Both friends were studying Russian at the time.
[8] *Ibid.*, p. 360.

first dealt with the outbreak of the war, and the attitude which the French and German workers (and the International) should take toward it. The second came after the fall of Napoleon and the proclamation of the French Republic. The third was issued immediately after the fall of the Paris Commune. Whatever the reticences and errors of the first and second addresses may have been, they are worth studying, for they contain in germ the most important prophecy Marx and Engels ever made, indeed, the one true prophecy of the many with which they were so ready in the course of a lifetime. The third address, of pamphlet length, subsequently published under the title of "The Civil War in France," has so completely formed the socialist image of what happened in Paris during the period from March 18 to May 28, 1871, that socialists and communists have never been able to see the Paris Commune as in historical fact it really was. These three addresses form a most important part of the Marxist heritage.

In the First Address on the outbreak of the war, as two admiring biographers of Marx have cautiously put it, "it was manifestly impossible for him to set forth all the arguments which determined his position."[9] He could neither denounce the "chauvinism deep in the heart of every Frenchman," nor say that "France needed a licking," nor that this would beneficently "transfer the center of gravity of the Labor Movement from France to Germany."

The Address put the blame for the war squarely on Louis Napoleon. It was but "an improved version of his *coup d'état* of December 1851," by which we must suppose Marx meant that it was another step in the development of "Bonapartism," and a surprise attack on Germany behind the backs of the French people. "On the German side, it is a war of defense." The implication was that the German people should rally to Prussia's support as long as she conducted the war as one of defense.

Having thus settled the question of responsibility to his satisfaction, Marx turned to prophecy. Here he was on firmer ground. No matter what happened, he said, the war would surely end with the downfall of the Second Empire of Louis Napoleon. But with that fall might come a new danger to the peace of Europe: "If the German working class permits the war to lose its strictly defensive character, then victory or defeat will be alike unwholesome." Then France will seek the return of whatever territory might be wrested

---

[9] Nikolaevsky and Maenchen-Helfen, *Karl Marx: Man and Fighter*, Philadelphia, 1936, p. 304.

from her, by preparing a future war. And, "in the background of this suicidal struggle, lurks the sinister figure of Russia."

For the rest, Marx did his best to give the document a balanced international flavor by quoting such resolutions as he could, from the French and German sections of the International. He welcomed warmly an antiwar declaration of the Paris Section, published a week before the war began, and a second, published three days after it broke out, which called the war "neither just nor national, but exclusively dynastic." These he matched with three statements of German socialists, all adopted on the eve of the war, in Braunschweig, Berlin, and Chemnitz. The Braunschweig resolution called it "a war of defense, into which we find ourselves obligated to enter as an inevitable evil." This was substantially the view of Marx and Engels themselves. The Berlin resolution was a mere return of greetings from the Paris Section. The Chemnitz declaration most nearly matched that of Paris, for it too called the impending war "an exclusively dynastic one," meaning that it was a war on Bismarck's part to promote the fortunes of the Hohenzollern dynasty. Marx found it convenient to quote it in order to preserve the "international balance" of his Address, but neither he nor Engels liked it, as their scornful letters concerning both the Address and its author, their disciple Liebknecht, make clear.[10]

It was awkward for Marx and Engels that their principal supporters were two members of the North German Reichstag elected from Saxony, in Southeastern Germany. Both Wilhelm Liebknecht and August Bebel opposed the war and the war's real aim, the unification of Germany under the hegemony of Prussia and the Hohenzollerns. Liebknecht wanted to vote against the war credits asked by Bismarck; it was only because Bebel persuaded him to compromise that they abstained from voting instead. How Marx and Engels felt we can gather from a letter of Engels dated August 15:

> The whole mass of the German people of all classes has perceived that it is precisely a matter of national existence in the first place, and has therefore leaped immediately into the breach. That, under such circumstances, a German political party should preach total obstruction à la Wilhelm [Liebknecht], and should put all sorts of side issues above the main one, seems to me impossible.

---

[10] The *First Address of the General Council on the Franco-Prussian War* is in *Werke*, Vol. XVII, pp. 3–8; an English translation is in Marx-Engels, *Selected Works*, Moscow, 1951, Vol. I, pp. 441–45.

Add to this that Badinguet [Louis Napoleon] would not have been able to wage this war without the chauvinism of the mass of the French population. . . . As long as this chauvinism has not been crushed . . . peace between Germany and France is impossible. . . . Now that the war is here, there is nothing left but for the Germans to do this themselves and at once.[11]

That the war was being led by Bismarck and would redound to his glory was a "secondary matter"—it was regrettable, but inevitable due to the lack of spirit of the German bourgeoisie. On that account to elevate anti-Bismarckism into the one leading principle would be absurd:

Now, as in 1866, B. is doing a part of our work, in *his own* way and without wanting to, but he does it all the same. As before, he is clearing the decks for us. . . . In general, à la Liebknecht, to want to turn back the entire history [of Germany] since 1866 because it doesn't please him, is stupid. But we already know these model South Germans. With these fools you can't do anything.[12]

On September 2, the main French army under General Mac-Mahon and the Emperor was smashed at Sedan and the imitation Bonaparte was taken prisoner on the field of war, to which his talents were so unsuited. Two days later, acting out the memory of the French Revolution and the heroic year 1792, a Paris mob invaded the Palais Bourbon, then the Hôtel de Ville. Under their pressure the Paris rump of the National Assembly proclaimed a Republic with themselves as a Provisional Government of National Defense of France. General Trochu, who had so recently sworn to die defending his Emperor, became President and Military Governor of Paris. Keratry remained as before Prefect of Police. But the Provisional Government was made up chiefly of men who had opposed Napoleon, their real leader being the dynamic liberal republican, Gambetta, who performed miracles in a vain effort to turn the tide in a war which was already lost.

Paris refused to believe the truth. Had not an aroused capital stirred all France in '92 and '93 to beat back all the federated powers of Europe? As Louis Napoleon had striven to emulate Napoleon Bonaparte, now radical republicans and assorted socialists, journalists, shopkeepers, artisans, workingmen, and nondescript mobs sought to imitate the Paris of the Great French Revolution, forget-

---

[11] *MEGA*, III/4, p. 365.
[12] *Ibid.*, p. 366.

ting the little detail that this time France was already beaten, and victorious Prussian armies were surrounding the last strong points, Paris and the Fortress of Metz.

For a moment, Gambetta electrified the imagination of Europe by escaping from the beleaguered city in a balloon to rouse the Provinces. Journalists and agitators of all shades came up with "military plans" for Paris to overwhelm the "thin gray line" of the Prussian besiegers with a "human wave" of the people of Paris (*la sortie torrentielle*). Inventors "rediscovered" Greek fire and calculated the number of Prussians it could consume per hour. They elaborated schemes for the poisoning of the Seine from which the Germans drew their water, and for the loosing upon them of all the ferocious beasts from the Jardin des Plantes. Jules Allix, later one of the leaders of the National Guard, then of the Commune, who ended up in a madhouse, expounded to the clubs the virtues of his invention, a "prussic finger," which was to protect the honor of Paris women and exterminate any Prussians who might get past the *sortie torrentielle*.[13]

Rochefort was the only radical in the new Provisional Government, but at the outset it had the support of virtually everybody. Thiers, one-time Orleanist who, with the downfall of Louis Philippe, had become a moderate republican, told the conservative majority of the old Chamber of Deputies:

> To fight this authority would be unpatriotic. We can neither oppose it nor enter into collusion with it. . . . It is impossible either to recognize a government born of insurrection, or to oppose it when it fights against the enemy.

At the other end of the spectrum, Blanqui, the permanent insurrectionist, with a dozen of his faithful disciples, signed a proclamation reading:

> In the presence of the enemy, no more parties, no more divisions. With a government which betrayed the nation, cooperation was impossible. The [new] government represents republican thought and national defense. That is sufficient. All opposition . . . must disappear to make way for national safety.[14]

Irritation and disgust at the loss of the war; contempt for the fallen Emperor who had strutted so ill in the cloak of Napoleon

---

[13] For a good account of the atmosphere in the club discussion of military problems, see Edward S. Mason, *The Paris Commune,* New York, 1930, pp. 79–82.

[14] Mason, *op. cit.,* pp. 60–61.

Bonaparte and been taken prisoner in his first big battle; patriotism, fed on the memories of France's military might during the great French Revolution; reluctance to face harsh reality; and a belief that some change of government would turn the tide of war—such were the causes of the Revolution of September 6, 1870. And they were the basic cause of each of the succeeding attempts at revolution, including the Paris Commune.

With the capture of the Emperor and the proclamation of the Republic in France, so far as Marx and Engels were concerned, the "war of defense" they had credited to Bismarck had come to an end. Had not the King of Prussia sworn, calling God to witness, that he was not fighting the French people but only defending his land against attack? Now his Chancellor arranged that the King should be "overwhelmed" by petitions demanding the annexation of Alsace and Lorraine as a "frontier guaranteeing security against future attack." To make the "will of the German people" unanimous, the Government arrested the Marxian Braunschweig Committee for issuing an appeal calling for working-class demonstrations for an honorable peace with the French Republic, and against annexations. To Marx's embarrassment, the Braunschweig Committee published along with their appeal large excerpts from a confidential letter he had written them in which he told them, too, that the defeat of France would have the salutary effect of transferring the center of gravity in the Western labor movement from France to Germany. Marx also received a letter from the Paris Section of the International asking him to draft a new Address on the new situation. To his intense irritation, "the fools in Paris" and particularly his future son-in-law, Charles Longuet, deluged him with "masses of their ridiculous chauvinistic manifesto . . . to send to Germany, probably to make clear to the Germans that they must first 'withdraw over the Rhine' before they reach their homes!" Worst of all Longuet was presuming "to send me telegraphic instructions . . . *how I must agitate in Germany!*"[15]

Despite these private irritations Marx set to work to write a new address for the General Council. He asked Engels for advice on the nullity of the claim that the annexation of Alsace and Lorraine would give Germany "military security." The rest he wrote himself. The *Second Address of the General Council on the Franco-Prussian*

---

[15] *MEGA*, III/4, pp. 381–82.

War is much superior to the first, indeed, one of the best political documents from Marx's hand.

It began by reminding its readers how soundly the First Address had prophesied the "death knell of the Second Empire," and how earnestly it had warned lest the German war should "lose its strictly defensive character and degenerate into a war against the French people." Now the "defensive war" was over, but King William and Bismarck were "turning" the war [as they had intended all along] into a war to strengthen the dynasty and to annex German-speaking but French-loyal Alsace-Lorraine.

Followed a long analysis, largely contributed by Engels, showing that the Alsatian town of Strasbourg had held out for six days against German bombardment, and that border annexations, far from giving military security, would merely sow the seeds of future wars.

In the name of the German working class "which resolutely supported the war it had not been in their power to prevent, a war for German independence and the liberation of France and Europe from the pestilential incubus of the Second Empire," in the name of the workingmen who had furnished the sinews of war, had made up its "heroic hosts," and suffered poverty and decimation, Marx demanded *"an honorable peace for France and the recognition of the French Republic."*

He "hailed the advent of the Republic," but he did not hold to Lenin's belief that a revolution issuing from defeat in war was likely to be a wholesome one. "That Republic has not overthrown the throne, only occupied its place made vacant by German bayonets."[16]

The truly notable passage of the *Second Address* was a warning by Marx to his own people on the danger to Germany's future (and Europe's) inherent in the projected annexation of Alsace and Lorraine:

Do the German nationalists [*Deutschtuemler*] really believe that the peace and freedom of Germany can be secured if they force France into the hands of Russia? If the fortunes of arms, the arrogance of victory, and dynastic intrigues, mislead Germany into robbing French territory, then only two ways lie open to her. Either

---

[16] In subsequent editions the "German bayonets" were omitted, and it was made to read "occupied its vacant place." The original text is in *Werke*, Vol. XVII, pp. 271–79, with variorum footnotes. An English version without the variorum notes is in Marx-Engels, *Selected Works*, Vol. II, pp. 446–52.

Germany must become the *open and public* servant of Russian expansion, or, after a short breathing spell, she will have to arm herself for a new "defensive" war, not one of those new-fangled "localized" wars, but a *war of the races*, against the allied races of Slavs and Latins.[17]

For the first time in their lives, the prospect of war with Russia inspired not hope but fear. Like Bismarck, they had now come to fear for Germany's fate in a two-front war with both Russia and France. With the coming of universal military service, and, increasingly, of universal suffrage, they sensed that changes were taking place in Europe that would make well· nigh impossible the limited, localized *Blitzkrieg* such as Bismarck had just fought with Denmark, Austria, and France. They foresaw that a new kind of war was in the making, a war involving not merely dynasties, professional armies and limited aims, but total in scope, aimless, or boundless in aims and passions, involving entire peoples, a war of "races" for their very existence. Slowly through the next decade, the feeling grew in the hearts of Marx and Engels that it would be better for socialism, for democracy, for European civilization, and for "the revolution," if this war could be averted. They began to lose their taste for war as an engine of progress. In this matter Lenin would follow their earlier and ignore their later years.

To be sure, the old warlike mood did not die out all at once. In 1876–78, when Russia and Turkey went to war over the Christian peoples of the Balkans and it seemed possible that England and Austria might leap into the fray on Turkey's side, there was a brief relapse.

This time their homeland was not involved, for France was still licking her wounds while Bismarck bluntly declared that Herzegovina was "not worth the bones of a single Pomeranian musketeer." Marx overestimated both Turkey and the prospect that England and Austria might join the war as Turkey's "protectors." The hope that "the gendarme of Europe" might be beaten kindled again in Marx's breast—for a brief moment, and the last time.

Marx had a spokesman in the German Reichstag—that same Wilhelm Liebknecht who had wanted to vote against war credits for Bismarck in the Franco-Prussian War. Now Liebknecht made an about-face, from antiwar to pro-war, denouncing Bismarck for lacking "a truly German spirit and German policy toward Russia." But

---

[17] *Ibid.*

in neither case was he, in Lenin's sense, defeatist for his own country.

With Marx's approval, Wilhelm Liebknecht carried their case to the people in a pamphlet entitled *On the Eastern Question, or Shall Europe Become Cossack?* The slogan, "the Balkans for the Balkan peoples," he declared, was a "Russian reptile product." The discontent of the Balkan Christians was "ninety-nine per cent made in Russia." The Western powers were "face to face with the alternative of either crying *Halt!* to Russia with drawn sword, or giving up as Great Powers." In Marx's spirit, too, Liebknecht "defended the English *people* against the charge that they are to be identified with the 'peace movement' of the Russian agent, Gladstone." It was not the English people but "the English *bourgeoisie* that was 'without a fatherland.'" The style and spirit was that of Marx's writings on the "Eastern Question" which had so won the approval of "the monomaniac," Urquhart.

When Marx saw the manuscript, he sent two approving letters to his disciple, both of which Liebknecht added as appendices to the pamphlet. In the first, Marx explained that he was pro-Turk because "I have studied the Turkish peasant" and find him "unconditionally the most industrious and moral representative of the peasantry in Europe." (It was the only peasantry who ever got a kind word from the man who coined the scornful city phrase, "the idiocy of rural life.") The Turks, Marx concluded, going out once more on the brittle limb of prophecy, will surely give the Russians such a licking that the throne will be discredited and revolution come to Russia.

Alas for Marx's certitudes, before the pamphlet was off the press Turkey had proved too poor to carry on a long war, while England and Austria, or so Marx charged in his second letter, had committed "treason" to their own "true interests." They failed to give Turkey military and financial support. Turkey "failed" to revolutionize herself, which was the only way to win a war. "A people who in such moments does not know how to follow a revolutionary course, is lost." By the time the pamphlet was out with its two letters, one prophesying victory, the other explaining the failure of the prophecy, the war was over.[18]

---

[18] The quotations from Liebknecht and the two Marx letters are cited in Kautsky, *Sozializten und Krieg*, Prague, 1937, pp. 229–36. They have so far been omitted from all available publications of Marx's letters issued behind the Iron Curtain, but will presumably appear in Vol. XXXIII of the Marx-Engels *Werke*.

The Liebknecht who went to jail for opposing Bismarck in the Franco-Prussian War, and the Liebknecht who reproved Bismarck for lacking a sufficiently warlike "German policy toward Russia," were both used as precedents by contending socialists in 1914. The same ambivalent use is made of the Marx and Engels who supported Germany in her "war of defence" in 1870, but opposed the same war when it was revealed that one of the objectives of Prussia was the annexation of Alsace and Lorraine.

Another passage in Marx's second letter on the Turkish War which was the subject of contention in 1914 was his criticism of the British working class as "corrupt" and its pacifism as unworthy:

These fellows [Marx wrote contemptuously of the English labor leaders and "small-time agitators"] howl in *majorem gloriam* of the Tsar Emancipator of People, following in a pack behind the Gladstones, Brights, Mundellas, Morleys. . . . The wretches! And the whole business was worthily crowned by the last votes in the House of Commons on February 7th and 8th . . . when most of the "Grand Liberal Party" . . . left their army in the lurch and disappeared when the vote was taken, so as not to compromise themselves too much.[19]

This is not the place to discuss all the things Marx and Engels learned in England, how the sight of a more democratic country than those on the Continent altered the views they had carried over from 1848, nor what they grasped and what they misapprehended in English life. But we must examine more closely their remarks on the "corruptness" of British labor since it had consequences for the fate of the First International, and was later interpreted in fundamentally differing ways by Kautsky and Lenin.

Marx and Engels could never get used to the fact that the best organized workingmen in Europe, indeed, the only ones with more or less permanent trade unions, were more concerned with keeping out of war, democratizing their country, getting a greater voice in the existing government, and improving their living standards, than in overthrowing the British constitution and "system."

Engels knew England more intimately than Marx, for he went

---

[19] The episode Marx refers to is as follows: Disraeli asked for 6,000,000 pounds to prepare for possible war with Russia. The vote in the House of Commons was 328 to 124, with half the Liberals simply walking out instead of voting. The coal miner, Burt, the only Labour member, voted with the Liberals against the credit. Marx was opposed both to voting against the war credits and to abstaining. He was for the appropriation and for the war.

there earlier. He wrote an excellent book on *The Condition of the Working Class in England in 1844*, and became first an overseer and then a partner and half owner of the textile firm of Ermen and Engels in Manchester, working very hard in the practical affairs of his father's (subsequently his own) business. It was from the "exploitation," to use Marx's term, of the textile workers in Manchester that Engels lived, and contributed substantially to the support of Marx and the latter's writing.

On October 7, 1858, Engels wrote his friend on how well the textile business was going, how high wages were, and how steady employment. He expected a new drive for wage increases soon. He had heard that even in China and India the textile business was at that moment flourishing. He continued with an attack on the British radical leader Jones, whom they had worked with in Chartist days and had always considered one of England's best. Jones was becoming "disgusting" and the English proletariat

. . . actually more and more *verbuergert* ("bourgeoisified") so that this most bourgeois of nations seems to want in the end to possess a bourgeois aristocracy and a bourgeois proletariat *alongside* its bourgeoisie. In a nation which now exploits the entire world, this is in any case to a certain extent justified. In this matter nothing will help except a few really bad years, and these are not so easily produced since the discovery of gold [in California].[20]

Such views are all very well in private letters. But in 1872, when Marx was engaged in packing the Hague Congress of the International Workingmen's Association for the purpose of expelling Bakunin and other opponents, he caused a public scandal by making the same attack on the leaders of the British workingmen to their faces. The occasion was a fit of anger when the spokesmen of the British delegation questioned the credentials of one Maltman Barry, an ex-cobbler, whom they had expelled from the British Labour Movement and who now mysteriously appeared with a credential from a German-speaking group in far-off Chicago, where Barry had never been.

The International Workingmen's Association was originally founded by the British Labour Movement in collaboration with some workingmen's delegations from France. Marx had been called

---

[20] *MEGA*, III/2, p. 340. Marx and Engels believed that the discovery of gold in California had so raised prices and stimulated industry and commerce that they could no longer count on an early and deep crisis to further their cause, which was linked in their minds with the troughs of the business cycle.

in at first as a respected emigré from Germany, with a revolutionary past and a doctor's degree, to help write a programmatic document for the new association. His influence had grown as the leaders of the big labor delegations neglected the affairs of the International for those of their own movements, until he became the leading figure on the General Council. Yet its congresses could and did outvote him and his faction, for Bakunin, Proudhon, and others who did not accept his every pronouncement, had more influence than he in France, Italy, Spain, Belgium, Holland, and Switzerland, while the English continued to have views distinctly their own. Marx had decided just before the Franco-Prussian War that he must pack a congress with his disciples, set it to be held in a country from which Bakunin was banned, strengthen the powers of the General Council over the affiliated movements, whose mere clearing-house and obedient servant it was originally supposed to be, then expel Bakunin and move the Headquarters of the General Council to far-off America, where Bakunin could not lay hands on it and where it would not require so much of Marx's attention and time.[21]

The strategy for packing the congress was such that even a Lenin might have envied it. Marx picked The Hague, to which Bakunin could not go because he was wanted by the police of both France and Germany. Engels paid the fare of five members of the General Council who would side with Marx. Marx wrote to Kugelmann in Germany and to Sorge in America to send the largest possible delegations of the faithful, and as many blank credentials as possible which he might fill in with suitable names. That is how Maltman Barry came as one of the delegates from a German group in Chicago. Other unconditional followers had similar credentials.

As if to make Marx's task easier, many Latin socialist and anarchist delegates became indignant at these and other measures of the Council and decided not to attend. From a publisher in Russia, Marx got a letter to be used against Bakunin to expose him as an "embezzler." All the letter really said was that Marx's great rival, and in many respects his admirer, had accepted a three hundred-

---

[21] This was the second time that Marx had moved an international organization outside the reach of opponents in order to bury it. The first such maneuver was carried out in 1850 when the German emigrés in London mustered a majority against him. By skillful and remorseless intrigue he managed to move the Communist League from London to Cologne, where it died. On that see Mehring, *op. cit.*, p. 233; Mayer, *op. cit.*, Vol. II, p. 2.

ruble advance against a translation of *Das Kapital* into Russian, and then had been so slow in delivering the text that the publisher had had to hire another translator. Bakunin, as is the wont of impecunious writers with advances, had spent the money and could not return it. Moreover, the unscrupulous adventurer Nechaev had promised Bakunin to "take care of the matter," which he did (quite without Bakunin's knowledge) by threatening the publisher's life if he should demand the return of the advance. This had happened in 1869. Though by 1872 Marx knew the true facts, he did not scruple to use the letter to give his rival the *coup de grace*. When the delegates assembled at The Hague, in a hall named by a mischievous fate, *Concordia*, all matters had really been settled by these preliminary maneuvers.[22]

Many of these preparations were unknown to the delegates until the battle over credentials began. When Barry presented the credential Marx had fixed up for him from Chicago, the English delegation, first through John Hales, Secretary of the Delegation and of the General Council, then through the British trade unionist Mottershead, objected to the mandate. At this point the unofficial German-language *Minutes,* kept by Heppner, record:

Mottershead asks why of all things Barry was elected by a foreign German Section whereas at home in England he does not belong among the leaders and is a nobody?—

Marx says it is none of their business whom the Section elects. Besides, it should be counted an honor to Barry not to belong among the so-called leaders of the English workingmen, for these are all more or less sold out to the bourgeoisie and the government.[23]

---

[22] On the packing of the congress, see Gustav Mayer, *Friedrich Engels,* The Hague, 1934, Vol. II, p. 247; *Briefe und Auszuege aus Briefen von Johann Philip Becker, Josef Dietzgen, Friedrich Engels, Karl Marx, und Anderen,* Stuttgart, 1906, p. 59; Franz Mehring, *Karl Marx,* p. 516; Hans Gerth, *The First International, Minutes of the Hague Congress of 1872 with Related Documents,* Madison, 1958, pp. vii, xvi, xvii; *La Première Internationale, Recueil de documents publié sous la direction de Jacques Freymond,* Geneva, 1962, Vol. I, pp. xx–xxvii, Vol. II, pp. 266–479. The ideas of expelling Bakunin and holding a congress in a place where he could not attend find their first expression in letters of Marx to Engels on July 27, 1869 and May 15, 1870 (*MEGA,* III/4, pp. 213 and 330). On the accusation that Bakunin was guilty of embezzlement, Marx's generally admiring biographer, Franz Mehring, writes: "That Bakunin was to be robbed of his good name in questions of *meum et tuum* was inexcusable." (*op. cit.,* pp. 516–17; Nikolaevsky and Maenchen-Helfen, *op. cit.,* pp. 349–51). [23] Gerth, *op. cit.,* pp. 29, 186, 262. The *Minutes* were supposed to be kept by four secretaries in four languages: German, French, English, and Dutch. Sorge and Heppner, the German Secretaries, were both followers of Marx. Barry

The attack on the British labor leaders was probably even sharper than Heppner's *Minutes* suggest, for the reports of both Barry and Guillaume quote Marx as saying: "the British leaders had all sold themselves to Gladstone, Morley, Dilke and others."[24]

After this insult to their chosen leaders and this close-up of Marx's methods of faction fighting, the British lost their last interest in the association they had founded. Marx lost interest, too. Having gotten the power he sought, and having used it to expel his leading opponents and to move the General Council to New York to be cared for by his follower, Sorge, Marx returned to his "scientific work" while the International died ingloriously far from the England in which it was born. We shall have to examine its troubled history further in another context. But now we must return to the questions of war and peace.

The first source of Marx's quarrel with the British labor leaders was their detestation of war, and their inclination to the more pacific Liberal Party, rather than the more bellicose Conservatives, in the Russian question. Marx's first public denunciation of British labor "corruption" was made in Liebknecht's pamphlet, published in 1877 during the Russo-Turkish War. That war, as we have seen, ended so swiftly that in any case it would have been impossible for England to intervene. Nothing remained but the possibility of European intervention at the peace table to see that Russia did not press her advantage too hard. In 1878, the neutral Bismarck undertook, in his own words, to "play the honest broker" between Russia and the other interested powers, a role which concentrated on him all the wrath of that small but articulate body of Russian public opinion which felt cheated of its expectations. Thus he helped to bring about what he (and Marx and Engels with him) now feared most, a readiness on Russia's part to consider an alliance with Republican France, which was still smarting at the loss of Alsace-Lorraine.

Thenceforward to the day of their deaths, Marx and Engels never wavered in their fear of a Franco-Russian alliance and a two-front "war of the races" which it might bring in its train. On Sep-

---

served many masters. At the congress he invariably voted with Marx. Despite the congress's decision, however, he reported its sessions in the *London Daily Standard*. Later he attached himself to the English Conservative Party. (Gerth, *op. cit.*, pp. ix, 298.) Gerth's book contains, besides the German minutes and an English translation, Barry's newspaper reports.

24 Gerth, *op. cit.*

tember 12, 1880, a little less than three years before his death, that
same Marx who in 1848 had urged his countrymen to take on Denmark, France, Russia, and Prussia together, wrote soberly to the
Russian economist, Nikolai-on (Danielson):

> I hope that there will not be a general war in Europe. Although in
> the long run the war would not be able to arrest social development (I
> have in mind *economic* development), but would rather intensify it,
> still it would certainly produce a useless exhaustion of strength for a
> more or less prolonged period.[25]

Despite his predilection for military strategy and tactics, "the
General" completely shared Marx's newborn fear. Because Engels
concerned himself with improvements in weaponry and mass manpower, he saw more deeply than Marx into the destructiveness of
modern warfare. After the latter's death, he continued to write such
warnings until, twelve years later, his voice was stilled. With every
writing, the outlines grew grimmer.

An exchange of letters between Engels and Marx in September,
1879, showed how swiftly their feelings were changing about war
with Russia. No longer does war seem a means to the revolutionizing of both Russia and Europe. Marx mocks at the way Bismarck
has stumbled into a quarrel with Russia, yesterday's ally. Engels,
without enthusiasm, rather somewhat complainingly now, observes
that Bismarck is "working with both hands and feet to bring about a
war with Russia." He expects that England and Austria may join
Bismarck, while Denmark and even France may remain neutral.
Anyhow, the Narodniks seem to be preparing a revolution in Russia
(he was misled by the few resounding acts of the terror), and then
the Russian-German alliance will be over. It would be better if a
revolution should come in Russia without war. In any case, there
was grave danger for Germany and for their movement:

> A simultaneous war against Russia and France would be a struggle
> for national existence [for Germany], and in the chauvinism kindled
> by it, our movement would be ruined for years . . .[26]

---

[25] The letter was written by Marx in English and signed for conspirative
reasons *A. Williams.* Here it is translated back into English from *Perepiska K.
Marksa i F. Engelsa s russkimi deyatelyami,* Moscow, 1947, pp. 86–87. The fear
that Europe would be exhausted and barbarized, and the reassuring phrase
about wars not being able "in the long run" to arrest the inevitable victory of
socialism, were from now on to appear in all the warnings of Marx and Engels
on the nightmare which would haunt them ceaselessly. It was not the nightmare
of "defeatists," or of men who did not love their native land.
[26] Letter of Engels to Marx of September 9, and of Marx to Engels of September 10, 1879, *MEGA,* III/4, pp. 495–98.

It is hard to believe that this is the correspondence of men who as late as a year or so back were still crying for all and sundry to join Turkey against Russia, and still crying *treason* at those who were for keeping the peace.

At the end of 1882, during Marx's last illness, Engels wrote a letter to Bebel which expressed the new mood of both:

> A European war I would consider a misfortune. This time it would be terribly serious. Everywhere it would inflame chauvinism for years on end, for each people would be fighting for its existence. The whole work of the revolutionaries in Russia, now on the eve of victory, would become useless, destroyed. Our party in Germany would momentarily be drowned in the flood of chauvinism and shattered, and the same would happen in France. . . . a Russian constitution, if it came as a result of misfortune in war would have quite another meaning from one gained by revolution, a rather more conservative meaning. . . .[27]

This was a far cry from Lenin's famous letter to Gorky that war between Russia and Austria would be a "great trick for the revolution," or that defeat of his country in war was the high road to social revolution in Russia and all Europe. It was a long way, too, from the Marx and Engels of the three preceding decades. But as a prophecy it was a genuine prevision.

In the eighties Engels had lost nothing of his earlier disdain for the lesser Slavic peoples; indeed, his deep concern with the danger of general war caused him to add a further stricture on them. It was an uprising of South Slavs in Austria that caused him to return to the subject.

In 1881, the Austro-Hungarian Empire tried to conscript its southern Slavs, including those of the newly acquired "protectorates" of Bosnia and Herzegovina. The result was a Slav rebellion. Both Bernstein and Kautsky, as editors of the German party organ, *Socialdemokrat,* unhesitatingly took the side of the Slavic rebels against their German rulers, warning "West European Democracy" that, if it did not rally to the support of the Slavic revolutionaries, they would turn to the Tsar for help.

On February 22, 1882, Engels wrote Bernstein urging that the journal change its policy. Western Democracy and Socialism should oppose the revolt, he thought, for the following reasons:

---

[27] Marx-Engels, *Briefe an A. Bebel, und Andere,* Moscow, 1933, p. 412.

. . . First, the danger of Panslavism . . . lies not in the periphery but in the center, not in the Balkans but in the eighty million Slavs from which the Tsar gathers his armies and finances . . .

Second, I don't want to examine how it came about that the little Slavic peoples see in the Tsar their only liberator. It is enough that they do . . . If there is a war, then all these interesting nationettes will take the side of Tsarism, the enemy of the entire developed bourgeois West. As long as this is so, I cannot take an interest in their *direct*, immediate liberation. They remain our direct enemies, just as much as their ally and protector, the Tsar. . . .

The victory of the proletariat will liberate them, truly and of necessity, not merely apparently and temporarily as with the Tsar. [Involuntarily, one is reminded of Stalin's "liberation" of these same peoples after World War Two.] Therefore, they who have hitherto not only done nothing for Europe and its development but have even been a hindrance, should at least have as much patience as our proletariat.

To kindle a world war for the sake of a couple Herzegovinians, a war which will cost a thousand times as many men as all those who live in Herzegovina—that is not my idea of a policy for the proletariat. . . .

If from the uprising of these fellows a world war threatens to flare up that will spoil our entire revolutionary situation, then they and their right to cattle-stealing must be mercilessly sacrificed to the interests of the European proletariat. . . .

The most interesting part of Engels's letter is the warning about a coming war with which he concludes it. You are too "lighthearted" about this, he lectures Bernstein. Remembering how Bismarck had taken in Marx and him in 1870, Engels admonishes Bernstein: "If it comes to war, Bismarck will easily manage to make Russia appear the attacker." Then, while Germany is fighting for her life in the East, France will seek revenge for the conquests of 1870:

Thereby, it seems obvious to me, Germany will fall into a struggle for its existence, and patriotic chauvinism will win the upper hand. . . . The outcome of such a struggle . . . is entirely incalculable, and I should not wish it to occur at any price.

On the other hand, if peace can be prolonged, Engels continues, things are going so well for our party that "we ourselves do not have to do anything, only let our opponents work for us." The Tsar will fall by revolt ("at most a matter of months"). With that, revolution will spread all over Europe. (Engels still clung to the belief that only the Tsar's intervention had caused the failure of the revolutions of '48.)

One thing could spoil this prospect: general war. Such a war would make the Tsar popular once more. All the work and sacrifices of the revolutionaries in Russia would be undone. In Germany, such a "patriotic howling" would be heard that Bismarck would find it easy to crush us, while "our own people will chime in with the howl. . . . Shall I wish for war under such circumstances? Certainly not. Not even if two hundred noble robber peoples should be ruined."[28]

The supreme prophecy on the danger of war on the part of Engels came in 1887, addressed this time not to a single party or class but to the German nation. For it he found more eloquent language than he ever had for the social revolution:

No other war is now possible for Prussia-Germany than a world war, and indeed a world war of hitherto unimagined sweep and violence. Eight to ten million soldiers will mutually kill each other off, and in the process devour Europe barer than any swarm of locusts ever did. The desolation of the Thirty Years' War compressed into three or four years and spread over the entire continent; famine, plague, general savagery, taking possession both of the armies and of the masses of the people, as a result of universal want; hopeless demoralization of our complex institutions of trade, industry and credit, ending in universal bankruptcy; collapse of the old states and their traditional statecraft, so that crowns will roll over the pavements by the dozens and no one be found to pick them up; absolute impossibility of foreseeing where all this will end, or who will emerge victor from the general struggle. Only *one* result is absolutely sure: general exhaustion and the creation of the conditions for the final victory of the working class.[29]

Engels's closing years were brightened by great electoral gains

---

[28] Cited from Kautsky, *op. cit.*, pp. 245–46.
[29] From Engels's introduction to the reissue of a pamphlet by Sigismund Borkheim. Borkheim's pamphlet, *Zur Errinnerung fuer die deutschen Mordspatrioten 1806–07* (*In Memory of the German Super-patriots of 1806–07*), was an analysis of the collapse of the German Army after the battle of Jena in 1806, and a warning to the German Nation not to let itself get intoxicated by the swift victory of 1870. Like Engels's own pamphlets on the Po Valley, it had no special "class angle." Borkheim had been a personal friend, and two years after his death, Engels republished it as a memorial to him, and a warning to the German people. The date of publication was 1887. The introduction is reproduced in *Werke,* Vol. XXI, pp. 350–51.

being made by the German Social Democracy, but darkened by the lowering shadow of war. From the middle eighties when he wrote the apocalyptic warning we have just quoted until the day of his death, the grim specter of the four horsemen would not let him rest. Sometimes he sought to reassure himself:

> It may happen [he wrote Bebel on Nov. 17, 1885] that the war machines will rebel, and refuse mutually to kill each other off for the sake of the lousy Balkan peoples. . . . But I confess, I hope it comes off without this slaughter; surely it is not needed.[30]

It was not the older great powers (with the exception of course of Russia) whose territorial ambitions Engels feared. It was the new-born Balkan lands that he found land-greedy, frivolous in the use of their newly-acquired guns and bombs, dangerously, lightheadedly aggressive toward each other. It was their struggles over disputed territories that might yet drag in the great powers, a danger greatly increased by Germany's seizure of Alsace and Lorraine, which put it before the dilemma of either supporting Russia in the Balkans, or, if it supported Austria, risking the consolidation of a Franco-Russian alliance and all the perils for Germany of a two-front war.

In the letter to Bebel just cited, Engels went over the whole worrisome dilemma once more. The land-greedy—the "imperialists" —he found in the young Balkan nations. It was their struggles to seize each other's borderlands, their quarrels over the Macedonian Highlands, the Adriatic Coast, the Slavic parts of the Austro-Hungarian Empire, which might somehow get the great powers involved in general war:

> These wretched, ruined fragments of one-time nations, the Serbs, Bulgars, Greeks, and other robber bands, on behalf of which the liberal philistine waxes enthusiastic in the interests of Russia, are unwilling to grant each other the air they breathe, and feel obliged to cut each other's greedy throats.[31]

In letter after letter Engels returns to this nightmare. If war

---

[30] Marx-Engels, *Briefe an Bebel, Liebknecht, Kautsky und Andere*, Moscow, 1933, p. 412.

[31] *Ibid.*, p. 411. So today India and Pakistan remain mobilized on each other's borders and unwilling or unable to come to an agreement for the partition of Kashmir, or the opportunity for the Kashmiris to determine their own fate. So Indonesia, hurling execrations at "imperialism," sends guerrilla armies into the neighboring states of Borneo, and the new Somalia seeks to annex a "Somalia irridenta" in Ethiopia. And even so, our General Tasker Bliss would look askance at the new nations born of the Treaty of Versailles in 1919, and write to his wife: "They appear to have been born with fangs, and in their cradles cry out for weapons with which to attack each other."

came, he foresaw "the inevitable ruin of our movement, and the need to start all over again, something like in 1850." He dwelt on the frightful shedding of Europe's blood and treasure, "desolation and finally exhaustion."

In one letter to Bebel, dated September 13, 1886, he tried to calculate the chances of such a war:

> The German army is unconditionally the best and the best led, but it is only one among many. As in everything, the Austrians are hard to figure out militarily, both as to numbers and as to leadership, but they have always known how to let their best soldiers fight. The Russians deceive themselves as always about their colossal strength on paper; they are extremely weak in an offensive, in the defense of their own land, strong. Their weakest point, besides the supreme command, is the lack of usable officers for such enormous masses. . . .

Then the letter goes on to the Turks ("the best fighters but with a high command that is miserable when not actually bought"); the French ("lacking officers because the French bourgeois is absolutely unwarlike"); the English—which side would they take?

> England's importance will grow as the war lasts (both because of her enormous fleet and her enormous resources). Though she may keep her soldiers in reserve at the beginning, an English army corps of 60,000 men could well deal the finishing blow. . . .[32]

In letters of Engels to Sorge and Liebknecht written in 1888 we find variations on these same themes. At the outbreak of war, Germany would be the strongest power, which was good, for he did not wish to see Bismarck overthrown by military defeat, at least until there had been a revolution in Russia (which he still expected to break out momentarily).

But he was pleased, too, with the new French fortifications, which the German army would find "a hard nut to crack." (In 1914, they would crack it by outflanking the forts through neutral Belgium.)

> As things stand now, Germany cannot beat France, nor France Germany. Excellent! If worst comes to worst, there will probably be a static war on the frontiers, with varying fortunes, which will impress both armies with respect for their enemy and make a passable peace easy to conclude.[33]

His opposition to a smashing defeat for Germany was as far from

---

[32] *Ibid.*, pp. 467–70.
[33] Mayer, *op. cit.*, p. 291.

Lenin's defeatism for one's own country as was his desire for a
stalemate and a decent peace without victory for either side. The
first Lenin would call social chauvinism in 1914 and the second
social pacifism, and both treason to Marxism and socialism! In such
sentences from Engels's pen one senses the spirit of a man who loves
his country and Paris and old Europe, and does not want to see their
values destroyed.

In most of these letters there is some phrase of ritual comfort,
repeated one feels with less and less conviction, to the effect that
"after the mass butchery on an unparalleled scale and the exhaustion
of all Europe to an unparalleled degree," after the brutalization,
plague, and famine, there would finally come "the collapse of the
old system."

But in notes found among his papers after his death, his thought
is gloomier, the ritual reassurance frequently missing:

Tragicomic conflict [reads one such note]: the state must wage
political wars, which never arouse national enthusiasm. And for them
it needs a national army, which is only reliable for national defence,
and for defensives directly following from it (1814 and 1870). In this
conflict, the Prussian state and the Prussian army go smash—probably
in a war with Russia, which may last for four years and in which
there is nothing to be gained but diseases and broken bones.[34]

Sometimes he felt that the alliances in Europe were really not as
stable as his prophecies suggested, but constantly shifting with each
new conjuncture, even each change of monarch or foreign minister.
The "millstone of alliances" that weighed so heavily on Bismarck's
neck, weighed heavily on Engels's heart.

It might be that the new Emperor (William II) would throw
open the way to Constantinople to the Russians in return for a free
hand against the French. But in that case, in the long run Germany
would find the whole world lined up against her, and in the end
would surely be defeated. "I hope this danger will pass," he wrote
gloomily to Liebknecht in April 1888. Again his papers sound a
darker note. Any war in Europe now was a leap in the dark, and
might sweep away many precious things which seemed so stable
and secure. In the case of such a war "American industry would be
victorious all along the line and would thrust upon us this choice—
either a relapse into pure agriculture on a subsistence basis (Amer-

---

[34] *Ibid.*, p. 291.

ican grain would prevent it from being anything more than that) or . . . a transformation of society."[35]

Another note reads:

A war? Easy enough to begin, but it defies conjecture to say what will happen once it has begun.[36]

Thus his private notes, like his letters to his closest comrades, were full of ever-deepening concern:

Impossible to conjecture . . . nothing to gain but disease and broken bones . . . plague, famine and exhaustion . . . the outcome is entirely incalculable . . . Europe reduced to subsistence agriculture . . . the desolation of the Thirty Years' War compressed into four years . . . general savagery taking possession of both armies and peoples . . . will devour Europe barer than any swarm of locusts ever did . . . I wish it would not occur at any price. . . .

The voice of foreboding grows stronger; the words of ritual comfort falter or disappear. Were ruins really the building blocks with which to construct a higher social order? Could a Europe with industry and cities in ruins, reduced to subsistence agriculture, undertake such a task? Was the prospect of years of universal brutalization and savagery and mass murder a proper preparation of man himself for an order more humane?

---

[35] *Ibid.*, p. 292.
[36] *Ibid.*, p. 292. Some of these manuscript notes are repeated verbatim in his letters and articles; others were intended either only for his own eyes, or he never got around to using them.

Chapter 4

FROM PEACE TO
THE DEFENSE OF
THE FATHERLAND

We have not forgotten the splendid example that France
gave us in 1793.
—Friedrich Engels to the French workingmen in 1892

ON NOVEMBER 17, 1885, when Engels wrote Bebel of his hope that
the armies of the civilized lands of Western Europe might refuse "to
kill each other off for the sake of the lousy Balkan peoples," he
added an additional thought which we noted previously in another
context:

I confess, I hope it comes without this slaughter; surely it isn't
needed. But if it must come, then I only hope that my old injury
doesn't prevent me, at the right moment, from mounting my horse
again.[1]

Did he want to mount his horse to fight his own government,
strive for its defeat and a revolution in wartime? Or to defend his
country against the outer foe?

Engels assumes that Bebel knew what he meant, and indeed,
Bebel did, and shared the hope and the patriotism of his teacher. As
early as 1880, Marx being then still alive, Bebel had gotten up in the
Reichstag after Bismarck outlawed his party, to say that despite this
new law against "the fellows without a country," in the hour of
danger, the Social Democrats would defend the country as well as
the best. Marx and Engels made no objection. Once more in 1891
under solemn circumstances, at the Erfurt Congress of his party, a

---

[1] Marx-Engels, *Briefe an Bebel*, p. 412.

congress closely watched and guided by Engels, Bebel told the delegates:

> If Russia, the refuge of cruelty and barbarism, the enemy of all human culture, attacks Germany in order to partition and destroy her . . . then we are as much interested, and more so, than those who stand today at the head of Germany, and we will fight against the attack.

Again Engels approved. As he hoped to be able to mount his horse again if need be, in the hour of Germany's mortal danger, so, many times, did old Bebel (the last was in 1907) repeat in solemn assembly, that in case of attack from Russia, "enemy of all the oppressed and of all civilization . . . I myself, old fellow that I am, am still ready to shoulder a rifle."[2]

In 1890, William II dismissed the aged Bismarck and became in effect his own Chancellor and Foreign Minister. For the father, Bismarck had been the creator of the Empire, but the son looked on it as a ready-made inheritance to be taken for granted. He had neither Bismarck's strength of character nor his practical sagacity; he was unaware of the danger of getting drunk on one's own phrases, or alarming one's neighbors by false bravado. He did not have Bismarck's tight control of generals and ministers, a fact that was to prove fatal in 1914. In foreign affairs and military plans, "he never really ruled, only interfered." Nor did he share Bismarck's misprision for overseas empire, suddenly become fashionable once more in the least promising part of the world, Central Africa, nor Bismarck's view that the Balkans "were not worth the bones of a single Pomeranian grenadier."

For William II history began with three successful *Blitzkriege*, each crowned with easy military victory, and increased popularity at home. His reign, he was sure, would bring "glorious days" to the German people and write golden pages in their history. But Engels wrote gloomily: "If Wilhelm crosses the Rhine, he will destroy a great empire."[3]

Alarmed by what he foreboded, on October 13, 1891, Engels wrote to Bebel, as the party's leading spokesman in the Reichstag:

> If we are convinced that it will break out next spring, we can hardly oppose on principle these requests for [military] appropriations. And then we would be in a pretty bad situation. The lickspittle

---

[2] As noted above; Bebel's biographer, Kluehs, in his *August Bebel*, Berlin, 1923, pp. 68–78, has brought together all these statements.
[3] *MELS*, Vol. II, Part 2, p. 1118, reprinted from the German-language *Sozialdemokrat*, London, March 8, 1890. It was another true prophecy.

parties will boast that they have been right, and that we have had to eat our words. And such an unexpected change of front would cause appalling friction within our party—and internationally, also.

But Engels was not one to quail before such difficulties when he thought that the main thing was to defend his country in the hour of peril to its existence. So he made the naïve proposal that the Party should offer to vote for the military budget provided the government would agree not to use the money for the formation of *new* cadres or the purchase of *new* types of equipment, "since neither could be carried out in time for war in the spring." The Party should further stipulate that it was ready to vote for an appropriation:

. . . which would bring the present army nearer to a people's militia, which will simply strengthen our ability to defend ourselves, which will train and arm all men who have not yet been enlisted, from seventeen to sixty, and organize them into fixed units [cadres] without increasing all that control. . . . We cannot demand that the existing military organization should be completely transformed while the danger of war persists.

If there is an effort to take the great masses of men who are fit for service but have not been trained, and to train them as well as possible, and put them into cadres—for real fighting, not for parading and all that nonsense—that is an approach to our idea of a people's militia which we can accept.

If the danger of war increases, we can tell the government that, if they made it possible for us by decent treatment, we would be ready to give our support against the foreign foe—on condition that they are ready to fight relentlessly and use every means, even revolutionary means. If Germany is attacked from both east and west, then any means of defense is good. Then the existence of the nation is at stake, and we too have a position to maintain, and a future which we have won by hard struggle.[4]

Few things make so clear the ambiguity of the heritage for the heirs of Marx and Engels as their treatment of this letter. Neither pacifists nor defeatists nor the Internationalists of the Zimmerwald Conference could use it. Only the defensists of 1914 could, in some measure.

Ryazanov, an honorable and scholarly student of Marx, set out to publish the whole of the work of Marx and Engels in his monumental *Marx-Engels Gesamtausgabe*. When he had finished the first

---

[4] Gustav Mayer, *Friedrich Engels*, The Hague, Vol. II, pp. 514–15.

fourteen tomes and prepared some additional material for publication, in the year 1931 he was expelled by Stalin from his Party and exiled to Siberia where he died in 1943. As Simone Weil once wrote of the Romans that their chief contribution to science in antiquity was the assassination of Archimedes, so Boris Souvarine wrote (I quote from memory): "The chief contribution of Joseph Stalin to Marxism is the purging of David Ryazanov."

Next V. V. Adoratsky, on a lower and more servile plane, took up the unfinished work of the Marx-Engels Institute, rechristened Marx-Engels-Lenin Institute. He issued a few volumes which his learned predecessor had prepared, but the courage, scholarship, and illuminating annotation gave way to brief, flat, timid, and apologetic footnotes, and explanations that explained away whatever was inconvenient. In 1933 he published the first part of an intended two-volume work called *Briefe an A. Bebel, W. Liebknecht, K. Kautsky und Andrere*. This carried Engels's letters to Bebel through the year 1886. Part Two never appeared, but Adoratsky disappeared, his scholarly career ending as Ryazanov's had, in Stalin's bloody purges.

Thereafter the Institute, taking cognizance of Stalin's great contributions to Marxism, became the Marx-Engels-Lenin-Stalin Institute. It published a work of the big four called *Marx-Engels-Lenin-Stalin zur deutschen Geschichte* (here referred to by the initials of its four co-authors as *MELS*). This professed, among other matter, to reproduce all the letters from Engels to Bebel or to anyone else which dealt directly or indirectly with German history. There are in it letters to Bebel antedating the one we have just quoted, and letters postdating it, but the letter of October 13, 1891 is not there. The Institute has also published the *Selected Letters of Marx and Engels* in English, and in German. Once more this letter is strangely missing. Even the scholarly, and dependably honest, Karl Kautsky does not appear to have found use for the letter in his thick book, *Sozializten und Krieg*, Prague, 1937.

With Stalin's death and subsequent expulsion from Olympus by his one-time lieutenant, the Institute changed its protean existence once more and became the Institut fuer Marxismus-Leninismus beim ZK der SED, offshoot of a similar Institute attached to the Central Committee of the CPSU. This time the works of Marx and Engels are appearing consecutively in the original German (or in German translation if originally written in English or French*);

---

* Ryazanov's *Gesamtausgabe* reproduced the texts in their original languages. And the German translation in *Werke* is sometimes tendentious.

each volume is introduced anonymously by the two Institutes without any indication of who is doing the editing. The guillotine has been out of operation for some time now, and it is hard to cut off the head of an anonymous Institute, hence we can hope that the letter will at last appear when they get to the corresponding volume. But so far, the only trace I have been able to find (the portions quoted here) is in Gustav Mayer's two-volume biography of Friedrich Engels.

Having spoken thus to his own party through August Bebel, Engels cast about for some proper means to speak to the French on the war which seemed to him close at hand. At that very moment, the more Marxist of the French Socialist Parties (le Parti Ouvrier led by Jules Guesde and Paul Lafargue) invited the old warrior to contribute something to their annual *Almanac* for 1892. "Something from Engels" was to be the icing on the cake, but the old man was too desperately in earnest for that. He wrote to Paul Lafargue and his wife, Laura (Marx's daughter)—a bit anxiously—outlining his intentions. Then he sent Bebel a summary of the intended article:

> People must realize that if France, in alliance with Russia, should declare war on Germany, she would be fighting against the strongest Social Democratic Party in Europe; and that we would have no choice but to oppose with all our strength any aggressor who was on the side of Russia. For if we are defeated, the social democratic movement in Europe is smashed for twenty years. If not, we shall come to power ourselves. The present system in Germany cannot possibly survive war.[5]

Engels's warning to the French nation through the pages of the *Almanac* was as frank as his summary suggests. Like other parts of his writing during the last five years of his life, collectively regarded as his "Testament," it began with an old man's backward glance over the years of his life and that of Karl Marx.

He spoke of the "disintegration" of Hegelian philosophy, out of

---

[5] Friedrich Engels, *Briefe an Bebel*. Besorgt vom Institut fuer Marxismus-Leninismus beim ZK der SED, Berlin, 1958, pp. 189–91. In English in Mayer's *Biography of Engels*, p. 311. Omitted from *Marx-Engels-Lenin-Stalin on German History*. The letters to and from the Lafargues on the *Almanac* article are in Friedrich Engels, Paul and Laura Lafargue, *Correspondance*, Paris, 1959, Vol. III, pp. 99, 101, 108–09, 115, 116–17, 118. Most of the letters were written in English, a French translation being appended. To Engels's relief, Lafargue wrote: *"il est magnifique,"* and Laura, that it was "what has been needed here." But they did not prove representative of French opinion.

which Marxism was born; of the fusion of Marx's doctrine with German working-class socialism, itself nourished on French socialist theories; of the conflicts with the Lassalleans and the ultimate fusion of the two German socialist currents. With pride he designated his own land as "the nation which begot the *Communist Manifesto.*" Then he boasted of Bismarck's failure to kill the German movement by outlawing it and of its growth from year to year, so that it was now possible "to fix with almost mathematical certainty the exact time when it will come to power." Even now the votes his party received made it the largest party in the Reich. But since German youth was more socialist-minded than its elders and a voter had to be twenty-five while an army recruit had only to be twenty, the party's strength in the army was far greater than the strength it showed at the polls.

> Today we have one soldier in five; in a few years we will have one in three; around 1900, the army . . . will be socialist in its majority. This advances unceasingly like a decree of fate. . . . The government sees it coming but is powerless. The army is slipping out of its hands.

Though his party was unwilling to take an oath that it would never again resort to illegal methods of work if the need arose, under the present circumstances it was not the socialists who would violate legality. Let *them* violate their own legality. When they try to provoke us into doing so, we say: "Please be so good as to shoot first, Messrs. Bourgeois!"

Thus the old man reviewed his battles, and repeated his time-table and his dream of certain victory.

Only in the final section did he come to the point that had motivated his choice of a subject. The peaceful political and economic development he had been describing, and the victory he declared to be so near and so certain, could be disturbed by only one thing: the outbreak of an internecine war that would tear Europe apart, ranging "France and Russia on one side, Germany, Austria, and perhaps Italy, on the other."[6] Had not Marx already warned Bismarck in 1870 that his annexation of Alsace and Lorraine might

---

[6] Marx and Engels were good enough Europeans to regard any war between Western nations as a kind of "civil war." Thus Marx wrote Engels in 1868 that "a war between France and Germany is a civil war for the profit of Russia." And he complained that his follower, Eccarius, had altered his formula to read that "any European war is a civil war." Because of its "semi-Oriental despotism" and its aggressiveness, Marx drew the line at Russia. *MEGA*, III/4, p. 92.

bring about just this catastrophe, "not a new-fangled 'localized war,' but a war of races, a war with the united Slavs and Latins?"

As compared with official imperial Germany, he did not doubt that the French Republic represented the revolution. But, he reminded his French comrades, there was another Germany for them to bear in mind: a socialist Germany, the Germany of the near and certain future.

As soon as that Germany came to power, of course it would return Alsace and Lorraine to France and northern Schleswig to Denmark, and it would liberate Poland.

It was only a matter of waiting some ten years more [he urged]. In France, in England and in Germany, the proletariat itself is still waiting for its emancipation. Shall the Alsace-Lorraine patriots not be able to wait a little longer, too? Because of their impatience, shall a whole continent be laid waste, and delivered in the end to the Tsarist knout?

But what if they would not wait, he asked, and if war should come under the present relation of forces? Then France and Germany would both be laid waste. Only the Tsar would gain. As for Germany:

. . . then it would be struggling for its simple existence. If it won, it would find nothing anywhere to annex; to west and to east of it there are only foreign-speaking provinces, and of those it already has more than enough. If, crushed between the hammer of France and the anvil of Russia, it is defeated, it will lose Old Prussia [i.e. East Prussia] and its Polish provinces to Russia, all of Silesia to Denmark, the entire left bank of the Rhine to France. . . . Reduced to the estate which Napoleon forced upon it at Tilsit, it could only continue to live by preparing another war for the restoration of the conditions for its national existence. . . . The Social Democratic Party would be suppressed. . . .

Now Engels came to his outspoken warning:

The German Social Democratic Party has conquered for itself such a place as no other socialist party in the world possesses, a place that guarantees that within a short time the political power will fall into its hands. Socialist Germany occupies the foremost, the most honorable, the most responsible post in the international labor movement. It has the duty to defend this post to the last man against any attacker. . . . In the interest of the European Revolution, they are obligated to maintain all the posts they have conquered, not to capitulate any more to the outer than to the inner foe. And this they can do only by fighting to the uttermost against Russia and all its allies, whoever they may be. Should the French Republic put itself at the service of His Majesty, the Tsar and Autocrat of All the Russias, then the German socialists will fight with sorrow, but fight they will. Compared with German Kaiserdom the French Republic *may* possibly represent the bourgeois revolution. But . . . against the Republic in the service of the Russian Tsar, German socialism unconditionally represents the proletarian revolution.

Finally, to stir French memories of their own revolutionary tradition and the revolutionary wars fought in its name, Engels revived once more the mistaken metaphor under the spell of which Marx and he had lived:

A war in which Russians and Frenchmen were to break into Germany would be for the latter a life and death struggle, in which it could assure its existence only by the application of the most revolutionary methods. The present government, unless it is forced to, will surely not unleash a revolution. But we have a strong party which can force it to, or if need be, replace it.

And we have not forgotten the splendid example that France gave us in 1793. The hundredth anniversary of 1793 is approaching. If the Tsar's thirst for conquest and the chauvinist impatience of the French bourgeoisie should stop the victorious but peaceful forward march of the German socialists, then the latter are ready—on this you can count—to show the world that the German proletarians of today are not unworthy of the sans-culottes of a hundred years ago, and that 1893 may be worthy of comparison with 1793. If then the soldiers of M. Constans set their feet on German soil, they will be greeted with the words of the "Marseillaise":

> Quoi, ces cohortes étrangères
> Feraient la loi dans nos foyers![7]

In his translation for the *Neue Zeit* Engels wrote of himself as one "whose position, won by fifty years of work, forbids me to take a stand for this or that national socialist party as against the other, even though it does not forbid me to remember that I am a German, nor forbid me to be proud of the position our German workers have

---

[7] M. Constans (Jean-Antoine-Ernest Constans), a second-string French political figure, in 1892 was Minister of the Interior. The article in the *Almanac for 1892* was written by Engels in French, then translated by him into German and published in *Neue Zeit*, X/I, pp. 580–87, so that the German party might also see what he had said to the French. Also in *MELS*, II/2, pp. 1137–45.

won for themselves before all the others."[8]

Most French socialists were shocked when the *Almanac* appeared. The article was everywhere contested. Could this be the internationalism of which their great tribunes spoke? Was this the pacifism which was even then being embodied in resolutions of the newly-formed Second International?

"It was," wrote Engels's biographer, Gustav Mayer, "because Engels considered a world war unnecessary and shrank from the idea, that in the last years of his life he was drawn to take a very active part in politics."[9] Was this then the meaning of his activities of these last years?

Engels wrote in his foreword to the German version that he had written the article as a duty to both the French and the German workers:

> To the French, because it must become known in Germany with what openness one can discuss with them the situation in which German socialists would unconditionally take part in a war even against France, and how free *these* Frenchmen are from chauvinism and thirst for revenge. . . . To the Germans, because the latter have the right to learn from me personally and in an authentic fashion what I have told the French about them.[10]

Engels's last words on war left an ineradicable mark on the thinking of German socialists concerning a two-front war in which Russian Autocracy and French Republic should have troops on their frontiers at the same time. Engels was not so much inspiring new views as giving expression to views latent in the German people, high and low, and showing once more how deep were the roots of feeling for the existence of their country in Marx and Engels themselves.

In France, where the echoes of the revolutionary patriotism born during the French Revolution and the imperial patriotism of the Bonapartes clashed with the easy and sonorous phrase radicalism of "*guerre à la guerre*" and "*pas un sous*" and "general strike against war"—an immediate debate broke out, opening afresh the not-yet healed, and never to be healed, rift between French Socialism and the "German Theory."

The leaders of the Parti Ouvrier were embarrassed, for they had asked for, approved, and published the article. As representatives on

---

[8] *Ibid.*
[9] Mayer, *op. cit.*, Vol. II, p. 464.
[10] *MELS*, Vol. II, p. 1137.

French soil of "the German theory, the only scientific theory of socialism," they had been assuring their followers and the French masses that they could count on German international socialism to oppose military budgets and war, actions which they, with less practical effect since they did not have a large parliamentary delegation like the Germans, had been preaching in France.

Vaillant, recent convert from Blanquism to Marxism, was indignant. Jules Guesde explained uncomfortably that the French workers, too, would be duty bound to defend their country if some other land "betrayed the peace of Europe." Bonner wrote Engels to say that if the Social Democrats were really so strong, they should be able to prevent such a war; if not, there was no call to proclaim their weakness.

The non-Marxist French socialists, syndicalists, and anarchists, the heirs of Bakunin and Proudhon, returned to their old charge that Marx and Engels were "Prussian Socialists" who had always wanted the supremacy of Germany on the continent and the supremacy of their theory in the International. Some noted that while the French socialists were revolutionaries and barricade fighters and had achieved their rights in street-fighting, the German socialists were submissive nationalists who had gotten suffrage and social security handed to them by the authorities.

In the face of this uproar, Engels held his ground. He did not try to explain further, or explain away, his forthright statement. Instead, he extended his position to the French, and by implication, to socialists everywhere:

If the French socialists do not expressly state that in a defensive war they would be willing to repel an attack by Kaiser Wilhelm, it is because this is so glaringly obvious and self-evident that it is not worth saying. There is not a single socialist in Germany who doubts that in such a case French socialists would simply do their duty in defending their national independence. Everybody would agree, and indeed, approve their action.[11]

For pacifists, antimilitarists, and internationalists à l'outrance, that only made matters worse. Fortunately for the peace of mind of Engels's defenders, no one in France, not even the Lafargues, knew that at that moment Engels was urging Bebel to have the party delegation in the Reichstag vote for the war credits "if we are convinced that the thing will start next spring," and if the money would

---

[11] Mayer, op. cit., II, p. 513.

go exclusively for the immediate training of "all men from seventeen to sixty" under limitations that, for all practical purpose, were meaningless. Bebel was too down-to-earth to follow this advice, and too discreet to argue with it or to make it public. But it left its impression all the same. For this letter, and the articles in the *Almanac* and *Neue Zeit* for 1892 constituted the last solemn word of Marx's old comrade-in-arms and posthumous interpreter, on war, peace, and national defense. These views, along with Engels's ardent desire to avoid war, and his discussion of barricades and elections (see Chapter XI) were built into the foundations of the Second International (1889–1914), through which Engels sought so earnestly to lay the specter of war that haunted his closing years. He was the chief legatee and executor of Karl Marx, and this was part of the ambiguous heritage which he in turn left in his *Testament*.

Chapter 5

WHAT LENIN MADE OF THE

TESTAMENT OF ENGELS

> Engels was the father of passive radicalism? Not true! Not
> at all. This you will never be able to show.
> —Lenin to Inessa Armand on January 19, 1917

WHEN THE VOICE of Engels was stilled, the heirs felt suddenly alone.
Who now would evaluate new social changes or propose new tactics? Marx and Engels had been authorized revisers of their own
doctrines and correctors of their own errors, but who was authorized
now to make changes in a doctrine on which great movements
rested, as an edifice rests on its foundations? Something like panic
seized the devoutest of the heirs lest their heritage be taken from
them.

Almost at once a great controversy broke out, centering around
Eduard Bernstein, friend of Engels's last years and his literary
executor. Bernstein's heresy was to suggest that the theories of the
increasing misery of the proletariat, of the growing polarization of
society, and the apocalyptic breakdown, were dogmas in need of re-
examination in the light of such phenomena as the development of
democratic institutions, a powerful and organized working class,
and a welfare state, and the continued persistence of intermediate
layers between the "handful" of supermagnates at one end, and the
rest of society supposedly reduced to misery and explosive wrath, at
the other. It is not my purpose to examine that "revisionist" controversy on which so much has been written. Something we shall
have to say in later chapters on the hesitant essays in revision of
parts of these doctrines by Marx and Engels themselves. Here we

83

will limit ourselves to the examination of the efforts of another "revisionist," one in whom the very sound of the word "revisionism" conjured up the furies. For in 1914, quite without prior warning or expectation, V. I. Lenin suddenly found it necessary to revise the whole basic attitude of his revered masters in the matters of war, peace, and national defense. Considered from the standpoint of its consequences for the history of our time, this was to prove the most important of the revisions made by any of the heirs.

The first thing to get straight, since it seems to have escaped the notice of commentators, Leninist and anti-Leninist alike, is that Lenin made his revision *ad hoc* in August 1914, and not before, although he was at great pains to give the impression that he had made it much earlier. This he did by a number of uneasy shiftings of the cut-off date on which the old era of "progressive capitalism" and "progressive wars," i.e., the days of Marx and Engels, had come to an end, so that their tactics could be revised or abandoned and new tactics adopted for a new period of which they had known nothing, the period of "decaying and dying capitalism." His writings, and the writings on this question of his lieutenant, Zinoviev, which he carefully edited, set the date variously as the end of the seventies, some time in the eighties, in the nineties, and around nineteen hundred. The uncertainty Lenin displays while groping for this date is revealing. With a little literary detective work, we can find out when, and why, and precisely how, he finally arrived at an exact cut-off date for the end of the old era and the beginning of the new.

The first war on which Lenin had to take a stand was the Russo-Japanese War of 1904–05. Japan and Russia were struggling over Manchuria, Mongolia, and Korea. It was, therefore, on both sides an imperialist war, fought to determine which of the two "imperialist powers" was to have the exclusive right to carve certain fat pieces out of the temporarily helpless Empire of China. No matter which of the attempts to find a cut-off date for the end of the era of "progressive capitalism" and the beginning of the new era of "decaying imperialist capitalism" we accept, this war was one manifestly occurring in the later of Lenin's two periods. Thus, according to the standards which Lenin himself proclaimed as self-evident in 1914, he should have been for the defeat of both Russia and Japan. But instead, in 1904 and 1905, he sought to follow the practice of Marx and Engels for the wars they had faced: he asked *which side he should favor and which oppose in the interests of "progress."*

The war occurred at a time when the Socialist International had become overwhelmingly pacifist, but three prominent Marxists gave open support to victory for Japan. They were the French Marxist leader, Jules Guesde, the British, H. M. Hyndman, and the Russian, V. I. Lenin.

The Russian Mensheviks took all three to task in the columns of *Iskra*, charging that they were unfaithful to the "Marxist antiwar heritage," and to the cause of the toiling people. Not a victory for one side, or the other, but the earliest possible peace without victory was what *Iskra* called for. Modern war, its editors felt, was an unmitigated calamity for the masses on both sides who had to fight it, while a decisive victory for either side was likely to prove the seedbed of future wars. "In your speculation on victory for Japan," *Iskra* chided Lenin, "you are forgetting that the Japanese, too, have a bourgeoisie."

Lenin's scorn was boundless for these false heirs who knew not the ways of the testators from whom they claimed to inherit. "The founders of scientific socialism," he admonished the *Iskrists*, had been "no pacifists," but had "taken sides" in every capitalist war of their day, always asking only one question: "*Whose victory will be more advantageous to democracy and socialism?*" Lenin did not trouble to defend himself personally, except indirectly, by his defense of the Marxism of Guesde and Hyndman.

It is perfectly understandable that these most consistent and decisive representatives of international revolutionary social democracy should express, without any *ifs* or *buts*, their sympathy with Japan, which is shattering the Russian autocracy. Though socialists are the enemies of all the bourgeoisies, this does not free them from the duty of distinguishing between historically progressive and historically reactionary representatives of that class.

When Port Arthur fell to the Japanese on January 2, 1905, Lenin broke into a veritable paean of rejoicing:

Yes, the European bourgeoisie has good reason to fear and the proletariat good reason to rejoice. . . . Progressive, advanced Asia has dealt an irreparable blow to backward, reactionary Europe.

This was not exactly in the spirit of Marx and Engels, who ambivalently loved and hated European civilization and thought of Asia as the center of a despotism Marx designated as "oriental." To give Lenin the benefit of the doubt, however, we might take his "reactionary Europe" in this context to mean Russia, and his "progressive Asia" to mean only Japan, which Marx had called not an "oriental despotism" but a land with a "purely feudal organization."[1] What is important is the fact that, like his teachers, Lenin was not afraid to take sides in a war, even though both sides were "bourgeois."

> Ten years ago [Lenin continued], this same reactionary Europe [now it is clear that he means not only Russia] was upset by the breaking up of China by Japan, and united to deprive her of the best fruits of her victory. . . . The return of Port Arthur to the Japanese is a blow dealt to all of reactionary Europe. . . .

Best fruits! That Port Arthur was a port of China, and not of either Russia or Japan, did not seem to concern him! At the beginning of 1905, Lenin was defeatist for his own fatherland, but he was not "anti-imperialist" in the sense of urging the defeat of both imperialist powers who were fighting over the prostrate body of that mighty giant, temporarily incapable of resistance, whose civilization, yes, and whose imperialism too, were older by a cycle of centuries than those of any of the Western powers. Far older, also, than the civilization and the imperialism of Russia and Japan.

If we bear in mind that Guesde, Hyndman, Lenin, and the Russian Mensheviks were all ardent, self-proclaimed orthodox Marxists, all claimants to the heritage exactly as it had been left to them, we can judge in what a parlous state that heritage was on the eve of the Great War of 1914.[2]

Once more in 1913, on the eve of the World War and in the very mêlée which turned out to be its prelude, Lenin made another "classic Marxist" attempt to pick himself a "progressive" horse in the Balkans. In a letter to Gorky he showed, as we have already noted, how little of the lover of peace there was in him. Written at the end of January 1913, it said:

> A war of Austria and Russia [over the Balkans] would be a very useful thing for the revolution all over Eastern Europe, but it is

---

[1] Marx wrote little on Japan. His characterization of it as having "a purely feudal organization" is a footnote on p. 745 of Das Kapital, as published in Werke, Vol. XXIII. There was a sense in which even a devout Marxist like Lenin might call Japan "progressive" in 1904, since it was in obvious transition from a feudal to a modern industrial society, with the two structures and ideologies inextricably intermingled.

[2] For Lenin's stand on the war with Japan and the fall of Port Arthur see Sochineniya, Vol. VII, p. 183; VIII, pp. 31–39, 238–40, 448–51.

hardly likely that Franz Josef and Nikolasha will give us that pleasure.[3]
Then on March 29, 1913, when the Bulgarians had taken Adrianople
from Turkey in a war in which Bulgaria, Serbia, Greece, and Mon-
tenegro were allied against the Turks, Lenin chose that moment to
pronounce Bulgaria's victory "a link in the chain of world events
which signify the collapse of the Middle Ages in Asia and Eastern
Europe."[4]
Since the proletariat was still weak in the Balkans, Lenin continued, it was natural that "these progressive tasks have been resolved by a war led by bourgeois and dynastic interests." But leadership by bourgeois and dynastic interests did not prevent the war
from being "progressive," and marking an important step:

> . . . in the creation of unified national states in the Balkans, the
> overthrow of the yoke of local feudalists, the final emancipation of the
> Balkan peasants of all the various nationalities from the yoke of large
> landed interests.

These fantastic words were scarcely out of Lenin's pen than he
wished them back again, for there was an immediate regrouping of
these land-hungry ("imperialist") young states, with Serbia, Greece
and Rumania joining "feudalist" Turkey against Bulgaria, thus making mincemeat of Lenin's analysis.

Thereafter, though *Pravda* was a daily paper in 1913, published
legally in Russia and providing an opportunity for daily comment on
events as they occurred, Lenin said not another word on the
Balkans. However fatuous his "analysis," it makes clear once more
that he did not in 1913 yet think of a "new era of imperialist capitalism" in which small states were mere puppets (parts of "the system
of states") and all sides alike reactionary—until August 1914
prompted him to construct new, retroactive "theoretical foundations" for the revision of the tactical practices of Marx and Engels
toward all the wars of their lifetime.

There is not a word about a coming world war in Lenin's writings for 1913 and 1914. When the International Socialist Bureau
called its last despairing emergency session to stave off the war, and
the Austrian army was already shelling Belgrade, Lenin did not
even put in an appearance. He was a member of the I.S.B., but he

---

[3] V.I. Lenin and A.M. Gorkii, *Pisma, Vospominania, dokumenty*, Moscow, 1958,
p. 91.
[4] In *Pravda* of March 29; *Sochineniya*, Vol. XIX, p. 19.

was thinking only of his own private war with the Mensheviks, and the International Socialist Bureau's attempts to unify the Russian factions; hence he ostentatiously stayed away from this session as from the previous ones. "They only want to scold me," he told his intimates, "their interference will spoil everything. . . . I'm not going."

In the years from 1912 to 1914, the years of the Balkan Wars and the pistol shot at Sarajevo, Lenin refused to go near an international conference. If war was really brewing "for a whole period since the end of the nineties," as he was later to maintain, certainly he himself had not noticed it. He sent Kamenev to represent him at one I.S.B. conference; Litvinov, lesser but tougher, to a second; Inessa Armand (*Petrova,* the "Rock Hard"), with iron-bound and detailed instructions, to disrupt a third attempt at unification. In the summer of 1914, he went to the country earlier than usual:

> Autumn is marvelous in the Tatras [he wrote to his sister Maria on April 22] . . . If it is fine this Autumn, we shall probably stay here in the country until October.[5]

On June 28, the heir-apparent to the Austrian throne was murdered. A month later to the day, Austria declared war on Serbia. The International Socialist Bureau went into its last, frightened emergency session. But Lenin sent his mandate to the Lettish Bolshevik, Berzin, who had stood firmly shoulder to shoulder with Inessa Armand at the last conference, and walked out together with her, still obdurately opposing an end to Lenin's war with the Mensheviks.

At the Emergency Session of the I.S.B. nothing was further from the minds of the heartsick participants than Lenin and his war with Menshevism. War had begun between Austria and Serbia, yet Lenin still did not seem to realize that this meant world war. He thought it would be, as he unwittingly made clear later when viewing the Austro-Serbian struggle in isolation, "a progressive, national war on the part of Serbia," and a reactionary war of conquest on the part of Austria.[6]

Then, all of a sudden it became clear that "Franz Josef and Nikolasha"—and many others besides—were really "giving us that

---

[5] Lenin, Vol. XXXVII, pp. 433–34.

[6] "The national element in the present war is represented *only* by the war of Serbia against Austria. . . . Were this war isolated . . . then all socialists would be *obliged* to wish success to the Serbian *bourgeoisie.*" (Lenin, Vol. XXI, pp. 209–10.)

pleasure." It would be "a great thing" not only "for the revolution in Eastern Europe" but a great thing for the revolution in all Europe. Capitalism, he decided instantly, has reached its *final crisis. They* have begun the war, but only *we* will finish it:

> *The present war is an imperialist war.* [Lenin told a packed hall at Lausanne] . . . The wars of the end of the eighteenth and the entire nineteenth century . . . were *national wars* which accompanied and assisted in the formation of national states . . . Such is the character of the wars beginning with the period of the French Revolution and continuing down to the Italian and the Prussian wars.
>
> . . . While the national wars of the eighteenth and nineteenth centuries signified the beginning of capitalism, the imperialist wars indicate its end. . . . How long this epoch will last we cannot say. There may be several such wars . . . But we must understand that [in this war] the tasks confronting the Socialists are different. . . . The historic era of national wars is past. We are now confronted with an imperialist war, and it is the task of Socialists to turn the "national" war into civil war. We have all anticipated . . . this imperialist war, we have all been preparing for it. . . . It is impossible to pass from capitalism to socialism without breaking national frameworks, as it was impossible to pass from feudalism to capitalism without adopting the idea of the nation.[7]

"*The historic era of national wars is past.*" It had run "*from the French Revolution down to the Italian and the Prussian Wars.*" That meant, down to 1872. But that was a perilous cut-off date, for in 1872, Marx and Engels were still alive. And in 1891 and 1892, Engels was still speaking out for the defense of the fatherland. . . .

Indeed, when had the old era passed and the new era begun? Lenin turned to Hobson's *Imperialism* for help. But that book was over a decade old. Why had he not noticed it before? As a matter of fact he had noticed it, and written a brief and negative review. Why

---

[7] Excerpts from Lenin's speech as reported in *Golos,* antiwar socialist journal which, in the same lecture, Lenin called "at present, the best Socialist paper in Europe." *Sochineniya,* 3rd Russian Edition, Vol. XVIII, pp. 49–53. It was omitted from the 4th Edition under Stalin, but included in the supplementary Vol. XXXVI, pp. 259–64, after Stalin's death and the subsequent "rehabilitation" of certain of Lenin's writings. As late as the summer of 1918 Lenin was still convinced, as he told the Fourth Conference of the Russian Trade Unions on June 27: "This war, which the imperialists began, these imperialists will not finish it, but other classes will finish it, the working class which in all lands and with each day is entering into an ever greater movement, discontent and revolt, which impels it to overthrow the rule of the capitalists" (*Sochineniya,* Vol. XXVII, p. 425).

had he not perceived that it proclaimed a "new epoch"? Hobson had set the year 1870 as "the beginning of a conscious policy of imperialism," a "movement which did not attain its full impetus until the middle of the eighties."[8] Both dates were awkward for Lenin's purposes.

If German imperialism manifested itself in the forcible conquest of Alsace and Lorraine, as Marx had repeated in three Manifestoes of the First International, then how could Engels still talk of defending the fatherland in the eighteen nineties? In the most famous of his "defensist" articles, that in the French *Almanac* of 1892, had Engels not spoken frankly of the German part of Poland, the northern part of Schleswig, and Alsace-Lorraine as illicit, i.e. imperialist, conquests, which a socialist Germany would be obligated to return to their rightful owners? Here was a prickly problem which Lenin did not completely solve until the autumn of 1916.

Meanwhile, he had to write and speak on "the new era," while opponents kept bombarding him with embarrassing quotations from Marx, and especially from Engels. He set Zinoviev, his closest intellectual collaborator during the war, to doing a fat book we have already referred to, in three sizable volumes, on the theme, *Voina i krizis sotsialisma* (War and the Crisis in Socialism). His purpose? To take up every war in Europe from the days of the French Revolution to the First World War, and to show that whatever Marx or Engels had said of any of those wars was, to the last syllable, justified. And the deeper aim—to analyze all those wars in such fashion as to prove the existence of two distinct epochs of capitalist conflicts—one from 1789 to 1870, when by and large all wars had been "progressive" on one side and "reactionary" on the other, and a second epoch (the present one) when all wars were, on both sides, reactionary and imperialist.

Under Lenin's schoolmasterly guidance,[9] Zinoviev managed his task of scholastic exegesis as best he could. But here, too, the problem arose of the appropriate cut-off date. Once more the solution

---

[8] Hobson, *Imperialism: A Study*, London, 1902, p. 19. For Lenin's negative review see his *Sochineniya*, Vol. IV, pp. 84–87.

[9] "The manuscript of the First Part [that is, the historical section] was read through by V.I. Lenin whose views exercised a decisive influence on this work," Zinoviev wrote in his "Introduction to the German Edition," p. 13. Since we are interested in Lenin's views rather than in Zinoviev's, which were in any case a mere echo, I have limited my quotations to the First Part. The German edition, used here, is in one fat volume of 659 pages, G. Sinowjew, *Der Krieg und die Krise des Sozialismus*, Vienna, 1924.

was unsatisfactory. Zinoviev wrote with Lenin's approval and using Lenin's own words:

We seldom meet a complicated phenomenon of public life in a pure unfalsified form. In spite of that, we have the right to characterize the period from 1789–1871 as that epoch in which absolutism was overcome and *the national states finally* arose in Europe—an epoch in which for the attainment of this goal a series of national wars were conducted. . . . By and large this period of [progressive] wars terminates with the year 1871. . . . The period from 1789 to 1871 is a period . . . of wars in which the bourgeoisie plays a progressive, often a revolutionary role. . . . Then the slogan, "defense of the Fatherland," possessed a historically progressive meaning. . . . The war of 1870–71 was the last big national war in Europe, in which, starting from the criterion of socialism and democracy one could apply the criterion of offensive and defensive war. The war of 1877–78 was a transition to a new era.[10]

The new era then, began in the seventies. On page 211, Zinoviev lists a series of "colonial or imperialist conquests since 1870," by England, France, Germany, Russia, and Japan. And on page 225, he makes the flat statement (overlooking, as needs he must, Lenin's stands of 1904–05 and 1913):

To call an imperialist war "just"—that only an agent of the bourgeoisie can do.

To be sure, no one remembered, nor thought of reminding Lenin of his "Marxist" stand of 1905 and 1913. But they did remind him of Engels's *Almanac* article and his letter to Bebel of the nineties, whereupon he would fall into a rage and resort to abuse.

Since a "new era" had begun, namely the "final crisis of decaying capitalism," no honest Marxist could continue to ask the question Marx and Engels had asked concerning all the wars of their day. Those who now asked "Whose victory will be more advantageous to democracy and socialism," or stressed, as the Belgians did, that their country had been invaded and was fighting for its independence, were philistines, lackeys of the bourgeoisie, ministerial socialists, agents of the imperialists, social patriots, social chauvinists, betray-

---

[10] Zinoviev, *op. cit.*, pp. 32–33, 61–62, 190–192. It is impossible in brief space to give any feeling for the hairsplitting casuistry employed in justifying the precise stand, errors and all, of Marx and Engels on every war. The book abounds in section headings such as "The German-French War of 1870–71 as an Example of a Defensive War from the Historical and an Aggressive War from the Diplomatic Standpoint." We must leave it to the reader to determine where this leaves the annexation of Alsace-Lorraine.

ers, traducers of the Marxist heritage. Lenin had no difficulty finding new labels for those guilty of the new heresies appropriate to the new era.

Worst of all to him, however, were those who asked the question that Marx and Engels (or so Lenin thought) had never asked themselves: Is not modern total war ("war of the races") the greatest possible evil for the masses and for European civilization, and hence for socialism? Would not the maintenance of peace, or the earliest possible peace without victory ("with each side still respecting the other," as Marx and Engels had put it), be preferable to a prolongation of war until Europe was laid waste? For those who asked such questions Lenin found the contemptuous labels, priestly (popish, from Russian *pop,* priest) pacifists or social pacifists.

In October 1916, Inessa Armand wrote to Lenin to tell him that he was contradicting his own position of 1913 and differing with that of Engels of 1892. Because of the closeness of their relationship, Lenin could not meet Inessa's challenge with abusive epithets. To make matters more complicated, she appears to have told him that he was right and Engels wrong in this difference of attitudes.[11] With unwonted patience and persistence, Lenin explained to his devoted follower, or explained away, his differences with Engels and the reasons for his new position. These letters lay bare the cracks in the structure of his position and the strain he was under in his casuistry, and they reveal certain essential components of his spirit.

Between November 20, 1916 and January 30, 1917, Lenin wrote no less than six letters to Inessa on this question, one of them occupying nearly six pages in his *Collected Works.* They are detailed, insistent, repetitive, sophistical. They leave Inessa unconvinced. From the time she forced this matter into his consciousness around mid-November, 1916, Lenin wrote to virtually no one else, the rest

---

11 Unfortunately, the Marx-Engels Institute, which has the letters of Inessa Armand, has withheld them from publication, and refuses to let any scholar who has not been housebroken consult them. But the points made above can be deduced from Lenin's letters to her which have been published. For an explanation of the unusual courtesy and patience of his letters to her, see my "Lenin and Inessa Armand," *Slavic Review,* March, 1963, pp. 96–114, or *Encounter,* London, February, 1964, pp. 83–91. For additional discussion of the theme of the present chapter, see my "Lenin Has Trouble with Engels: A Heretofore Unanalyzed Source of Lenin's Theory of Imperialism," *Russian Review,* July, 1956, pp. 196–209.

of his correspondence being one brief letter to Arthur Schmidt, Swiss Socialist, to convince him of the rightness of one of Lenin's formulas, and a note to Pokrovsky, to collect money due for the legal publication of *Imperialism* in Saint Petersburg.

Lenin was striving not only to convince Inessa, though that was important to him, but in a deeper sense to convince himself. His orthodox and dogmatic temperament made him regard every word of his masters as part of a sacred canon. He justified to the last detail all their calls for war, their expectations as to the course of each conflict, their stands supporting one side or the other in every "capitalist war" occurring in their lifetimes, their pledges to defend the fatherland. Even Engels's unpleasantly nationalistic *Po und Rhein* and his talk of "great vital nations capable of life which had swallowed up whole series of small nations not capable of life" in order that the great nations might attain their "natural frontiers," gets its justification from Lenin.[12]

Yet Lenin is bent on using other formulas and following a completely different course now that the outbreak of "the war of the races" so feared by his masters has convinced him that capitalism's "final crisis" has begun. This striving to combine *orthodoxy* and *novelty,* to be at once the most orthodox, indeed the only orthodox disciple, and at the same time to make the most drastic of all revisions of the attitude of the founding fathers toward war—provides the central problem of Lenin's wartime Marxism.

When Inessa sought in mid-November 1916 to convince him of the contradiction between his orthodoxy and his novelty, and even between his pre-1914 writings on war and those after 1914, he answered:

> In the matter of the fatherland, you want to establish a contradiction between my earlier writings (when? 1913? when precisely? what precisely?) and my present ones. I don't think there are contradictions. Find the exact texts, then we'll try again. Of course, between the orthodox and the opportunists there have always been differences on the understanding of the fatherland. . . . That the defense of the fatherland is permissible (when permissible) only as a defense of democracy (in the appropriate epoch), this is also my opinion. . . .[13]

---

[12] *Sochineniya,* Vol. XXII, p. 309, where Lenin quotes these words with approval.
[13] Letter of November 25, 1916, Vol. XXXV. The letters will be referred to by their dates and can be found, dated, in Vol. XXXV.

Inessa was not satisfied with this vague reference to the "appropriate epoch," for on November 30 Lenin writes:

Marx and Engels said in the "Communist Manifesto" that the workers have no fatherland. But the same Marx *called* for *national* war more than once: Marx in 1848, Engels in 1859 (end of his pamphlet, *Po und Rhein* where the *national* feelings of the Germans are openly inflamed and they are openly summoned to a national war). Engels in 1891, in view of the then threatening and advancing war of France (Boulanger) plus Alexander III against Germany, *directly* recognized the "defense of the fatherland."

Were Marx and Engels blunderheads, saying one thing today, another tomorrow? No. In my opinion the recognition of the "defense of the fatherland" in a national war *completely* accords with Marxism. In 1891, the German *Social Democrats* really *would have had* the duty of defending the fatherland in a war against Boulanger plus Alexander III. That would have been a peculiar variant of a *national* war.

It is obvious that Lenin knew the sacred texts better than he did French history, while Inessa, despite her French childhood, did not know enough of the history of her native land to challenge his preposterous use of General Boulanger to justify Engels's stand on the defense of Germany in 1891 and 1892.

Boulanger was a comic-opera Bonaparte of the eighties who dreamed of seizing power by a *coup d'état,* then waging war to recover Alsace and Lorraine. But he had reached the climax of his ineffectual bid for power in 1886, and, on January 27, 1889, he missed his last possible chance to try to lead some troops against a government temporarily discredited by scandal. Having seen two Bonapartes come and go, many Frenchmen really expected him to try. When he failed to move, his popularity collapsed, the scornful humor of the French replacing their former fear or expectation. The elections of that year were a smashing victory for the Republic. As the new government moved to try Boulanger for treason, he fled ignominiously to Belgium, while the country laughed. On September 30, 1891, he committed suicide on the grave of his mistress. As early as October 3, 1889, Engels had written: "In any case, Boulangism is finished (*kaput*)."[14] When Engels wrote his letter to Bebel in favor of voting the defense budget, and his article for the French *Almanac,* Boulangism was indeed *kaput* and Boulanger was

---

[14] *Wilhelm Liebknecht Briefwechsel mit Karl Marx und Friedrich Engels,* The Hague, 1963, p. 347.

dead. Moreover, it was not France that Engels feared, but Russia. When he drew up his blistering indictment of the foreign policy of Russian tsarism for Plekhanov's journal in Geneva, Boulanger had faded from the scene.

Whatever Inessa may have known of Boulanger, she was not overawed by Lenin's "historical" explanation. On December 25, 1916, he felt compelled to make a longer, more complete and "systematic" explanation of how both he and Engels could be right while taking such contradictory stands on the defense of the fatherland in time of war:

A war of France plus Russia against Germany in 1891. You take "my criterion" and apply it *only* to France and Russia!!!! Please, where is the logic in this? I say that *from the side of France and Russia* this would have been a reactionary war (a war for the purpose of reversing the development of Germany, of pushing her back from national unity to fragmentation).

And from the standpoint of Germany? You are silent. But this is the main point. From the standpoint of Germany in 1891 there was not, and there could not be, an imperialist character to the war. [Marx and Engels had thought otherwise in their attacks on the annexation of Alsace and Lorraine].

You have forgotten the main thing: in 1891 there was no imperialism in general (I tried to show in my pamphlet that it was born in 1898–1900 and not earlier), and it was not an imperialist war on the part of Germany.

Here then, we have the cut-off date! Not in 1872 or 1876, not beginning in the eighties, nor in the closing decades of the nineteenth century, as Hobson's, Lenin's, and Zinoviev's earlier formulations had put it. Anything prior to the death of Engels would have been too embarrassing either to Lenin's orthodoxy or to his novelty. This letter, with its marvelously precise dating of the "birth" of imperialism as occurring "in 1898–1900 and not earlier"—at least two years after Engels's death and not earlier!—throws a flood of light into Lenin's spirit, the genesis of his famous pamphlet, and the mechanism determining what Soviet historiography likes to call his "periodization."

Are we to conclude then that Lenin was not aware of the fact that the greatest ages of empire were in the past? Surely he had had a solid enough education to know of the ancient empires of Egypt and Babylon, Assyria and Phoenicia, Persia and China, Greece and

Rome, and to know that the very word *empire* was Roman both in origin and by antonomasia. He knew, too, of the two Romes: on the Tiber and on the Bosphorus; and of the Holy Roman Empire whose ghost had haunted the Middle Ages.

Coming to modern times, he could not help but know that the great age of empire-building occurred in the fifteenth, sixteenth, and seventeenth centuries, when Spain and Portugal, France and Holland and England, spread out over all the continents and the Seven Seas, and great colonial, i.e. imperialist, wars were fought over the Americas, Southern Asia, the Spice Islands, and the control of the continents and oceans. How could he ignore, since he had written about it, Russia's own imperial expansion during three centuries over so much of Europe and Asia and into the ancient Empire of China? Could he be so ignorant of recent history that he did not know that France had acquired her great Empire in North Africa in the middle of the nineteenth century, begun her conquest of Cochin China in the sixties, and finally, in 1893, with Engels still alive and watching over the course of history, established her protectorate over Laos? There was scarcely a year of the adult life of Friedrich Engels when some colonial or imperialist war was not going on.

And Napoleon's Empire? Lenin himself wrote of it in these unequivocal words:

A national war can be transformed into an imperialist war, and *vice versa*. For example, the wars of the Great French Revolution started as national wars and such they were. They were revolutionary wars against a coalition of counterrevolutionary monarchies. But after Napoleon had created the French Empire by subjugating a number of large, vital, long established national states of Europe, the French national wars became imperialist wars, which *in their turn* engendered wars for national liberation against Napoleon's imperialism.[15]

So Lenin did know! It is fascinating for the student of the vagaries of the human mind to note that Lenin wrote this last passage in a polemical article against Rosa Luxemburg ("On the Junius Pamphlet"), as the very next piece of written work after completing his *Imperialism as the Highest Stage of Capitalism*! But, since Rosa Luxemburg was antiwar, and since she, along with Hilferding and Hobson, was his teacher in the matter of a "new era" of "imperialism," he did not have to polemicize with her about that. Hence, unwittingly, he let his guard down on the matter of "periodiza-

---

[15] Lenin, *Sochineniya*, Vol. XXII, p. 295.

tion"—at the very moment in 1916 when he had at last worked out the cut-off date precisely.

And again on December 10, 1917, when he was preparing an "Outline of a Program for the Peace Discussions" with the representatives of Germany at Brest Litovsk, Lenin defined *annexations* in his slogan, *peace without annexations or reparations,* in these terms:

> An annexation is any acquisition of territory, the population of which in the course of the last decades—since the second half of the nineteenth century—has expressed its dissatisfaction with the uniting of its territory to another state, or its inclusion in a state, and regardless of whether this dissatisfaction is expressed in literature, in the decisions of representative bodies, municipalities, meetings, and similar institutions, in state and diplomatic acts called forth by the national movement of these territories, in national frictions, disorders, etc.[16]

Here the cut-off date of the middle of the nineteenth century was obviously intended to include Germany's seizure of Alsace-Lorraine as an act of imperialist conquest.

In their last years, Marx and Engels did begin to sense a new situation in Europe: not Lenin's new period of parasitic, decaying, imperialist capitalism, but a period with contradictory trends. On the one hand Marx and Engels became aware of new democratic institutions, the power of organized labor, the growth of social reform—matters to be considered in Chapter XI. On the other, they felt a new tension in the air, a more dangerous lineup of the great powers after 1870, a titanic arms race, the growing danger for Germany and for Europe of a "war of the races," that might involve whole populations, devastate Europe and destroy her civilization, so that there would be no foundation left on which to build a "higher social order."

As far as empire-building was concerned, the energies stored up in the wars for national unification, and the industrialization of other powers than England, led to new claims "for a place in the sun." Marx and Engels, especially the latter, lived through several decades of this belated flare-up of empire-building. No longer were the stakes the riches of the Indies and the gold and silver of the Americas. The colonization of equatorial Africa, begun by France in

---

[16] Lenin, *Sochineniya,* Vol. XXVI, p. 313.

Marx's day, and witnessed by Engels for several decades, gave
promise only of poor areas which have always required a greater
outlay by the "mother country" than the yield they gave.

To discuss what was "new" in this "new period" would require a
special study and it will not be undertaken here. In any case, it was
an arrant absurdity for Lenin to say that in 1891 and 1892 "there
was no imperialism in general," and that "there was not and could
not be an imperialist character" to the war which Engels contem-
plated with dread and in which he pledged his party to defend the
fatherland. What made Lenin uncomfortable and gave Inessa Armand the courage to talk back was the fact that the war which
broke out in 1914 looked suspiciously like the very war Marx and
Engels had been predicting since 1870, the very war in which Engels had chosen his side when he thought it was coming in the
nineties. This did not trouble Inessa as much as Lenin, for her
revered leader was not Engels but Lenin himself.

Politically and psychologically it was necessary for Lenin to find
a formula which would submerge or dissolve such "details" as the
fact that the war of 1914 began out of the very nibbling by the
"historyless" Southern Slavs at the Hapsburg Empire, of which
Engels had said that the Eastern Germans and the Hungarians
"would not permit themselves to be torn to pieces like a loaf of
bread that has been gnawed by rats." It was the land-greedy new
Balkan nations and the wars of these "lousy Balkans" with each
other over their own second-rate imperialist claims that Engels had
feared might bring on a "civil war of the Western powers with each
other for the benefit of Russia." It was the assassination of the heir-
apparent to the Hapsburg throne by a young Bosnian terrorist
helped by some high officials in Serbia, which had dragged the great
powers, even as Engels had feared and prophesied, into the general
"war of the races." Lenin needed a formula that would dissolve
these "details" as in acid, dissolve, too, the fact that the Hapsburg
multinational empire, threatened by dissolution, had struck back,
even as Engels had urged, at these "historyless little bandit peoples"
who were "gnawing at her Empire"; the fact that Austria had sent
such an ultimatum to Serbia as no sovereign power could accept and
still remain sovereign; the fact that Germany had violated the territory, the neutrality and the independence of Belgium with no other
excuse than *inter armas silent leges,* the law of military convenience;
that England, which Engels hoped would stay out of the war he

envisaged, had come in only after Belgium's neutrality was violated. Above all, Lenin's formula had to dissolve the sharp outlines of the vision Marx and Engels had had of a total or "race war" which would come, as that of 1914 did, out of an alliance of France and Russia against Germany and the terrorism and contentiousness of the Balkans.

In his heart, of course, Lenin knew this, but his heart required him not to know it. There are passages in his wartime writings when he admits, nay urges, that the war of 1914–18 was "for decades" preparing, hence was the precise war which Engels had been fore-telling.[17]

In June 1918, with Lenin now safely in power but the war not yet over, he boasts that its outlines were foretold "to the letter" in Engels's "prophetic words" of 1886–87. He quotes the apocalyptic prophecy of Engels of the laying waste of Europe, "the devastation of the Thirty Years' War compressed into three or four years . . . the famine, pestilence, demoralization . . . general bankruptcy . . . general exhaustion . . ." But he is quoting now to console the Russian people for the breakdown and famine and demoralization in the land over which he rules. Had not general ruin, and disease and famine "all been foreseen"? And was not this a guarantee to those made faint of spirit by the universal ruin and suffering, that the rest of "Engels's scientific prophecies" concerning socialism in all Europe were also bound to be fulfilled?[18]

But in 1916, in his earnest argument with Inessa Armand (and with his own spirit), he could make no such admission. On January 19, 1917, he wrote her:

> In Western Europe has been constructed a *system* (this N.B.! [nota bene!! make special note of this] think that over!! don't forget that!! we live not only in separate states, but in a certain *system* of states; anarchists are permitted to ignore that; we are not anarchists), a *system* of states, in general, constitutional, national. *Alongside of*

[17] For example, in "Opportunism and the Bankruptcy of the Second International," Lenin writes of "the series of economic and political conflicts which were preparing this war during the course of decades, and revealed themselves fully in 1912 [the outbreak of the First Balkan War], and which called forth the war of 1914."

[18] Lenin wrote this "consoling" article entitled "Prophetic Words" after drafting the decree for a resolution on "The Struggle Against the Famine." *Sochineniya*, Vol. XXVII, pp. 408, 455–60. The decree on the famine was dated June 4, the consoling article published in *Pravda* on June 29, 1918.

them there is the mighty, unshakable, pre-revolutionary tsarism, robbing and oppressing over hundreds of years, putting down the revolutions of 1849 [in Hungary] and 1863 [in Poland]. Germany (of
1891) the land of *advanced* socialism. And this land is threatened by
tsarism in union with Boulangism! The situation is not at all, not at all
that of 1914–1917, when tsarism is undermined by 1905 and Germany wages a war for rule over the world. That's a cloth of *another*
color. To identify, even to regard as similar, the international situation
of 1891 and that of 1914—is *supreme* unhistoricity. . . . Engels was
the father of "passive radicalism"?? Not true! Not at all. This you will
never be able to show.

In the same letter, Lenin warns Inessa "in comradely fashion"
that those who think to blacken the name of Engels disgrace only
themselves:

Your attacks on Engels, in my opinion, are highly unfounded. For-
give me for my frankness: it is necessary to prepare yourself much
more seriously before writing in that fashion! Otherwise it is easy to
bring disgrace upon yourself—I am warning you of this *entre nous,* in
a friendly way, just between the two of us [*s glazu na glaz,* i.e.
looking into each other's eyes], in case you should ever want to speak
thus at any time either in print or at a meeting.

In the same fashion, a little earlier, on December 25, Lenin had
written her:

Engels was right. In my time I have seen painfully many accusations against Engels for opportunism, and my attitude toward this is
sceptical in the extreme: Try, say I, just to prove once that Engels
was wrong!! You will never be able to. . . . No. No. Engels is *not*
infallible. Marx is *not* infallible. But to prove their "fallibility" one
will have to do better than that. Verily, verily, much better. And in
this you are a thousand times wrong.

On January 30, 1917, Lenin felt impelled to turn to the subject
yet again. Once more, Lenin's letter contains a passionate confession
of faith in the infallibility of the "not infallible."

I am still "in love" with Marx and Engels, and will not tolerate
any slander against them in silence. No, these are real people! From
them we must learn. From *this* ground we must not depart. . . .

On this note, the argument comes to an end, though it is not
clear that Inessa is convinced. As a matter of fact, they will soon
have other things to think of, for before two months were up, the
Tsar was to fall, and Lenin and Inessa were on the "sealed train"

that was bringing him into the land which he himself pronounced to have "the freest government in the world."[19]

With that, Lenin's differences with Engels's stand for the defense of the fatherland take on an entirely new aspect, for now he must decide whether he should still be for the defeat of his country when it has become a democracy and is the freest government in the world, and still at war with an invader which, as Lenin had insisted to Inessa, is "imperialist and waging war for mastery of the world"— a Germany, moreover, which occupies large areas of Russian soil.

Even before he arrived at the Finland Station, Lenin had made up his mind. In fact, he made up his mind when he decided to accept the help of the enemy General Staff to get back to his free and democratic and beleaguered land. For all his asservations of literal orthodoxy, here is one claimant of the heritage who puts his real emphasis not on the inherited formulas but on the prospect of taking power. Sensing that power is loose in the streets and will turn out as easy to seize "as lifting up a feather,"[20] he opts not for Engels's formula but for the continuation of his own. *For the defeat of your fatherland*—until you yourself have power—this is the sum of Leninism on war in 1917.

---

[19] Lenin, Vol. XXIV, pp. 4, 61; Vol. XXV, p. 338; Vol. XXVI, p. 174.
[20] Lenin, Vol. XXVII, p. 76.

PART III

The Paris Commune:
An Ambiguous Revolution

It is time people understand the true meaning of this Revolution; and this can be summed up in a few words: the government of the people by the people. It was the first attempt of the proletariat to govern itself. . . . The establishment of the Commune meant not the replacing of one form of class-rule by another, but the abolishing of all class-rule. It meant the substitution of true cooperative, i.e. communistic for capitalistic production, and the participation in this Revolution of workers of all countries meant the internationalizing, not only the nationalizing of private property. . . .
  —Eleanor Marx Aveling in her introduction to Lissagaray's
   History of the Commune of 1871

He who tells the people revolutionary legends . . . is as criminal as the geographer who would draw up false charts for navigators.
  —Lissagaray

Well and good, gentlemen, do you want to know what this dictatorship looks like? Look at the Paris Commune. That was the Dictatorship of the Proletariat.
  —Engels in 1891

Chapter 6

MARX'S WARNING

> The entire French Branch is getting ready to commit stupidi-
> ties in the name of the International. They want to over-
> throw the Provisional Government [and] establish a *Com-
> mune de Paris*.
> —Karl Marx to Friedrich Engels, September 6, 1870

THERE IS no event in the history of the nineteenth century that more truly leads a double life than the Paris Commune. On the one hand it appears as a small, bloody, rearguard action in the response of the French people to ignominious defeat. On the other, it is the source of a stirring socialist and communist legend that has had more influence on the events of the twentieth century than the historical facts themselves. Perhaps no dichotomy presents more sharply the pet problem of the philosophy of history: is history "the events as they really happened" or what subsequent historians and historical interpretations have made of them? As both an awareness of the event *"wie es eigentlich gewesen"* and the source of the legend itself, are in the writings of Marx and Engels, here are some of the greatest ambiguities in the heritage they left to their heirs.

Marx's hostility to the French socialist leaders is an old story. The socialists who participated in the Commune were not Marxists but Proudhonists, Blanquists, Bakuninists, and followers of such moderates as Lerroux and Louis Blanc, whom Marx had been fighting for a number of years before 1870 in the International Workingmen's Association.

On June 20, 1866, before the International was two years old, Marx wrote a letter to Engels describing a stormy debate in the General Council, and expressing his contempt for the French and their notion that socialism might be brought into being by a free federation of Communes. By what Trotsky was later to call the technique of "amalgam," he added two detestable tendencies together, and called their view "Proudhonized-Stirnerism." He found the French "gentlemen's heads" full of "the emptiest Proudhonian phrases." They were "ignorant, vain, presumptuous, chattering, and arrogant." He was particularly indignant with their idea that "all nationality and nations" are *"des préjugés surannes"* [obsolete prejudices]:

> . . . to be dissolved into little *"groupes"* or *"communes,"* which should then form an "association" but not a State. Moreover, this "individualizing" of mankind, and the corresponding "mutualisme," was to take place while history stopped in all other lands and the entire world waited until the French were ripe to make a social revolution. Then they will show us how to perform the experiment, and the rest of the world, overcome by the force of their example, will follow suit. . . .

Marx was particularly scornful of a young student delegate named Paul Lafargue (later to become his son-in-law) and he boasted of the cheap laugh he got from the large English delegation by telling "our friend Lafargue who had just abolished nations, that he had spoken to us in *French*, i.e. a language which nine-tenths of the assemblage did not understand." To Kugelmann Marx wrote explaining that the French had more delegates than their membership warranted, and that these "empty phrasemongers" were either not workingmen (as in the case of Lafargue) or, where they did represent the workers of Paris, they "were unaware of the fact that these were luxury workers who belong to the old crap."[1] Thus Marx's view of the French idea of a Federation of Communes was anything but enthusiastic.

Neither in the Address that Marx drafted at the outbreak of the Franco-Prussian War, nor in his letters to Engels before Napoleon III was captured, are there any explicit thoughts about what the French workingmen should do if and when Napoleon fell. Only after the Emperor surrendered at Sedan did Marx and Engels suddenly realize that France was headless, and that almost anything might happen.

They began to write anxious letters to each other expressing the belief that the French workingmen were not equal to the task of

---

[1] *MEGA*, III/3, p. 341; *Letters to Kugelmann*, pp. 28–29.

combining a republican revolution with the defense of their invaded country.

> If a revolution breaks out in Paris [Marx wrote on August 8, 1870] then it is questionable if they have the means and the leaders to put up a serious resistance to the Prussians. . . . Twenty years of Bonapartist farce have been enormously demoralizing. One can hardly count on revolutionary heroism . . .[2]

Both Marx and Engels thought of the Republic which was then being set up as a mere transition to a future Orleanist dynasty. Their letters and their public writings continued to express this attitude toward the French Republic for several years. Nevertheless, Engels, with his usual interest in military planning, began to work out strategy and tactics for the defense of defeated France and of the new-born Republic. On August 15, he wrote Marx:

> The debacle in France seems horrible. . . . Still a revolutionary régime [he meant republican not socialist], if it comes *soon*, need not despair. However, it must abandon Paris to her fate and carry on the war from the South. Then it is not impossible that it may be able to hold out until new weapons have been purchased and new armies organized to drive the enemy gradually back to the frontier. That would really be the true ending of the war: that both countries should mutually demonstrate the proof of their unconquerability. But if that doesn't happen soon, the comedy is over. Moltke's operations are really models . . .[3]

And the same day he wrote to Mrs. Marx:

> The worst thing is—in the case of a real revolutionary movement in Paris who should be at its head? Rochefort is the most popular and the only usable person. . . .[4]

Engels's proposal to "leave Paris to her fate" and his selection of the French radical journalist, Victor-Henri Rochefort, Count and Marquis de Rochefort-Lucay, as the "only" viable leader in Paris, alike make clear that he was thinking not of a socialist but of a republican revolution. Rochefort had no interest in social and economic questions: like many a French journalist, he was a perpetual crusader for many and startlingly diverse causes. He was against Bonaparte and for the Republic. He supported the Commune yet was one of its severest critics. For a few months in 1870, he opened the columns of his journal, *La Marseillaise,* to the French members

---

[2] *MEGA*, III/4, pp. 358–59.
[3] *Ibid.*, p. 367.
[4] *Ibid.*, p. 368.

of the International, regardless of faction. Later he became an enemy of socialism and, as the sardonic and cantankerous editor of *l'Intransigeant*, he denounced the Republic, supported a military dictatorship by General Boulanger, and fought stubbornly against the Dreyfusards. Born in 1830 he died in 1913, convinced at the end that what France needed was the restoration of a monarchy. Marx must have shared Engels's favorable view of him, for Jenny Marx, answering the latter's letter, wrote:

> How bad all the news from Paris is. If the *g-r-r-r-a-a-nde nation* had struck in good time, they would not have the régime of [Empress] Eugenie and [General and Count] Palikao. Isn't it disgraceful that they let Rochefort sit quietly [in jail], the only political head in young France? Really, they deserve the Prussian chastising more than we can imagine.[5]

From this point on, the letters of Marx and Engels express steadily deepening concern lest the workingmen of Paris, or the Paris chapter of the International, exasperated by the humiliating defeat of France, should take part in some sort of uprising against the newly-formed republic. Now that the French "aggression" against Germany had been defeated and the Republic proclaimed, both men genuinely desired a peace without victory, and without annexations, preferably peace by a stalemate which would teach each side to respect the other. Nothing could be further from Lenin's view of how war should end than this, but it expressed their genuine internationalism now that they were convinced that Germany's integrity had been safeguarded.

Engels, as was his wont, began excitedly to work out military plans for the Republic's defense, going so far as to send his analyses through Lafargue to Gambetta, the real leader of the "Government of National Defense." Marx urged diplomatic intervention on England to protect France from any dismemberment; then, spurred on by Engels, he urged less realistically that England should intervene with armed force. When a former member of the Communist League, the Prussian official Johannes Miquel, let Marx know that the Prussian army was having a hard time that winter, through Lafargue Marx passed the intelligence on to Gambetta.[6] Also through Lafargue, Engels sent Gambetta a plan for the fortifying of the slopes of Montmartre and the lifting of the siege of Paris. He became so absorbed that he wanted to offer his personal services to

---

[5] *Ibid.*, p. 370.
[6] Nikolaevsky and Maenchen-Helfen, *op. cit.*, p. 318.

the French Government of National Defense, but Marx dissuaded him. "Do not trust these bourgeois republicans," Longuet quoted Marx as saying, "if anything goes wrong, whether you are responsible or not, at the first hitch, you will be shot as a spy."[7]

On August 20, Engels wrote to Marx:

I believe the annexation of the German-French [i.e. the Alsatians] is now a settled matter. If a revolutionary government had been set up in Paris even last week, something might still have been done. Now it would come too late, and only make itself ridiculous, a miserable parody of the Convention.[8]

In the letter Engels explained in detail the technical difficulties involved in an attempt at a revolutionary republican defense of Paris.

In contradistinction to the sympathy of Marx and Engels for Gambetta's efforts to defend France, Bakunin and many French members of the International were all for overthrowing the new government of national defense and imitating the example of the Convention of 1792 and '93, which had succeeded in mobilizing the country and standing off the allied forces of all Europe coalesced against it.

In the *Second Address of the General Council of the International on the Franco-Prussian War*, prepared by Marx between the sixth and ninth of September, he solemnly warned the French workingmen not to yield to the voices urging them to overthrow the new Republican Government of National Defense:

The French working class finds itself in an extremely difficult position. Any attempt to overthrow the new government when the enemy is even now almost knocking on the gates of Paris, would be an act of desperate folly. The French workingmen must do their duty as citizens, but they must not let themselves be dominated by the national memory of 1792 as the French peasants let themselves be deceived by the national memory of the First Empire. It is not their task to repeat the past, but to build the future. Let them quietly and with determination utilize the means which republican freedom gives them to carry on systematically and thoroughly the organization of their own class . . . On their strength and wisdom depends the fate of the Republic.[9]

---

[7] *Ibid.*, p. 319.
[8] *MEGA*, III/4, p. 371–72.
[9] *Werke*, Vol. XVII, pp. 277–78.

Marx's Manifesto ended with the words, *Vive la république!*
Thus the private misgivings of Marx and Engels about any attempt
to follow the Commune of 1792 became a public warning to the
workingmen of Paris.

On September 12, Engels returned to the worrisome subject in a
letter to Marx:

If anything can be done [by us] in Paris, it should be to stop the
workers from starting anything before the peace.

The workers must be held back even if that meant that Bismarck
would take Paris without a serious attempt at defense:

However peace may come about, it must be concluded before the
workingmen can do anything. If they should win now—in the service
of the national defense—then they would have to take over the
heritage of Bonaparte and the present lousy republic, and they will be
beaten uselessly by the German army and thrown back by twenty
years. They can lose nothing by waiting. . . . To fight against Prussia for the bourgeoisie would be madness. . . .

It is too damn bad [Engels continued] that people are so scarce
in Paris who dare to want to see into the present state of affairs as
they *really* are. Where is there a single man in Paris who so much as
dares to think that the active power of resistance on the part of
France is broken so far as this war is concerned, and therefore any
chance of driving out the invader through a revolution, is gone. Just
because people do not *want* to hear the truth, I am afraid it may
come to that.[10]

And on the thirteenth he complained to Marx:

In general, the war is bit by bit taking on a disagreeable form.
The French still haven't gotten enough of a beating, and the German
asses have already been much too victorious. . . .[11]

For his part, Marx strove to restrain the French members of the
International from engaging in foolhardy and anti-republican adventures. On September 6, he wrote Engels that he was giving instructions to Seraillier, a French emigré living in London and acting as
Belgium's Secretary on the General Council, and an unconditional
follower of Marx. The latter was despatching him to Paris to see
what he could do to "arrange matters with the *International* there
(Conseil Fédéral de Paris)."

This is especially necessary because today the entire *French Branch*

---

[10] *MEGA*, III/4, pp. 383–84.
[11] *Ibid.*, p. 386.

is getting ready to commit stupidities in the name of the *International*. "They" want to overthrow the Provisional Government, establish a *Commune de Paris*, name Pyat as French Ambassador to London, etc.

Félix Pyat was an old Republican revolutionary of 1848, a journalist, dramatist, and amateur politician, easily made drunk by the sound of his own phrases. He was not a socialist but a democrat in the style of the Paris of 1848. Marx detested him.

Marx ends his letter with a statement that he personally has written to the Federal Council in Paris and "undertaken the disagreeable task of opening their eyes to the real state of affairs."[12]

To this Engels replied ironically that the French section was "completely under the dominion of the phrase." They had been able to endure the despicable Louis Napoleon for twenty years, but now

> . . . these people are demanding . . . that the Germans should immediately leave the sacred soil of France, or else: *guerre à l'outrance!* It is nothing but the old fanciful idea of the superiority of France, of the soil made holy by 1793, which no later French *Schweinereien* [swinish acts] can desanctify: the sacredness of the Republic of the phrase. . . . To sacrifice the workers at this moment [for the purpose of continuing the war] would really be strategy à la Bonaparte and à la MacMahon; before peace is concluded they can do nothing under any circumstances, and after peace, they will still have as their first need time to organize.[13]

Engels expressed the hope that "after they have gotten over their first delirium," they will have second thoughts, "for otherwise it would become damned hard to have any international relations with them." He has had a talk with Dupont and they have agreed that the program of the moment of the French section of the International should consist of two things:

> To make use of the freedom inevitably given by the Republic in order to organize the party in France. . . . To hold back the International in France until peace has been concluded.[14]

---

12 *Ibid.*, p. 378.
13 *Ibid.*, pp. 379–81.
14 *Ibid.* Eugéne Clovis Dupont, a maker of musical instruments, Corresponding Secretary for France on the General Council. He was a veteran of the insurrection of June, 1848. He lived in London from 1862 on, but at the moment of Engels's letter was in Manchester where Engels lived. He supported Marx and Engels in all their faction fights with the Proudhonists, the Blanquists, and the

In his letter to Marx of September 12, Engels advances for the first time the idea which in another context we met in Chapter IV (in his "testamentary" article in the French *Almanac* for 1892):

The French workingmen won't lose anything by waiting. Whatever alterations in the borders there may be are in any case only provisional and will be again overthrown [i.e. by a socialist Germany].

But won't they let themselves be carried away again under the pressure of foreign attack and proclaim the social republic on the eve of the storming of Paris? It would be horrible if the German army as its last act of war should have to fight a barricade war with the Parisian workingmen. This would throw us back fifty years and distort everything so that every one and everything would appear in a false position, and the national hatred and the dominion of the phrase that would *then* appear among the French workingmen!

. . . since, as it seems, in any case *something* will be annexed, it would be timely to reflect on the form in which German and French workingmen could come to an understanding that everything should be regarded as *nul et non avenu* [null and void] and when the opportunity comes, be reversed. My idea was that this would have been useful at the outbreak of the war. Now however when the fate of ceding ground has hit the French, it is necessary or the fellows will otherwise cry blue murder [*moerderlich schreien*].[15]

About the middle of September (probably on the thirteenth), Mrs. Marx wrote Engels that the Marx-follower, Seraillier, in place of converting the Parisians, had been converted to their furious madness and delusion:

Seraillier says one is almost torn to pieces if he tells the truth, and even the better ones and the best ones are living on the memories of 1792. He is completely bewitched by Rochefort, with whom he met twice, and has let himself be recruited into the defense company *du cher Gustave*. Perhaps it is better not to let Dupont know for the time being that Seraillier is helping to defend *le sol sacré*. In the end he

---

Bakuninists. In 1874 he emigrated to the United States. After his talk with Engels he wrote to the Lyons Branch of the International: "The role of the workers . . . is to let the bourgeois vermin make peace with the Prussians (for the shame of doing so will adhere to them always), but not to indulge in outbreaks which would only consolidate their power, but to take advantage of the liberty which circumstances will provide, to organize. . . . [For the text of this letter, see Nikolaevsky and Maenchen-Helfen, *op. cit.*, p. 312.]

[15] *Ibid.*, p. 384.

too might have *le coeur gros* and want to leave, too. *Et à quoi bon?*
Dupont with his excitability would be in a fine fix there.[16]

On September 16, Marx sent Seraillier's letter to be shown to
Dupont. And, on the sixteenth, "in all haste," he urged that Dupont

. . . in the name of the General Council, answer the Marseillers
(including both their letter and their Manifesto) and give them a
good rubdown; at the same time he should send them *our* Manifesto.
If he needs it, I can send him new Manifestoes from here.[17]

And then suddenly, to the dismay of the historian, the correspondence of Marx and Engels, that marvelous window into their
souls, breaks off altogether!

Engels had at last managed to buy his way out of "capitalism."
For several years now, his life had been lived on the treadmill of
managing the Manchester branch of Ermen and Engels (by no
means the position of "well-to-do idling" that Marx described as the
life of the capitalist in *Das Kapital*).[18]

Now at last Engels persuaded his partner, Ermen, to make him
(and Marx with him) well-to-do idlers, for Engels was to receive not
a single cash sum for his share, but a life annuity for himself, and
another, more modest, for Marx. It was wonderful for Engels, who
got rid of the drudgery of running a large factory, and the visible
reproach that he was an "exploiter" of workingmen. He could now
join his friend Marx in London, serve on the General Council of the
International, devote himself to the revolution or socialist letters as
his profession. It was wonderful for Marx too, who could give up the
humiliation of begging letters and pinched means, and receive an
assured income of three hundred fifty pounds sterling per annum
(no small sum for those days), plus insurance to cover all "extraordinary expenditures due to illness and other unforeseen happenings,"
while all his past debts were at the same time erased.

For the historian, however, their happiness has its negative side,
since their frank, arrogant, and impulsive letters to each other supply a constant illumination in depth for their more public acts and
documents. Engels himself called the letters "a correspondence
worthy of historical examination." When he suspected—wrongly, of

---

[16] *Ibid.*, p. 385.
[17] *Ibid.*, p. 388.
[18] "Since I have become the boss, everything has become much worse because
of the greater responsibility," Engels had written to Marx on April 27, 1867
(*MEGA*, III/3, p. 386). Marx's description of the owners of the machines as
"well-to-do idlers" is in a footnote to page 405 of the English edition of Vol. I
of *Capital*.

course—that the British government might be opening their mail, he wrote to Marx:

> The government of dogs can in any case not want for a better means of informing itself on the activity of the whole proletarian party than our correspondence. They will also find in it a great deal that they can make use of with their continental colleagues.[19]

Down to the last letter, it was clear how deeply Marx and Engels were opposed to all the actions which were involved in the setting up of the Commune of Paris, and to the very idea of such a commune.

---

[19] *MEGA*, III/4, pp. IX, X, 130–32.

Chapter 7

THE WOMEN OF
MONTMARTRE

> Poor Versailles! It no longer remembers the 5th and 6th of
> October, 1789, when the women of the Commune alone
> sufficed to catch its King.
> —Félix Pyat in *Le Vengeur*, April 1, 1871

IN ORDER to understand why Paris refused to believe in France's
defeat, we must go back to the memories cherished from 1792. The
armies of many nations were on French soil then, and one French
general after another was deserting to the invading coalition as a
protest at the execution of the King. When all seemed lost, Paris
instituted a *levée en masse* (the first example of a modern mass
army). Under the leadership of the great military engineer, Lazare
Carnot, the armed people lifted the siege of Paris, drove the invaders out of France, occupied Holland, chased the British into
Hanover, defeated the Spaniards in the Pyrenees, pursued the Prussians across the Rhine. Then the Corsican corporal, Napoleon Bonaparte, built his empire with this armed people and subjugated most
of Europe.

From 1792 to 1794 the French Revolution passed through many
confusing and contradictory stages: from absolute monarchy to limited monarchy, to regicide and constitutional republic, to the dictatorship of the Committee of Public Safety, and then of the Jacobin
clubs, and their leader, Robespierre.

Conservatives, clerics, and provincial notables had reason to remember with horror how, before the troops raised by the Commune
of Paris left for the front, nameless executioners killed 2,000 clerics

115

and real or supposed royalists in the prisons of the city. Thereafter the hungry guillotine, fed by frenzy and fear, and those who denounced others lest they be denounced themselves, began to devour young and old, men and women, rich and poor, extreme leftists like the followers of Herbert, moderates of the Girondin clubs, then Jacobins, including the Minister of Justice, Danton, and finally Robespierre himself, before its hunger was assuaged.

Next had come the Directory, stilling the terror, filling its pockets, suffering defeat in war. Then military dictatorship and empire. Full circle from Monarch to Emperor, from the Terror to the Code Napoleon, with French armies under Napoleon the masters of the Continent.

Frenchmen were bitterly divided as to this confusion of events, and so they are even today. But Paris remembered with unquenchable pride that its mass armies had made France into a nation, and their nation the dominant power in Europe. Until Napoleon III was taken prisoner at Sedan, no patriotic Frenchman (and according to the letters of Marx, Engels, and Jenny Marx, all Frenchmen were "chauvinists," even "the best of them") was able to conceive that the single, obscure, provincial kingdom of Prussia could beat the armies that had beaten the coalesced armies of all Europe.

Even then, matters did not seem hopeless to the Parisians. When Empress Eugenie received the telegram: "The Army has been defeated and captured; I myself am a prisoner. *Napoleon,*" Paris felt that all it had to do was depose the counterfeit Napoleon, proclaim a Republic and a Government of National Defense, and raise new armies by a *levée en masse,* in order to repeat once more the miracle of 1792–94.

Once more a Paris mob stormed the Tuileries and the Hôtel de Ville, once more "Jacobin" clubs sprang up and "Jacobin" journals. But despite the oratory of the clubs and the eloquence and scorn of the journals, despite Gambetta's balloon journey and his superhuman efforts in the provinces, the tide of war did not turn. Neither the colorful and disorderly armies that he scraped together, nor the feeble attempts at sorties in torrents, nor any of the sober and fantastic schemes of inventive journalists and amateur crackbrains in Paris, could halt the inexorable advance of the well-armed, well-led Prussian armies. Having taken Strasbourg and Sedan and the armies of MacMahon, they took Metz and the armies of Bazaine, then laid siege to the capital.

Bismarck was not one to waste the bones of his grenadiers unnecessarily. The gray Prussian line blocked all the approaches to the city and waited for the populace to starve. First Paris consumed its horses at the rate of seven hundred a day, then its cats and dogs; finally prime rats were going in the market at three francs apiece.[1]

On the 28th of January, the 135th day of the siege, Paris capitulated. The spirit of the city remained high, its external defenses intact. Paris refused to believe in France's defeat, or in its own. But it did believe in its hunger, and grudgingly accepted capitulation, while it looked for scapegoats, and sought for new means of renewing the war.

Paris was required to surrender its forts, pay an indemnity of 200 million francs within fifteen days, submit to the disarming of its 250,000 troops. But Bismarck agreed to the retention of arms by 12,000 troops for service within the city, and by the National Guard. The sense of humiliation was keen; bitterness toward the Government of National Defense possessed all classes of the populace. No one, as Marx and Engels had written to each other, and as Seraillier had written from Paris to Marx, was willing to look reality in the face.

Bismarck chose not to occupy Paris, nor would he treat with the Government of National Defense which had been set up by revolution with the express purpose of continuing the war. Instead he chose to keep his troops where they were until France should elect a new government authorized to sign the terms of peace. He permitted the French to hold their elections without interference. The issues were two: to decide the nature of the new government of France and legitimatize its authority; and to decide whether to try to fight on, or accept the terms of a dictated peace.

Gambetta led the desperate last-ditch war party to which Paris now gave its votes. The "realists" in the capital who were willing to recognize the truth of defeat, occupation, and the capture of their armies, were few. But in the provinces, that had known not merely siege but the invasion itself at first hand, their numbers were overwhelming. The peace party buried its differences as to the future form of government, to include in its ranks moderate republicans, most of the officialdom and clergy, the peasants, and monarchists of all shades (Orleanists, Bourbonists, and the few remaining Bonapartists). Out of some 600 delegates to the new National Assembly,

---

[1] Edward S. Mason, *The Paris Commune*, New York, 1930, p. 93.

about 400 were monarchists of various kinds, whose differences with each other were to block the possibility of a monarchy, and some 200 were Republicans, radical and moderate. Paris alone voted with stubborn blindness for war *à l'outrance*—"to the bitter end"—a phrase without real content, for the bitter end had already been reached.

Paris elected thirty-seven of the war party, mostly journalists and club orators, and six of the peace party. After the long and desperate siege, the humiliation, and the weird dreams, Paris was still too keyed up to accept the reality of defeat. The monarchists, distrustful of each other, joining with the moderate republicans of the new National Assembly, settled on Adolphe Thiers, in his youth an Orleanist, after the fall of Louis Philippe in 1848 a moderate republican, to become Chief of the Executive, with a cabinet of three moderate Republicans, two Orleanists, and three Legitimists (supporters of the main Bourbon branch). Upon him devolved the patriotic but uncomfortable duty of signing an unpopular peace and paying off the indemnity as soon as possible, so that the Prussian troops would withdraw. To its resentment at his signing the peace, Paris added distrust of his republicanism, a distrust shared by Marx and Engels. But whatever else was to be said against Thiers, he was to remain faithful to his proclaimed view that "the Republic is the form which divides us least." By the time he was forced out in 1875, he had convinced moderate Frenchmen that the Republic would not produce another reign of terror. The monarchists remained strong yet deadlocked by their rival candidates for the throne. The Third Republic was to last into the next century.

Thiers published the peace terms forced upon him by Bismarck. Then Paris added to its sense of humiliation and injured patriotism, fresh indignation at the fact that Thiers was transferring the meeting place of the National Assembly from Bordeaux to Versailles, and not to Paris. "The City of Light" of all Europe was being dethroned as the capital of France!

To be sure, the National Assembly had its reasons for avoiding Paris as its meeting place, for it too had its memories of 1792 and '93: mobs invading the Tuileries and Hôtel de Ville, and imposing their will on the Assembly of the Nation; blind and undiscriminating terror by categories or by anonymous denunciation; the sharp blade of the guillotine.

Yet, in classic French petit-bourgeois fashion, it was a measure of the National Assembly concerning the purse strings which finally set virtually all Paris at odds with the Assembly, and raised in decisive fashion the question of whether the Assembly of the Nation or the City of Paris should rule France.

Obsessed by the huge indemnity France had to pay to Prussia before its troops would be withdrawn, and having decided that the war was really over in spirit and in fact, the majority of the National Assembly, with undue haste, tampered not with Republican institutions, but with the pay of the National Guard, and with the moratorium on the payment of debts and rents that had obtained during the siege of Paris.

The National Guard of Paris was not so much a means of keeping order (for which purpose Bismarck had left it its arms), and still less a means of defense of the city against the Prussians. It was in fact a dignified means of unemployment relief. Demobilized soldiers and deserters, journalists and artisans and workingmen, and all sorts of unemployed, filled out its ranks. Its small wage—thirty sous (one franc, fifty centimes) a day—were paid irregularly, yet for most of its 300,000 members there was, in the midst of the ruined economy of a city so long under siege, no other way to exist.

Still worse, the National Assembly at Versailles quite senselessly, hastened to pass a new "law of maturities" ending the moratorium on debts. With that the shopkeepers of Paris, merchants large and small, artisans and industrialists, were faced with immediate bankruptcy. Even the city's conservative journals protested. The National Assembly's own Committee of Inquiry later admitted that "the maturities fixed on March 13th placed a considerable section of the business men of Paris in a position of inevitable failure, that is to say, of ruin and dishonor."[2]

The National Guard, 300,000 strong, was still armed. Its ranks were depleted by the exodus of propertied and conservative citizens to the quieter climate of the provinces, and swelled by those now threatened with dispossession for nonpayment of rent, or with bankruptcy for nonpayment of debts. Thus the new recruits were largely from the *petit-bourgeoisie enragée*. The regular fighting troops of the line, disarmed, disgusted, weary, smarting under the awareness

---

[2] *Ibid.*, p. 103: cf. Marx, *Der Buergerkrieg in Frankreich, Werke,* Vol. XVII, p. 328: "Dufaures Gesetze wegen der verfallnen Wechsel und Hausmieten, die den Handel und die Industrie von Paris mit dem Untergang bedrohten."

that they had been badly armed and badly led, flocked into Paris to swell the ranks of the jobless, the homeless, the discontented.

The radical opposition, led mostly by journalists, and to a far lesser extent by Blanquist and Proudhonist members of the French Section of the International, concerning whom Marx and Engels had been so uncomplimentary in their letters, now transferred their criticisms and their animus, without interruption, from the Government of National Defense to the National Assembly.

"The more I think about it," wrote Henri Maret in *Le Mot d'Ordre* of March 11, "the more I become convinced that we are attaching too much importance to the decisions of the six hundred cow fanciers who ornament our National Assembly." Thus the spokesmen of Paris viewed the Assembly, the legally elected government of the country. And the "cow fanciers," had they possessed the same facility for barbed verbiage, would have responded that Paris was filled with vagabonds, insolvent debtors, demagogic leaders, and irresponsible mobs.

At that moment Bismarck demanded either the surrender of the commanding Fort of Belfort or the symbolic humiliation of France by a triumphal entry into Paris. Favre and Thiers worked earnestly to save Paris this indignity, but the surrender of Belfort seemed to them a greater evil. Entry was conceded for two days only. During this period the excitement of Paris was at fever pitch. Still refusing to recognize that the war was lost, many wanted the poorly armed and poorly trained National Guard to attack the "invaders" in the hopes of renewing hostilities. But cooler counsel prevailed: The National Guard merely removed its cannon and other military equipment from the artillery parks to the heights of Montmartre, Chaumont and Belleville "for greater safety."

Mussolini has written, "the revolution is an idea which has found bayonets." Lenin would perhaps have added "the revolution is an idea which possesses organization and has found bayonets." In the National Guard Paris found its bayonets. In its Central Committee it found its organization. In the journalists, its idea . . . or at least, its voice. In the *petit-bourgeoisie enragée* it found a sense that all classes in Paris were against the National Assembly of the Republic. All that Paris needed now was to find the "idea" which was to employ the bayonets and the organization and the strident voice. Its idea, insofar as it had one, was embodied in its memories of the

Commune of Paris of 1792, from which had come the rule of Paris over all France, and the organizing force and mass armies to combat all of coalesced reactionary Europe.

All the grumbling and discontent in Paris would not have been sufficient to make a revolution, only riots and rebellions. But the situation was so tense in March 1871 that almost any act of the National Assembly against the City of Paris could have aroused riots. The National Guard, quite without intending it, provided the pretext for the riots, and then, the organization to turn spontaneous rebellion into revolution.

The Government of National Defense had arranged for the National Guard to elect its own officers, with results disastrous to discipline, but useful to the Radical Opposition. The men of the eloquent phrase on whom Marx and Engels had spent so much irony, the journalists of the acid-dipped pen, the notables, or as Mason aptly calls them the "notorieties," of revolutionary Paris, were selected in large numbers, particularly in the poorer working-class quarters, to head regiments. Only after these commanders (a minority) were discovered on October 31, 1870 to be marshaling their troops, not for the defense of Paris against the Germans, but against the Government of National Defense itself, were sixteen chiefs of battalion removed. Between September 17, 1870 and March 18, 1871, thirty-six battalion commanders, one hundred seventy-one captains, fourteen adjutant-majors, one hundred forty-seven lieutenants, one hundred nineteen second lieutenants, and a number of lesser officers, were discharged. These remained as spokesmen at the clubs, as writers in the journals, as orators at mass meetings, and as potential leaders of discontent.[3]

In connection with the elections to the National Assembly, the National Guard formed a temporary "Central Committee." The invitation to elect delegates was sent to all the regiments of the Guard "in no exclusively partisan spirit," but it was the veteran radicals, the articulate journalists and agitators, the experienced club orators, who came in numbers. They endorsed radical candidates in the elections, including a few from the International. So many organizations had come and gone, but this time, impressed with the possibility of concerted action by two hundred-odd battalions in the defense of the Republic (they were all without exception defensists and pa-

---

[3] Mason, *op. cit.*, p. 88.

triots), this organization decided not to dissolve when its occasion, the electoral excitement during the war-or-peace election, had died down.

The International had had no hand in the formation of the Central Committee but it was later invited to send four of its members. It was delighted, for its influence, never much, had been fading rapidly. The Parisian workers, being unemployed, had neither been paying their dues, nor subscribing to the little sheets of the International. When they could afford it, there were more exciting journals. In the Central Committee, though a small minority, the four representatives of the International could contribute experience and ideas, and advertise their organization. Engels had written to Jenny Marx that the very name of Blanqui, long in prison, was completely forgotten in Paris.[4] Now Varlin, a devoted Blanquist serving on the Central Committee, was able to revive it.

The acts of the Central Committee, however, were completely free of socialist intention or implication. It was on their initiative that the cannon had been withdrawn to the Hill of Montmartre and other "safe places," when the German triumphal entry occurred. On March 3, the Central Committee of the National Guard laid claim to the right to discharge any battalion commander who refused to obey it, a claim which violated both the electoral principle for each regiment, and the governmental powers of the National Assembly. And it adopted a resolution declaring that if the National Assembly deprived Paris of its title as capital of the nation, the Committee would declare the Department of the Seine an independent republic![5]

Between February 26 and March 12, the Central Committee began taking over the equipment of the demoralized organizations of the troops of the line in the capital. These acts of quite unpremeditated sovereignty aroused alarm both in conservative circles in the city, and in the National Assembly at Versailles. A suspicion arose that secret and sinister forces were at work in the National Guard, a conjecture given color of truth by the fact that most of the names signed to the decrees were unknown to the public, while the handful of known names were Blanquists like Varlin. Aside from those decrees, its only program, posted on the walls on March 10, was to represent the "general will" of the people of Paris, to disband the regular army, and to retain its own arms, the possession of which

---

[4] MEGA, III/4, p. 368.
[5] Mason, op. cit., p. 111.

meant safety to the people of Paris, and thirty sous per day to each possessor. In the words of Edward S. Mason:

> The Federation would admit of no government other than the Republic; within the Republic it would admit of no armed force other than the National Guard; within the National Guard it would admit of no authority other than that elected by the rank and file.[6]

Obviously, this was no social program in Marx's sense. But it was a political program of armed force and sovereignty. As long as the Central Committee had the backing of the majority of the National Guard, and the National Guard had fighting equipment strategically disposed on the hills of Paris, the National Government of France could not be sure of its own position or its sovereignty in its principal metropolis.

The National Guard of Paris had at no time played any part in the war. Yet now, after the armistice, it was the only considerable body of men with arms, and, once it had formed its Central Committee, the only armed force in the country with an independent organization.

The Commune of Paris, on the contrary, was, so far, nothing but a vague slogan of a handful of intellectuals, journalists, and club orators.

The National Guard was an armed force of 300,000 men. Without its decision, the word "commune" would have remained a fading memory of 1793. Even in the clubs, Mason writes, no one appeared to have a definite conception of what that memory was or what the slogan meant. Marx, in his Second Address of the International on the War, had specifically warned against it as a false and dangerous slogan from the vanished past. At the Club Favier, an orator challenged his hearers to define the term:

> I'll wager that even here at the Club Favier, three-quarters of the audience does not know what the Commune means. [Protests, denials, tumult, shouting. "He's a police spy!" Others: "Well, go ahead and tell us what it is."] The Commune is the right of the people, it is equal treatment for all, it is the *levée en masse* and the punishment of traitors; the Commune, finally, is the Commune.[7]

Actually rebellion began in Paris neither as the work of the

---

[6] *Op. cit.* p. 115, where each of these assertions is documented by a corresponding decree.
[7] Cited in Mason, *op. cit.*, p. 119.

Jacobin clubs nor the Socialist clubs, nor the few members of the French Section of the International, nor the National Guard. Its occasion was a badly planned attempt of the National Government to remove the cannon parked on Montmartre and other strong points of Paris to the École Militaire. Only three days before the attempt was made, the Vigilance Committee of the Montmartre National Guard was seriously considering the voluntary surrender of the cannon, but a delegation sent by the Federation of the National Guard assembled at the Vauxhall persuaded the local committee to reject the request. Still, the National Guard made no attempt to guard the cannon.

On the night of March 17 to 18, Thiers dispatched 15,000 troops of the line and 3,000 police, split into some ten or twelve sections, for a simultaneous march upon the cannon scattered in various parts of Paris. If the troops under General Vinoy had been fully reliable and the task quickly accomplished, the operation would have succeeded without a hitch, for the cannon lay in the moonlight unguarded. On Montmartre alone there were 171 cannon. At three A.M. troops marched up Montmartre without disturbance, and took the entire lot. But their prize could not be removed until horses arrived. By the time the horses arrived, it was eight o'clock in the morning!

The proletarian quarter of Montmartre rose early, disturbed by the sound of marching men and shouted orders. The soldiers were soon surrounded by the women and children of Montmartre and deluged with insults and reproaches. By morning the National Guard of the quarter was aroused and rushed to the scene. The 88th Battalion of the Army, demoralized by the frustrating wait in the darkness and the surrounding tide of the women of the quarter, refused to obey General Lecomte's order to fire on the approaching Guard. The police, disorganized too by the crowds of women in their midst, fired but few shots. Then the Regulars fraternized with the Guards, while General Lecomte was seized by the crowd and conducted to the Guard Headquarters on the Hill. Some of the cannon were dragged by horses and loyal troops halfway down the Hill before crowds cut the traces and dragged them up again. The same spontaneous action of the mobs occurred at other strong points. By eleven o'clock, small volunteer detachments of the National Guard were everywhere guarding the artillery parks, and barricades were springing up all over the excited city, which felt it was once more the Paris of '93! At noon, none other than the Minister of the Interior of Paris, Picard, posted a placard calling upon the National Guard to resist the National Government of France, to defend "your homes, your family, your property" against these men, "obeying unknown leaders, who are directing the cannon destined for the Prussians, against Paris itself."

All that afternoon the bulk of the National Guard remained passive, while their elected officers tried to restrain the crowds, largely acting, as unorganized crowds do, on impulse. In the middle of the afternoon, the imprisoned General Lecomte and another captive, General Clement Thomas, were moved to the Headquarters of the Vigilance Committee of the Eighteenth Arrondissement (Montmartre) for the purposes of questioning. But the Vigilance Committee stayed away from its own quarters, while the mob, finally roused to a frenzy, took the two generals into a garden behind the house where Committee Headquarters were, and shot them. It was the first bloodshed and, as blood so often does, it opened an abyss between Paris and Versailles.

At this point Thiers, who had come to Paris to direct the operation, ordered General Vinoy to sound a retreat and lead his detachments back to Versailles. The retreat was conducted in perfect order. The National Guard could not have harassed them if it wanted to for it was not yet mobilized nor had its Central Committee taken any decision on the riotous day. (Marx would contend later that if they had pursued the "demoralized troops" they could have taken well-garrisoned Versailles and control over all France.)

The issue between Versailles and Paris was joined late that afternoon. Part of the Central Committee of the Guard met, then dispatched its members to various precincts to take command of what had been until that hour a spontaneous and sporadic movement of mobs, supported here and there by individual Guardsmen and Guards Officers. As it took over from the mobs, the Central Committee had no idea that it was thus assuming responsibility for what had occurred and opening, despite its intentions, a civil war.

Chapter 8

THE COMMUNE IN

HISTORY AND LEGEND

The Commune is the form "at last discovered" by the proletarian revolution under which the economic liberation of
labor can proceed. . . . the first attempt of a proletarian
revolution to *break up* the bourgeois state machinery . . .
the political form "at last discovered" which can and must
take the place of the broken machine. . . . The Russian
Revolutions of 1905 and 1917 . . . continued the work of
the Commune and confirmed the historic analysis made by
the genius of Marx.

—V.I. Lenin in *State and Revolution*

They wrote with their blood an indelible page in history
. . . but themselves could not decipher this page. . . . Its
leaders were Blanquists and Proudhonists, its policies moderate and timid, it had no socialist program and whatever aims
it professed were vague and ill-defined. Nevertheless it was
socialist because *the proletariat can fight for no other cause
than Socialism.*

—I. Stepanov, in *Parizhskaya Kommuna*,
Moscow, 1921

The Commune was merely the rising of a town under exceptional conditions, the majority of the Commune was in no
sense Socialist, nor could it be. With a small amount of
common sense, they could have reached a compromise with
Versailles. . . .

—Karl Marx to Domela Nieuwenhuis,
February 22, 1881

WHEN the Central Committee met on the evening of March 18, it found that power had been thrust upon it by the flight of the Government and the action of the Paris mobs. The Central Committee certainly had not organized the revolution. In fact, it had not even met for over a week, that is, since the tenth of March. Mobs, and spontaneously formed groups of insurgents, had seized the principal strong points in Paris, and murdered Generals Lecomte and Thomas without a trial and without the Committee's knowledge.

But the Government at Versailles held the Committee responsible for all that happened that day, and charged that the Committee of the Guard was composed of antipatriotic revolutionaries "nearly all affiliated with the International." Nothing could be further from the truth, for the Committee was composed of smallish men, elected haphazardly, fanatically patriotic and anti-Prussian. Only four, or at most five, were affiliated with the International. Moreover, power had been thrust upon it by spontaneous uprisings all over Paris, some participated in by Guardsmen or Guards detachments but none ordered or directed by the Committee, and still less by the International.

The Central Committee could repudiate the insurrection, leaving Paris and itself in defenseless chaos, or it could take over as the only authoritative body in Paris, at least until it could get the city to elect its own representative body. It chose the second course, for it did not dream of a third.

On the nineteenth it issued a proclamation actually claiming credit for what had been thrust upon it both by Paris and Versailles. Its posted proclamation read, somewhat incongruously:

> You have charged us with organizing the defense of Paris and the preservation of your rights. We are conscious of having fulfilled this mission; assisted by your generous courage and admirable sang-froid, we have overthrown the government which betrayed us.

Commissions were delegated to take over the National Press and the Official Journal, and to administer the services abandoned by the Government: telegraph, interior, finances, police, war. But at the same time the Central Committee announced that it had no intention of assuming governmental power. It was "not a Government" and "did not intend to take the place of those whom popular opinion has displaced." On the very same day, the nineteenth of March, the Central Committee, dismayed by the tasks thrust upon it, hastily set elections for the twenty-second, only three days away.[1]

---

[1] Mason, *op. cit.*, pp. 132–33.

On the twentieth it assumed the governmental function most important to its own existence: it guaranteed the regular pay of that part of the National Guard which supported the Committee. As to the battalions that supported the National Government, "there was no objection to their collecting from the Government at Versailles."

Next it appointed forces to supervise ex-convicts who had drifted into Paris, posted a threat of death to all thieves caught in the act, postponed the maturity of business obligations for a month, abolished the right to evict tenants for nonpayment of rent until further notice, and provided for the discharge of all public employees who did not return to their duties by the twenty-fifth. Varlin, the Blanquist, and Jourde, who was to become prominent in directing the finances of the Commune, managed to assure the payment of the National Guard salaries by negotiating a loan of half a million francs from Rothschild, and an advance of a million francs from the Bank of France.[2] Neither the House of Rothschild nor the Bank of France thought of itself as financing a proletarian revolution.

The elections so hurriedly set for the twenty-second had to be postponed for technical reasons to the twenty-sixth. In the meanwhile, the Central Committee fluctuated

> . . . between revolution and legality, between governing and resigning, between inaction and action. . . . A bewildered group of incompetent individuals found themselves at the head of, and responsible for, a movement which had far outrun its original intentions. Unwilling to go forward and incapable of going back, the Committee was forced by circumstances to govern illegally while frantically striving to achieve legality. It attempted at the outset to shift both power and responsibility to an assembly elected by the municipality. . . .
> It proposed [meanwhile] to limit itself to purely municipal affairs but continually and irresponsibly neglected this limitation.[3]

For eight days the Central Committee exercised its reluctant sovereignty while striving to terminate its rule by the earliest possible elections. It had no more idea of what the magnetic slogan, the Commune of Paris, might mean than did the club orators or the populace, but it had a naïve faith that elections would settle everything, hence it called on Paris to elect its municipal assembly, or "Commune."

Voices were raised—the majority of the mayors of arrondisse-

---

[2] *Ibid.*, p. 134.
[3] *Ibid.*, pp. 136–37.

ments and the majority of the press—in favor of securing a legal cloak for the elections by a compromise with Versailles. Some spokesmen for Versailles expressed a hesitant willingness to conduct the voting if it were postponed to April 3. Mayors and other deputations scurried up and back between the Assembly and the Committee. For a few days it seemed as if both sides might accept April 1 as a compromise date. But on both sides there was obduracy and distrust. The end result was that the mayors finally threw a cloak of greater legality around the elections by their own last-minute endorsement, while many provincial cities were alienated from the capital by its refusal to postpone the elections while seeking agreement with the National Assembly.

The radical journal, *La Commune*, expressed the general feeling of Paris on the day of voting when it wrote:

The peace is made. The blood of Parisians will not be shed in this great capital of civilization. Universal suffrage will speak and the whole world will bow respectfully before its decision.

And the veteran republican revolutionary, Félix Pyat, whose phrase radicalism Marx and Engels so detested, told the citizens of Paris:

You have made a revolution without example in history. Your revolution of the eighteenth of March has a particular quality which distinguishes it from all others. Its especial grandeur lies in its being completely popular, entirely collective, communal—a revolution *en commandite* [corporate, as in a joint stock company], anonymous and unanimous, and, for the first time, without directors [*gérants*]."

This, too, was published in *La Commune* on March 27. On the twenty-eighth, the installation of the Commune of Paris was a festival of rejoicing. In front of the Hôtel de Ville orators addressed the populace and the "Federals," as the Guard was now rechristened. The *Marseillaise* was sung. The spirit of 1793 was declared resurrected. Paris felt that she was once more master of herself, and, as in 1793, leader of all France. Herein lay the real ambiguity in the term, Paris Commune. Was it simply the legally elected municipal council of Paris in a federal France? Or was it the reincarnation of the Jacobin dictatorship of 1792, the dictatorship of Paris over France? The Central Committee transferred to the Commune the authority that it had exercised so reluctantly with the words:

Today, we have had the privilege of viewing the most glorious popular spectacle that has ever met our eyes or stirred our souls; Paris greeted and acclaimed its Revolution; Paris opened a white page of the book of History and thereon inscribed its puissant name.[4]

Before a month had passed that white page would be charred with smoke and red with blood. This was the "dominion of the phrase" which Marx and Engels had feared and warned against; the ghost come back to haunt France from the holocaust of 1792. Now that the Commune was here and, whatever its intentions, was going to be forced to defend itself bloodily against bloody assault, it was necessary for Marx to determine what attitude he, and the General Council of the International which he controlled, should take toward it.

Since there are no longer letters of Marx and Engels to go by, it is harder to trace with exactness the change in Marx's reactions. But a letter from him to Kugelmann, dated April 12th, suggests that he at once began the preparation of a hymn of praise, a claim on the heroism of the Commune, an excoriation of Thiers, and a catalogue of tactical errors which would help to explain the downfall of the Commune which from the first day (and even earlier!) he foresaw as inevitable.

If you read the last chapter of my "Eighteenth Brumaire," [Marx wrote him], you will find that I declare to be the next effort of the French Revolution no longer as it has up to now to hand the bureaucratic-military machine from one hand to another, but *to break it up*, and this is the prerequisite of any genuine revolution on the continent. This is also the attempt of our heroic Parisian party comrades. What elasticity, what historical initiative, what capacity for self-sacrifice there is in these Parisians! After a six-months long starvation and ruin through internal treason more than through the foreign foe, they rise up, under the Prussian bayonets, as if there had never been a war between France and Germany and the enemy were not before the gates! History has no similar example of similar greatness! If they go down, then nothing is at fault for it except their "good nature." The thing to have done was to march immediately on Versailles after first Vinoy and then the reactionary part of the Paris National Guard had cleared the field for them. The right moment was passed out of scruples of conscience. They did not want *to open a civil war*, as if the mischievous *avorton* [abortion], Thiers, had not already opened the civil war with his attempt at the disarming of Paris! Second error:

---

[4] *Ibid.*, pp. 154–62.

The Central Committee gave up its power too soon to make way for the Commune. Again out of too "honorable" scrupulousness! However that may be, this present insurrection of Paris—even though going under before the wolves, swine and vile dogs of the old society—is the most glorious deed of our Party since the June insurrection. Compare this storming of the heavens by the Parisians with the slaves of heaven of the German-Prussian Holy Roman Empire with its posthumous masquerades, smelling of barracks, church, *Krautjunkertum* [country bumpkin squirarchy] and above all philistinism.[5]

Marx did not write to Kugelmann again until June 18, after the Commune had fallen and the General Council had issued the celebrated Address which has come to be known as *The Civil War in France.* Then Marx wrote him:

You know that during the whole time of the Paris Revolution I was denounced as the "grand chef de l'Internationale" by the Versailles sheets and *par repercussion* by the local journals. And now there's the *Address* which you have probably gotten! It makes a devil of a noise and I have the honor of being *at this moment the best calumniated and the most menaced man of London* [in English in the original]. That really does one good after the tedious twenty years of stagnant idyll. The Government sheet—the *Observer*—threatens me with persecution in the courts. *Qu'ils osent! Je me moque de ces canailles là!*[6]

The most interesting thing in these letters is Marx's claim to the action, against which he has been warning, as "the most glorious deed of our Party." And the apparent relapse, after two decades of comparative realism, into the romantic-utopian mood of 1848, when a little handful of communists could hope to penetrate and dominate a democratic movement and take the heavens by storm.

But the majority of the leaders of the Paris Commune were not members of the French Section of the International. Insofar as that leadership was socialist at all, it was a united front of Blanquists and Proudhonists, only a small number of whom were members of the International. Not one of them was a Marxist, unless perhaps one delegate could be so accounted, the Hungarian-Jewish refugee, Leo Frankel. Even of the second-string delegates to the Communal Assembly only one, by stretching it, could be called an adherent of Marxism, namely, Seraillier. Marx, as the reader will remember, had

---

[5] *Letters to Kugelmann,* pp. 96–97.
[6] *Ibid.,* p. 99. The last two sentences are in French in the original: "Let them dare! I mock at those scoundrels!"

sent him to Paris from London to dissuade the members of the International from attempting to overthrow the Provisional Government or set up a Commune, and he had immediately fallen under the spell of the Radical Republican, Rochefort.

The most exhaustive attempt thus far to analyze the "social-class" and political inclination of the members of the Communal Assembly is a series of brief biographical sketches appended to Volume Two of the two-volume translation into Russian of the *Minutes of the Paris Commune* (*Protokoly Zasedanii Parizhskoi Kommuny*), published by the Moscow Academy of Sciences in 1960. The biographical sketches take up some twenty-odd pages and offer the following breakdown:

Proudhonists or semi-Proudhonists	20
Blanquists or semi-Blanquists	20
Neo-Jacobins	5
Bourgeois Radicals and Democrats	5
Uncertain or unclassified	24
Bakuninist (Cluseret)	1

Of the above, one is listed as having been expelled from the International in 1868, ten as members of the International who were Proudhonist, three as members who were semi-Blanquist, and ten as Internationalists with no other qualifications.

The members of the Commune, of course, ceased to exercise their normal professions, i.e. were "declassed." But the *Biographical Sketches* list 33 as workingmen, 24 as journalists and writers, 6 as office workers, 5 as artists (including the great Courbet), 5 as salesmen or sales clerks, 5 as doctors, 5 as lawyers, 1 merchant, 2 officers, 1 pharmacist, and 1 professional revolutionary (Blanqui, who remained in a prison of the Government at Versailles). There is some overlapping; a few workers and many professional men had actually ceased for some time to exercise their trades and professions in favor of journalism. There were a few teachers, but all of these had become journalists. Of the eighty-nine people thus sketched, a little over a third were workingmen or rather former workingmen, and almost all of these artisans, not factory workers, while slightly more than half were journalists and professionals. Less than one-quarter were members of the International.

In addition to the above, seventeen biographies are studied of delegates who were elected to the Communal Assembly but, by way of protest or disagreement with some of its declarations or acts, withdrew before April 2. This group includes six merchants, two officers, one teacher, two industrialists, two doctors, two lawyers, one concert conductor, and one workingman or former workingman. Thus the workingmen, in mass, stuck it out, but never formed a majority of the Commune.

Even those who called themselves members of the International had hesitated until the very last moment before they allied themselves with the Central Committee of the National Guard, for fear of linking the fate of the International with the fate of the Revolution. Only in their sessions of March 23 and 24 did they finally come out with a proclamation wholeheartedly espousing the cause of the Central Committee.

Their endorsement was posted on the walls of Paris and published in the *Journal Officiel*, along with a brief statement of principles and lists of candidates of the socialist clubs of various arrondissements. It was the election of many of these, and the entrance of socialist formulations into various official documents that enabled both the reaction in Versailles and Marx in London to maintain that the Commune was the work of "our party" or of Marx's International Headquarters in London. Thenceforward, contemporaries at both extremes of the spectrum were inclined to see in the insurrection of March 18 as well as in the Commune Assembly elected on the twenty-sixth an attempt to overthrow existing society.[7]

The conservative Paris daily, *Le Bien Public*, which had opposed the elections for the Commune, in its edition of March 28 was the first to put this idea into clear words:

This is no political revolution but a social revolution. The leaders do not see this—they are looking at it politically. But they do not know the nature of the forces they are leading.

Like Marx, the editor of *Le Bien Public* seemed to hold that there was something in the nature of the proletariat which foreordained that wherever it was in a majority with the right of suffrage, and able to choose its own representatives, it must by the nature of things be socialist.

And indeed, there was much socialist language and many socialist ideas floating in the air, if not as Marx defined socialism, then as Proudhon, Blanqui or Bakunin defined it. Thus the Paris sections of the International, in announcing their adherence to the cause of the

---

[7] Mason, *op. cit.*, pp. 156 ff.

Central Committee of the National Guard, declared that the independence of the Commune of Paris would "put an end to class antagonism and assure social equality."

> We have demanded the emancipation of the working class [its statement of principles continued] and this communal assembly is its guarantee, for it gives to every citizen the means of defending his rights, or controlling in a satisfactory manner the representatives charged with the care of its interests, and of determining the progressive application of social reforms.[8]

The socialists of Paris were articulate and eloquent orators, verbose and excitable journalists, past masters of the vague and stirring phraseology of socialism. The word *socialisme* was born in Paris, as were *collectivisme, mutualisme,* and *solidarité,* not to mention *égalité* and *fraternité* which could boast of over three-quarters of a century of life. Socialist phrases had filled the air since the days of Babeuf and his Conspiracy of the Equals. In the first half of the nineteenth century the city was an incubator of utopias. Its banking system was the work of disciples of Saint-Simon. Even its emperor, Louis Napoleon, had written his *L'extinction du pauperisme* in 1845, won the votes of the workingmen for his *coup d'état* of 1851, and had, as emperor, been appealed to by Proudhon to "carry out without restrictions or equivocation the social revolution." As the Revolution of 1848 had proclaimed the "social republic," so the counter-revolution of 1851 had called forth Proudhon's *La Révolution sociale démontrée par le Coup d'État du Deux Décembre,* a vision of the "social empire."[9] This variety of socialisms, with their many minor fractions and factions and their many personal chiefs, was as characteristic of the ideological air of Paris as the many minor parties, personal leaders, and perpetually shifting governmental combinations were of the Chamber of Deputies throughout the Third Republic. Without taking into account the grandiloquence, the infantile candor, and the phrase-radicalism of journalists and politicians, "socialistic" bankers and the "socialistic" emperor, one cannot begin to understand the politics of France.

One of the ablest of the editors of the *Journal Officiel* was the Proudhonist journalist, Charles Longuet, later to marry Marx's daughter and become a leader of one of the moderate wings of French socialism. In the *Journal Officiel* Longuet treated the spon-

---

[8] Mason, *op. cit.,* p. 158.
[9] Proudhon's book was published in 1852.

taneous insurrections and riots of March 18 as a class struggle of the proletariat for its emancipation from its bourgeois masters. Yet his formulations were far from socialist in any sense that Marx would recognize. Typical is his characterization of the uprising of March 18:

> The proletariat, confronted with a permanent menace to its rights, with an absolute negation of all its legitimate aspirations, with the ruin of the country and all its hopes, has conceived as its imperious duty and its absolute right the taking in hand of its own destinies and the assurance of its own triumph by the assumption of power. That is why it has answered by means of a revolution the criminal and insensate provocation of a blind and culpable government, which has not hesitated to let loose a civil war in the presence of a foreign invasion and occupation.[10]

But before we consider the social character of the Commune, we must return to Karl Marx who was claiming it as the "most glorious deed of our Party since the June Insurrection."

As soon as the Insurrection occurred, Marx began work on his own interpretation of it, which was to take form as an *Address of the International,* better known under its subtitle of *The Civil War in France.* He began to fill notebooks with excerpts from the reports in the British press and the journals of Paris and Versailles. On April 18, he proposed to the General Council of the International that it should issue an Address to all its members in all lands on "the general tendency of the struggle" in France, whereupon he was commissioned to prepare it. In the second half of April he began his first draft, working on it until approximately May 10. The framework of his interpretation of "the general tendency" was already there, but the draft was too long—122 pages. He finished a second draft in a few days, by the middle of May, beginning work at once on the third and final one. This he had ready to submit to the General Council on May 30, two days after the last barricade in Paris fell. Just as he had started work before the Commune was elected, so he intended to complete the Address before it fell, for from the beginning he foreknew its fate and had decided on his own intended interpretation.

On May 23, the Minutes of a meeting of the General Council record that "Citizen Marx declares that he has been ill and therefore

---

[10] *Journal Officiel,* March 21: Mason, *op. cit.,* p. 159.

unable to complete the promised Address, but hopes to have it ready next Tuesday." That "next Tuesday" was May 30. Marx read his Address then and had it approved. It was in English, thirty-five pages long, and in this form it was published on June 13.[11]

The chief concern of the Central Committee of the Guard, as of the Communal Assembly, was the defense of the city once it became clear that war had broken out between Paris and Versailles. From the start this defense was handled badly.

The first Commander, a drunken fool and loudmouth named Lullier, neglected to occupy the key fortress of Mont Valerien, commanding the principal routes from Paris to Versailles. Until April 3, Paris remained on the defensive, doing nothing to follow the demoralized troops retreating with Thiers. Even if the Paris National Guard had pursued them, given its lack of training and discipline, its poor equipment and incompetent elected officers, it is doubtful that it could have taken Versailles from the regular army, though this is of course speculation. In any case, after over two weeks of delay its effort to assume the offensive proved pitiful. On the third of April, under elected generals, three columns marched out gaily from Paris as if the taking of Versailles were a sort of excursion. When they got under the guns of Mont Valerien, the fortress opened fire; two of the columns broke ranks and fled in opposite directions. The attempt to take Versailles ended in bitter defeat, with the result that in Paris itself, many elected members resigned from the Commune as confidence in it waned.

The Commune ceased to give its trust now to "the shouters" and elected generals, seeking instead the services of professionals. Chief of these was General Cluseret, whose military works, hallowed by the Commune, Lenin was to translate into Russian in 1905. This vociferous and not too skillful French soldier and politician undoubtedly loved the turmoil of revolutionary war. In June 1848, General Gallifet had entrusted to him the crushing of the workingmen's uprising. Then he participated in the Crimean War, served in the conquest of Algeria, fought under Garibaldi in Italy, became an American citizen and took part in the Civil War in the ranks of the Union, where he attained his generalship. Next he participated in the Fenian movement in Ireland, and was condemned to death *in*

---

[11] The three drafts are all available in German in *Werke*, Vol. XVII, pp. 319–64, 493–571, 572–610. The relationship between the drafts and the dating of the work on them is given on pp. 703–04 and 735–36.

absentia in England. In 1868, returning to France where he published his *L'Armée et la Democratie,* he got himself jailed by the Imperial Government, and entered the International as its lone Bakuninist. With Bakunin he attempted to overthrow the Provisional Government of National Defense first in Lyons and then in Marseilles. He did not join the Commune's armed forces until his generalship was recognized, then served as its Military Delegate or Minister of War to the National Guard from April 2 to April 20. Since he did not show any ability to turn the tide of battle, he was jailed on the thirtieth of April for the loss of Fort Issy. Exonerated of treason on May 21 just before the Commune fell, he escaped France to participate in an Albanian uprising against Turkey. He returned after the amnesty of 1880, was jailed once more, then elected a member of the Chamber of Deputies. His turbulent life was typical of the romantic soldier-of-fortune and freedom of the nineteenth century. He was the professional military analogue of the professional revolutionary, Bakunin. He was symbolic of the military character of the Commune, and his jailing by the Commune had something typical in it, too, for he had been preceded in his trip from commander to "traitor"-in-prison, by General Bergeret, and was followed on the same route by General Rossel, who escaped prison only by going into hiding. General Rossel was the most professional of the Commune's commanders, a conservative who offered his services out of disgust with what he considered Thiers's cowardly and unpatriotic retreat from Paris to Versailles with the troops of the line. Neither the professional nor the soldier-of-fortune could turn the undisciplined and disorderly National Guard with its elected chiefs into an effective fighting force.

In Versailles, Thiers steadily built up his army. Aided by easy victories, professional leadership and training, better equipment, and by the release of war prisoners to swell their ranks, the morale of the Versailles troops rose as that of the National Guard fell.

On the night of May 21–22, troops entered Paris without firing a shot, through an unguarded breach in the walls. There followed seven days of the bloodiest street battles in the entire history of the nineteenth century. By defection of the moderate, the prudent, the timid, and the unwilling, the defenders were reduced for this last-ditch defense to bands of true revolutionary fighters, including many women and children as well as men. From behind 500-odd barricades, with the homes of their own quarters at their backs, they fought with desperate courage, retreating from street to street and from barricade to barricade, burning suspect houses, shedding their blood unstintingly, leaving behind them a heroic memory, and a wide breach between the poor and the well-to-do which is still felt in France.

The Government of Versailles took a brutal revenge for the fright it had suffered. There were firing squads, mob violence, summary courts-martial, mass arrests and trials. As on March 18 it had been the women of the poorest quarters who were most energetic in their actions, so now women of the well-to-do showed the greatest fury against the captives.

The number of the dead has never been settled. Estimates range from 10,000 to 70,000. Mason, reviewing the evidence, places the figure at more than 10,000 and less than 15,000. E. L. Woodward places at 17,000 the number of Communards killed and 38,000 those arrested, of which 13,450 were sentenced to jail or deported to penal colonies.[12] Including all arrests from the beginning of hostilities to 1875 when the fury had spent its force, Mason estimates the total figure to be 50,000. At least 35,000 were taken to Versailles. "During the May days, long columns of worn-out, feverish, and despairing prisoners marched through Paris between lines of soldiers and crowds of jeering and vindictive spectators howling for their death. At Versailles they were herded into improvised prison yards before being distributed among the penitentiaries along the coast."[13] Conservative British papers like the *Times*, which had viewed the Commune with horror, were "sickened" by the ferocity of the reprisals.

The last meeting of the Assembly of the Commune was on May 22. It was always a question whether the Commune, which depended on the National Guard, or the Central Committee of the Guard itself, really held the power. Now, however, power devolved upon the armed units, the barricade fighters' control of each street and quarter, the bloody-minded Committee of Public Safety, and random mobs. There had always been a minority in the Commune who were more anticlerical than anti anything else. On the evening of the twenty-fourth, the Archbishop of Paris, the Curé of la Madelaine, the former President of the Senate, and three priests were executed. Next day twelve Dominican monks were killed. On the twenty-sixth, 52 remaining hostages were killed despite the plea to

[12] E. L. Woodward, *French Revolutions,* Oxford, 1939, p. 228.
[13] Mason, *op. cit.*

the mob by the old Blanquist Communard Varlin. All told 70 innocent hostages were thus killed in the last days by the now ungovernable revolutionary mob. But this paled into insignificance before the vengeance taken by more elegant mobs in Paris, supported by the soldiery of Versailles. On both sides, it must be added, the mobs were more bloodthirsty than the organized troops.

Many leaders of the Commune escaped through the advancing armies, and the German lines surrounding the city, with the Germans pretending not to notice the fugitives. These turned up in Switzerland, Belgium, and England, where, despite Marx's contention that the whole bourgeois world was united against the Commune, the "bourgeois" governments gave the refugees asylum, rejecting French demands for their extradition. Marx and Engels spent the next year raising funds for the refugees of the Commune in England, including those who had never formed part of the International. And the year following, the two friends spent in fighting against most of the French leaders of the International.

It is the bloodshed, and the heroism of the last barricade battles that gives the Commune its revolutionary aura. But they do not determine to what extent the Commune was Socialist, or whether it aimed primarily at a radical republican and democratic, a patriotic-defensist, or a social revolution. Only by examining this question can we determine whether the uprising of March 18 was a last, forlorn rearguard action of Paris to express its resentment and humiliation at the defeat of France in the Franco-Prussian War, or a first vanguard action in the scientifically preordained war between the proletariat and the bourgeoisie which was to culminate in the victory of socialism—whether it was a relatively simple if bloody episode in the history of France, or an all-important and programmatically complex event in the history of socialism.

If we turn to *The Civil War in France*, we find the Commune pictured as a conscious creation of the Paris proletariat on March 18. "On the dawn of the 18th of March," Marx writes, "Paris arose to the thunder burst of *Vive la Commune!*" Rhetorically this is splendid, but it is hard to recognize in it the frustrated delay of the soldiers from three A.M. to eight, as they waited for horses to be brought up to drag the cannon down the Butte of Montmartre, hard to catch the visages and picturesque language of the women of the Fauborg of

Montmartre, surrounding and infiltrating the lines, cajoling and confusing the soldiers, and cutting the traces of the horses halfway down the hill. It is hard, too, to find the bewildered Central Committee of the National Guard, looking askance that same evening at the power that had been thrust into their hands, seeking to push it off from themselves into the hands of an Assembly that it hoped to have legally elected within three days.

In place of these vivid scenes, what we have is a preconceived three-stage abstract schema of Marx concerning "the Revolution" in France:

The first stage, in 1789, "the bourgeois republic," followed by the thrusting of power "by the bourgeoisie" into the hands of the Emperor Napoleon;

The second stage, in February 1848, "the social republic," first proclaimed, then short-circuited in June 1848 by the suppression of the proletariat of Paris, and replaced once more by "Imperialism," i.e. the Empire of Napoleon III. ("Imperialism" is defined by Marx as "the most prostitute and the ultimate form of the State power which nascent middle class society commenced to elaborate as a means of its own emancipation from feudalism, and which fullgrown bourgeois society finally transformed into a means for the enslavement of labor");

The third stage is the realization of "the social republic" on March 18, 1871 in the form of the Commune.

The direct antithesis to the Empire [Marx sums up] was the Commune. The cry of "social republic" with which the revolution of February [1848] was ushered in by the Paris proletariat did but express a vague aspiration after a Republic that was not only to supersede the monarchical form of class rule but class rule itself. The Commune was the positive form of that Republic. . . .

Paris could resist [the National Assembly at Versailles]only because, in consequence of the siege, it had got rid of the army, and replaced it by a National Guard, the bulk of which consisted of workingmen. This fact was now to be transformed into an institution. The first decree of the Commune, therefore, was the suppression of the standing army, and the substitution for it of the armed people.

The Commune was formed of the municipal councilors, chosen by universal suffrage in the various wards of the town, responsible and revocable at short terms. The majority of its members were naturally workingmen, or acknowledged representatives of the working class.

The Commune was to be a working, not a parliamentary body, executive and legislative at the same time.[14]

For several pages Marx paints in glowing colors the thoroughgoing democratic character of the Commune: election of all councilors and officials by universal suffrage; all officials responsible, subject to instructions or imperative mandate by their electors, subject to recall; judges to be "elective, responsible and revocable . . . divested of their sham independence"; the breaking of "the parson-power" by separation of church and state and secular education; all functionaries to do their jobs at workingmen's wages,[15] making the "catchword of bourgeois revolutions, cheap government, a reality"; depoliticalizing and communal control of the police [actually a constant complaint in the Communal Assembly was that the police under the bloody terrorist Rigault was a law unto itself in defiance of the Commune]; abolition of the standing army in favor of an armed citizenry which would automatically be in its majority workingmen, etc. All this Marx summed up by paraphrasing Lincoln's famous definition of democracy: the Commune "supplied the Republic with the basis of really democratic institutions . . . Its special measures could but betoken a government of the people by the people [in the first draft: "it is the people acting for itself and by itself."].

---

[14] No page and edition is given for these and the following quotations from *The Civil War in France* because of the many editions in current use. I have used throughout the text as given in the Moscow English-language edition of the Marx-Engels *Selected Works*, Vol. I, which bears the notation: "Printed according to the text of the English pamphlet of 1871." For quotations from the First and Second Drafts I have used the German-language *Werke*, Vol. XVII. There is no real evidence extant that the majority of the National Guard consisted of workingmen, although this is not unlikely, given the nature of the Paris population, the large numbers of unemployed, and the guaranteed pay. The majority of the elected officers consisted not of workingmen but of journalists, club orators, and what Marx himself called "shouters." The same is true of the majority of the delegates to the municipal assembly or Commune. As the Commune lost ground, moderate and "respectable" elements withdrew and the specific gravity of the revolutionaries grew steadily greater, but the majority of these and above all their spokesmen were Jacobins rather than socialists, who had learned their arts of speaking and writing as journalists and club orators. The evidence of this is scattered throughout Mason's *The Paris Commune*, and the Inquiries conducted by the victorious Versailles Government, which was inclined, like Marx, but for its own reasons, to exaggerate the socialism of the Commune.

[15] Actually the 6000-franc annual wage the Commune deputies voted themselves and set as a maximum for state officials was nearly twelve times the amount being paid to members of the National Guard who were defending Paris.

All of these are no more than democratic reforms, most of them part of the "democratic litany" of French radicalism. They might make the institution of social and economic transformations easier, but only provided the majority did indeed, by the laws of history, inevitably tend toward socialism, as Marx assumes, rather than demonstrates. The Commune, he sums up, is "the political form under which to work out the economic emancipation of labor." This last Marx proves by citing the angry charges against the Commune coming from Versailles, and by a piece of "logical" deduction: "Except on this last condition, the Communal Constitution would have been . . . a delusion . . . The Commune was therefore to serve as a lever for uprooting the economical foundations upon which rest the existence of classes. . . ."

Unfortunately for Marx's logic, the Commune itself, as he elsewhere admits, had not begun to take any socialist measures. In the First Draft he declared that "the actual 'social' character of the Commune consists only in this, that workmen govern the Paris Commune." And in the final draft: "The great social measure of the Commune was its own working existence."

In any case, Marx consoles his socialist readers:

The working class did not expect miracles from the Commune. They have no ready-made utopias to introduce *par decret du peuple.* They know that in order to work out their own emancipation, and along with it that higher form to which present society is irresistibly tending . . . they will have to pass through long struggles, through a series of historic processes, transforming circumstances and men. They have no ideals to realize, but to free the elements of the new society with which the old collapsing society itself is pregnant.

These are familiar Marxist formulas that do not carry us one whit further in our examination of the actual social and economic measures of the Commune. When Marx gets to these measures, they turn out to be the following:

The Commune saved the great bulk of the middle class—shopkeepers, tradesmen, merchants . . . by a sagacious settlement of . . . the debtor and creditor accounts . . .

Its special measures could but betoken the tendency of a government of the people by the people. Such were the abolition of the nightwork of journeymen bakers; the prohibition . . . of fines; the surrender, to associations of workmen, under reserve of compensation [to the owners], of all closed workshops and factories. . . .[16]

To this can be added the law holding up the payment of rents and evictions, and the law forbidding pawnshops to sell their forfeited pledge objects. And that is all! But not one of these measures is incompatible with the continuance of a "bourgeois order." The modern welfare state has many more and far more sweeping laws regulating working conditions, setting minimum wages, maximum rent ceilings, giving tax exemption to cooperatives, and a host of other measures which, strange indeed to nineteenth-century France, today are commonplace. Even the taking over of abandoned workshops and factories is rather a wartime measure of a beleaguered city than an attack upon the system of ownership, as is proved by the phrase of Marx, "under reserve of compensation."

All European socialists and anarchists, each in his own way, took the side of the Paris Commune, the first rousing example of barricades and street fighting since 1848. Socialism in Europe was inclined to favor such thoroughgoing democratic measures as universal suffrage, still unknown on the Continent, imperative mandate, right of recall, substitution of the armed people for the standing armies. The heroic fight of the last-ditch Communards provided a "glorious tradition," as did the sufferings and martyrdom of the captives. Following Marx's example, the First International everywhere gave welcome and financial support to the escaped Communards, and claimed their exploits as those of "our party."

Marx had been preparing in 1870 to do battle with Bakunin and the anarchist forces in the International. He had gone so far as to set the Congress of 1870 to meet in Mainz, where Bakunin was an outlaw and where German delegates could pack the Congress, when suddenly the Franco-Prussian War intervened to stop these preparations.[17]

After the fall of the Commune, Marx resumed his plans to oust the anarchists from the International. Now the Communards, who had settled in England, Belgium, and Switzerland, threw themselves energetically into this struggle, bringing to it the prestige they bore

---

[16] Both the prohibition of night work for bakers, and the attempt to turn the abandoned workshops into cooperatives (with some "Proudhonist" credit advances from the Bank of France) were proposals of the lone Hungarian refugee and solitary "Marxist," Leo Frankel, who was in charge of Labor and Industry.
[17] Marx to Engels in *MEGA*, III/4, p. 330.

as "heroes of the Commune." They served only to add to the rancor and disorder, for the Communards differed as much among themselves in exile as they had in Paris, and differed no less with Marx. The Blanquists having settled in London, Marx spent much time with them trying to remake them into Marxists and win their support against Bakunin. In this he was reasonably successful. But they were to turn on him as soon as they found out about his plan to move the General Council of the International to America.

With other factions among the Communards Marx had less luck. On November 9, 1871, he wrote a bitter and unpleasant account of this to Sorge in America:

> Among the refugees has been built here a *French refugee* Section of the International, *Section Française de 1871* (about 24 persons), which at once got into a squabble with the General Council, because we requested some changes in their statutes. It will probably come to a *split*. These fellows work together with part of the French refugees in Switzerland, who in turn intrigue with the members of the *Alliance de la Democratie*, which we have dissolved. The targets of their attacks are not the governments and ruling classes of Europe which are allied against us, but the General Council of London, and especially my humble person. This is my recompense for having lost nearly five months in working on behalf of the refugees, and for having saved their honor through the *Address on the Civil War!*[18]

Bakunin, too, to employ Marx's language, did what he could to "save the honor" of the Commune, for he interpreted it as the noblest and most heroic effort of Anarchist Socialism. He accused Marx of having "annexed" the Proudhonist (and Bakuninist) plan for a federation of Communes, as a means of using the prestige of the "glorious" Commune of Paris to strengthen his own centralist

---

[18] The italicized words are in French and English respectively in the original. The letter is in *Briefe und Auszuege aus Briefen von Joh. Phil. Becker, Josef Dietzgen, Friedrich Engels, Karl Marx u. A. an F. A. Sorge u. Andere,* Stuttgart, 1906, p. 33. The Alliance de la Democratie Socialiste was an organization led by Bakunin which favored atheism, equalitarian democracy, and related measures and rejected all forms of political activity that did not aim directly at securing the victory of labor over capital. It applied as a body to join the International, its application being forwarded and supported by Marx's follower, Johann Philip Becker, who aroused Marx's instant wrath by saying in his accompanying letter that the Alliance was anxious to make good the lack of "idealism" in the International. The Council not only rejected the application but stipulated that Bakunin and other members would have to dissolve it in order to be admitted to the International. A fair account of the Alliance can be found in Mehring's *Life of Marx* (New York, 1935), pp. 434–40.

and statist brand of socialism. His interpretation did for socialist opinion of the revolution in the Latin countries what Marx's *Civil War in France* did for socialist opinion in Germany, England, and the United States. Bakunin saw in the Commune a movement for anarchist federalism; "an audacious negation . . . of the State"; a step toward "the future social order [which] must, from top to bottom, be made only by free association first, then in communes, in districts, in nations, and, finally, in a great international and universal federation." These were the ideas of Proudhon, but of a Proudhon to whom Bakunin had added his own revolutionary fire. They had never been the ideas of Marx, and within a few years, he and Engels were expressly repudiating them once more.

Bakunin, like Marx, found a way to attribute socialism to the Commune. He recognized that the socialists, led by the Blanquist Varlin, were opposed by an overwhelming Jacobin majority. But the Jacobins, controlled by "the logic of events," could not escape becoming socialists. Here his "logic" is as deductive as that of Marx:

> These generous Jacobins, at whose head was placed naturally Delescluze, a great soul and a great character, desired before everything else the triumph of the revolution; and as there is no revolution without the masses, and as the masses today are filled with the socialist instinct and can make no revolution other than an economic and social revolution, the Jacobins, permitting themselves in good faith to be carried along by the logic of the revolutionary movement, ended by becoming socialists in spite of themselves.[19]

Thus in Bakunin as in Marx, the final episode in the humiliating defeat of Imperial France by Prussia, the post-bellum insurrection of exacerbated patriots in Paris against a government believed to have betrayed them and suspected of wishing to restore the discredited imperial régime—a minor if bloody episode in the history of France —was immediately overlaid by a legend which made of it the beginning of the so long awaited war of the world proletariat against the world bourgeoisie.

> Paris [wrote Bakunin] inaugurated a new era, that of the emancipation, definitive and complete, of the masses and their solidarity henceforth really established across and in spite of the frontiers of states. Paris killed patriotism and established on its ruins the religion of humanity; Paris proclaimed itself humanitarian and atheist, replacing

---

[19] Mason, *op. cit.*, pp. 301–03. Bakunin's disciples, Élisée Reclus, himself a Communard, Guillaume, and Kropotkin, all repeated the same formula.

divine fictions by the realities of social life, and faith in science.
And his disciple Kropotkin wrote:

The Commune's moving spirit was the idea of a social revolution; vague certainly, perhaps unconscious, but still the effort to obtain at last, after the struggle of many centuries, true freedom, true equality for all men. . . . Communal independence was but the means for the people of Paris; the social revolution was their end.[20]

Marx for his part said:

Workingmen's Paris, with its Commune, will be forever celebrated as the harbinger of a new society.

As an episode in the history of France, the Paris Commune left little trace on France's future, except perhaps, as I have suggested, to deepen the gulf between the well-to-do and the Paris poor, and to write finis to an age of Paris insurrections that ran from 1789 through 1830, 1848, and 1871.

But as a legendary event in anarchist, socialist, and communist history, the Commune left an imprint the importance of which is hard to exaggerate. The Commune was accepted by Lenin's opponents with as much ardor as it was by Lenin himself, although the contradictory uses they made of Marx's famous pamphlet, and Engels's introduction to the edition the latter issued twenty years later, testify once more to the ambiguity of the Marxist heritage. Indeed, in this case, both Engels and Marx have testified to that ambiguity themselves!

Writes Gustav Mayer, Engels's biographer:

When Engels republished the Address twenty years after its first publication, the historical Commune had already been transformed into a myth for the class-struggling proletariat under [the Address's] influence, a myth which led its own historical life, and which did not completely correspond with the events as they actually occurred. Engels knew of the origin and the existence of this myth. On New Year's Day, 1884, he confessed to Bernstein that in Marx's work "the unconscious tendencies of the Commune were credited to it as more or less conscious plans," and then he added that this "under the circumstances was justified, even necessary."[21]

Marx himself went much further than Engels in his reappraisal of the Commune. On February 22, 1881, he wrote to Domela Nieuwenhuis:

---

[20] Mason, *op. cit.*, pp. 303–04.
[21] Gustav Mayer, *Friedrich Engels,* The Hague, 1934, Vol. II, p. 228.

The embarrassments of a government which has suddenly come into being through a people's victory have nothing specifically "socialist" about them. . . . One thing you can at any rate be sure of: a socialist government does not come into power in a country unless conditions are so developed that it can above all take the necessary measures for intimidating the mass of the bourgeoisie sufficiently to gain time—the first desideratum for lasting action.

Perhaps you will point to the Paris Commune; but apart from the fact that this was merely the rising of a town under exceptional conditions, the majority of the Commune was in no sense socialist, nor could it be. With a small amount of common sense, they could have reached a compromise with Versailles useful to the whole mass of the people . . .[22]

Here we are back to the opinion Marx and Engels had been expressing to each other in 1870 and 1871, part of which Marx had included in his public warning against a Commune in the *Second Address of the International*. But this verdict contradicts both the express statements and the entire spirit of Marx's *Civil War in France*. It reduces the Paris Commune to

. . . the rising of a town under exceptional conditions . . . a majority in no sense socialist . . . [and lacking in that] small amount of common sense that could have reached a compromise with Versailles, [a special case of] the embarrassments of a government which has suddenly come into being through a people's victory, [embarrassments which] have nothing specifically socialist about them.

This was Marx's last recorded word on the Commune.

----

[22] Marx-Engels, *Selected Correspondence,* New York and London, 1935, pp. 386–87.

PART IV

Democracy
or Dictatorship?

Both Marx and Engels came to socialism from *democracy,* and the democratic feeling of *hate* for political arbitrariness was extraordinarily strong in them.
　　　—Lenin in 1895 writing on the death of Engels.

Chapter 9

THE REVOLUTIONARY WILL OR

THE OBJECTIVE FACTS?

(MARX AND BLANQUI)

It has been possible for Social Democrats and Communists
alike to appeal to Marx's authority; and for good reason.
The contradictions latent in his outlook were fused into a
doctrine which Janus-like confronted the beholder whatever
his angle of vision.

—George Lichtheim

THE PERIOD that opens with the *Communist Manifesto* and ends
with the *Address of the Central Committee to the League of Communists* in March 1850 is the period in which Marx expected a social
revolution to take over Europe by direct storm attack. It is the
Sturm und Drang Periode of Marxism. Marx was completely under
the spell of the barricade and conspiracy traditions of Paris, the
Paris which had stormed the Tuileries and the Hôtel de Ville, taken
the Bastille, set up the guillotine to decapitate the counterrevolution
(and, in the end, the revolution too), the Paris which had driven out
the Bourbons from one day to the next in 1830, and done the same
to the "Citizen King," Louis Philippe in February, 1848, the Paris of
the workingmen's uprising of June 1848. Marx's socialism during this
period was the romantic, equalitarian, street-fighting, barricade, and
seizure of public-buildings brand of socialism of the Paris conspirators, Babeuf, Buonarrotti, and Blanqui. It was a socialism that
looked forward to an insurrection which would take the world by
storm, keep the revolution going in permanence, abolish private

property, set up a revolutionary dictatorship, remake society into a realm without private property, without classes, without exploitation or oppression or antagonisms, and without frontiers. It would win the battle for democracy, then make democracy itself superfluous, since with the disappearance of classes the state itself, even the democratic political state, would become superfluous, yielding to the "administration of things." It was to be the same romantic storm attack as earlier Paris revolutions, but armed with "scientific" knowledge of what it must do. And led by a new class, more consistently revolutionary than the bourgeoisie because there was no class below it to inspire fear and compromise. This class hitherto had always fought for others, brought others to power, and been cheated by them. This time it would take power for itself.

As the revolution lost in Paris, in Frankfurt and Berlin, in Vienna and Budapest, Marx's mood became black and he "unpacked his heart with curses" and consoled himself with threats of terror and revenge. He persisted in believing that the revolution was not over. At any moment it would flare up anew. "There is only one way to *shorten* the murderous death agonies of the old society, only one way to shorten the bloody birth pangs of the new society," Marx wrote on November 5, 1848, ". . . only *one means*—revolutionary terrorism." And as his new year's greeting in the NRZ for January 1, 1849, he predicted with the same grim hope: "*Revolutionary upheaval of the French working class, World War*—that is the table of contents of the year 1849."

All through 1849, Marx broke into occasional hymns to "the fist" and "the terror" and threats of ruthless vengeance on those who had suppressed the revolution. Even in March 1850, in exile in London and with the Continent manifestly quiet once more, Marx did not abandon hope: an imminent economic crisis in London (overdue by his time-table) would call forth a new earthquake in France. It was then that he made a united front with the Blanquists and wrote the most extreme of all the documents to come from his hand, as if conspiracy and extremism would revive the struggles of a society that had grown weary and passive once more.

This *Circular*, the spirit of which was to be repudiated by Marx only six months later, and never returned to for the rest of his life, would nevertheless lie like an undetonated time bomb on the Marxian road, to be joyously dug up by Lenin in the next century, and used with explosive force as a Marxian manual of Leninist strategy and tactics.

The *Circular* of March 1850, bears upon it the stamp of the conspirative tradition of Blanqui. Marx was sending conspirative emissaries to the various capitals to revive the branches of the Communist League. He was using some of Blanqui's followers as his agents in these missions. The new uprising would come as a result either of a new insurrection of the Paris workingmen, or through "an attack of the Holy Alliance."

In Germany the Liberals had disgraced themselves. Their role was played out, hence, according to the *Circular*, the leading role would now be taken over by the democratic petty bourgeoisie, who call themselves "the Red Party"—"Democrats" in Germany, and "Socialists" in France. The workingmen must assist them to take power, which Marx seemed to think would be a swift and easy task, but "must oppose them in everything by means of which they seek to consolidate their power."[1]

We have already considered some of the instructions in this March *Circular* in Chapter One.[2] Here our interest is primarily in the "Blanquist" strain in early Marxism which the *Circular* reveals and which we must consider now in connection with the well-known pronouncement of Marx on Blanqui, published in the very same month of March 1850. The connection between the pronouncement and the *Circular* seems more than accidental.

The *Circular* urges that the workers arm themselves (with the help of the Democrats who will need their backing), and then keep their arms when the Democrats come to power. Alongside the new democratic government, they must set up "their own revolutionary workers' governments in the form of workers' clubs and workers' committees" or, where they control an industrial center, "municipal councils or municipal committees." (Here one is reminded of the many clubs Blanqui formed, of the Jacobin clubs of the 1790s which were his model—and no less of his Jacobin centralism and his conviction that Paris should control and decide for all France.)

The Democrats, the *Circular* continues, should be out-trumped

---

[1] The *Circular* or *Address* as it has been variously translated (actually it was a circular letter of instructions, not a public document) is in *Werke*, Vol. VII, pp. 244–54. Suggestions that conspirative agents of Blanqui were being used as bearers of the commissions of the Central Committee to the various local branches are to be found in a second *Circular* dated June 1850, in *Werke*, Vol. VII, pp. 305–12. See also the comment of Boris Nikolaevsky in Nikolaevsky and Maenchen-Helfen, *op. cit.*, pp. 208 ff.

[2] See above, p. 18 ff.

in every demand for social reform by the Communists' pushing for a more extreme demand, incompatible with their continued rule. And, as they would sit in their official new governmental institutions they must be made to feel over their shoulders, overseers who would "supervise" and "threaten," "authorities backed by the whole mass of the workingmen."[3]

In this *Circular,* too, comes the climax of Marx's centralism, his statism, and above all, the streak of terrorism that then possessed him:

> The workers must above all things during the conflict and immediately after the struggles, just as much as they possibly can, work against the civil [or *bourgeois*—the word *buergerlich* has both meanings in German] pacification and force the Democrats to carry out their present terrorist phrases. Far from opposing the so-called popular excesses, the examples of the peoples' revenge against hated individuals or public buildings which have only hateful memories connected with them, the Communists must themselves take the leadership of these actions into their own hands.

In these words echo the storming of the Bastille, the clubbings to death with rifle butts, the heads raised on pikes, and rise and fall of the sharp blade of the guillotine. Here the line from Babeuf, through Buonarrott to Blanqui leads to the Marx who has been brooding on and studying the Great French Revolution and all the lesser revolutions and conspiracies of Paris that sought to fulfill the most sweeping of its promises. At the very moment Marx was writing it, he was writing the much quoted and much disputed praise of Blanqui in his *Class Struggles in France 1848 to 1850:*

> . . . the proletariat groups itself more and more around *revolutionary socialism,* around *communism,* for which the bourgeoisie itself has invented the name *Blanqui.* This socialism is the *declaration of the revolution in permanence,* the *class dictatorship* of the proletariat as a necessary transition point to the *abolition of class differences altogether,* to the abolition of all the relations of production on which they rest, the abolition of all social relationships which correspond to

---

[3] Lenin was to see in them, as in the Paris Commune, prototypes of the Russian workingmen's councils (Soviets) of 1905, and of the Councils of Workers' and Soldiers' Deputies of 1917. In the overseers breathing down the necks of the new democratic officials, supervising and threatening them and acting as "authorities backed by the whole mass of the workingmen," Lenin saw the image of his own commissars and vanguard élite.

these production relationships, the transformation of all ideas which arise from these social relationships.[4]

While the democratic petty bourgeoisie will be inclined to bring the revolution to as speedy a conclusion as possible[the *Circular* continued]. It is our interest and duty to make the revolution permanent until all the more or less propertied classes are forced from power, the state power is seized by the proletariat, and the partnership of the proletarians of the world has advanced to such an extent that competition between the proletarians has ceased, not just in one country but in all the principal countries of the world, and at least the vital forces of production are concentrated in the hands of the proletariat.

No longer able to get at the ruling powers in their native land, the refugees fell to tearing at each other. Marx was seduced by a plausible agent-provocateur, the Prussian-Austrian spy, Colonel Bangya, into writing a series of mordant and scandalous profiles of the democrats and moderate socialists of the Central Committee of European Democracy, particularly its German members who called themselves by the resounding title, the Central Buro of the Entire German Emigration. It took Marx three months of research and gossip-gathering, and the help of his wife, of Engels, and of a number of disciples, to produce a lengthy and tedious manuscript entitled *Die grossen Maenner des Exiles* (The Great Men of the Exile). From the police agent, Marx received an honorarium of twenty-five pounds and an assurance of early publication in Berlin. It took him almost a year to realize that Colonel Bangya had no publisher and no intention of publishing, but had merely turned in this detailed report on the German exiles to the Prussian police. At that Marx must be accounted fortunate, for had it been published it would not have brought its author any credit or honor. Out of piety, first Engels, and then his literary executor, Eduard Bernstein, decided against its publication, the latter even going so far as to remove all references to it from the *Marx-Engels Correspondence* when he published their letters. But it finally fell into the hands of the Marx-Engels Institute in Moscow and now appears in slightly over one hundred unreadable (except in the line of duty) and inglorious pages of Volume VIII of the *Werke,* where it testifies

---

[4] What was later to be published by Engels under the title *Class Struggles in France* was originally published by Marx in two numbers of the *Neue Rheinische Zeitung. Politisch-oekonomische Revue,* Hamburg, and in one number of a later *Revue* published abroad. The part quoted was published in March 1850.

to the bitterness and blackness of the night of exile and the depths
to which the greatest of the exiles could descend in the course of
their feuds.[5]

The bitter atmosphere of the "sleepless night of exile" was made
more bitter because yesterday's captains were reluctant to see that
the battlefields were indeed deserted and the armies dispersed and
returning to the pursuits of every day. They quarreled over programs and tactics, and responsibilities for the defeats that all their
movements had sustained. Since they awoke at different moments to
the darkness of the empty theater, great was the tumult as they
shouted at each other their predictions of fresh upheavals, their
charges of error and desertion, their attempts to make up for the
disappearance of the masses by combining their respective groups
into new "universal organizations." For a few months at least this
activity brought together two main groupings of yesterday's leaders,
the Central Committee of European Democracy and the coalesced
Marxist and Blanquist Communists. Resounding titles and federations of fragmentary remnants took the place of the revolutionary
actions of 1848 and '49.

The Central Committee of European Democracy published a
monthly with the characteristic name, Le Proscript, Journal de la
République Universelle. (Among its leaders were Mazzini, Ledru-
Rollin, Kossuth, Delescluze, Ruge, and other less well-known figures
of 1848.) Blanqui was as usual in prison, but the Blanquists and
Marxists in London closed their ranks in April (the month after
Marx's "Blanquist" Circular) to form the Société Universelle des
Communistes Révolutionaires. It was a super-conspirative "universal" organization, for even the rank and file of the federating
secret organizations did not become members of this new universal
secret society. Thus it was a secret society to the second power, the
officer staff, for which the federating societies should serve as armies,
a "universal" Communist Federation and conspiracy to offset the no
less rootless conspiracy of the "Universal Republic."

The statutes of the Universal Society of the Revolutionary Communists was signed by six men, Vidil and Adam, representing the

---

[5] The best short account of the Colonel Bangya affair is in that remarkable little
work of condensation of Marx's life by Werner Blumenberg, Karl Marx: In
Selbstzeugnissen und Bilddokumenten, Hamburg, 1962, p. 102. A somewhat
apologetic account is in Mehring, op. cit., p. 246; a more detailed one in Mayer,
op. cit., Vol. II, pp. 19–24. The text itself is in Werke, Vol. VIII, pp. 232–335,
and an explanatory account in a note (n. 143) on p. 627.

London Blanquist organization in exile, Marx, Engels, and Willich, representing the German Communist League, and Julian Harney, representing what was left of the British Chartists. These six men constituted the Central Committee and the "General Staff." They could adopt no measure except by a two-thirds vote. If they met and adopted any decisions, which is doutbful, these were kept secret in this conspiracy to the second degree.

The Blanquists, true to form, were engaged in secret preparations for an armed uprising in 1850 and '51 just as they had been all through the thirties and forties, and would continue to be in the sixties and seventies. Always they hoped to gain power by a surprise attack, then set up a revolutionary dictatorship to win over the whole people and transform society. Such was Marx's mood at this moment that for several months he accepted this concept of revolution.

He still protected the autonomy of his group by the two-thirds veto rule since he had three members out of six on the new Central Committee. But his March *Circular,* his June conspirative emissaries, his climactic praise of Blanqui in the *NRZ Revue* in March, and the aims to which he subscribed in the Statutes of the Universal Society, all point in the same direction. Defeat of the democratic revolution in Germany and of the proletarian revolution in France had for the moment made Marx into a Blanquist and Blanqui in Marx's eyes into the living incarnation of the movement of "revolutionary socialism or communism."

> The aim of the association [read the Statutes to which Marx subscribed and which judging from the language, he must have taken a leading part in drafting] is to make an end to all the privileged classes, to subject these classes to the dictatorship of the proletariat by maintaining the revolution in permanence until the complete realization of communism, which ought be the last form of the constitution of the human family.

And the immediate goal of this super-secret confederation was to establish

> . . . bonds of solidarity among all the fractions of the revolutionary communist party by causing to disappear the divisions of nationality according to the principle of republican fraternity.[6]

---

[6] The best account of this society is in Nikolaevsky and Maenchen-Helfen, *op. cit.,* pp. 208–11. This account is the more remarkable in its testimony and documentation in that this whole period in Marx's development is profoundly distasteful to the authors of the biography, inclined as they are to see Marx as a

Setting on one side the attitude toward democracy implied in the directives of the March *Circular*—something we may properly do since in 1850 democracy was more a theoretical than a practical matter, there are two things wrong with the *Circular*.

First, there was no revolution to keep going in permanence, stillness having settled over storm-tossed Europe.

And second, though Marx found the whole outlook incongruous a few months later, he never acknowledged that his own estimate had been mistaken, but merely condemned the same estimate and some of the same deductions in his followers in September, after he had changed his mind. In his change of front, he could not carry the Communist League with him. He and Engels did have a narrow margin in the Central Committee. His last act in the Communist League was to use his control to transfer the League headquarters to Germany, where the triumph of reaction meant its certain death.

At the moment of the break with the Communist League, the second stage of Marxian thought began. It has been customary for Social Democrats and democratic socialists to divide Marxian thought into two distinct and separate periods: that of the young, romantic, Paris-barricade, revolutionary Marx, and that of the "mature Marx." Most nonsocialist commentators on Marxism make the same division. Insofar as the division is justified, the dividing line is quite clear. It is the moment when Marx and Engels withdrew from the Communist League in September, 1850, at which moment Marx pronounced the programmatic words which distinguished him and Engels from Willich and Schapper, and indeed from almost all his comrades of the past three years. With these words, he laid down

---

democratic and scientific socialist and a natural opponent of Blanquism. The authors write:

> The fact that Marx accepted this kind of revolutionism, which he condemned so violently both before and afterwards, and was so utterly foreign in every way to the essential nature of the proletarian revolution, the fact that he formed an alliance with the Blanquists, proves better than anything else the extent to which his judgment had been affected by the breakdown of his immeasurable hopes (*Ibid.*, p. 210).

To which we can only add: Were not those "immeasurable hopes" of 1848–50 themselves an evidence of the romantic revolutionary "Blanquist" streak in the character of the Marx who first proclaimed the *Communist Manifesto* as a supposedly realistic program for '48 and then wrote the *Circular* of March, 1850, as the last echo of those immeasurable hopes, before he submerged them into the underground of his subconscious where they persisted as the nourishing soil from which would spring up the luxuriant growth of his "scientific" endeavors to prove that the revolution was all the same "inevitable"?

the approach which was to serve him for the rest of his life. Just six months earlier he had been prophesying a new uprising, praising the name of Blanqui, and proclaiming *the revolution in permanence.* Now he grandly told the "Minority" (the minority in the Central Committee, that is, which possessed the support of almost the entire membership of the Communist League):

> The minority replaces critical observation with dogmatism, a materialist attitude with an idealist one. It regards its own naked will as the driving force of the revolution instead of the real facts of the situation. While we say to the workers, "You must go through fifteen, twenty, fifty years of war and civil war, not only to alter existing conditions but to alter yourselves and make yourselves fit to take over political power," you on the contrary tell them, "You must seize political power immediately, or go to sleep!" While we especially call the attention of the German workingmen to the undeveloped character of the German proletariat, you crudely flatter their national feelings and caste prejudices, and that is naturally more popular. Just as the Democrats made of the word *people* a holy being, so you do with the word *proletariat.*[7]

Here was the beginning of a new Marx. Though he spoke of "fifty years of war and civil war," he knew that the age of revolutions, with its dream of revolutionary wars and its reality of counter-revolutionary interventions, had come to an end. For a moment, in 1871 while the Paris Communards were fighting on 500 barricades, perhaps he half persuaded himself that it had come again. But if so, he soon discounted that mirage, his letter to Domela Nieuwenhuis making it clear that the picture he had painted in his *Civil War in France* was a myth.

It is intriguing to note, however, that immediately after he published his *Address* on the Paris Commune, he entered into a second brief period of united front with the Blanquists.

In September 1850 he had written off "naked will" as the demiurge of revolution, and for it had substituted "the real facts of the situation." Thus the Marx of revolutionary voluntarism yielded to the Marx of scientific inevitability or fatalism. But in 1871, when the old war horse smelled gunpowder, he pawed the ground, impatient for battle. For the rest of his life, the battle never came. Nor in Engels's lifetime either. Marx's letters to Engels show how he detested his "scientific studies," but what else was there to do?

---

[7] *Werke,* Vol. VII, p. 614.

He tried to break out of the loneliness of the British Museum and the torment of the forever unfinished masterpiece in 1864 when he wrote the *Statutes* and the *Inaugural Address* of the International Workingmen's Association. But this was the work not of the romantic young Marx of the barricades of Paris but of the "mature Marx" who repudiated "sects," found a real movement "worth a dozen programs," wished to base socialism on the organized labor movement and the working class as a whole, proclaimed the "emancipation of the working class" to be "the work of the working class itself." The "mature Marx" recognized the fundamental importance of organized labor, of the use of democratic institutions where they existed, both to win reforms like the ten-hours bill, and to conquer political power. He looked forward to a party of the working class which would develop its numbers, its organization, its solidarity, its class consciousness, its awareness of its "true role," and its understanding of "the law of motion of capitalist society" along with its knowledge of the "inevitability" of socialism.

But was the break between the mature Marx and the young revolutionary Marx really so complete as the Social Democratic heirs have claimed and the majority of Marx commentators have assumed? Since we cannot read a man's passions, nor his pride in his past (or conversely, his rejection of it), nor enter into the recesses of a man's spirit, nor know to what extent the youth continues in the mature man, we can only guess at the answer.

To me it seems that the subterranean stream that overflowed its banks in 1848 still supplied its dark waters to the roots of Marx's spirit all the days of his life. It is their passions and juices that water the roots of his spirit in the arid desert of the British Museum, that keep him at the disappointing and frustrating work of a lifetime, searching for the evidence that the cataclysmic moment of revolution when the expropriators are to be expropriated must one day come. He became a "Marxist" in the gathering storms of 1844–48. As the storm broke for a moment he could imagine that he and his "party" were wielding the thunder and the lightning and generating the storm. He was the first among the revolutionary exiles whose sense of realism told him that the storm had ended and that they must substitute a study of the "objective facts" for the "naked revolutionary will." But the "objective facts" concerning what, if not the manner and the moment of the coming of the next period of storm? This and this alone explains the passion with which he pursued the apparently dispassionate research in the dry and arid tomes, and the passion with which he disputed every difference of social and economic history with those who disagreed with him. This and this alone explains the startling contradiction between the rich empirical material in *Das Kapital* and the apocalyptic ending of the closing chapter on the *General Law of Capitalist Accumulation.* But that discussion must be reserved for a later chapter.

The "mature Marx" declares himself in favor of the democratic, organized labor movement which will create out of itself the party of the working class. But he quarrels angrily with the most authentic labor movement in the First International, the British, denounces its pacifism, charges all its chosen leaders with corruption, repels it by the character of his defense of the Paris Commune, then alienates those English labor leaders who did not desert him on the issue of the Commune, by reiterating his charges of corruption in an open meeting of the International.

In the same passionate way Marx rejected the authentic workingman's party of Lassalle in Germany and strove mightily to prevent the union of his own faction and the Lassalleans after the latter's death. So, too, he fought the next most important socialist movement in the International, the French (the International was founded by British and French workingmen) and continued his war on it both in polemics and in the surreptitious planting of his own program and a faction of his own among the multiple socialist factions of Paris.

Because Marx never expressly repudiated the extremist circular of March 1850, never re-evaluated publicly the more extreme and outdated parts and formulations of the *Communist Manifesto,* and because he imposed by the vividness of his picture of the Paris Commune a revolutionary legend on the growing Social Democratic movement that was incompatible with its practical program and day-to-day activities, he developed in the new movement that posthumously revered him and continually invoked his name, a schizoid personality—revolutionary extremism and voluntarism in the "Marxist classics" and the holiday commemorations, and practical reformism, and respect for democratic process in its daily work.

Over Marx's grave, as the reader will remember, Engels pronounced him the Darwin of social science, and in the next breath declared that all his life, "above all Marx remained a revolutionist." In his last years, with Marx's darker and more passionate temperament removed from the scene, Engels developed the "scientific" and "inevitabilist" side of the schizoid doctrine further in the direction of "scientific socialism." But he somehow kept the other side alive in the glowing shadows of memory. In his last writings he remembered Marx's and his early battles, told their story afresh, with some "corrections" that time had made, but remembered other things with pride, "explained" and justified them. One by one, he republished or published for the first time "the classics of Marxism," each introduced with a bit of history that was never the whole story.

Most interesting of Engels's reminiscences are those in his introduction to a new edition of Marx's *Enthuellungen ueber den Kommunistenprozess zu Koeln* (Revelations on the Trial of the Communists in Cologne) which Engels brought out in 1885, two years after Marx's death, for in these reminiscences we once more stumble over the traces of the imprint of Blanqui and Blanquism on the early Marx.[8]

The *League of the Communists (Kommunistenbund)* Engels explains, was an outgrowth of the *League of the Just,* which in turn grew out of the *League of the Proscribed (Bund der Geaechteten).* This earliest of the successive organizations was founded by a group of German refugees in Paris in 1834, under the direct influence of Blanqui. Thus the real family tree of the Communist League for which Marx and Engels wrote the *Communist Manifesto* runs from Babeuf and his Conspiracy of the Equals through Babeuf's disciple and chronicler, the Italian refugee Buonarrotti, to Blanqui.

In 1836, the more extreme and more proletarian elements of the romantically entitled League of the Proscribed seceded to form the League of the Just. The latter, Engels continues, was "half propaganda league, half conspiracy," and, though it held its sessions in German, in revolutionary matters it learned "to speak French" and was little more than a "German offshoot of the French working-class communism which derives from Babeuf." Its members formed part of Blanqui's conspirative groups. At the same time, influenced by Paris utopian socialism, it strove to enter directly into the future by living according to the principles of equality, community of goods, and justice. To be sure, it hoped that some day its activities would spread to the native land of the German journeymen tailors who made up most of its membership, but in actual fact it lived and dreamed in Paris and was "not much more than the German branch of the French secret society founded by Blanqui and Barbès, the Société des Saisons."

---

[8] Engels called his introduction *A Contribution to the History of the League of Communists.* It may be found in the corresponding volume of *Werke,* or in Marx-Engels *Ausgewaehlte Schriften,* Vol. II, pp. 314–32.

It was in the League of the Just that Weitling developed his doctrines. It was in the League of the Just, rechristened the Communist League, that Marx and Engels found their first "party," to which they belonged (except when Marx arbitrarily dissolved it in the Rhineland) from 1847 until September 1850. It was in this League that Marx acquired his short-lived admiration for Weitling (at the moment in Switzerland) and his lifelong admiration for the person of that incarnation of revolutionary will, revolutionary dictatorship, and the revolution in permanence, August Blanqui. And it was for the Communist League that Marx and Engels wrote the two key documents of early romantic revolutionary Marxism, the *Communist Manifesto* and the Jacobin-Blanquist (one is tempted to say, Leninist) *Circular* of March 1850.

We are now in a better position to understand that mixed bag of incompatible doctrines, the *Communist Manifesto*. For on it are the imprint of Marx's philosophical past in Germany, the impression made upon him by Paris socialism in all its forms and particularly the socialisms of Saint-Simon and of Blanqui. And in it are the germs of Marx's future doctrine, his concern with economic evolution, his materialist conception of history.

All the heirs have gone to the *Communist Manifesto* to claim the heritage. Each has reduced it to consistency by selection of some parts and ignoring of others. Since each sonorous phrase has ringing overtones and undertones, each heir can make do with very little, enlarging the selections by repetition and exegesis. The *Communist Manifesto* can be all things to all varieties of socialists, for in it are voluntarism and fatalism, Marx's past and Marx's future, Blanquism and democratic socialism, conspiracy and propaganda slogans, the art of insurrection and the science that guarantees its victory. It is the very incarnation of the ambiguity in Marxism.

But March 1850, the moment of the eulogy of Blanqui, of the Universal Communist Association, and of the most thoroughly Blanquist document from Marx's hand, is quite another matter. Lenin pounced upon it with glee as the masterpiece of tactical directives, the prime classic of Marxism, the quintessence of the Master's revolutionary spirit. The other heirs preferred to forget this *Circular,* or to regard it as an isolated aberration. Had not Marx recovered from this momentary aberration by September of the same year? Had he not then substituted "the objective facts" and "prolonged evolution" both in society and in the working class itself for the revolutionary voluntarism of the *Circular?* Had he not gradually come to recognize the basic role of the labor movement, the usefulness of reforms like the ten-hours bill, the value of democratic institutions, the need of scientific investigation of reality, the need to win the agreement of the majority of society?

But had he repudiated his own revolutionary voluntarism, or only criticized its untimely, obstinate and wrongheaded manifestation in Willich and Schapper? Were not the stormy passions and the utopian hopes of the Paris days the dark soil which kept alive his tenacious will to prove the inevitability of the coming of the apocalypse in the fullness of time? These questions probe at the core of the ambiguity in Marxism; they are the heart of his mystery.

In any case, Lenin had his fixed points on which to chart his trajectory, and so did Kautsky. Kautsky had a far greater volume of texts by actual word count and content analysis. And he had the support and encouragement of the aging Engels. But Lenin had texts enough, each of them electrifying. The more stirring parts of the *Manifesto;* Engels's discussion (at that time attributed by his daughter to Marx) of the military tactics proper to an insurrection;[9] the eulogy of Blanqui in *Class Struggles in France;* the second sentence of Engels's two-pronged obituary of Marx; the recrudescence of the Blanquist spirit in Marx's picture of the Paris Commune; and above all, the precise directives, Marx's praise of terror and popular excesses, and the fiery and ultra-extremist Blanquist spirit of the *Circular* of March 1850.

When his opponents accused him of compounding his doctrine from the terrorism of the Narodnaya Volya, the Jacobinism of the "bourgeois" French Revolution, the centralism, revolutionary élitism, and revolutionary voluntarism of Blanqui, he accepted the accusations with pride. What is Marxism, he asked, but Jacobinism "fused with the working-class movement"? Was not Marx in love with the great days of 1789–95? Had he not sought to revive those days in 1848? Had he not praised their revival in 1871? The great years would return, sloughing off the dull detritus accumulated during the dead years of civil peace and capitalist expansion. Then the great years would be combined into one—1789–93, 1848, and 1871—all fused together. That, Lenin dreamed, was what he was doing when his own year came, the fateful year, 1917.

---

[9] See Lenin's article of 1917 on "Marxism and Insurrection," *Sochineniya,* Vol. XXVI, pp. 4–9 and 105–06.

Chapter 10

DEMOCRACY AND DICTATORSHIP

IN 1848

> To treat political ideas as the offspring of pure reason would
> be to assign to them a parentage about as mythological as
> that of Pallas Athene. What matters most is the underlying
> emotions, the music to which the ideas are the mere libretto,
> often of very inferior quality; and once the emotions have
> ebbed, the ideas established high and dry, become doctrine
> or at best innocent clichés.
>
> —Sir Lewis Namier in *Human Nature and Politics*

ALONG with Marx's taste for war as an engine of progress, his taste
for terror diminished, too. But in this field there was a peculiar
division of labor: in the stormy period of '48 and '49, it was Marx
who exalted violence and terror and thundered threats of vengeance. But in the seventies and eighties, and continuing after
Marx's death, it was Engels who did the reconsidering.

Far from thinking of war and civil war as brutalizing, Marx as
we have already noted professed to tell the workers in 1850:

> You must go through fifteen, twenty, fifty years of war and civil war
> not only to alter yourselves and make yourselves fit to take over
> political power. . . .[1]

But in 1870 with Paris besieged and the two friends worrying
lest the Paris workingmen overthrow the Provisional Government,
Engels advanced in a letter to Marx a completely new view of terror
in general, and of the Reign of Terror in Paris in 1793:

---

[1] See above, Chapter 9, page 159.

From these perpetual little *panics* of the French [he wrote] . . . one gets a much better idea of the Reign of Terror. We think of it as the reign of people who instill terror. But quite the contrary, it is the reign of people who are themselves terrified. *La Terreur* is for the most part useless cruelties perpetrated by people who are themselves frightened, for the purpose of reassuring themselves. I am convinced that the blame for the Reign of Terror, Anno 1793, falls almost entirely on the over-nervous bourgeois acting the patriot, on the little, philistine petit-bourgeois soiling his pants in fright (*kleinen hosen-scheissenden Spiesbuerger*) and on the riff-raff mob, making a business out of the terror. The present little terror comes from precisely the same classes.[2]

On the other hand, in the late seventies, when Professor Duehring told admiring audiences of Berlin socialists that force possesses an evil potential which may affect the character of the user, and therefore it should be used circumspectly by the proletariat lest it corrupt the society they hoped to build, Engels could still haughtily remind him:

That force also plays another role in history, a revolutionary role, that, in the words of Marx, it is the midwife of every old society that is pregnant with a new one, that it is the instrument with which the social movement realizes itself and shatters political forms which have grown rigid and moribund. . . . Only with sighs and groans does he [Professor Duehring] admit the possibility that for the overthrow of the system of exploitation perhaps force may be necessary—unfortunately—for every use of force may demoralize its user! And this in the face of the high moral and spiritual upsurge which is the consequence of every victorious revolution! And this in Germany, where a violent clash, which of course may be forced upon the people, at least has the advantage of extirpating the servility which has permeated the national consciousness as a result of the humiliation of the Thirty Years' War. And this gentle, soft, and powerless preacher's way of thinking makes the claim to impose itself upon the most revolutionary party that history has known![3]

This is an echo of the mood of '48, which confidently expected

---

[2] Letter of Engels to Marx, September 4, 1870, *MEGA*, III/4, p. 377. The italicized words are in English and French respectively in the original.

[3] *Werke*, Vol. XX, p. 171; an English translation is in Engels's *Herr Duehring's Revolution in Science*, London and New York, no date, pp. 209–10. The translation used here is my own and closer to the original.

Germany to be "cleansed, purified and made manly" by war and force. The Great War of 1914–18, with its habituating of Everyman to use a gun and deal death lightly; its aftermath of street fighting, irregular armed forces, political murder, and Nazi terror; then the second total war which taught Everyman to use a telegraphic rifle sight; and now the monstrous wall across the center of the capital city of the German people to keep the inhabitants of East Germany immured in their prison-paradise, and the moral wall raised by the cold-blooded shooting of those whom barbed wire, watchtowers, and land mines cannot stop—all this suggests that perhaps Professor Duehring had a clearer vision of what the use and exaltation of force might do to Germany than did the man who wrote the massive polemic against him.

Be that as it may, hymns to force were more infrequent now in the writings of Marx and Engels and lacking in their earlier fervor: dim sparks from a dying fire. After Marx's death, Engels returned to this theme for the last time in 1887–88. He planned a book on the role of force in history. It is a symptom of his mood and priorities that he never finished it. All he completed was the intended "fourth section," a manuscript of some sixty-odd pages, dealing with force in German history, with special attention to its use by Bismarck. Its aim, Engels says, is to show that:

> . . . the praxis of force, of blood and iron . . . had to succeed for a certain time, and . . . in the end, had to fail.[4]

Closely allied to the inclination to use force in order to give history a shove, is the inclination to use dictatorship to accelerate history. Hence we must examine the meanings to Marx and Engels and their contesting heirs of the term, *dictatorship,* and more particularly, the term, *dictatorship of the proletariat.* In the literature of Marxism there has been no formula more controversial than this.

Fortunately, we have an illuminating examination of both the general term and the special one, and of all the relevant passages from Marx and Engels, in a recent study by Hal Draper. He has given Marx the benefit of the doubt in the matter of rational consistency and democratic inclination, but his combing of the writings of the two founding fathers of Marxism is thorough and dispassionate, and, it seems to me, his interpretation sound, insofar as an *ism* can be pinned down in texts and exegeses. The present chapter

---

[4] *Werke,* Vol. XXI, p. 407.

makes substantial use of his study, but in any case, the texts and contexts must speak for themselves.[5]

Marx and Engels became revolutionists in Germany under the influence of the ideas of the French Revolution, which they devoutly hoped was about to repeat itself on a more advanced scale. Their hearts were possessed by the dream of Babeuf: "The French Revolution is the precursor of another, more magnificent revolution, which will be the last." It was through the distorting prism and many-colored spectrum of that dream that Marx beheld the uprisings of 1848. He was, so to speak, an advocate of a French Revolution for Germany, and then, for all Europe. We can understand neither the *Communist Manifesto,* nor the calls for revolutionary war in the *Neue Rheinische Zeitung,* nor the *Address of the Central Committee of the Communist League* of March 1850, if we fail to bear in mind this distorting prism through which they viewed events.

When Marx got to Paris in 1844, the word *dictatorship* itself was a term in flux, being used in various contexts with varying meanings. Today we have tended to settle on one of those meanings: we regard dictatorship as a synonym for permanent dictatorship, personal dictatorship, autocracy, despotism, tyranny, absolutism, authoritarianism, or totalitarianism. That is a wide range, yet all these uses imply some form of permanent and uncontrolled autocratic rule, a meaning quite different from that which prevailed throughout much of recorded history.

"Dictatorship," Lenin said on December 5, 1919, in a moment of frankness, "is a harsh, heavy, and even bloody word." He did not shrink from exercising it in that spirit. When he wrote from the vantage point of power (on October 20, 1920), "the scientific concept *dictatorship* means nothing more nor less than unrestricted power, not limited by anything, not restrained by any laws, nor by any absolute rules, and resting directly upon force, *that, and nothing else but that,* is the meaning of the concept, dictatorship,"—Lenin may not have been as "scientific" as he thought, but he was fully in accord with the semantic uses of our day, expressing them with marvelous precision and clarity. But the usage of our day, as I have

---

[5] *Marx and the Dictatorship of the Proletariat,* by H. Draper, published in English in *Études de Marxicologie,* No. 6, special supplement of the *Cahiers de l'Institute de Science Economique Appliquée,* Paris, Sept. 1962, 68 pp. plus an unsigned one-page summary, possibly by M. Rubel, general editor of the studies.

suggested, is one quite different from that which prevailed when the term was first conceived, and throughout much of its subsequent history.

The term *dictatura* is of course Latin. It originated in the early Roman Republic, where it had a long and honorable life as a way of designating a temporary-emergency delegation of power by the Republic to a trusted servant, to meet a crisis requiring special unity, unusual energy, and exceptionally complete mobilization of the forces of the Republic. The dictatorship of the Roman Republic was distinguished by a number of features which our present usage has lost, features which make it in many ways the direct opposite of Lenin's "scientific" definition:

(1) It was constitutional. The constitution provided for this office in emergencies, defined the qualifications of those who might be chosen and the limits of their powers.

(2) It was temporary. The period of a dictatorship was a maximum of six months, but the dictator surrendered his powers earlier if the emergency ended.

(3) The dictator had control of the army, and the power of life and death. He could abrogate the laws and the ordinary rights of citizens, as Lincoln did the right of *habeas corpus* during the Civil War. But he could not make *new* laws, alter the constitution permanently, or even touch the treasury, without the authorization of the proper constitutional body.

(4) When he surrendered his powers he was accountable for any arbitrary and unjust use he might have made of them.

(5) The dictatorship system worked for three centuries—until it was abolished by that permanent and self-chosen dictator, the Roman imperator or emperor, raised to absolute power on the shields of his legions. With its death died the Republic. But as long as the Republic lived, dictatorship stayed within the republican, constitutional, legal framework, and did not degenerate into tyranny.

Thus the classic Roman Republican *dictatura* corresponds not to the modern dictatorial régime, but to the modern institutions of temporary *state of siege*, proclamation of *martial law* in a distress area, or some other form of *crisis-and-emergency government.* These make the same constitutional assumptions as the *dictatura* of

---

* In connection with the enforcement of integration and the Civil Rights Act, and the checking of race clashes and looting in our big cities, we have recently prohibited crowds, sealed off areas, called out state troopers or National Guard to protect a Negro student, or enforce a court order; to uphold a provision of the Constitution itself by extaordinary, emergency measures.

the Roman Republic, namely, that they can abrogate certain rights for an emergency period, but can neither make new law nor destroy these rights permanently. "Not only is this consistent with democracy, but when directed against a power conceived of as threatening liberty, it appears as the very shield and buckler of democracy."[6]

When the French revolutionists, both those of 1789 and those of 1848, wrapped themselves in Roman togas, it was in this sense that they at first used the term, *dictatura*. But, in an age of continuous revolution, terms and institutions change continually, acquiring ever new meanings. Alongside of, and displacing each other, arose the *dictatorship of the Convention*, the *dictatorship of the Commune of Paris*, the *dictatorship of the Committee of Public Safety*, and the *dictatorship of Robespierre*. Robespierre himself was a "Roman" who did not associate the concentration of vast power in his own hands with the term *dictatorship* in the new sense which it was even then assuming. On the contrary, "with his neck already on the block," he said:

> . . . this word, dictatorship, has magic effects; it stigmatizes liberty; it villifies the government; it destroys the Republic; it degrades all revolutionary institutions, which are presented as if the work of a single man; it traduces national justice, which is presented as if instituted for the ambition of a single man; it concentrates at one point all the daggers of fanaticism and the aristocracy. What terrible use the enemies of the Republic have made of just the name of a Roman magistracy![7]

When Marx found the word and used it in various contexts for his varying purposes, all these meanings were jostling each other as definitions of a concept in flux. Marx himself uses the term in all these senses, before he hits upon the formula, "dictatorship of the proletariat." Thus Draper cites a letter to Engels of March 31, 1851, in which he writes:

> You must admit that all this crap is not very pleasant, and that I am up to the ears in petty-bourgeois filth. And besides all that, they have me exploiting the workers and striving for a dictatorship![8]

Again Marx uses the term, dictatorship, to attack Comte:

---

[6] Draper, *op. cit.*, p. 7. On the nature of the Roman Republican dictatorship see any standard history of Rome.

[7] Draper, *op. cit.*, p. 11.

[8] *MEGA*, III/1, p. 179.

Comte is known to the Parisian workmen as the prophet in politics of Imperialism (of personal *Dictatorship*), of capitalist rule in political economy, of hierarchy in all spheres of human action, even the sphere of science, and as author of a new catechism with a new pope and new saints in place of the old ones.[9]

Marx first used the term *dictatorship of the proletariat*, as we have seen, in March 1850 in his *Class Struggles in France 1848–50*. In that work, and the next one, *The Eighteenth Brumaire of Louis Napoleon*, he also uses the term dictatorship in five other contexts and different senses. He speaks of the dictatorship delegated temporarily to Cavaignac to crush the insurrection of the workingmen of Paris in June 1848. This is a temporary, military, or state-of-siege dictatorship exercised *by* bourgeois society "by means of the saber," but not a dictatorship "by the saber" *over* bourgeois society. It is also a dictatorship of a representative body, namely of the Constituent Assembly, which has delegated this power to Cavaignac. Next, Marx speaks of the successive stages in the dictatorship of Louis Napoleon. When he is elected President, he represents "the legislative dictatorship of the united royalists . . . the parliamentary dictatorship of the Party of Order," *and* "the dictatorship of the bourgeoisie." When the bourgeoisie, however, repudiates universal suffrage, it openly confesses, according to Marx, that:

Our dictatorship has hitherto existed by the will of the people; it must now be consolidated against the will of the people.[10]

Thereby, the dictatorship of the bourgeoisie brings about its own downfall; the Emperor becomes an irresponsible dictator *over society and over the bourgeoisie.*

Thus Marx has successively recognized that there is the possibility of *a class* dictatorship, of the dictatorship of *a representative institution*, and of the dictatorship of *an individual*, which may be delegated, temporary and limited, or may be permanent and unlimited. It is only in this last case that it becomes a true despotism, raising the state over society and the autocracy of the Emperor over

---

[9] *Werke*, Vol. XVII, p. 555. This is a section of Marx's first draft of *The Civil War in France*, and shows Marx as an opponent of personal dictatorship and hierarchy. He identifies the former with "Imperialism," by which he means the personal dictatorship of the Emperor, Louis Bonaparte.
[10] *Werke*, Vol. VII, p. 93.

the class or classes that raised him to power, and over society as a whole.

If we turn from Marx's use of the term dictatorship in general to his use of the term in connection with his predilect class, the proletariat, we find that Marx, and with him Engels, normally use not dictatorship (*Diktatur*) but rule (*Herrschaft*). There are two brief periods in Marx's life, 1850–51, and 1872–75, when Marx several times replaces *Herrschaft* by *Diktatur*. And there is a third period, long after Marx's death, when Engels employs the word *Diktatur* in 1890–91 in some retrospective musings on the period from 1872–75. This substitution of one term for the other or their simultaneous use for short periods raises a number of ambiguities for us and for the heirs.

Are the terms synonymous? Were there any special reasons for using one term in preference to the other several times during two brief periods of their lives? Did the term come into Marx's vocabulary from his association with Blanqui? Was it Blanqui's term or Marx's? Was *Diktatur des Proletariats* the dictatorship of a class? of a party claiming to speak for that class? of a conspirative élite?

Was it merely a *Woertchen,* an unimportant little word that Marx let slip once or twice, as Kautsky maintained? Or was it what he meant all along, but only occasionally translated from German into Latin, as Lenin maintained? Is it a synonym for the "democratic rule of the immense majority in the interests of the immense majority," a synonym which, however, puts emphasis on the *energetic character* of the measures taken by that rule to maintain itself and to establish a new political constitution, or a "new social order"? Or is it the dictatorship of a single party, then of its leading committee, then of a single infallible interpreter of its infallible doctrine, as Lenin, Stalin, and Khrushchev have conceived it?

In the earliest of their joint political writings, the "German Ideology," 1845–46, Marx and Engels wrote:

> . . . every class which is struggling for rule (*Herrschaft*), even when its rule, as in the case of the proletariat, postulates the abolition of the old form of society in its entirety and the abolition of *Herrschaft* itself, must first conquer for itself political power. . . .[11]

---

[11] *MEGA,* I/5, p. 23. It is interesting to note how the word *Herrschaft* has been translated in this passage by R. Pascal for the International Publishers' translation, New York, 1947, p. 23: ". . . every class which is struggling for

A year before the *Communist Manifesto* was published, Engels wrote for a German-language journal in Brussels:

The Communists, far from starting useless quarrels with the Democrats . . . themselves prefer at present to take a stand as democrats in all practical party matters. Democracy brings with it in all civilized lands the political rule (*Herrschaft*) of the proletariat as a necessary consequence, and the political rule of the proletariat is the first prerequisite for all Communist measures. As long as democracy has not been won therefore, Communists and Democrats fight side by side, and the interests of the Democrats are also the interests of the Communists.[12]

This conviction that universal suffrage and other democratic institutions would inevitably mean the victory of the proletariat or the Communists in their struggle for power, was to remain with Marx and Engels all their lives, growing stronger in their last years. It was inconceivable to them that the proletariat, once it had the vote and formed the majority of the population, should fail to vote for the dismantling of the existing order and its replacement by a new *system* called socialism.

When Marx and Engels were working on the *Communist Manifesto,* Engels's main contribution was a rough draft in the form of a Communist Catechism, known as *Grundsaetze des Kommunismus* (Principles of Communism). The eighteenth question reads: "What will be the course of development of this revolution?" Engels answers:

First of all it will establish a *democratic constitution*, and thereby, directly or indirectly, the rule of the proletariat. Directly in England, where the proletariat are already a majority of the population. Indirectly in France and Germany, where the majority of the people consists not of proletarians alone, but also of small peasants and petty bourgeois, who are just beginning to be caught up in a transition to proletarians and to become more and more dependent on the proletariat in all their political interests, and must therefore soon adapt themselves to the demands of the proletariat. Perhaps this may cost a second struggle, which however can only end with the victory of the proletariat.

---

mastery, even when its *domination,* as is the case with the proletariat, postulates the abolition of *mastery* itself, must first conquer for itself political power. . . ." Each of the three terms I have italicized is expressed in German by the word, *Herrschaft*.

[12] *MEGA,* I/6, p. 289.

Democracy will be useless to the proletariat if it does not use it immediately as a means to the realization of measures directly attacking private property and making secure the existence of the proletariat.[13]

Clearly then, the word *Herrschaft*, or rule, of the proletariat, signifies to Marx and Engels a democratic government of the working class, or the working class and those small proprietors, etc. who are being driven into its ranks. Further, it is a government which will be *energetic* in its own defense, in its attacks upon private property and on the existence of the old "ruling classes." It is, moreover, given the limited suffrage of that day, a government not likely to be achieved by democratic process but by a pro-democratic revolution.

In the *Communist Manifesto* this proposition is expressed by Marx in the following language:

> All previous historical movements were movements of minorities, or in the interest of minorities. The proletarian movement is the self-conscious, independent movement of the immense majority. The proletariat, the lowest stratum of our present society, cannot stir, cannot raise itself up, without the whole superincumbent strata of official society being sprung into air.
> . . . the first step in the revolution by the working class is to raise the proletariat to the position of the ruling class, to win the battle of democracy.[14]

When Marx and Engels got back to Germany in 1848, although it was a Germany in insurrection, they did not find it ripe for the rule of the working class. Hence, when Marx put on the masthead of the *Neue Rheinische Zeitung* the words, "Organ of Democracy," he was not merely trying to conciliate his financial backers and stockholders. He was also, he thought, adjusting his aim to the realities and possibilities of the moment, which obliged him and his handful of disciples to conceal the "proletarian" program he had just drafted, and to back, encourage, and drive forward, the "bourgeois" democratic movement then on the march in Germany. So far did this concealment or tactical reticence go that he made no reference to and used no formulation from the *Communist Manifesto*, and made

---

[13] *Ibid.*, p. 514.
[14] *Ibid.*, pp. 536, 545.

no use either of sixteen of the seventeen points contained in a circular just drafted by him as an address of the Communist League to the German workingmen. Only the first point, "All Germany is declared a single, indivisible republic," was of any use to him as the editor of the German "Organ of Democracy." When Engels wrote him from Barmen:

> The mood of the bourgeoisie is really despicable. The workers are beginning to move a little, still very crudely, but on a mass scale. They immediately formed unions. But that certainly doesn't suit *us* (Das aber ist *uns* gerade im Wege)—

Marx agreed. In fact, the NRZ published no reports whatsoever about the labor movement and its activities.[15]

To have called then for the as yet unformed German working class to take power, Marx felt, would be a fruitless exercise in self-isolation, and a way of frightening the bourgeoisie away from the revolutionary role history had assigned to it.[16] Hence he called on the liberal and democratic "middle class" to take power and use their rule energetically to make a clean sweep of the old régime, to make a French Revolution in Germany.

What infuriated Marx, and rightly so, was the lack of energy, courage, and understanding of what to destroy and what to build, shown by the majority of the democratic Frankfurt Assembly, which the insurrections of 1848 had called into being. The Assembly suffered from "parliamentary cretinism," timid constitutional prejudices and illusions. It was voluntarily donning the straitjacket of the old constitution which reaction and counterrevolution were using to prepare the dispersal of the new Assembly itself. What was needed,

---

[15] The letter of Engels is in *MEGA*, III/1, p. 100. The authority for the statement that NRZ published nothing about the labor movement is Franz Mehring, both in his biography of Marx, p. 189, and in a special study for *Archiv fuer die Geschichte des Sozialismus und der Arbeiterbewegung*, Vol. I, p. 119, where he explains that "Socialist theory and even the proletarian class struggle still greatly receded behind the revolutionary struggle of the German nation against the reactionary classes." His "German nation" or "German people" (Volk) gives a sounder picture of the variegated movement than does Marx's class term, *bourgeoisie*.

[16] Marx was inclined to distinguish between a class which exists *in itself* (*an sich*) and the same class as existing *for itself* (*fuer sich*). The first was a physical or objective fact, the second a matter of the class having become conscious of its existence, its interests, and its role in history. In 1848 Marx found the German working class unformed even in the first sense.

Marx wrote, was "a revolution which had first to establish constitutional principles of its own."

> Every provisional state set up after a revolution requires a dictatorship and an energetic dictatorship at that. From the beginning we have reproached Camphausen [the Premier designated by the Frankfurt Assembly] for not acting dictatorially, for not immediately shattering and eliminating the remnants of old institutions.[17]

Thus once more Marx speaks of, and calls for, a "revolutionary dictatorship" of a democratic institution, a representative body, to be exercised by an agent responsible to it. Once more dictatorship and democracy are not opposites but dictatorship is an energetic way of action by the new democratic institutions to abolish the old undemocratic ones, and to safeguard the new democracy's own existence and extension. Only a dictatorship of "the bourgeoisie" and of its democratic representative assembly could save democracy and the German Revolution. Since such energy was lacking, the revolution failed.

With these uses of the word dictatorship in mind—as the dictatorship of a class, as the dictatorship of a democratic assembly, as a dictatorship temporarily entrusted to its commissioners, as energetic rule consistent with Marx's idea of democracy—we can now examine his use of the term in connection with the proletariat.

All through the stormy years 1848 and '49, Marx continued to speak of the rule (*Herrschaft*) of the proletariat. Only in March 1850, as we have seen, when the tide had ebbed but Marx would not admit it to himself, did he for the first time employ the term *dictatorship of the proletariat*. And the first use of *Diktatur* was in a passage dedicated to Blanqui as the incarnation of revolutionary socialism. Let us examine more closely the passage in *Class Struggles in France* in which this seeming identification of the name of Blanqui with the dictatorship of the proletariat occurs:

> . . . the proletariat groups itself more and more around *revolutionary socialism*, around *communism*, for which the bourgeoisie itself has invented the name *Blanqui*. This socialism is the *declaration of the revolution in permanence*, the *class dictatorship* of the proletariat as a necessary transition point to the *abolition of class differences altogether*, to the abolition of all the productive relations on which they rest, of all social relations which correspond to these production rela-

---

[17] *MEGA*, I/7, pp. 361-62.

tionships, the transformation of all ideas which arise from these social relationships.[18]

Taking Marx at his word, Marxicologists have generally assumed that it was from Blanqui that Marx got both the idea of the proletarian dictatorship and the term itself. We are indebted to Mr. Draper for having gone painstakingly through all the published writings of Blanqui, and then through all those who have written seriously about this apostle of the revolutionary conspiracy in permanence (some of whom used his unpublished manuscripts as well), and for coming up with the information that Blanqui never used the term *dictatorship of the proletariat!* This leads Mr. Draper to conclude that in the cited passage Marx was not defining "Blanquism" but expressing his own views, the "revolutionary socialism or communism" which he himself advocated, and to which the bourgeoisie has given (invented) the name of Blanqui. Obviously, Mr. Draper's "solution" of the enigmatic passage raises as many problems as it solves.

On the one hand it helps to keep separate (too separate as we suggested in the preceding chapter, Marxism and Blanquism, the names and views of Marx and Blanqui). For when Marx wrote it, he was entering into his *Association* with the Blanquists; he was agreeing to, or more probably he was writing, virtually the same formula into the joint statement of principles; he was issuing his peculiarly "Blanquist" *Circular;* and he was using Blanquist conspirators as emissaries to the branches of the Communist League.

On the other hand, Mr. Draper's distinction helps to keep in focus the important fact that even at his most "Blanquist," Marx was not for the revolutionary dictatorship of a conspirative élite of professional revolutionaries, but, as he himself underlines, for a *"class dictatorship* of the proletariat."

But at the moment the two formulas looked suspiciously alike. The proletariat in Paris was beaten. The proletariat in Germany was unformed, so that Marx had worked there with the Liberals and Democrats of other classes. The "Universal Association" in practice looked more like a Blanquist conspiracy than like the rising of a class. It was led by a conspiratorial élite of self-chosen "professional revolutionaries," for, though they did not use the word, that is what they were. Blanqui was indifferent to the workers' organizations as

---

[18] Clearly this is another rendering of the language which appears in the statement of aims of the Universal Communist Association of Marxians, Blanquists, and Chartists, discussed in the preceding chapter.

such while there were elements of Marx's doctrinal theories which even then pointed at the future labor movement and the working class as the repositories of socialist doctrine, as the class destined to rule, and by its revolutionary dictatorship, to keep the revolution going in permanence until society had been completely transformed.

Thus at the moment when Marx was joining forces with the Blanquists and proclaiming his unstinting admiration for the old conspirator, there were two things they possessed in common and one which separated them: Marx had acquired from Blanqui his formula of the "revolution in permanence" and an intensification of his penchant for a "revolutionary dictatorship." But he was not able then, nor during their second united front after the Paris Commune, to persuade the Blanquists of the importance of the working class or the need for the revolutionary dictatorship to be a class dictatorship of the proletariat. As a matter of fact, in 1872 Marx was to spend many days and nights expounding this idea to the Blanquists in London. His lectures briefly "infected" their proclamations, but then for the second time he broke with Blanquist formulas for the social revolution, and they dropped their interest, always superficial, in the working-class movement and the formula of the dictatorship of the proletariat. The formula disappeared from his writings and from theirs within a year or a little more.

Neither united front with the Blanquists lasted very long. Actually, the "Universal Association" never really got going in 1850; within a few months Marx quarreled both with the Blanquists and with the spirit of "the permanent revolution" in his own organization. By September he had come to the conclusion, although he never acknowledged it as his own error, that the Communist League was living in a dream world and playing with conspiracies to bring back the revolutionary atmosphere that fresh winds of prosperity had blown away.

In place of repudiating his own erroneous estimate he made the sharp attack on Willich and Schapper which we have already quoted, charging them with "dogmatism," an "idealistic" refusal to take account of "the real facts of the situation," a reliance on "naked revolutionary will," a refusal to wait for the working class to mature and a new objective revolutionary situation to ripen. It is this utterance of Marx that is the take-off point for "mature Marxism," for what Engels was to christen "scientific socialism," and in general, for the orthodox Marxist, non-Leninist claimants to the heritage.

Marx and Engels further clarified their new view in a final double number of the short-lived *Neue Rheinische Revue,* published in November of 1850. Here we find the famous hymn to the prosperity of America after the discovery of gold in California, the prophecy of a canal through the Isthmus of Panama (one of the many dreams of great public works out of the book of Saint-Simon), the prediction that the Pacific Ocean would now become what once the Mediterranean and then the Atlantic had been, the great highway of world commerce, with the ports of the Americas as the new "great emporiums of world trade." The civilized countries of Europe would now become a backwater unless, by means of a "social revolution," Europe should "transform the modes of production and transport in conformity with the technological requirements of modern production, thus releasing fresh productive forces, securing the superiority of European industry and canceling the disadvantages of geography. . . ."[19]

In retrospect Marx and Engels in this review attribute the uprisings of 1848–49 one-sidedly to an economic crisis, ignoring or greatly underestimating the national tensions and discontents, the growth of democratic movements and conspiracies, the various socialist currents in Paris that had played so large a formative role in the fashioning of the doctrines of Marx himself. This new emphasis on the state of the economy as crucial to the "real facts of the situation" which determine the appropriateness and timeliness of political actions, conspiracies, uprisings, expectations of proletarian rule or proletarian dictatorship, the *Revue* finds the source of crises (and hence of revolutions) on the Continent in the economic situation in England. Follows a glowing account of the strength of the British economy, the bright side of the picture which Marx was to paint more darkly in *Das Kapital.* The key passage on the relation of politics to economics is the following:

> In view of the general prosperity which now prevails and permits the productive forces of bourgeois society to develop as luxuriantly (*ueppig*) as is possible within the limits of bourgeois relationships, there can be no question of a real revolution. Such a revolution is possible only in a period in which these *two factors,* the *modern*

19 The general survey of the economic and political situation from May to October 1950 is unsigned, but style and ideas suggest that it is primarily the work of Engels, written in consultation with and with the approval of Marx. It is in *Werke,* Vol. VII, pp. 421–463. The new situation of America is treated on pp. 434–37.

productive forces and the *bourgeois forms of production,* have come into *conflict* with each other. . . . *A new revolution* is only possible as a result of a new crisis. *But the former is also just as certain as the latter.*[20]

With this, the interests of Marx and Engels shifted to the scrutiny of the economy of England, "the demiurge of the bourgeois cosmos." The great expansion of the productive forces of society by the bourgeoisie which the *Communist Manifesto* had celebrated so eloquently had not reached its end then, as the *Manifesto* had assumed.

Marx and Engels had had their revolutionary ardor, or at least their belief in the all-sufficiency of the revolutionary will, dampened by their first-hand contact with the prosperity and the self-confident optimism of Victorian England.[21]

Anxiously, Marx and Engels began taking the pulse of British prosperity. Again and again they saw "the next crisis" about to come, predicted it, and waited for its revolutionary effects on the Continent, and on England herself. When the crisis kept delaying its appearance, they sought and found explanations. At last, when it came, it failed to bring with it a new 1848.

With this discovery that "bourgeois society is still in the ascendant,"[22] the rift in Marxism between the sense of fatality and the exaltation of the omnipotence of the revolutionary will to change the world, became complete—or as complete as the irreducible revolutionary passion in Marx's temperament could make it. As early as September 1850, when the two friends split with the Communist League, and November 1850, when they published their *Revue,* the isolation of Marx and Engels was complete.

Reluctantly, Engels left London for Manchester, where he joined his father's textile firm once more, this time sticking with it until he became its director. And with distaste and rage, Marx began the long mole's work of burrowing through the mounds of economic literature to find the nature and probabilities of crises, the conditions and "law of motion" which, in spite of everything, must one day put revolution once more on the order of the day, and, this time, make its triumph inevitable. In place of trying to run a revolution

---

[20] *Ibid.,* p. 440.
[21] On the extent to which they had become dissident "Victorians" see the chapter in Lichtheim, *op. cit.,* pp. 133–40, entitled "Victorian Watershed."
[22] Letter of Marx to Engels, Oct. 8, 1858. *MEGA,* III/2, 342.

that was no longer there, he began to dig a scientific tunnel—a tunnel through modern industrial or "capitalist" society, at the end of which he hoped to see the daylight of the social revolution. The task was still unfinished when death came.

Often only the need to make a living by journalism, or merely to come up for air from the deep tunnel shafts of his "scientific work," caused him still to take cognizance of day-to-day affairs. But it was the "scientific work" which in his eyes and Engels's had the priority, and the only real importance.

Feeling nothing but contempt for the rest of the emigration (their letters to each other about the German emigrés are hair-raising), Marx and Engels constituted themselves as an independent propaganda center of communism or scientific socialism, a personal union around which the broken and scattered remnants of German communism should gradually gather (insofar as they were worth anything) into a force to be reckoned with, a kind of pre-party, to do the slow educational and organization work which corresponded to Marx's scientific labors, and to form at last the working class itself into a party of the class. The little lonely "party" of two righteous and self-righteous men, and the party of the entire working class— these were the two poles of the dialectic that would rule the rest of their lives.

As we read Marx's savage utterances in public documents, his strictures on bourgeoisie and petty bourgeoisie, on bourgeois democrats and petty bourgeois democrats, on republicans and socialists, all of them portrayed as lacking in revolutionary spirit, consistency, courage, understanding of their "tasks" and their "role in history"; as we add to the published discussion of the immaturity of the German workingmen the harsher and more contemptuous judgments of Marx and Engels on their own "communist élite" in letters to each other written during the '48 period—all this testimony adds up to an overwhelming proof

> . . . that in Germany there was neither a bourgeoisie nor a proletariat in the ideal-typical form and full development of antagonisms such as the *Communist Manifesto* had assumed.[23]

Actually, the stormy year 1848 produced neither a bourgeois revolution nor a proletarian revolution nor a revolution in permanence. It proved to be a great and contagious explosion of national-

---

[23] Blumenberg, *op. cit.*, p. 87.

ism and democracy (only in Paris did the workingmen give it a somewhat different character with their demand for a guaranteed right to work and national workshops), and it was followed by dynastic, absolutist and bureaucratic counterrevolution rather than "feudal" reaction.

Thus the *Communist Manifesto* was a stirring fantasy in the French manner, with little relationship to the actual events of 1848 or the subsequent history of Germany and Europe. Marx himself put it on ice when he went to Germany in 1848. By the autumn of 1850, he was excoriating (with Willich and Schapper as the targets) his theory of the imminent petit-bourgeois democratic revolution and the proletarian revolution in permanence. With that ended the first heroic, or romantic, period of Marxism, and the more patient and less dramatic heroism of "scientific investigation" engaged his powerful mind.

Yet, as a fantasy seductive in its inner coherence, strong in the impact of its aphorisms and slogans, memorable in its phrasing, and most memorable in its dream of a utopia bedecked in the parti-colored raiments of science and prophecy, the *Communist Manifesto* continued to possess the imagination of millions in coming generations. So, too, the *Circular* on extremist tactics and revolution in permanence more unreal than the *Manifesto,* issued in March of 1850 and recalled and condemned by its author that same summer, was to provide the chief stock-in-trade of Trotsky and Lenin in the twentieth century. Nothing makes so manifest the ambiguities in the heritage and the ambiguities in the heirs than the contrast in the fate of those two documents in the hands of their progenitor, and in the hands of the rival claimants to the legacy.

Chapter 11

DICTATORSHIP OF CLASS, PARTY,

OR DOCTRINE?

If we do not allow freedom in chemistry, why should we
allow it in morals or politics?

—Auguste Comte

FROM Gracchus Babeuf, the Jacobin who organized the "Conspiracy
of the Equals" in 1796, through Filippo Buonarroti to Louis Auguste Blanqui, Paris had an almost continuous tradition of armed
revolutionary conspiracy, aiming at a revolutionary dictatorship.
There was nothing in the life of Berlin, or Vienna, or the Rhineland
that even remotely resembled this tradition.

Louis Auguste Blanqui (1805–81) was a declassed law student
who first electrified France, when, being tried with other conspirators, he gave his occupation as "proletarian." This self-chosen title
was the most "socialist" thing about him. He participated energetically in every popular movement against the monarchy or the
empire, and for the republic. When no such movement was afoot, he
kept building a succession of secret societies for which he evolved
some of the conspirative techniques later employed by Lenin. His
instructions to those societies included military training, pseudonyms known only to a trusted handful of picked leaders, a trium-
virate or *troika*, and the *de facto* personal dictatorship of Blanqui
himself. The organizations bore such names as *Société des Droits de
l'Homme, Société des Familles, Société des Saisons*. Their structure
was robed in fantasy, but their aim was always the same, the seizure
of power on behalf of the discontented, the declassed, and the popular masses, by a little band of resolute armed men. These were to set

up a revolutionary dictatorship—with Blanqui as Supreme Dictator
—which must then be trusted by the masses to work progressively
for their welfare.

The uprisings were invariably abortive, although some of them
preceded by only a few days uprisings of a wider character that
were successful. Blanqui as invariably landed in jail, spending all
told over thirty-seven years of his adult life in prison. It is thus that
his name became a legend. It was with the legend rather than the
man that Marx twice made an alliance.

The reaction believed in the legend, too. Released by the Provisional Government in 1870 after the fall of Louis Napoleon, Blanqui
made two abortive attempts to overthrow it as not energetic enough
in the war against the Prussians, then was arrested once more just
one day before the National Guard took control of Paris. The Commune of Paris offered seventy-four prominent hostages which it had
taken, including the Archbishop of Paris, in exchange for the single
prisoner, Blanqui. Thiers answered: "To return Blanqui to the insurrection would mean to send it a force equal to an entire army corps."
The equivalent of the army corps was then a tired old man of sixty-
seven, with little energy left even to dream. Yet he was tried again
after the fall of the Commune, condemned for life, then released by
the Republic in 1889, two years before his death.

Marx made his brief alliances, in 1850 and 1872, not with Blanqui but with Blanquists, men whom the legend had gathered around
Blanqui's name. Though the alliances did not last Marx never ceased
to admire in Blanqui his tireless energy, his devotion to the idea of
revolution, his inability to recognize defeat.

In his first experiment with a united front with Blanquists in
1850, Marx was struggling against the recognition of the defeat of
the Revolutions of 1848 and '49. He was seeking by more extreme
programs and by union with conspirative remnants to make up for
his own isolation and the sudden disappearance of the masses from
the scene. In the second case, after the Paris Commune, Marx had
need of an alliance for quite different reasons: a joint fight of Blanquists and Marxists, both of whom believed in the use of the centralized State for revolutionary dictatorship, against that other colorful
figure, Bakunin, and the Bakuninists, against the anti-statist followers of Proudhon, and all the assorted Communard refugees who were
giving Marx a hard time in the International.

On both occasions, but more particularly in 1872, after the Paris
Commune, Marx attempted to "re-educate" the Blanquist emigrés,

to induce them to substitute his idea of "the dictatorship of the proletariat," which Marx considered synonymous with the "winning of the battle for democracy," for Blanqui's "revolutionary dictatorship" of an élite, conspirative minority. At least, so Engels has explained the matter.

In 1874, Engels wrote:

Blanqui is essentially a political revolutionary, a socialist by feeling, sympathizing with the suffering of the people, but he has neither a socialist theory nor definite practical proposals for social improvements. In his political activity he has been essentially a "man of the deed," of faith that a little well-organized minority which at the right moment attempts a *coup de main* (*Handstreich*), can stir up the masses by a couple of early successes and thus make a victorious revolution.

Engels underlined the difference between the revolutionary dictatorship of a handful of conspirators or a minority conspiratorial organization, and the dictatorship of the proletariat as a class, such as Marx had advocated in 1850 and such as Marx in 1871 ascribed to the Paris Commune.

From Blanqui's conception of every revolution as the *coup de main* of a small revolutionary minority, it necessarily follows that a dictatorship is needed after the success of the revolution: the dictatorship, it must be made clear, not of the entire revolutionary class, the proletariat, but of the little handful of those who have made the *coup de main* and who in turn are themselves under the dictatorship of one or of several individuals.[1]

It seems clear then that Marx and Engels make their use of the term *dictatorship of the proletariat* in the period immediately after 1872, for the purpose of emphasizing their difference with the Blanquist concept of the dictatorship of the minority, of a small conspirative élite, or its leaders or leader.

Draper, who counts any work with one or more uses of the term, *dictatorship of the proletariat*, as a single *locus*, records one such locus in Marx during this period and two in Engels. In one of these references, Engels explicitly derives Marx's view from the *Communist Manifesto*, showing that he sees no difference between "the dictatorship of the proletariat" and "the rule of the working class."

---

[1] Engels, *Program of the Blanquist Commune Refugees*, published in the *Volkstatt*, June 26, 1874, shortly after the break of the Blanquists and the Marxists. *Werke*, Vol. XVIII, p. 529.

In general, it must be said that Marx and Engels were believers in the idea that entire classes can and do rule. This fundamental preconception they never took the trouble to question or seriously examine. At least as far as the bourgeoisie and the proletariat were concerned, Marx thought that if the class in question did not rule, it was only when the state set itself above society with some dictator such as a Bonaparte, above the classes and dictating to all of them. Though one class, or even more than one, may have sponsored it, the distinguishing feature of "Bonapartism" for Marx is that it was a personal dictatorship in the form of a "state above classes," as against the normal "class state." It was the only "state above classes" that Marx could recognize in a "class society," and his recognition took the form of intense and passionate hatred, Louis Napoleon being more hateful to him than the Emperor of Germany.

When Marx found in England workmen and manufacturers both supporting the same party and program, he did not question his theory of the ultimate identity of class and party. Instead he exploded in wrath against the workingmen for benighted "backwardness," and against their leaders for having "sold themselves."

Engels, somewhat more subtle, and, one is tempted to say, more "Marxist," in this matter, expresses sadness rather than anger and seeks to work out a "materialist" or "economic" explanation of a less demeaning character.

England was his first love. Here Robert Owen had written of "The New Society" and striven to establish cooperative industrial villages in the early years of the century. Here Engels had made his hopeful study of *The Condition of the Working-class in England in 1844* (published in 1845) even before Marx and he formed their lifelong union. This was the land of great industry and the great misery attendant on the early stage of industrialization. Here the Chartist Movement had arisen, the "first real party of the workingmen," and here the first and only firmly organized trade unions developed. Above all, in England the workingmen, by Engels's count, possessed an absolute majority. They might make a social revolution, or, with universal manhood suffrage, vote socialism in, without any uncomfortable problems such as concessions to dubious allies from the peasantry and other classes. All through his life Engels wrote unhappily to friends and disciples about the failure of the British working class to develop a "working-class consciousness," or, after Chartism died, a working-class party, or to show any interest in the doctrines of Marx. Writing to the latter from Manchester, that most industrialized of cities, on October 7, 1858, Engels said:

> . . . actually more and more *verbuergert* ("bourgeoisified") so that this most bourgeois of nations seems to want in the end to possess a bourgeois aristocracy and a bourgeois proletariat *alongside* its bourgeoisie. In a nation which now exploits the entire world, this is in any case to a certain extent justified. In this matter nothing will help except a few really bad years, and these are not so easily produced since the discovery of gold [in California].[2]

A witty, and, in its way, a "Marxist" explanation. But the British workingmen have since formed their own party, known their "thoroughly bad years," seen their country lose its privileged position as the world's workshop, counting house, merchant, shipper, insurer, and empire; and the workingmen's party has even been in power— yet the workingmen of England still refuse to take to their hearts the doctrines and the writings of Marx, or to make an all-out, total statification or "socialization" of industry.

One of Engels's two uses of "dictatorship of the proletariat" immediately after the Paris Commune is aimed at the followers of Proudhon rather than of Blanqui. It is interesting not for its target but as an example of how easily Engels slides up and back from *class* to *party* and from *rule* to *dictatorship*. He is polemicizing against one Muehlberger, to whom he attributes the following Proudhonist view and criticism of the Marxian system:

> "We" do not pursue any "class policy" [Engels pictures "Friend Muehlberger" as boasting] and *we* do not strive for "class domination." But the German Social-Democratic Workers' Party, just because it is a *workers' party*, necessarily pursues a "class policy," the policy of the working class.

To this Engels answers:

> Since each political party sets out to establish its rule in the state, so the German Social-Democratic Workers' Party is necessarily striving to establish *its* rule, the rule of the working class, hence "class domination." Moreover, *every* real proletarian party from the English Chartists on, has put forward a class policy, the organization of the proletariat as an independent political party, as the primary condition

---

[2] *MEGA*, III/2, p. 340; and see above, p. 60.

of its struggle, and the dictatorship of the proletariat as the immediate aim of the struggle.[3]

In broad outlines, the writings of Marx and Engels on this subject spell out many things which should make one school of heirs
uncomfortable, namely, the Marxist-Leninists. Both men make it
clear that they oppose "sects," small minority organizations, or parties made up of a revolutionary élite, that seek to "raise the state
above society," impose their sectarian prescriptions on the working
class, substitute themselves for the working class as a whole, substitute the party for the class or the movement.

To be sure, it is Engels rather than Marx who concerns himself
steadily with this matter, and, notwithstanding the pious legend to
the contrary, the two men are not always identical in their views.
But the declarations of Marx concerning class and party are not out
of line with those of Engels.

In the *Communist Manifesto*, Marx wrote:

Communists do not form a separate party conflicting with other working-class parties. They have no interests apart from those of the
working class as a whole. They do not put forward any special principles according to which they wish to mold the proletarian movement.[4]

Again in 1864, when Marx drafted a second basic document, the
Statutes of the International Workingmen's Association (the First
International), he declared:

. . . the emancipation of the working class must be the work of the
working class itself. . . .

Since . . . the success of the workingmen's movement in each land
can only be assured through the strength of unity and combination
. . . the members of the International Workingmen's Association
should devote all their forces to the unification of the fragmented
labor associations of their respective countries into national bodies,
represented by national central organs.

. . . In its struggles against the united power of the possessing
classes the proletariat can only act as a class if it constitutes itself into
a separate political party, opposing all other parties previously formed
by the possessing classes.[5]

Commenting on the First International, Marx wrote to Bolte on

---

[3] Marx-Engels, *Selected Works*, Vol. I, pp. 613–14.
[4] *MEGA*, I/6, pp. 537–38; English translation by Eden and Cedar Paul for the
Marx-Engels Institute, New York, 1930, p. 42.
[5] *Werke*, Vol. XVI, pp. 14–16.

November 23, 1871, in that chop-suey of languages which he liked to affect:

> Das political movement der Arbeiterklasse had natuerlich zum End-zwecke die Eroberung der political power fuer sie, und dazu ist natuerlich eine bis einem gewissen punkt entwickelte previous organization der working class noetig, die aus ihren oekonomischen Kaempfen selbst erwaechst.[6]

This notion that the working class is not ripe for the development of a party of its class until it has developed some degree of previous organization as a class out of its economic struggles sounds like the rankest expression of that dread heresy, "Economism," against which Plekhanov, Axelrod, Martov, and most especially Lenin, pronounced their anathema.[7]

In the same letter to Bolte, Marx added:

> The *International* was founded to set the real organization of the working class in the place of the socialist or semi-socialist sects. . . .
>
> On the other hand, the International would not have been able to maintain itself [it seemed to be flourishing when Marx wrote this], if the course of history had not already broken up the sectarian system of existence. The development of socialist sectarianism and that of the real labor movement always stand in inverse ratio to each other. As long as (historically) the sects are justified, the working class is still unripe for an independent historical movement. As soon as it has reached this ripeness, all sects are in their essence reactionary.

In the view of Marx and Engels, most clearly expressed in their letters to German followers who had gone to America, the important thing was not first to draft an ideal program and ideal statutes and then gather around them a group, large or small, that would accept them down to the last detail. Rather the thing to do was to gather great numbers, ultimately the class as a whole, in large organizations on even the most fragmentary and imperfect program. Experience in action would deepen both their solidarity and understanding, teach them to correct the defects and make good the shortcomings in their program. Again and again Marx, and much more frequently,

---

[6] "The *political movement* of the working class naturally has as its final goal the winning of *political power* for itself, and for this purpose it needs naturally a certain degree of *previous* organization growing out of its economic struggles themselves." The letter is in Marx-Engels, *Ausgewaehlte Werke*, Vol. II, p. 349.

[7] For the best discussion of the "Economism" controversy to date, see Jonathan Frankel, "Economism: A Heresy Exploited," in the *Slavic Review*, June 1963, pp. 263–84.

Engels, warned the German-American Marxists not to make their Marxism a shibboleth which would isolate them from the main stream of American labor. Whether it was the Knights of Labor or the American Federation of Labor, or some third party movement which gave promise of developing into a labor party, the German Marxist emigrés were urged to join it, work within it, win its confidence, and help it to benefit by its own experiences—the "only way entire classes can learn."

Yet, when it came to the German labor movement, the pride that beset them and their dislike of Lassalle prevented Marx and Engels from following the advice they had given their followers in America.

During his first period of exile, in December 1845, Marx had thought it smart to renounce his Prussian citizenship so as to prevent the Prussian police from interposing against him with the governments of the various lands in which he sought refuge. In the early sixties, when the German workingmen at last began to organize in earnest, he was not able to return to Germany. It was the more romantic and charismatic Lassalle, idolized by the German workingmen, whose whirlwind energies and eloquence and feeling for the psychology of his auditors, brought into existence the first large-scale organization of German labor, the General Workers' Union.

> The development of the German workingmen's party [writes Marx's biographer, Blumenberg] . . . was carried on entirely without Marx's collaboration. He, like Engels, was excluded from any active political participation, and they followed the development with unconcealed ill-will and mistrust. . . . Even later, when they advised the German Party in individual matters, an advice that was by no means always followed, they were still scarcely able to rid themselves of their mistrust. Engels really lost it only a few years before his death, under the influence of August Bebel and the electoral victories of the German Social democracy, which legitimated Bebel's tactics as "correct."[8]

This mistrust was the more pitiful since it ran not only against the main conceptions of Marx on the relation of class and party, but because Lassalle himself was an admiring if self-directed disciple, extremely anxious to get Marx's approval and help in his popular agitation. "But Marx," in the words of his biographer, Mehring, "was never completely able to overcome his prejudice against the man whom the history of the German Social Democracy will always

---

[8] Blumenberg, *op. cit.*, p. 126.

mention in the same breath with him and Engels, and even the mitigating power of death had no permanent effect."[9]

When, after Lassalle's death, Lassalleans and Eisenachers finally prepared to unify their forces to form the German Social Democracy, Marx and Engels first attempted to prevent the unification, then raised all sorts of theoretical objections to the procedures of the unity congress and the program adopted by it. In their various letters to their followers in Germany, together constituting the *Critique of the Gotha Program*, impressive generalizations and matters of some moment alternate with unjust criticism, unfounded conjecture, and petty semantic caviling. There are sections which might give the candid reader the idea that one programmatic formulation is worth a dozen strides forward in working-class unity. Indeed, in some parts of his criticisms of Lassalle, Marx jumps on formulations and proposals which the unsuspecting Lassalle had actually borrowed from the *Communist Manifesto* (the idea of "the iron law of wages" and workers' cooperatives with state credit). And Marx attributes to the Lassalleans formulations which his own followers, the Eisenachers, had suggested for the Gotha Program.

The Eisenachers responded to this ill-timed and ill-tempered attack by simply ignoring it, and refusing to publish it in their journals. In the end, Marx was reconciled to the united party, while Engels in his late years came to identify himself with it and glory in its victories. Even such a devout biographer as Mehring concludes that Marx and Engels had lost touch with German conditions and the moods of the German workingmen, "their judgment clouded by their undiminished distrust of Lasalle and everything Lassallean."[10]

Time has taken its revenge for this display of irrational passion and prejudice. A century after Lassalle conceived his organizing campaign, the German Social Democracy solemnly declared that "it traces its origin back to the General Workers' Union which Ferdinand Lassalle founded in Leipzig in 1863, and not to the Social Democratic Workers' Party, which was brought into being in Eisenach some six years later."[11]

Marx's attitude toward Lassalle and all his ways and works, and his grudging attitude toward the unification congress and program of Gotha, must not be taken to negate Marx's basic attitude toward

---

[9] Mehring, *op. cit.*, p. 340.
[10] Mehring, *op. cit.*, pp. 332–41 and 531–34, gives a fair account of the whole Marx-Lassalle relationship and the unification controversy.
[11] See Introduction, note 8.

the relation of class to party. Even in the midst of his sharp letters on the Gotha Program we find one of the most famous of his pronouncements on the value of working-class unity in a single party. In his letter to Bracke of May 5, 1875, he writes, and underlines the words:

Every step of the real movement is more important than a dozen programs.

And he urges that, if the Eisenachers cannot get the Gotha Congress to adopt their own Eisenach program, then it would be better to make a *"simple agreement for joint action* against the common foe."[12]

Thus the ambiguity is not in the rational principles or theories on the question of party or class, but represents a distortion of those principles by Marx's irrational feelings toward Lassalle and everything Lassallean. If further proof is needed, we can find it in the continuing injunctions of Marx, and more particularly of Engels, to their followers in America. In 1886, a good decade after the smoke of the Gotha Program controversy had cleared, Engels wrote two characteristic letters on program and movement, party and class, to Sorge and Florence Kelley. In the letter to Sorge, dated November 29, 1886, he said:

The Germans have not understood how to use their theory as a lever which could set the American masses in motion; they do not understand the theory themselves for the most part and treat it in a doctrinaire and dogmatic way as something that has to be learned by heart, which will then satisfy all requirements forthwith. To them it is a credo and not a guide to action. . . . The first step of importance for every country newly entering into the movement is always the constitution of the workers as an independent political party, no matter how, so long as it is a distinct workers' party. . . . That the first program of this party is still confused and extremely deficient, that it has raised the banner of Henry George, these are unavoidable evils but merely transitory. The masses must have time and opportunity to develop, and they can have the opportunity only when they have a movement of their own . . . in which they [can] learn through their mistakes. . . .[13]

---

12 *Briefe an A. Bebel und Andere,* Teil I, p. 117.
13 *Letters to Americans, 1848–1895,* by Karl Marx and Friedrich Engels, New York, 1953, pp. 162–63. Henry George, the founder of the Single Tax Movement, ran for mayor of New York in 1886 with the support of the United Labor Party and the Socialist Labor Party.

When Sorge objected that the *Communist Manifesto* had exercised great influence on him when he first read it although he was only a boy at the time, Engels answered:

. . . forty years ago, you were Germans, with a German capacity for theory, and that is why the *Manifesto* had an effect at the time, whereas, though it was translated into French, English, Flemish, Danish, etc., it had absolutely no effect upon the other peoples.[14]

In his letter to Florence Kelley of December 28, 1886, he developed many of the same points in slightly different language:

It is far more important that the movement should spread, proceed harmoniously, take root, and embrace as much as possible the whole American proletariat, than that it should start and proceed on theoretically perfectly correct lines. The great thing is to get the working class to move *as a class*. . . . Therefore I think also the K. of L. [Knights of Labor] a most important factor . . . which ought not be pooh-poohed from without but revolutionized from within, and I consider that the Germans there made a grievous mistake when they tried, in the face of a mighty and glorious movement not of their own creation, to make of their imported and not always understood theory a kind of *alleinseligmachendes* dogma [dogma from which alone can come salvation], and to keep aloof from any movement which did not accept that dogma . . . A million or two of workingmen's votes next November for a *bona fide* workingmen's party is worth infinitely more at present than a hundred thousand votes for a doctrinally perfect platform. . . . Anything that might delay or prevent that national consolidation ["of Georgites, K. of L., trade unionists and all"] of the workingman's party—on no matter what platform—I should consider a great mistake. . . .[15]

To those familiar with Lenin's *What's to Be Done?* and his other basic pronouncements on the relation of party to class,[16] it is obvious that intellectually Marx and Engels stand poles apart from Lenin on this question. From 1902 on, Lenin opposed the idea that the Social Democratic Party (later Communist Party) should be a broad party of the working class or that it should, as Marx and

---

[14] Letter of May 4, 1887, *ibid.*, pp. 184–85.
[15] *Ibid.*, pp. 166–67.
[16] On this see the chapter entitled "Lenin's Organization Plan" in my *Three Who Made a Revolution* (New York, 1964) and my paper, "A Party of a New Type," in *Highlights of the Comintern: Essays, Recollections, Documents,* Milorad Drachkovitch and Branko Lazitch, Editors, Leiden, 1965.

Engels thought, consolidate unions and labor parties with rudimentary and mistaken programs ("Georgites, K. of L., trade unionists and all") into a single party including as far as possible the entire working class. Lenin from the outset favored not a party *of* the class but a party *for* the class. It was to be a self-appointed élite party of declassed revolutionary intellectuals and, where they were of suitable quality, it might add declassed workingmen, in a narrow, exclusive, élite, or self-styled vanguard organization of professional revolutionaries.

Lenin never accepted the idea that the emancipation of the working class was to be the work of the working class itself, moving as a class, learning from its mistakes, gaining ever more complete consciousness and ever more complete and wider union from its experiences, its struggles and its errors, until it had made all little, doctrinally pure, self-appointed sects "superfluous and reactionary," because the working class itself constituted the workers' party. He never accepted the *Communist Manifesto's* idea that "The Communist Party does not form a party distinct from the other working-class parties." Nothing was further from his dogmatic, authoritarian, orthodox temper than Marx's pronouncement that "one movement is worth a dozen programs." The man who split the *Iskra* editors and *Iskraites* at the Second Congress in 1903 on the niceties of two slightly differing definitions of a member of the party in the first paragraph of the draft statutes, and laid the foundation of a separate party of pure Leninists on that issue, would never be in a position to understand or approve the idea that it was "far more important that the movement . . . should spread, take root, and embrace as much as possible of the whole proletariat . . . than that it should start and proceed on theoretically perfectly correct lines."

If Marx could have heard Lenin invoking his name while discoursing on "opportunism in the organization question," the self-appointed vanguard, the proletariat which left to itself was "inevitably petty bourgeois," or any other of Lenin's pet "orthodox Marxist" dogmas on the organization question, he would have repeated once more the wry *bon mot*, "then I myself am no Marxist."

After Marx's death Engels continued to make many pronouncements on party democracy, party discipline and party organization that cannot be reconciled with Lenin's views on these questions. Here are a few typical utterances of Engels, the first dating from 1880, while Marx was still alive, the others made after his death.

They are numbered consecutively here for the purposes of easier annotation:

(1) "The looser the organization [of the party] the firmer it is in reality."

(2) "The organization itself [of the Communist League] was thoroughly democratic, with elected and removable officials, and that alone was enough to bar all the lust for conspiracy which means dictatorship. . . ."

(3) "It is high time that people should at last stop handling party officials—their own servants—with those eternal kid-gloves, and stop standing before them submissively instead of critically."

(4) "What is the difference between you people and Puttkammer [the Prussian Minister of Police from 1881 to 1888] if you pass antisocialist laws against your own comrades? It does not matter to me personally. No party in the world can condemn me to be silent when I am determined to speak. But I think you should reflect whether you would not be wise to be a little less sensitive and a little less Prussian in your behavior. You—and the party—need socialist science, and such science cannot exist unless there is freedom in the party."

(5) To Sorge, Engels complained that Liebknecht was forever talking of "expelling people," and that even Bebel let himself be carried away by the same mood. He was determined to make them see that "only when there were striking proofs of acts injurious to the party, and not mere oppositional activity [Oppositionsmacherei]" could there be any ground for expulsion. "The greatest party in the Reich cannot exist without all shadings within it enjoying complete representation or expression [vollauf zur Geltung kommen]."

(6) To Liebknecht he wrote: "Show that freedom to criticize prevails, and if there must be expulsions, then this should occur only in cases where there are quite striking and completely provable *acts* of vileness [Gemeinheit] and betrayal."[17]

Of these quotations—and they could be matched by others like them—it is noteworthy that the first was written in 1880, the second in 1885, and the others in the nineties, that is, in the last years of

---

[17] Point (1) is from a letter to Johann Philip Becker, April 1, 1880; (2) from "On the History of the Communist League," in *Werke*, Vol. XXI, p. 215; (3) from a letter to Karl Kautsky, in Kautsky, *Aus der Fruehzeit des Marxismus, Engels' Briefwechsel mit Karl Kautsky*, Prague, 1935, p. 271; (4) Gustav Mayer, *Friedrich Engels*, Vol. II, p. 481; (5) Letter to Sorge of August 9, 1890, in *Briefe an Sorge*, pp. 343–44; (6) *Wilhelm Liebknecht Briefwechsel mit Karl Marx und Friedrich Engels*, The Hague, 1963, p. 376.

Engels's life. There was no longer a Blanqui or a Bakunin to argue with, but a powerful German Social-Democratic Party to which, in this as in other fields, Engels wanted to leave his spiritual testament before he died. Clearly, this was Engels's image of a proper democratic party, even as the quotations from the *Communist Manifesto* and the "Statutes" of the First International given above seem to show that it was Marx's.

Such were the statements on "the party" written for the eyes of others. When Marx and Engels corresponded privately, they wrote sharply, even mockingly, concerning "the party," which the Marxist-Leninist claimants of the heritage tend to deify.

Thus one cannot by the wildest stretching of the imagination think of Lenin's using such language concerning "the party" as Marx and Engels used in letters to each other at the beginning of 1851, when they found themselves isolated from the bulk of the German Communist emigration in London and read out of the group (or "party"—the Communist League) which they had been leading from 1847 to 1851, and for which they had drafted the *Communist Manifesto*. On February 11, 1851, Marx wrote to Engels:

. . . I am greatly pleased by the public, authentic isolation in which we two, you and I, now find ourselves. It corresponds completely with our position and our principles. The system of mutual concessions, the halfway positions tolerated for appearances' sake, and the duty in the eyes of the public of assuming responsibility for a share of the nonsense of the party along with all these asses—all that has now come to an end.

To which Engels replied on February 13:

At last we have again—for the first time in a long while—an opportunity to show that we do not need any *support* from any party of any land whatever, and that our position is totally independent of such trash [*Lumpereien*]. From now on we are responsible only for ourselves, and when the moment comes when these gentlemen need us, we are in a position to be able to dictate our own terms. Until then we have at least tranquility. To be sure, also a certain solitude. . . .
Basically we have no ground for complaint that these petits grands hommes shun us. Have we not acted for so and so many years as if every rag-tag and bob-tail were our party, when we had no party at all, and when people whom we reckoned as belonging to our party, at least officially, *sous reserve de les appeler des bêtes incorrigibles entre nous*, didn't even understand the beginnings of our business? How do

people like us, who flee from official posts as from the pest, fit into a "party"? What is the meaning to us who spit on popularity, who mistrust ourselves when we begin to get popular, what to us is a "party," i.e. a band of asses who swear by us because they think us the likes of them? Actually it is no loss if we no longer serve as "the correct and adequate expression" of those limited dogs with whom the last few years have thrown us together.

A revolution is a pure phenomenon of nature that is led more by physical laws than by the rules which in ordinary times determine the development of society. Or rather, these rules acquire a more physical character in revolution, the material force of necessity comes more powerfully into the foreground. And, as soon as one appears as the representative of a party, one is drawn into the whirlpool of unceasing natural necessity. Only by keeping one's self *independent* while one remains in *essence* more revolutionary than the others can one for a time at least maintain one's independence as against the whirlpool, though of course in the end one is drawn in.

This position we can and must take in the next such event. Not only no official *government* post, but also as long as possible no *party* post, no committee membership, no responsibility for asses, merciless criticism for every one, and . . . then the entire business of conspiracies of muttonheads will at least not get hold of us. And that we can do. In essence we can always be more revolutionary than the phrasemakers, because we have learned something and they haven't, because we know what we want, and they don't, and *because after what we have seen for the last three years, we shall take it a great deal more coolly than any one who has an interest in the business.*

The main thing for the moment is: the possibility of getting our things into print; either in a quarterly, in which we directly attack and defend our positions against *persons;* or in thick books, where we can do without having so much as to mention any of these spiders. . . . What will come of all this clatter and chatter which the entire emigration mob is making concerning you when you answer it with a work of economics?[18]

In truth, it is hard to imagine Marx and Engels as party leaders. Each of them lacked that most elementary prerequisite: the art of handling men. Their friendship with each other from the outset was

---

[18] *Werke,* Vol. XXVII, pp. 184–85, 189–90. With the exception of the words, *government and party,* all the italicized words in the letter of Engels are in English in the original.

in some measure built on the expression of the most arrogant contempt for all those with whom they had to deal. They are acid-sharp in discussion, scornful of any expression of sentiments and ideals on the part of their comrades-in-arms, haughty and unyielding in all their intercourse with their fellows. The world of German revolutionary emigrés is pictured in their letters as a world of "idiots" and "asses" "cattle" and "pigs"—a whole menagerie of contemptible animals. This for those with literary and intellectual pretensions. When it comes to the workingmen, Engels writes that they understand nothing, that you cannot even argue with them, nor cleanly break with them. In a letter to Marx of January 14, 1848, Engels gives this description of the cream of the cream, the élite workingmen of the Communist League:

> With the League things go miserably here. Such sleepy-headedness and petty rivalry of these fellows with each other is something I could never have imagined. The Weitlingerei and Proudhonisterei [contemptuous expressions for the ideas of the two socialist workingmen, Weitling and Proudhon] are really the supreme expression of the living conditions of these asses, and so there is nothing that can be done about it. Some are genuine *Straubinger* [tramps], aging *Knoten* [louts], the rest in the way of becoming petty bourgeois. A class which lives like the Irish by driving down the wages of the French, is totally useless. I shall now make one more last attempt, si cela ne réussit pas, je me retire de cette espèce de propagande. [if that doesn't succeed, I shall retire from this sort of propaganda, i.e. among German revolutionary workers in exile in Paris].[19]

Actually, Marx and Engels were intellectual snobs, with contempt for all the literary and intellectual emigrés with whom they had to work, and haughty scorn for the poor exiled journeyman workers who in France could get employment only at odd jobs. Engels thus habitually refers to them as *Straubinger,* that is to say, journeymen who continue their journeyman period, the old German custom of wandering from job to job, all their lives, never succeeding in becoming full-fledged master workmen. They were "tramps" and "louts" with the intellectual limitations of a ludicrous, lifelong journeyman-apprenticeship. Such were the individual workingmen-in-the-flesh with which Marx and Engels found themselves together in the Communist League.

But when it came to the workers-as-a-class, a *class-in-itself* on the road to becoming a *class-for-itself,* Marx and Engels assigned to

---

[19] *Ibid.,* p. 111.

them the highest role ever allotted to any class in the history of man! To this strange ambiguity, this contradiction between personal reactions to individual workers-in-the-flesh and social theories as t the role of the workingmen-as-a-class we shall have to return. In an case, their instinctive and ever-present haughtiness made these tw friends unfitted for the task of day-to-day leadership of a real party-in-being made up of such *Straubinger* and *Knoten*.

But for Marx there was a real party, living like one of the ideal patterns of Plato in the brain of their conceiver, which was something quite different from the little circles of the Communist League which Marx so readily and arbitrarily dissolved, to which he and Engels referred with such scorn, and from which they broke away in the autumn of 1850 with a genuine sense of relief. Alongside this transient *party-of-the-moment*, a mere pallid reflection of the image in Marx's mind, there was *the* Party, the only *real* party . . . music of the future, foreknown, imagined, anticipated, impatiently awaited, sure to come in the fullness of time: the organized movement of the proletariat as a whole, the party in the grand historical sense on the scale which History demanded and scientifically based prophecy foresaw.

When the poet Freiligrath refused to help Marx in his libel suit against the Berlin *Allgemeine Zeitung*, which had published the slanderous assertion of Karl Vogt that Marx and his followers in the Communist League had been conspirators secretly connected with the Prussian police, Marx appealed to the poet's sense of solidarity with the Communist League to which he had belonged, "as your old party comrade and old personal friend." Marx disliked writing in sentimental terms and he did so stiffly when he attempted it. But in his appeals of February 8 and February 23, 1860 to Freiligrath, he wrote with unfamiliar sentiment. The second letter reminded the poet that

> . . . each of us in his own way put aside private interests and from the purest motives for years waved high over the philistines the banner on behalf of the *classe la plus laborieuse et la plus miserable.* . . .

It was the honor of the party, which had been proud to number Freiligrath among its members, that Karl Vogt was now impugning; Marx was sure that the poet could not stand aside, indifferent.

To this Freiligrath answered that he had felt a positive release when the *Bund* was dissolved in 1852. "My nature," he said, "and that of every poet, needs freedom! The party is a cage, too, and one sings, even for the party itself, better outside of it than within."

Marx responded on February 29 with an attempt to explain to his former comrade-in-arms the difference between the insignificant and transitory party called the Communist League, to which they had both belonged, and the platonic ideal of a party that was in his head and in gestation in the pregnant womb of history:

> First of all I want to observe that from that moment when, in November 1852, *on my motion*, the League was dissolved, I have *never* again belonged either to a *secret* or to an *open* association, and therefore, a *party* in this entirely ephemeral sense of the word doesn't even exist for me for the past eight years.

The lectures he delivered after his book on political economy appeared in 1859, Marx explained, were before *open* organizations of workingmen to which he did not belong. When a German Communist emigré turned banker had written from New York urging Marx to revive the Communist League, Marx answered curtly that "since 1852 I am *not* connected *with any* organization and am deeply convinced that my theoretical labors bring greater advantage to the working class than participation in organizations the time for which has passed." So too when Gustav Levy came to him from Düsseldorf to urge that the workingmen of the Rhineland were ready for insurrection if Marx would summon them, "I sharply opposed such a useless and dangerous piece of *folly*," and for his pains he was denounced in Germany for his "doctoral indifference." Now he comes to the core of his thought:

> And so of a *"party"* in the sense in which you write of it, I know nothing *since 1852*. If you are a *poet*, then I am a *critic*, and really I have had quite enough of the experience [inside the party] between 1849 and 1852. The "League," like the Société des Saisons in Paris, like hundreds of other organizations of the kind, was only an episode in the history of the party, which everywhere forms itself like a phenomenon of nature growing spontaneously out of the soil of modern society. . . . I have tried to dispel the misunderstanding that by "Party" I mean the "League" that has ceased to exist since eight years ago, or the editorial board which went out of existence twelve years ago. By party I meant the party in the great historical sense.[20]

---

[20] I have translated the letters to Freiligrath from the Russian, as given in *K. Marks i F. Engels, Sochineniya*, Isdanie vtoroe, Tom XXX, Moscow, 1963, pp. 362, 373–76, 398–407. Excerpts from Freiligrath's letters (not given in the Marx-Engels *Sochineniya*) may be found in the original German along with excerpts in German of Marx's replies in Werner Blumenberg, *op. cit.*, p. 124. The "editorial board" referred to in Marx's letter is that of the *Neue Rheinische Zeitung* to which Freiligrath belonged.

Such then is the party as conceived by Marx and Engels; such the law of its anticipated spontaneous growth "like a phenomenon of nature" out of the elementary class struggles of the working class until, in the fullness of time, the class itself has developed out of experience and error, full solidarity, full consciousness, and full unity of the class as a whole in an all-inclusive workingman's party.

Surely it would seem that all these ideas of the party are at the opposite pole of social thought and social optimism from Lenin. At the opposite pole, too, from Trotsky's self-destroying statement to the Thirteenth Congress of his party in 1924: "My party—right or wrong. . . . I cannot be right against the party . . . for history has not created other ways of the realization of what is right." At the opposite pole from the Marxist-Leninist deification of the *apparat,* the party machine, and its discipline (when Lenin, or one of his successors, is dishing it out). At the opposite pole from Lenin's readiness to split the party and the class again and again into smaller and smaller self-selected "ruling bodies," that profess no matter how few they number, that they have the right to speak for "the majority," for "the party," and "the class"; from Lenin's readiness to split on a single phrase in the program, or a single clause in the bylaws, on a single *alleinseligmachende* dogma, or tactical move, or interpretation. At the opposite pole, too, from Lenin's exclusive, self-selected élite that is to use the working class to realize the élite's ideas, not to serve the working class in realizing its own ideas; is to inject socialist ideas into the working class in spite of the latter's "petty bourgeois" instincts; that is to rule in the class's name, dictating to the working class what it is proper for workingmen to want, and dictating in the name of the working class over all other classes in society.

Lenin's idea of the relation of class to party and Marx's can be reconciled to each other intellectually, or rather verbally, by four acts of Leninist legerdemain, four feats of semantic juggling, four fundamental falsehoods achieved by four acts of arbitrary redefinition.

The first is the confusing of the proletariat with the people. The second is the confusing of the Party with the proletariat. The third is the confusing of the Party machine (the Central Committee, the Politburo, the Presidium, the Secretariat, the Apparat) with the Party. The fourth is the confusing of the *Vozhd* or leader with the Central Committee and the *Apparat.* All four are inventions of

Lenin. All four represent examples of what Isaac Deutscher has (rather reluctantly and awkwardly) termed "substitutionism." The trick of substitution has grown stale by endless repetition, but Lenin's heirs do not dare dispense with any of the four substitutions, or their world would come tumbling down. All four represent a strange fulfillment of a prophecy made by the young Leon Trotsky in his more orthodox-Marxist and anti-Leninist period when he foretold that Lenin's methods of organization, if followed, would bring about a situation where "the organization of the Party takes the place of the Party itself; the Central Committee takes the place of the Organization; and finally, the Dictator takes the place of the Central Committee."

It would seem eminently clear then that the ambiguities in the matter of the relationship of party to class and of the dictatorship of a class to the dictatorship of a party, are ambiguities in one branch of the claimants to the heritage (the Marxist-Leninists), but not in the heritage itself. And yet . . . And yet . . .

First, there is the magnificent presumption of Marx's claim to base his prescriptions and prophecies on the knowledge of the scientific laws of history and society. At the moment when Marx was, so to speak, just becoming a Marxist, he was already telling the proletariat that it was predestined to fulfill a mission which he foreknew, and which was determined for it by history and science:

It is not a question [he declared] of what this or that proletarian, or even the entire proletariat at one time or another *imagines* to be its goal. It is a matter of what [the proletariat] is, and what in accordance with that *being*, it will historically be forced to do.[21]

This foreknowledge, a feeling masked as scientific knowledge that he was privy to the arcane reality beneath the superficial appearances, would seem to be a part of Marx's temperamental makeup, for in September 1843, before he had discovered either socialism or the proletariat, he was telling something strangely similar not to a class but to "the world." In an open letter to Arnold Ruge, intended for publication in Ruge's *Deutsch-Franzoesische Jahrbuecher* as part of "An Exchange of Letters for 1843," Marx wrote:

We do not approach the world in doctrinaire fashion with a new principle: Here is the truth, kneel down here! We develop for the

---

[21] *Werke*, Vol. II, p. 39.

world out of the principles of the world new principles. We do not say to it: Leave off your struggles, they are a silly thing; we will cry out to you the true slogan for the struggle. We only show it why it is really struggling, and that consciousness is something which it *must* acquire even if it does not desire to do so. The reform of consciousness consists *only* in this, that one makes the world master of its consciousness, that one awakes it from its dream about itself, that one *explains* to it its own actions. . . .[22]

Second, there is the "energetic, revolutionary dictatorship" that Marx thought must follow any revolution, whether democratic or socialist.

To understand this better, let us examine his criticism of the Frankfurt Assembly in 1848 for being neither energetic nor dictatorial enough.

The Frankfurt Assembly arose out of insurrections in a number of German towns, and particularly barricades in Berlin and Vienna. The German nation was then a congeries of assorted despotisms, states much stronger than the social units over which they ruled through police, armed forces, and bureaucracy responsible only to the rulers. There was censorship, prohibition of organization, no legal right of opposition, no provision for the advocacy and accomplishment of constitutional, legal, peaceful change. What democrat can doubt that under these conditions revolution was justified?

Having arisen out of a democratic revolutionary movement, the Frankfurt Assembly conceived of its task as that of a Constituent Assembly, charged with writing a new constitution and providing a new representative and responsible government for Germany. Once this task was accomplished, it would conduct appropriate elections under the new constitution, then hand over its powers to the new democratic government. In short, it was a government such as democratic revolutions produce, having the self-limiting virtue—a simple test of democratic revolutions—of regarding itself as a provisional government, and desiring to give up its powers as soon as possible to the legitimate democratic government which its pre-legitimate, constitution-making functions would call into being.[23]

From the standpoint of elementary political wisdom, Marx was

---

[22] *Werke,* Vol. I, pp. 345–46.
[23] For the excellent term *pre-legitimate* as applied to a provisional government which has sprung from the rupture of monarchic-absolutist legitimacy and aims to establish a new democratic legitimacy to which to hand over its powers, I am indebted to the Italian historian, Guglielmo Ferrero.

undoubtedly right in his criticism of the Frankfurt Assembly. A government that arose out of a democratic revolution and aimed to draw up a democratic constitution (in this case a limited monarchy and a representative parliament vested with the powers that spring from popular sovereignty), had the duty to safeguard its existence by reorganizing the administrative and military apparatus in order to prevent court, generals, officials, and their supporters from restoring the old order whose defeat had called it into being. In Marx's words, it required:

> . . . a dictatorship, and an energetic dictatorship at that . . . to shatter and eliminate the remnants of old institutions . . . to proclaim the sovereignty of the people . . . work out the new constitution on the basis of the popular sovereignty of the German people . . . and from the existing conditions in Germany eliminate everything which contradicted the principle of popular sovereignty . . . to take the necessary measures to safeguard its own existence and the conquests of the revolution from all attacks.[24]

In short, democracy and dictatorship, as we have already suggested in the preceding chapter, are not opposites: there is such a thing as a *democratic dictatorship*, whatever abuse Lenin may have made of the term. But its hallmarks are (1) that it considers itself provisional and acts accordingly; and (2) that it uses energetic measures to prevent conspirators, whether they profess to call themselves "Right" or "Left," from overthrowing it and establishing a new despotism.

The Provisional Government of 1917 which Lenin overthrew, had the grace to regard itself as provisional, but it did not meet the second test. It did not have the energy or the understanding to prevent the overthrow of the nascent democracy which was simultaneously attacked from "right" and "left." It has been argued that it did not have the force-in-being for such a defense, yet I cannot help thinking that what it really lacked was the will to call such a force into being and to use it energetically. Its will was paralyzed by the fateful shibboleth that has paralyzed the will of so many provisional governments of liberal democrats and democratic socialists, the shibboleth which proclaims *Pas d'ennemi à gauche!* The terms, right and left, now approaching their two-hundredth birthday, having

---

[24] These proposals and others like them are scattered through the various articles Marx wrote in the *Neue Rheinische Zeitung*, beginning with its first issue on June 1, 1848. That first lead article, entitled "The Frankfurt Assembly," is in *Werke*, Vol. V, pp. 14–17.

arisen out of an accident of seating in an assembly hall, became meaningless even during the French Revolution itself, as the parties shifted their stands on such fundamental matters as the terror, autocratic and personal dictatorship, equalitarianism, mob rule, and a host of other problems. They have been emotion-arousing labels ever since, an obstacle to clear thought in politics, sociology and history, not to mention everyday journalistic analysis. In any case, from the standpoint of a democratic revolution and its aim of establishing democracy, both a "right" conspiracy and a "left" conspiracy represent an autocratic, dictatorial counterrevolution, followed by ruthless terror, and the abolition of popular sovereignty.

Having followed Marx in his criticism of the Frankfurt Assembly, let us carry the matter one step further. Suppose the Assembly had been energetic in breaking up the apparatus of counter-revolution, and, having written a democratic constitution and held elections under it, had succeeded in handing over its powers intact to the new democratic government. What then?

Here Marx has nothing to offer. If he regarded democracy as valuable in itself, he has little to say on it. But to democrats it should be obvious that once a democracy has been created and has introduced procedures for peaceful and lawful change by ordinary majorities won by peaceful persuasion, once it has introduced the assumption that one's opponents are also human, and the idea that the party in power must recognize responsible limits in the measures it takes to keep itself in power and defeat the opposition, and that the opposition must accept responsible limits in the methods it uses to oppose the party-in-power and to seek its own victory—it should be obvious that such a democracy has the right, nay more, the duty to defend itself. Since the procedures just enumerated represent some measure of consensus as well as difference, this defense is normally taken on both by government and opposition, for to both the consensus is precious as are the civilized, tolerant and responsible ways of settling differences; the respect for the humanity of one's opponents; the freedom to organize, speak and write in advocacy of one's views; the control of the state by society through its component organizations, electoral procedures, and procedures for the redress of grievances; and the pluralism and openness of democratic society.

On those who regard these things as precious landmarks in man's efforts to improve the organization of his society, and his government of himself, devolves the duty to defend these achievements against any party or movement aiming to subvert the democratic process itself. Nothing is more paralyzing than the loose thinking which leads conservatives to say *pas d'ennemi à droite* and liberals and democratic socialists, *pas d'ennemi à gauche*. For such antidemocratic parties, even when they claim with unction that they are themselves using democratic process, aim only to use the rights granted them until they attain power by whatever method, whereupon they abolish the multiparty system, the right of organization, advocacy, and opposition, and other democratic rights, first for all other parties, and then (although this may not be their intention) inside their own party. This last is but natural for, if they permitted opposition and groupings within their single party, the rest of the population, deprived of its right to form parties, would center its hopes on one or another grouping in the single ruling party, whereupon the pluralism of the multiparty system would tend to break through the crust of single-party despotism once more.

Against such a counterrevolutionary conspiracy whether of "right" or "left," democracy must use effective means and means worthy of itself. But such means involve a wider range than is generally imagined: from the outlawing of conspirative organizations, to martial law, state-of-siege, temporary delegation of emergency powers to the responsible executive, according to the degree of need or peril.

Those who conspire to destroy freedom for others (and, though they know it not, for themselves) forfeit among men who cherish freedom any right to conspire to destroy it. If they are permitted to organize and preach their antidemocratic doctrines and engage in their antidemocratic conspiracies, the degree of that permission should be measured by the convenience and safety of democracy itself. In any case, it can only be so long as and to the extent that their activities do not constitute a real, "clear and present danger" to democracy.[25]

When Mussolini fell in 1945, the masses of Italy having been so long cut off from political air and light, there was great danger that the country would stumble out of fascist totalitarianism into communist. At that point all the democratic parties from conservative to

---

[25] Many of these matters are examined and argued with great cogency and sophistication in several works of one of our leading political philosophers, Sidney Hook, namely: *Heresy, Yes—Conspiracy, No* (New York 1953); *Common Sense and the Fifth Amendment* (1957); *The Paradoxes of Freedom* (1962).

Christian Democrat and Democratic Socialist united to advance one single, common slogan: *Votate adesso o non votarete mai!* (Vote now, or you may never vote again!)

And indeed, a democratic party, whether conservative or radical or socialist, may win any number of elections, and always there will be another election. But once a totalitarian party wins, whether communist or fascist makes no difference, it abolishes all other parties along with democratic pluralism, and openness. It abolishes, too, the whole electoral machinery, or still worse, humiliates the populace by forcing it to participate in the mockery of one-party "elections."[26]

Third, we must take a closer look at the "scientific" certitudes of Marx and their implications for dictatorship and democracy, and for the relationship between class and party and government.

"It is not a question," Marx tells us, "of what this or that proletarian, or even the entire proletariat imagines to be its goal. It is a matter of what it is . . . and what it will historically be forced to do."

And what if History fails to force the working class to accept the goal that Marx's science has assigned to it? What if enslavement and degradation, or corruption, or willfulness, or caprice, should be such as to unfit it for, or cause it to reject, the mission of redeeming all mankind? What if the proletariat stubbornly continues to choose other goals or other methods than this "science" prescribes?

Assuming as Marx does, that all rule is class rule: how does the rule of a party or a class which comes to power armored with a scientific doctrine concerning politics, economics, and society, differ from the rule of a government which lacks such certain knowledge? Once such a government, by whatever means, comes to power, can it permit its decisions and its actions, based as they are on science, to be challenged, or outvoted, or reversed by ignorant numbers from whatever class or classes? If it knows what is right and what is good and what is historically necessary for society, can it permit society blindly to interfere with the right, the good, and the historically foreordained and necessary?

Are the certitudes which go with the possession of an infallible doctrine (more infallible, less tentative, and less alive after Marx's

---

[26] *Cf.* the statement of Maurice Thorez, General Secretary of the French Communist Party: "Some day the Premier will be a Communist. Perhaps after I am gone. All that matters is that it shall be the last cabinet in France." (Cited in the obituary of Thorez, *New York Times,* July 13, 1964.)

death than in his lifetime) any longer subject to challenge? Are
these certitudes of the same order as the certitude (if that's the word
for it) that democratic process is worth defending against its enemies? Does not the kind of certitude which carries with it built-in
answers to the problems of man-in-society foreclose many and significant questions which the kind of certitude that merely concerns
itself with the value of democratic process tends to leave open? Does
the possession of all the answers to all the major questions lead
logically and psychologically to a closed society? Does not the possession of an infallible doctrine lead to the need for an infallible interpreter, lest the party and its single truth fall to pieces in a war of
rival sacred texts and rival interpretations?

Finally, there is the question of the very possibility of the dictatorship of an entire class, or for that matter, how and to what
extent an entire class can ever rule in a complex government. Has
the political history of modern times ever known a party which
embraces a whole class? Can this be said even of the British Labour
Party with its trade-union affiliation and its local clubs, a party
which comes nearer to being that of a class than any other? It was
precisely this "class party" that Marx and Engels treated with contempt. And countless workingmen, affiliated or no, have always
voted the Conservative or the Liberal ticket.

What does it mean to say "the organization of the proletariat as
an independent political party"? Is this a matter of membership or
ideology? Does the entire proletariat, more or less, enter the party,
pay dues, select officers, determine candidates, determine policies
and program, accept the tenets of the unchallengeable social science
and science of history? How does an entire class dictate? rule? exercise its *Herrschaft*?

And what of those workingmen who disagree with the doctrine
as applied in action? What if they be numerous? What if for decade
after decade they are silent or recalcitrant, except under compulsion?

What of those countries where each party continues to be an
interclass or a multiclass party, and, so far as we can tell, incurably
so? Or where the party programs and support come from congeries
of interest groups, sectional interests, differing attitudes toward
large political questions, differing tempers and temperaments? What
of the countries where a particular religion is a rallying point for a
party, Catholics and Protestants, Christian Democrats and Secu-
larists, Christians and Moslems, Hindus and Moslems, differing lin-

guistic and cultural areas, rural areas more or less classlessly united against urban areas, linguistic rivalries? Shall all these varieties of nonclass or multiclass parties be disfranchised though they represent significant segments of the popular will, until they have been made to see the light of the science which bids them believe that parties must represent classes, that each class must have its party, one party and no more, and that parties must be ranked respectively as representing the past, the present, and the future? And what of those democracies where there are innumerable parties, all of them minority parties, and a workable democratic government is possible only through ever-shifting compromise and coalition?

The flood of questions wells up endlessly from the depths of political and historical reality. But the answers are not to be found in the science of the founding fathers. Nor are the questions either, for the two founders were not very sophisticated politically, and little given to empirical political investigation and reflection on their presuppositions. Moreover, only near the end of their lives did they even have a chance to watch the developing and multiform mechanisms of democracy which were to arise in rich and varying forms in various countries only after their death.

Though in the last decade or so of Marx's life and in the last two decades in the life of Engels, they began to attach an additional importance to democracy (something we shall consider in the next chapter), they found no answers to such questions as the above, nor did they come to attach any great importance to the questions. Yet all these questions call in question the scope of their own democratic views, the limits they set upon democracy, and the self-confident priority which they gave to other, supposedly overriding, aspects of their science.

Certainly, the claimants of the heritage in the twentieth century have felt the force of these questions and the ambiguity or inadequacy of the Marxian heritage to give answers. Some have reacted by rejecting the democratic aspects of Marxism in favor of totalitarian dictatorship; others have diluted the certitudes to the point where they are compatible with democracy as understood by those not possessed of a "science of society." Others have rejected Marxism as a "materialist science" in favor of a return to a view of social goals and values as matters of ethics. Some have abandoned Marx's recipe for irreversible and final verdicts on the direction in which history must go. Some have dropped the totalist elements in favor of pluralism, give-and-take, compromise, tireless piecemeal renovation and reform as a never-ending task in which each reform may create its own new problems to be corrected. Some have abandoned total nationalization for a mixed economy and a welfare state. Some have rejected the mystery of the State which by seizing and running everything was miraculously to wither away. And there are many other shadings which move imperceptibly toward the end of the political spectrum where stand the nonsocialist believers in a democratic society. But, except for those who have seized upon, and monstrously enlarged the dogmatic, "certitudinous," holistic, totalist, authoritarian and dictatorial elements in Marxism, few of the others have continued to call themselves *Marxists*. Where they do, it is largely a matter of inertia or residual piety.

Chapter 12

CATACLYSM OR CONTINUING

REVOLUTION?

> That period of social development in which democratism
> and socialism were fused in one indissoluble, indivisible
> whole (as was the case in the epoch of Chernshevsky) has
> fallen into eternity without chance of return. Now there is
> already and decisively no soil for that idea—which up to this
> moment has in some places persisted among Russian social-
> ists, which has had extremely harmful influence both on their
> theory and their practice—that in Russia, supposedly, there is
> not a deep qualitative difference between the ideas of the
> democrats and those of the socialists. Quite the opposite
> is true: between these ideas lies an entire abyss, and it has
> long been high time that Russian socialists understood this,
> understood the INEVITABILITY and THE URGENT NE-
> CESSITY OF A FULL and FINAL BREAK with the ideas
> of the democrats.
>
> —Lenin in September 1894

IN THE LAST decade of his life Marx became aware of a change
taking place in the institutional structure of Western Europe,
namely, its political democratization. Engels survived Marx by another dozen years, almost to the end of the nineteenth century,
hence he lived to witness the further spread of universal manhood
suffrage, the continuing erosion of tax and property qualifications
for voting, and the growth of the power of representative parlia-
ments over the administrative machinery of the Western countries.
These changes compelled Marx and Engels to re-examine many of

the formulas they had taken from their image of the Great French Revolution, or carried with them as intellectual impedimenta from the stormy years, 1848 and 1849.

In his pamphlet on the Paris Commune, the actual measures Marx chose to praise were measures of democratization: the direct election of all councilors and officials by universal suffrage; officials responsible to their electors through instructions or imperative mandate and the right of recall; judges to be "elective, responsible and revocable . . . divested of their sham independence"; the separation of church and state and the secularization of public education; cheap government; depoliticalization and communal control of the police; abolition of the standing army and its replacement by a popular militia; appointment of administrative heads by the municipal council, etc. "The Commune," Marx writes, "supplied the Republic with the basis of really democratic institutions. . . . Its special measures could but betoken a government of the people by the people."[1]

If the experience of both democracies and dictatorships suggests that the independence of the judiciary from sudden upsurges of popular passion or from the intervention of the executive or a ruling party is neither "a sham" nor an evil, none of the measures Marx lauds is incompatible with democracy. All of them are to be found in one or another of the effective democratic governments of our day.

Both by temperament and by the formative influences of his reaction to German particularism, Marx was no believer in federalism as a democratic device, yet he felt he could not choose but praise the proposal of the Paris Commune to make France into a Federation of Communes.

Switzerland has made such federalism the very foundation of its constitution; Sweden in the twentieth century permitted Norway to exercise the right of self-determination to the point of secession; many of our own western states have introduced the initiative, referendum, recall, and the right of repeal of a law by referendum, without shaking the fabric of democracy.

As for the social welfare measures Marx praised, abolition of nightwork for journeyman bakers and the prohibition of fines as deductions from factory wages, these are trifles compared with the sweep of protective labor and social-security legislation in any mod-

---

[1] See above, Chapter VIII.

ern democratic state. If the Commune with its universal suffrage and other democratic measures was indeed "the political form under which to work out the economic emancipation of labor," as Marx wrote, still one would think that it was up to labor to determine whether it desired to use its suffrage to "shatter" the existing order, or, with the assent and support of other classes of voters, to reform it by incorporating into law and practice such measures as the collective bargaining, labor protection, and social welfare legislation which the workingmen have since won.

Marx's appraisal of the democratic measures adopted by the Paris Commune was published as an Address of the General Council of the International Workingmen's Association in June 1871. The Franco-Prussian War and then the Commune commanded all the attention of the International, so that no meetings of the representatives of its various sections were held in 1870 or 1871. Marx and Engels, both in London now, devoted their full energies to the reconstruction of the International. Their conception of "reconstruction" involved the adoption of a clear resolution in favor of the formation of an independent political party of the working class in each country, and a change in the Statutes of the International which would give the General Council power to expel any national section which disobeyed its decisions. The faction fight which broke out on these two questions ended only with Marx's capture of the Hague Congress of 1872 (examined elsewhere in the present work) and his transfer of the General Council to America for inglorious burial.

On September 8, 1872, just one day after Marx and his faction had thus violated internal democracy in the hitherto federalist International by packing the Hague Congress and expelling Bakunin, he made the most striking of his statements on political democracy in society as a whole. A mass meeting in honor of the Hague Congress had been arranged by a pro-Marxist local of the International in Amsterdam. The speakers included Marx himself, Engels, Lafargue, Sorge, Becker, and other lesser known Marx-followers. What was said there remains unrecorded except for the words of the "Red Terrorist Doctor" who had earned his sobriquet and become front-page news since his espousal of the fallen Commune. Accounts of his address appeared in the *Algemeen Handelsblad* of Amsterdam and *la Liberté* of Brussels, and, somewhat later, in the Social Democratic *Volkstaat* of Leipzig. These accounts differ from each other in secondary details, but in the things that concern us here, there is general and striking agreement. Marx declared that the working class must conquer political power in all countries in order to establish a "new organization of labor."

But we do not assert [Marx continued] that the way to attain this goal is the same in all countries. We know that the institutions, the customs, and traditions of the various countries must be taken into account, and we do not deny that there are countries like England and the United States, and, if I understood your institutions better, I might perhaps add Holland, where the worker may attain his object by peaceful means.

Thus the speech is reported in the *Volkstaat* of October 2, 1872. In the Brussels *Liberté*, the same declaration that political control may be won peacefully by the workingmen in England, the United States, and perhaps Holland, is followed by a sentence reading:

Though this may be true, we must recognize that in most countries of the Continent violence must be the driving force of our revolution.

In the report of *Algemeen Handelsblad*, published the day after Marx spoke, indirect discourse is used throughout:

The speaker defends the use of violence, where other means do not help. In North America, barricades are unnecessary because there, if they do but want to, the proletariat can win victory at the polls. The same applies to England and some other countries where the working class has the right to speak out. But in the great majority of states revolution has to be substituted for legality because otherwise—by a wrong generosity, or a falsely directed sense of justice—one could not attain one's ends.[2]

All the accounts make one thing clear, that Marx had come to the conclusion that violence and barricades are necessary only in lands where there is no universal suffrage and no democratic institutional set-up. It was not the first time that he had spoken of violent revolution and the shattering of the existing state machinery as necessary to "any real revolution on the Continent." But by adding Holland as a possible example to England and America, concerning which he entertained no doubts, Marx shows that he has begun to extend the concept of peaceful political action to any land with universal suffrage and plenary parliamentary powers. Almost a

---

[2] All three versions are reproduced in *Bulletin of the International Institute of Social History,* Leiden, No. 1, 1951, and, in a condensed version in Gerth, *op. cit.*, pp. 236–37.

quarter of a century of life in England and a close watching of the rise of the antislavery party in the United States had convinced him that in such lands the task of the socialist movement is that of persuasion rather than conspiracy. They must win the support of the majority of workingmen, organize them in trade unions, cooperatives, and an independent political party of labor,[3] and seek to win the support of other feasible sections of the population. This is an important revision of the barricade Marxism of 1848–50, and a recognition of a fundamental element in the political structure of two, or perhaps three, democratic countries.

In 1891 Engels explicitly added France to the list of such countries, something which neither he nor Marx could have done in the seventies, when the fate of the French Republic was still in doubt. The same extension of universal suffrage and supreme parliamentary power was, or was soon to become, true of Belgium, Denmark, Norway, and Sweden, all of whom were later to vote peacefully into power Social Democratic, or Labor Party, or Socialist-coalition governments. In short, as universal suffrage, parliamentary prerogative, and civil liberties were extended in land after land, and as monarchy gave way to republic, or the powers of the monarchs were reduced to symbolic functions, peaceful democratic and social change seemed possible to the two old barricade-fighters in constitutional monarchies and democratic republics alike.[4]

The real puzzler for Engels in his last years was his own native

---

[3] In his *Inaugural Address of the International Workingmen's Association* Marx suggested the following order of development: (1) organization of labor in unions; (2) struggle for labor legislation; (3) organization of cooperatives on a national scale; (4) the conquest of political power.

[4] As an American nurtured in the tradition of perfervid antimonarchism, I can remember the astonishment I felt when I found myself telling a class of students that the "best governed and least corrupt countries in the modern world were England, Belgium, Holland, Norway, Sweden, and Denmark," monarchies all. In recent times labor governments have come to power peacefully in all of them. These governments have introduced a substantial degree of nationalization and government regulation of private enterprise and finance, sweeping systems of social welfare and labor legislation, and favorable conditions for independent, nongovernmental cooperatives. These provisions, for well or ill, have been left untouched, sometimes even further enlarged, by subsequent conservative or nonlabor governments, when the continuing "peaceful revolutions" of democratic elections turned labor out of office. Whether, or at what point, this combination of nationalization, economic regulation, welfare-state measures, planning and cooperatives, can be termed "socialism," I leave to semanticists to decide. Those who have another idea of what socialism means have simply not been able to convince a majority of voters, or any considerable number of workingmen-voters either, in any of these countries.

land. Germany, as he well knew, was a semi-absolute monarchy, with absolute power for the Emperor in the appointment of generals, command of the Army, and selection of a Chancellor for the Reich. De facto he controlled the *Bundesrat*. In Prussia a system of weighted or plural voting gave the privileged representation out of all proportion to their numbers, and the poor startling under-representation. In the same article of 1891 in which Engels added France to the roster of democratic countries, he warned that Germany was badly in need of constitutional reform, without which the institutional structure might "have to be broken as violently as a crab has to break its old shell."

> One can conceive [he continued] that the old society can grow peacefully into the new in countries where popular representation concentrates all power in itself, where one can do constitutionally what one will as soon as one has the majority of the people behind one; in democratic republics like France and America, and in monarchies like England . . . where the dynasty is powerless against the will of the people.[5]

In his last years Engels was increasingly stirred to pride by the great forward-strides of the German Social Democratic Party in each succeeding election, and the ever-larger aggregation of Social Democratic Deputies appearing in the Reichstag. He looked with ever greater hope on the army, too, whose ranks conscription was filling each year with larger numbers of socialist voters and card-carrying young Social-Democratic workingmen. The figure of speech of a crab molting its old shell as it grew in size was after all an organic one: he could not bring himself to believe that archaic constitutional barriers could withstand the swelling might of the party that was the pride of his old age. Before we examine Engels's last writings on this subject, it might be well to take a closer look at the structure of the German Empire as it was before 1918.

The new Germany that Bismarck had fashioned by his three lightning wars was a federation of over twenty previously autonomous kingdoms and principalities. By excluding Austria, Bismarck had contrived that Prussia should outweigh the other twenty-three.

---

[5] Friedrich Engels, "Zur Kritik des sozialdemokratischen Programmentwurfes," 1891, in *Marx-Engels-Lenin-Stalin zur Deutschen Geschichte*, Vol. II, Part 2, Berlin, 1954, pp. 1133–34; also in *Neue Zeit*, Vol. XX (1901–02), pp. 5–6, 9–13.

Only Bavaria and Saxony had sufficient size and standing to serve as even partial counterweights. It was Prussia that had won the victories, and with them the new all-German loyalty of the Empire's inhabitants. Five-eighths of the population of the new Reich was Prussian. The ruling house of Prussia, the Hohenzollerns, became the ruling house of the Reich. The core of the army was Prussian. Only Prussia possessed the requisite economic resources to build a modern state. The chief minister of the Hohenzollern court was usually appointed Imperial Chancellor by the Emperor, for the Emperor had the right to appoint and remove the Chancellor at will. All proposals to change the army, navy, taxes, had to have Prussia's approval. Berlin was the capital both of Prussia and the Empire. Only Bavaria, because of its special position as the leading kingdom of Catholic South Germany, was permitted to retain control over its own army and its own foreign service.

The new Imperial Parliament, the Reichstag, seemed an impressive enough body. It was chosen (unlike the Prussian Landtag) by equal, universal, male suffrage, and it represented the nation as a whole. But its powers were limited by the powers retained by the Emperor, and still more by the fact that it was only the lower house of a bicameral legislature, of which the upper house was a weird patchwork of survivals from medieval particularist Germany.

The *Bundesrat* or Upper House (Federal Council) represented the German princes, twenty-two monarchs and three free cities. The Emperor, as King of Prussia, possessed seventeen votes in the Council! And three more as trustee for Alsace and Lorraine! The King of Bavaria came next with six votes, then the King of Saxony with three. No wonder German revolutionists like Marx and Engels detested the only federalism they knew and were such ardent centralists! Moreover, Marx's centralism was reinforced by the authoritarian streak in his own character, by his desire for a nationwide stage on which a nationwide party of the working class might act, and his notion that industry would have to be centrally nationalized or "socialized" and centrally planned and directed in the new order he envisaged.

To add to the constitutional fetters on German democracy enumerated above, there was the fact that the parliamentary body of the ruling state, Prussia (like the Russian Duma later to be modeled on it) was chosen by a system of weighted or plural voting. The voting was by classes or estates whose representation was weighted according to wealth or the census of taxes paid by each group. Thus the tiny minority of the wealthiest, since they paid one-third of all taxes, got one-third of all the votes in the Prussian Landtag, while the many million-headed lowest third of taxpayers got no more than one-third of the representatives, despite its over-whelming numbers. In the year 1900, the Social Democratic Party of Prussia was already able to win a majority of all the voters in Prus-sia, yet it got only seven seats out of four hundred in the Prussian Diet!

For the Reichstag or lower house of the All-German parliament Bismarck had provided a system of universal male suffrage—one man, one vote. It was his way of enlisting the interest of all Germans in the new national union. Here in the Reichstag the Social Demo-crats became a truly formidable force, not a majority to be sure, but the largest party in the parliament and in the Reich.

In the Reichstag the military budget was voted, and the govern-ment's actions boldly judged, though not controlled. The imperial prerogatives, the medieval and undemocratic Bundesrat or upper house, the undemocratically chosen Landtag of Prussia, all com-bined to frustrate the will of the peoples' representatives. Bismarck had already showed in the sixties that he could finance the army of Prussia without the approval and against the vote of the Prussian Landtag, and though it was less likely now, some emperor and his chancellor might try it again. In 1914 the Kaiser could, and did, send the German Army into France and Belgium before convening the Reichstag to vote the war appropriations. Hence the problem of the military budget presented itself to the largest party in the Reichstag on August 4, 1914 as one of deciding whether the men already called up and entering into action—millions carrying socialist membership cards in their pockets—should be voted supplies by their own party, or "left in the lurch."

This freedom of the Kaiser and the Imperial and Prussian state machinery from popular control Marx had summed up with telling irony in his *Critique of the Gotha Program*. That program called, among other things, for a "free state and a socialist society." Marx's comment on the first phrase read:

A free state—what is that?

It is by no means the aim of the workingmen to make the state "free." In the German Empire, the "State" is almost as "free" as it is in Russia. Freedom consists in changing the state from an organ superior to society into an organ subordinated to society . . . state forms are freer or less free in proportion as the "freedom of the state" is restricted.[6]

This was captious criticism, for the authors of the Gotha Program meant by freedom what Marx meant, but since Marx was determined to show that no good could come of a union with the Lassalleans, he was not above scoring a point by semantic juggling. Yet what he said of the German state was true (as it is even more true of the "Marxist" Russian state of today): the German state was much too free from control from below.

As the Social Democratic vote grew from year to year, as the parliamentary fraction of socialists in the Reichstag came to surpass all other parties in numbers and in the talent of its spokesmen, and as the Social Democrats won an absolute majority of the popular vote in Prussia, Engels became more and more taken with the possibilities of nonviolent change in this hobbled quasi-democracy. In each year's increasing vote he saw a measure of the ripeness of the country for a socialist takeover, and gave less and less importance (in the end I think, too little) to the constitutional obstacles to a peaceful assumption of power by the German Social Democracy under the Constitution Bismarck had fashioned.

The final, and most complete statement of the view of Engels on this vexed problem appears in his introduction to a reissue of Marx's *Class Struggles in France, 1848–50*. The introduction is dated *London, March 6, 1895*—a mere five months before his death.

The introduction begins with a backward glance over his own life and Marx's. Their wild and unjustified hopes of 1848—Engels acknowledges—had been nurtured by their being "under the spell" of the French Revolution of 1789 and the Paris barricade and street fighting of 1830 and 1848.

> History has shown us to have been wrong . . . our point of view at that time to have been an illusion. . . . It has done more . . . [it has] completely transformed the conditions under which the proletariat has to fight. The mode of struggle of 1848 is today obsolete in every respect, and this is a point which deserves closer examination. . . .

In 1848 the bourgeoisie had not been played out, as Marx and he had thought, nor had the capitalist economy reached the end of its

---

[6] For the criticisms by Marx and Engels of the Gotha Program see *Werke*, Vol. XIX, pp. 3–33.

capacity for development, nor was the economy then "ripe" for the elimination of capitalism. The *national* revolutions then in gestation were not destined to be "revolutions from below, but revolutions from above." Thus things had turned out quite differently from the confident predictions in the *Communist Manifesto* and the other fighting works of 1848–50.

Both capitalism and democracy were then on the eve of a period of great expansion, a two-fold expansion which would bring in its train, among other things, a revolution of quite another kind, a revolution in the art of warfare.

The recruitment of the whole of the population capable of bearing arms into the armies that could henceforth be counted only in millions, and the introduction of firearms, projectiles, and explosives of hitherto undreamed of effectiveness, created a complete revolution in warfare. This revolution . . . put a sudden end to the Bonapartist war period, and insured peaceful industrial development by making war an impossibility, except as a world war of unheard of cruelty and absolutely incalculable outcome.

Engels spoke next of the rapid growth of German industry, the German working class, the socialist vote. "Thanks to the intelligent use which German workingmen have made of the universal suffrage introduced [by Bismarck] in 1866," the influence of the Social Democratic Party has grown astonishingly. "The hand of the state has been paralyzed . . . government and ruling classes have given tangible proofs of their impotence." Thereby

. . . the German workers have rendered a great service. . . . They have supplied their comrades in all countries with a new weapon, and one of the sharpest, by showing how to make use of universal suffrage. . . . [in ways] that have served as a model for the workers of all countries. Thus, in the words of the French Marxist program, the franchise has been *transformé de moyen de duperie qu'il a été jusqu'ici en instrument d'emancipation.*[7]

---

[7] The words quoted by Engels from a "French Marxist Program" were secretly written into that program by Marx himself. He and Engels, with the aid of the newly converted Marxist, Jules Guesde, and Marx's son-in-law, Paul Lafargue, drafted the program on the occasion of a visit of Guesde and Lafargue to London in the spring of 1880. Marx did not have his way in everything, however, for he wanted to exclude the demand for a minimum wage law, which he considered shameful. He declared that if the French proletariat was still childish enough to need such bait, it was hardly worth while drawing up a program at all. But Guesde was obdurate. Today no advanced working-class organization would agree with Marx on this but with Guesde, and minimum wage laws have been adopted in a number of countries. The entire preamble of

Universal suffrage, Engels continued, was a measure of strength and a guide to adjusting the party's tactics to that strength. But it was more than that. It provided as well "an entirely new method of proletarian struggle." It enabled Social Democrats to penetrate state institutions, to capture posts in Diets, municipal councils, industrial arbitration courts. With its help the Socialists can fight for every post for which voting determines the outcome.

And so it has come to pass that the bourgeoisie and the government have become much more afraid of the legal than of the illegal action of the workers' party, more afraid of the results of elections than of those of rebellion.

The older road to power through street-fighting, Engels found "to a significant extent obsolete." Even in 1848, victory in a barricade fight had come only as "one of the rarest exceptions" which depended more on the demoralization of the army, or the direct unreliability and defection of troops, than it did on barricade-fighting as such. The barricades and surrounding crowds had served largely only as a way of delaying the troops long enough so that the problem of their loyalty could arise within them.

In any case, by 1849 the spell of virtual unanimity in urban insurrections had broken, as by then "the bourgeoisie had thrown in its lot with that of the government."

Since that stormy period drastic alterations have been made in the physical layout of the cities, with new broad avenues down which cannon can be fired to pierce barricades and reduce them to fragments. The developing art of warfare has given decisive superiority to the weapons of the army over such arms as the populace might obtain. Things have changed "in favor of the military while on the insurgents' side conditions have grown worse." The middle layers of the population will probably never again group themselves around an insurrectionist proletariat to form a united people ranged against a reaction that has been isolated. Street-fighting must not now be altogether ruled out, but it must be regarded under these circumstances as at best exceptional and ancillary to the later course of a developing revolution. Moreover,

---

the program, including the sentence which Engels here quotes, was dictated by Marx to Guesde. His large role in the authorship of the "first French Marxist program" was kept secret so as "not to offend French sensibilities," a secrecy which enabled both Marx and Engels to quote Marx's own words with approval on more than one occasion. On the authorship of the program, see Engels to Bernstein, October 25, 1881; *Werke,* Vol. XIX, pp. 238, 570–71; Mehring, *op. cit.,* p. 548.

The revolutionist would have to be mad to himself choose the new working-class districts in the North or East of Berlin for a barricade fight. . . . The time is past for revolutions carried out by small conscious minorities at the head of unconscious masses. . . .

Even in France, Engels continued, that France in which for a hundred years governments had been made and unmade in uprisings and every party had used them—now "the socialists are realizing to an ever great extent that no lasting victory is possible unless they first win the great mass of the people, in this case, the peasants." In France, too, Socialists are learning, and must learn, to use elections.

Whatever may happen in France or elsewhere, in Germany the Social Democracy occupies a special position. It has become "the decisive *shock troops* of the international proletarian army. . . . By the end of the century (at our present rate of growth), we shall win the greater part of the middle strata . . . and become in the land the decisive power before which all other forces will have to bow."

For these reasons it is important to keep that force growing by the same methods as have so far proved so effective, important to avoid frittering away the best forces in vanguard skirmishes or permitting ourselves to be provoked into a situation which would furnish a pretext for blood-letting.

The irony of world history turns everything upside down. We, the "revolutionists" and "subverters"—are thriving far better on legal methods than on illegal methods and subversion. The Parties of Order, as they call themselves, are perishing under the legal conditions which they themselves have created. Despairingly they cry . . . *la légalité nous tue,* legality will be the death of us. Whereas under this legality we acquire strong muscles and rosy cheeks and have the look of life eternal. And, if *we* are not so mad as to let ourselves be driven to street-fighting in order to please *them,* then in the end there is nothing left for them to do but themselves break through this fatal legality.[8]

---

[8] An excellent translation of Marx's *Class Struggles in France, 1848–50, With an Introduction by Frederick Engels* was done by Henry Kuhn for publication by the Socialist Labor Party, New York, 1924. I have used here the more pedestrian translation done in Moscow in 1951 for the Marx-Engels *Selected Works,* Vol. I, pp. 109–27 (with only minor stylistic improvements in noncontroversial passages), because the Marx-Engels Institute made the charge, with great fanfare, that the Kuhn translation was "subjected to great distortion by the opportunist leadership of the German Social-Democratic Party."
Actually there were three versions of Engels's *Introduction:* (1) as it was

The Social Democracy, Engels asserted firmly, would not let itself be provoked. If the reaction should break its own rules of legality, it would only fare the worse, for in that case the Social Democracy "would be free to do with you as it pleases." Moreover, what force would the reaction use? Even now the army was gradually ceasing to be a serviceable instrument of the Government and the ruling class. Before long the army's majority would consist of Social Democrats. Thus the triumph of Social Democracy is as inevitable as was once in the Roman Empire the triumph of Christianity.

In much the same spirit, three years earlier Engels had written in *Neue Zeit* that more impressive and significant than the striking increase in the Socialist vote was the increase of Social Democrats in the army. Since the bourgeoisie is unable to get along without universal military service and takes young men at twenty but doesn't let men vote until they are twenty-five, the German army is more and more being "infected" with socialism. By 1900 or so, that "most Prussian element in Germany, the Army, would be in its majority Socialist." Thus "legality works so splendidly for us that we would be fools to break it. . . . We can afford to let them break their own laws. In the meanwhile [we politely say to them]: 'Be so good as to shoot first, *meine Herren Bourgeois!'* "[9]

Carried away by his joy at the rise of his once obscure party into the leading political party of Germany, and by his unexamined belief that a majority of workingmen in the army would make the armed forces cease to be an instrument of absolutism and bureaucracy, Engels in the last years of his life increasingly exaggerated

---

originally written by Engels; (2) as condensed by Wilhelm Liebknecht in 1895 for publication in *Vorwaerts,* a condensation which undoubtedly involved some distortion and aroused the wrath of Engels; and (3) a version published in *Neue Zeit,* by Karl Kautsky, in which certain excisions were made with Engels's express approval, for the sake of not jeopardizing the recently won legality of the hitherto outlawed Social Democratic Party. Mr. Kuhn used this third version, approved by the author, whereas the Moscow edition is an English translation of the galley proofs of Engels before the excisions were made. The fuss raised by Moscow is an attempt to reduce the awareness of the degree to which Friedrich Engels is the Number One "revisionist" of Marx's and his own violence, terror, and barricade views of 1848. The interested reader will find an account of the "falsification" charges and countercharges in Alexander Trachtenberg, "The Marx-Engels Institute," an article in the *Workers' Monthly,* Chicago, Nov. 1925, and in a pamphlet of the Socialist Labor Party entitled *Who Are the Falsifiers?* New York, 1926.

[9] *MELS,* Vol. II, pp. 1140–41. This statement is in the article Engels wrote for the *Almanac* of the French Parti Ouvrier for 1892. (See above, Chapter IV.)

the power that came with mere growth in the numbers of members, voters, and "red" soldiers. Hypnotized by these statistics, he began to underestimate the obstacles that the Bismarck constitution put in the way of the expression of the popular will.

In West Germany today, a mere majority vote would bring the Social Democrats into control of the government. In the Weimar Republic there were moments when this might have been possible, too. But it is hard to believe that within the legal framework of the First Reich any party or combination of parties could, by purely parliamentary methods, have put through a republic, or anything that Marx and Engels would have been willing to recognize as socialism. Not a single class merely, but a decisive majority of the German people would have had to want such change so intensely that it would press for it both by electoral-parliamentary and extra-parliamentary methods of considerable scope, before any basic constitutional reform could have been secured in the face of the fetters of imperial prerogatives, imperial veto, imperial control of the General Staff, the bureaucracy, and the Upper House of Princes, plural voting in Prussia, and countless other obstacles.[10]

In an occasional and somewhat too casual aside, Engels suggested that he was aware of this, as, for example, in his *Almanac* article, when he observed that his party was unwilling "to take an oath that it will never again resort to illegal methods of work if the need should arise." But such asides passed unnoticed. They were surely not of such character as to keep his party morally armed and ready for extra-parliamentary action. Moreover, Engels frowned on the very idea of a general strike[11] and gave no thought to any other

---

[10] It never occurred to Engels to ask to what extent a socialist vote represented a vote for the full program and principles of socialism, how intense the vote was, to what extent it implied that the voter would support the party in mass demonstrations, political general strikes, disobedience to superior officers in the army. In general, political science has never been able to devise a means of measuring the intensity, the scope, and the meaning of a given vote, which may range from mere habit, dislike of an opposing candidate, vague protest, or a feeling of being fed up with the other party, to last ditch support or even to going beyond the party for which the citizen has voted. For that matter there is no measure either of the intensity and meaning to a party member of his membership.

[11] See for example Engels's letter to Sorge of April 8, 1891, in which he wrote: "The Paris Miners' Congress almost broke up because of the Belgian stupidity (Bloedsinn) of a general strike. To avoid this, the English demanded that a vote be taken by numbers of workingmen which each delegate represented. That would almost certainly have given the English an absolute majority, and at this

type of extra-parliamentary action to win a democratic constitutional reform, lulling his fancy by the dream that "legality was killing" the "party of order" and the imperial structure.

Whether Engels overshot the mark or no in the case of Germany, it is abundantly clear that in their last years both he and Marx were convinced that, where there is a truly democratic constitution with universal suffrage, "where popular representation concentrates all power in itself, where one can do constitutionally what one will as soon as one has the majority of the people behind one, in democratic republics like France and America, and in monarchies like England where the dynasty is powerless against the will of the people," there "the old society can grow peacefully into the new."[12]

Lenin was at great pains to explain away these views of the democratic process in countries like England and America, Holland, Belgium, Norway, Sweden, Denmark. He did not care so much about the smaller countries of Europe, but after he came to power, England was in his mind "the main enemy." So on more than one occasion this would-be "orthodox" heir felt called upon to be, in the matter of democratic process, a drastic revisionist. In debates with Kautsky, in discussions with Bertrand Russell, in polemics against the Independent Labour Party of Great Britain, he sought to prove that the British Constitution was now such that the Labour Party

---

the others rebelled. I almost wished that the Walloon coal-miners, who this time started the whole General Strike nonsense, would actually have brought it to the point of a general strike in Belgium for universal suffrage. They would have been incurably beaten and the nonsense would have been buried." (*Briefe Friedrich Engels, Karl Marx u. A. an F. A. Sorge und Andere*, Stuttgart, 1921, p. 362.) Twelve years later, the Belgian workingmen did carry off successfully just such a strike for universal suffrage.

When Inessa Armand called this view of Engels to Lenin's attention in the course of her argument against Engels's proposal to defend his fatherland against a joint French and Russian attack, Lenin simply could not believe that Engels had ever opposed the tactics of a general strike. "Engels was right," he protested about the defense of the fatherland in 1892. "In my time I have seen painfully many hasty accusations against Engels for opportunism and I have felt extreme lack of confidence in them. Try, I say, let's see you first try to prove that Engels was wrong!! You won't be able to!! . . .

"His declaration on the Belgian General Strike? When? Where? How? I never heard of it.

"No. No. Engels is *not* infallible. Marx is *not* infallible. But to prove their 'noninfallibility' you will have to go about it differently, verily, verily, altogether differently. And in this you are a thousand times wrong." (Letter to Inessa Armand of December 25, 1916.)

12 See above, the statement of Marx in Amsterdam in 1872 and the statement of Engels of 1891 in *Zur Kritik des sozialdemokratischen Programmentwurfes.*

could never come to power peacefully. On this history has given the verdict to Marx and Engels and Kautsky, not to Lenin.

Yet if Marx and Engels began to appreciate democracy as an instrument which their movement could use for its purposes, it was those purposes, and not democracy as such, on which their attention was concentrated. In a letter to H.M. Hyndman of December 8, 1880, written by Marx in his stiff and slightly uncertain English, he makes that abundantly clear:

> If you say that you do not share the views of my party for England, I can only reply that that party considers an English revolution not *necessary*, but—according to historical precedents—*possible*. If the unavoidable evolution turns into a revolution, it would not only be the fault of the ruling classes, but also of the working class. Every pacific concession of the former has been wrung from them by "pressure from without." Their action kept pace with that pressure, and if the latter has more and more weakened, it is only because the English working class know not how to wield the power and use the liberties, both of which they possess, legally. In Germany the working class were fully aware from the beginning of their movement that you cannot get rid of military despotism but by revolution.[13]

A little later Marx told Hyndman in one of his monologue conversations that "England is the one country in which a peaceful revolution is possible; but," he added after a pause, "history does not tell us so." Though Marx was willing to have it come peacefully, both he, and history, would have nothing short of "the revolution" and nothing other than "the revolution" as he envisaged it. Nor did his appreciation of the chance for a peaceful revolution make him any more tolerant of other proposals or other views, no matter by what democratic process they might be arrived at. Writes Hyndman:

> I remember saying to him once that as I grew older I thought I became more tolerant. "Do you," he said, "*do* you?"[14]

If the British workingmen did not use their undoubted powers and liberties to make the revolution peacefully, it would have to come anyway. There were no two ways about that. At this point, Marx's qualifications as a democrat reached a dead end. For it did

---

[13] H.M. Hyndman, *The Record of an Adventurous Life,* London, 1911, p. 283.
[14] *Ibid.*, pp. 271, 273.

not occur to him, nor would his pre-possessions permit him to tolerate the idea, that workingmen, in a land where they represented a numerical majority and where they were powerful and free, might choose to use the democratic process in order to change the world in directions other than those that Marx's "scientific" system laid down for them. Though he showed moments of fragmentary comprehension, as when he eulogized the ten-hours' law, or of fragmentary incomprehension, as when he gagged at the very idea of a minimum-wage law, it never occurred to him that the British workingman, often with the support of the majority of society as a whole, might use his powers and freedoms to introduce state regulation of economic life; a mixed economy, in which what was nationalized and what was not would be a matter of pragmatic experiment; legalization of the right to organize, bargain collectively and strike; laws providing a minimum wage, maximum hours and other labor regulations; insurance coverage for sickness, accident, unemployment, and old age; medical care from womb to tomb; and all the other sweeping defenses against extreme poverty, misfortune, and disadvantage for the individual worker in the "sale of his labor power."

It must be noted that these changes were not introduced solely by labor into the English political and social structure. Labor's needs and pressure were significant factors, but England, even in Marx's day as the Parliamentary Bluebooks he used made clear, was developing a general, i.e. classless, social conscience. Most of the alterations came now from the Tory, now from the Whig majority, or from the Conservative and Liberal Parties that succeeded them.

As late as 1937, Harold Laski was still proving with Marxist clichés that the Labour Party could not possibly take control of England without a physical struggle, but at the end of World War Two the British Labour Party emerged as the leading social democratic party of the world, and, in 1945, received an overwhelming majority in Parliament, and, without let or hindrance, formed its own government. The Government of Prime Minister Atlee ruled for six years and passed two truly significant measures: It granted independence to India, thus putting an end to the Empire, and it enacted a program of comprehensive medical care from womb to tomb. Then, just as quietly, it was turned out of office in 1951. But the Conservatives made not the slightest attempt to undo what Labour in office had accomplished.

Whatever the "system" should be called that has been built in England, it is surely not the "capitalism" of Marx's schemata, nor the "socialism" with which he was so certain capitalism must be pregnant. The English people, workingmen and non-workingmen alike, have striven in their own fashion to build Jerusalem in their green and pleasant land. They have solved many of the problems that faced them in Marx's day, creating ever new problems in the process and seeking new solutions. It is not Jerusalem either, any more than it is the capitalism or the socialism of Marx's "science." Nor would any empirical social scientist of today venture to say of it as Marx did so confidently when speaking to his own country: "The industrially more developed land does but show the less developed the image of its own future: *De te fabula narratur!*" On the contrary, to us it seems likely that each land moves toward its own future in terms of its own traditions, its own institutions, its own temperament, and its own past, borrowing to be sure from the spirit of the age and from other lands, but even as it borrows, selecting and transforming what it incorporates into the living body of its own history.

Though Marx and Engels were laudably open to the awareness that the absolutist state was changing under their eyes and that the extension of democratic institutions and democratic process made a great difference in the way men settled their contests with each other—a difference so great that it compelled the two of them to jettison much of the intellectual baggage they had acquired from 1793 and 1848—yet one of the greatest Marxist errors has been absurdly to simplify and absurdly to underrate the socio-economic consequences of political democracy. And absurdly to deny to the working class and to society as a whole the autonomy to decide for themselves how they wanted to solve their own problems.

Lenin found an easier solution for the ambiguity involved in Marx's partial recognition of democratic process than did the rival claimants to the heritage. It was enough for him to ignore the discovery by Marx and Engels of political democratization and peaceful change embodied in the thought of the last period of their lives from 1872 to the death of Engels in 1895. All Lenin needed was to repeat and gloss endlessly the more violent and horrendous quotations of 1848–50. Selected passages from the *Communist Manifesto*, from the pamphlets of Marx and Engels on the clashes of 1848, from the *Circular* of March 1850, and from the Paris Commune—these made up his Bible, his catechism, and his litany of sacred texts. When his opponents reminded him of the later pronouncements, he had perforce to become a "revisionist" in this too, claiming absurdly that the England and America of his day were more like the Europe of 1848 in their tactical requirements than like the Europe of the eighties and nineties. The England of the twentieth century, he insisted, was not the England of the late nineteenth. This, of course, is undeniable, except that the change is one toward a less imperialist, a more democratic and equalitarian, and politically a still more open society.

But Lenin's opponents could not so easily make do with the handful of quotations on democracy which Marx and Engels had left them. These might provide enough *obiter dicta* to embarrass Lenin, but they were pitifully inadequate to suggest the sweep and significance of the democratic process as it has developed, and the social and economic changes which political democracy and the pressures of history have brought in their train. The continuing revolution, the mixed economy, the welfare state, the society institutionally open to continuous, peaceful, and piecemeal change—these escape completely from the constricting dogmas of Marx's frame of reference as they mock at his certitudes concerning the law of motion, the direction that social development must take, and the cataclysmic nature of the single dramatic moment of systemic revolution.

Lenin had a favorite admonition of Mephistopheles which he loved to quote in "closing a discussion" with opponents in his own camp. It is an admonition which he might well repeat to the rival claimants to the Marxist heritage, and, with even greater force, recite to himself, concerning the settlement of problems of the twentieth century by the application of sacred texts from the great social thinker of the nineteenth whose disciple he felt himself to be:

> *Theory is gray, my friend,*
> *But green is the golden tree of life.*

PART V

The Flaw in
the Foundation

There are at least as many socialisms as there are great nations.
—Georges Sorel

Chapter 13

THE MARVELOUS YEAR

> Paris is the heart and brain of the world . . . the queen of cities, in which European civilization unfolds to its fullest bloom, in which all the nerve fibers of European history converge, and from which at intervals electric impulses are discharged that make the entire world tremble.
>
> —Friedrich Engels

WHEN in late October 1843, Karl Marx took his newly-wedded bride to Paris, he was still anticommunist. He had a job waiting, as co-editor with Arnold Ruge of an international democatic journal which Ruge was to finance. The *German-French Yearbooks* had the ambition to unite German philosophy with the French revolutionary-democratic tradition in a common effort at the further enlightenment of Europe.

There was no little presumption in the proposal of Ruge and his young disciple of the moment, for France was the hearth and beacon of revolutionary radicalism, democratic political theory, and socialist doctrine, while Germany stagnated in its medieval particularism and theological and political authoritarianism. The German Enlightenment was no more than intellectual approval of the revolutionary upheavals occurring, or dreamed of, in France. It involved only a theoretical acceptance of those upheavals (or some portions of them) by a handful of schoolmen who did nothing about them at home beyond translating them into eager and complicated disputations in the cloud-realm of philosophy. It was Frenchmen who strove and suffered and dreamed, and tried to turn the world upside-down, while Germany continued to watch meditatively, and its philosophers, in cap and gown or nightcap and slippers, tried to

233

take—and now had come to give the French—theoretical account of what they were up to.[1]

Up to the time of his arrival in Paris, Marx himself had used the term *communism* only disparagingly. The best example was his retort to the editor of a rival paper, who in October 1842 had hinted that he and his journal, the "bourgeois" *Rheinische Zeitung*, showed some weakness for communism in their published reports by Moses Hess on French communism, and the journal's editorial notes thereon. Marx's idea of a proper retort was to say that it is you, the editor of the *Augsburge Allgemeine Zeitung*, who sound communistic in your comments on us. To this he added by way of confession of faith:

> We do not allow even *theoretical reality* to Communist ideas . . .
> still less wish to see their *practical realization*. . . . We intend to
> subject those ideas to a fundamental critique . . . but surely the
> *Augsburge Allgemeine Zeitung* must recognize that you can't criticize
> such writings as those of Leroux, Considérant, and above all the
> penetrating work of Proudhon, off the top of your head with casual or
> superficial ideas, but only after long, persistent and thorough
> study. . . .
>
> We have the firm belief that not the *practical attempt* but the
> theoretical exposition of Communist ideas constitutes the real danger.
> For practical attempts, even on a mass scale, can be answered with
> *cannon* as soon as they become dangerous, but *ideas*, which conquer
> our intelligence, which master the feelings that conscience has fused
> with our reason, these are chains which one cannot break away from
> without breaking one's heart, they are demons which man can only
> conquer by submitting to them.[2]

This was Marx's only significant comment on communism before he reached Paris, significant for what it suggests of the temper of his intellect: his need to make a profound study of the socialist doctrine before he criticized it; his subconscious yet vividly expressed fear lest his intelligence, conscience, and heart be caught in its toils; his

---

[1] Even after Marx made his striking synthesis of French political radicalism and socialism, British economic theory and German philosophy, the French remained unimpressed. From the French Revolution to the defeat of France by Prussia in 1870, Paris continued to be the City of Light, the beacon of revolutionary radicalism for all Europe and Latin America.

[2] "Der Kommunismus und die *Augsburge Allgemeine Zeitung*," editorial article by Marx in the *Rheinische Zeitung* of October 26, 1842, reprinted in *Werke*, Vol. I, pp. 105–108.

penchant for replacing "the weapon of criticism with criticism by weapons," a penchant which would thus seem to antedate his conversion to socialism.

Now here he was in Paris, exactly one year later, with the opportunity to make at first hand "the long, persistent, fundamental study of the ideas of Leroux, Considérant, the penetrating Proudhon," of Saint-Simon, Fourier and Cabet, and all the other socialist thinkers who filled the air of Paris with their theories and dreams. Suddenly he found plenty of time on his hands, too, for almost immediately he lost the job that had brought him to Paris.

The ambitious publishing venture had never really gotten started. The eminent French thinkers ignored their invitations to contribute, as did the eminent thinkers inside Germany. Marx and his co-editor-patron, Ruge, thrown together in the silence of isolation, found that their temperaments clashed, as did their private households, and even their ideas. One double number, badly delayed, and filled with contributions by other German exiles, came out in February 1844. Thereafter publication ceased. It was at this moment, as an acute biographer of Marx has pointed out, that "this German exile, deprived of material resources, without definite profession, exposed with his family to the hazards of fortune, discovered the proletarat."[3]

Along with the proletariat, in the same flash of lightning he discovered socialism, and, from the charged atmosphere drew most of the views he was to expound during a lifetime. In the next few chapters I shall have much to say of the debt Marx owed to French socialism, the French Enlightenment, and French "bourgeois historians." An awareness of this debt is important to the analysis of Marxian thought and an understanding of the conflict between "French socialism" and the "German theory." But it should not be taken to deny originality to Marx's powerful mind and unique doctrine. Those writers who have piled up parallel passages in an attempt to reduce his imposing structure of thought, analysis, passion, and prophecy to a rubble heap of mere plagiarisms are like those who have thought to reduce Shakespeare to a mere plagiarist by matching passages from Holinshed and Plutarch.

Later Marx's debt to these French thinkers was to be obscured

---

[3] Maximilen Rubel, *Karl Marx: Essai de Biographie Intellectuelle*, Paris, 1957, p. 52.

by bitter quarrels—his break with Proudhon, the rivalry which developed between French socialism and "our German theory," and Engels's dividing line between the socialist theorists whom he labeled *utopian,* and the doctrine of Marx for which he reserved the term *scientific.* It was then that the two friends were to discover how devastating a weapon the epithet *utopian* can be, not merely on the lips of opponents of socialism, but no less in the struggle for predominance among socialists themselves. It was to be, in the words of Martin Buber, an early example of the "Marxian device of annihilation by labels."[4]

Yet the claim to be *scientific* was part of the common coin of Paris socialism. Saint-Simon, Engels's prototype of the utopian socialist, to whom Marx, Engels, and Lenin all owed a substantial debt, wrote that "politics is the science of production," that as against "feudal and theological systems the maintenance of liberty was bound to be an object of primary attention," but now these had been overcome, it was necessary to "establish the industrial and scientific system, since this system must necessarily . . . bring with it the highest degree of liberty in the temporal and social sphere." In his *Lettres d'un habitant de Genève,* Saint-Simon wrote: "Social relations must be considered as physiological phenomena . . . treated absolutely in the same way as any other scientific question." Because Newton was still lord of science when Saint-Simon wrote, he called his own critique of existing society and vision of a better social order "the science of universal gravitation," which was but Marx's future "law of motion" in a different metaphorical context.

Proudhon, too, called his doctrine "scientific socialism," and Comte, after his break with Saint-Simon, whose secretary he had been, became the father of "the science of society."

When Marx published his *Zur Kritik der Politischen Oekonomie* in 1859, Darwin was just publishing his *Origin of Species.* Hence Marx called his study "the anatomy of civil society" much as Saint-Simon had spoken of the "physiology" and the "science of universal gravitation." By the time Volume One of *Das Kapital* was published in 1864, Darwin had become the very paradigm of scientific method. Marx had his doubts about Darwin, and Darwin his doubts about Marxism, but this did not prevent Engels from conferring on his friend the title of the "Darwin of the social sciences," while Marx

---

[4] Martin Buber, *Paths in Utopia,* Boston, 1949, p. 6.

himself wrote Darwin offering to dedicate to him the work he had just completed. The latter politely rejected the honor, pleading ignorance of economics and stressing as courteously as he could the one thing the two men had in common, "a desire to advance the sum of human knowledge."[5]

In two letters to Engels, Marx expressed preference for Trémaux's *Origine et Transformations de l'Homme et des autres Êtres* as "a significant advance over Darwin." In another letter Marx mocked at Darwin's projection of his biological ideas into society, though Marx himself indulged in social Darwinism of another stripe, seeing in "natural selection the biological basis of the class struggle," and in Darwin's emphasis on the organs of animals and plants support for his own emphasis on technology and the "means of production." But Engels never wavered in his admiration for both Darwin and Marx. Over Marx's grave he said: "As Darwin discovered the law of evolution in organic nature, Marx discovered the law of evolution in human history." It was the "scientific" rather than the voluntarist side of Marx's doctrine that Engels continued to develop when Marx was dead.[6]

Yet in a sense Marx's claim that his doctrine was scientific was there from the very beginning. We saw it in his letter to Ruge before he became a socialist ("We develop for the world out of its own principles, new principles. . . . We show it why it really struggles"). We saw it in his first announcement to the proletariat of what it would "historically be forced to do." But if this was a part of Marx's arrogant temperament, it was not at the outset the core of his voluntaristic, revolutionary doctrine. It was little more than an expression of certitude concerning the "essential nature of the world" (i.e. of "generic man") and of "the proletariat," by way of reinforcing the basic social optimism of his views and strengthening the will to struggle.

But after the revolutionary wave of 1848 had manifestly receded,

---

[5] On the exchange of letters between Marx and Darwin see Isaiah Berlin, *Karl Marx*, New York, 1949, p. 232. The letters will appear in *Werke*, Vol. XXXI, now on press.

[6] *Werke*, Vol. I, pp. 345–46 and Vol. II, p. 39. For the more important letters of Marx and Engels on Darwin see *MEGA*, III/2, pp. 447 and 533; III/3, pp. 61, 62, 355 and 460; see also Marx's letter to Kugelmann, June 27, 1870, to Lassalle in *MEGA*, III/3, pp. 77–78, and *Capital*, Vol. 1, Chicago, 1909, pp. 391 and 406n. For a more critical appraisal of Darwin by Engels, see *Dialectics and Nature*, New York, 1940, pp. 7, 13, 19, 208–09, 235–36.

the conviction that his doctrine was scientific became a consolation for the ever-lengthening chain of postponements of the "final crisis." Then, insensibly, as time dragged on and the revolution did not come, it became a mode of deducing the inevitability of socialism from "laws" which needed less and less intervention of human values and a struggling revolutionary will.

From 1844 until the upheavals of 1848 died away, revolution was in the air. Even the stagnant air of Prussia and Austria was blown clean for a while by the storms of revolution. It seemed to Marx that one great revolutionary effort would break the chains that bound Prometheus to his rock, and set him free. For freedom, Hegel had taught, was of the essence of the nature of man, and his unceasing goal. If man could but live his philosophy and realize it in life, all the institutions and superstitions that stood in his way and kept man from being himself would crumble. Then man would be made whole and attain at last his true human stature. Thus, for all his claims to positive knowledge of the truth, the heart of Marx's views until the middle of 1850 was an optimistic picture of man's "essential nature," an ardent, activist faith in the capacity of the human mind and the human will. The problem was only one of finding the "material force" that could "realize" this philosophy.

But in September 1850, when Marx broke with the majority of the revolutionists of the Communist League and lectured them on the need to take account of "objective conditions," on the need of a further period of evolution before the bourgeois order would be played out and a new revolutionary crisis come, and scolded them on the wrong-headedness of mere revolutionary voluntarism—then a new Marx was born. "The main thing now," Engels wrote him, "is that you appear again before the public with a thick book. . . ."[7] That thick book was the content of the second stage in the development of Marxism.

The third stage is more properly attached to the name of Engels than that of Marx, and to the "orthodox socialists" whom he trained and who succeeded him in the guardianship of the heritage. In this stage overt moral values, revolutionary activism, the anxious search for the outbreak of the "next revolutionary situation," and a vision of the society of the future, are all resolutely pushed into the background. Even to dwell on them is utopian. The foreground is filled

---

[7] Letter of November 27, 1851, *Werke,* Vol. XXVII, p. 374.

to overflowing with a new doctrine linked to Marx's name and writings, yet altered, transformed, made learned and even scholastic, and baptized *scientific socialism*.[8]

But we must return to Paris and the year 1844. It was for Marx a marvelous year, doubtless the most important in his life, for it was the ideas in the Paris air and the revolutionary impulses which streamed over Europe from the City of Light that made Marx into a "Marxist."

During that year, as we have already noted, Marx discovered the proletariat and socialism, and filled his head with the social criticisms of the world as it was and the generous utopian visions of the world as it should be, as expressed by Saint-Simon and Fourier and many lesser men.

From German philosophy, more specifically from Hegel, Marx brought with him to Paris the view that history has an objective meaning, that it unfolds by stages toward the fulfillment of that meaning, each stage leading by its very nature to the next. That meaning could be grasped by the intellect (before the year was up Marx was sure that his own intellect had grasped it). Its unfolding was to culminate in man's freedom and the attainment of his full humanity. In this there is as much of Condorcet as of Hegel. The belief that "generic man" is by nature rational and good, that to attain his full human stature he need only be freed from the institutional obstacles and irrational superstitions that bind him, that the process of social evolution is unilateral and forward-moving, that each successive stage in man's development brings him nearer to the rational ideal and that the new day of the reign of reason was now at hand—these views out of Condorcet and the Enlightenment he had absorbed from his father and his future father-in-law, Ludwig von Westphalen, in the days of his impressionable youth. Many of them stayed with him all through his life, fusing with and permeating the world-view he shaped in his maturity. But it is well to remember that Condorcet became a Girondin, Marx a "Jacobin."

From certain French "bourgeois historians," and most notably from Guizot and Thierry, as Marx himself declared, he absorbed the

---

8 The best analysis of these successive stages in the development of Marxism is in Lichtheim, *Marxism*, New York, 1961, the chapter on "Engels" and the two succeeding chapters. My only reservation is that his analysis does not take account of the extent to which Marx's own temper and conviction of scientific certitude contributed to the conception of "scientific socialism."

notion, then so fashionable in French historiography, that all history is the history of class struggles, that revolutions are but the nodal points in history when one class displaces another in power, and that the French Revolution was completely intelligible as a "bourgeois revolution." This notion developed in Marx the tendency to reduce individual man in all his variety, and "generic man" in all his abstract humanity, to yet another configuration-obliterating abstract construct, namely, class man. And it sharpened his awareness of the proletariat, for now history needed a new class to give it its next push forward.

He began a fascinated study of the Great French Revolution, its ideology, its leading figures, the origins of its "leading class," its terror, the miscarriage of the hopes of its more radical and plebeian supporters—until his mind was possessed by the French Revolution as the prototype of events that were destined to occur in his own country and all over the Europe of his own day.[9]

From Babeuf's *Conspiracy of the Equals* as narrated by Buonarrotti, Marx derived the dream that "the French Revolution is the precursor of another, more magnificent revolution, which will be the last." More magnificent, because this time it would spread from France to Germany, and from Germany roll back to France and throughout all Europe. More magnificent, too, because from the socialist air of Paris, Marx had gained the conviction that the role of the bourgeoisie was now played out. Since in a revolution one ruling class must replace another, this time it would be the turn of the proletariat, the last oppressed class in history, whence its elevation to power would truly be the "last revolution"—the end of classes, class struggles and class rule.

From the dramatic figure of the hero-martyr, Blanqui, perpetually in prison and perpetually in rebellion, Marx absorbed the idea

---

[9] Marx himself acknowledges this debt "to French bourgeois historians" and specifically to Thierry and Guizot. The historian Guizot, the self-same Guizot who as premier, albeit somewhat reluctantly, signed the order for Marx's expulsion from Paris in January 1845, writes: "Not only can one claim no credit for recognizing the existence of a class struggle, but it is almost ridiculous to deny it." One of the interesting features of French nineteenth-century historiography is the tendency of its practitioners to identify themselves with parties and classes, and to take partisan sides in their discussion of the searing events of the French Revolution. It is likely that the closer a society is to the period when it was structurally divided into estates, the greater is apt to be the persistence of a strong feeling of class, which is a modification of the notion of estates. That perhaps is why the United States, which never knew such estates, is so lacking in a feeling of class.

of revolutionary dictatorship and of the revolution in permanence until the world was completely transformed.

In March Marx met the Russian romantic revolutionary, Bakunin, and planned joint work with his future rival. In Paris, mostly from Proudhon, Marx himself acquired that incongruous touch of anarchism which made him all his life insist on the ultimate disappearance of the state, even while he was doing everything possible to extend its powers and sphere and centralism.[10]

Even earlier, before Marx had yet come to socialism, some six months before Marx and Engels had formed their partnership, Engels was writing in Robert Owen's *Moral World:*

> The most important writer [in the field of French communism] is Proudhon, a young man, who two or three years ago published his work: *What Is Property? (Qu'est-ce que la propriété?);* his answer to that question reads: *La propriété c'est le vol,* Property is theft. This is on the part of the communists the most philosophical work in the French tongue, and if I wanted to see any one French book translated into English, this would be it. The right of property, the consequences of this institution, competition, immorality and misery, are here developed with the force of reason and in truly scientific investigation, as I have never found it since in any other book. Along with that he makes very important observations on the forms of government, and after he has proved that every form of government is equally questionable [*anfechtbar*, contestable], whether it is a matter of democracy, aristocracy, or monarchy, that all rule by force, and that even in the best of all possible cases, the majority oppresses the weakness of the minority, he comes finally to the result: *Nous voulons l'anarchie!* What we need is anarchy, the rule of no man, the responsibility of each individual to nobody but himself. (*Werke,* Vol. I, pp. 455, 488; 566-67, 608.)

It was Engels, rather than Marx, who was the author of the much-quoted aphorisms concerning the "dying out" (*absterben*, generally translated *withering away*) of the State, and its final ignominious end in a museum of antiquities alongside the spinning wheel. (On the influence of Proudhon on Engels's early thought, see Mayer, *op. cit.,* Vol. I, pp. 143 ff.)

---

[10] During 1844 Marx had many long talks with Proudhon during which he "injected" Hegelianism into the Frenchman, and the latter "injected" anti-Jacobinism and antistatism into him. Neither vaccination took, and by the time Marx came to review his relations with Proudhon of that memorable year, he forgot the role the latter had played in this aspect of his thought. (On this, see Rubel, *op. cit.,* p. 106 n).

Saint-Simon is the author of the formula concerning the rule over persons giving way to the administration of things. Most of these formulations came from Engels, but since the heirs largely took Marx and Engels to be a single unity-in-duality, the formulations of Engels were what they puzzled over and glossed and took to be an essential constituent of "the Marxian doctrine of the State."

That year in Paris Marx met his first workingmen, and his first intellectuals who had come out of the working class (no small matter, for he was not to meet many workingmen during a lifetime dedicated to their cause). From those few meetings he drew striking conclusions concerning the role of the proletariat in the making of history and the making of "their own" philosophical theory. One Dr. Ewerbeck, a medical doctor from Danzig who had won influence over a league of German Communist artisans in Paris known as the League of the Just, took him to meet his first German workingmen. Moses Hess, the gentle, humanist socialist and future Zionist who had just converted Engels to Communism, introduced him to some meetings of French workingmen's secret societies. After a few such meetings, so few that they can be counted on the fingers of one hand, Marx wrote to Feuerbach:

You would have to attend one of the meetings of the French *ouvriers* [for some time Marx couldn't bring himself to call them *Arbeiter*] to believe in the virginal freshness and the nobility that stand out in these worn out men.

And in his *Economic-Philosophical Manuscripts,* a sort of memorandum to himself which he never published, he wrote:

When communist *workingmen* associate with one another, theory, propaganda, etc. is their first end. But at the same time, as a result of this association, they acquire a new need—the need for society—and what appears as a means becomes an end. You can observe this practical process in its most splendid results whenever you see French socialist *ouvriers* together. Such things as smoking, drinking, eating etc., are no longer means of contact or means that bring together. Company, association, and conversation, which again has society as its end, are enough for them; the brotherhood of man is no mere phrase with them, but a fact of life, and the nobility of man shines upon us from their work-hardened bodies.[11]

---

[11] The letter to Feuerbach, who was unconvinced, is dated August 11, 1844, which helps us to fix a probable date for the notebooks or *Manuscripts*. For the letter see *Werke,* Vol. XXVII, pp. 425–28. The Manuscripts are in *MEGA,* I/3, pp. 29–172. For an English translation see Karl Marx: *Economic and Philosoph-*

If this was Marx's conclusion from two or three visits to French workingmen's secret societies, his acquaintance with one German ex-journeyman tailor who had gotten his socialism in France, and with two French ex-printers, declassed workingmen become fullblown theorists and system-builders, Wilhelm Weitling, Pierre Leroux, and Pierre Joseph Proudhon, Marx derived the further conclusion that revolutionary feeling was "natural" to the working class and that "the workers make of their revolutionary activity the greatest joy of their lives."[12] That generalization at any rate was true of these three ex-workingmen, as it was to be true henceforward of the man who was even then appointing himself chief advocate for, and chief theoretician to, the proletariat. By the end of July 1844, Marx had written for the German-language *Vorwaerts*, published in Paris, this estimate of the theoretical capacity of the German proletariat:

As to the state of education or the capacity for education of the German workingmen in general, I remind you of Weitling's writings of genius (*geniale Schriften*) which in respect to theory often even go beyond *Proudhon*, however much they are inferior to him in their execution. Where does the bourgeoisie—including its philosophers and its learned scribes—have a work to show concerning the emancipation of the bourgeoisie, its *political* emancipation, that is a match for Weitling's *Garantien der Harmonie und Freiheit?* When one compares the sober and small-voiced mediocrity of German political literature with this *incomparably* brilliant debut of the German workingman; when one compares these giant-sized *children's shoes* of the proletariat with the dwarfishness of the worn out political shoes of the German bourgeoisie, then one has to prophesy for the *German Cinderella* the *frame of an athlete*. One has to admit that the German proletariat is the *theoretician* of Europe, as the English proletariat is its *national economist* and the French proletariat its *politician*. One must admit that Germany has just as much of a *classical* vocation for the *social* revolution as it has *political* incapacity. For the impotence of the German bourgeoisie is the *political* impotence of Germany, just as the endowments of the German proletariat—even leaving on one side German theory—are the *social* endowment of Germany. The disparity between philosophical and political development in Ger-

---

ical Manuscripts of 1844, Moscow, 1961, translated by Martin Milligan for the Institute of Marxism-Leninism of the Central Committee of the C.P.S.U. where the passage is on pp. 124–25. I have restored the French word *ouvriers* as used in the original German.

[12] *MEGA*, 1/6, p. 471.

many is not an *abnormality*. It is a necessary disparity. Only in socialism can a philosophical people find its corresponding practice, hence only in the *proletariat* the active element in its liberation.[13]

The German proletariat the theoretician of Europe! An audacious claim! And with little enough proof to rest on, for as soon as Marx and Weitling met face to face next year, Marx began an onslaught on "this workingman genius's" doctrine as sentimental and unscientific, and on yesterday's "young giant of theory" as an "absurd apostle" perhaps suited to influence "absurd young men in Russia," but with no useful role to play among the theoretically more advanced German workingmen.[14]

To understand Marx's claim for the scattered, unformed, uncultured, and semi-medieval artisanry of backward Germany to be the theoretician of Europe, we must note some of Marx's still unspoken assumptions.

He was after all a German. Despite his cosmopolitan outlook and his brooding on the French Revolution, what he longed for was a "French Revolution" in backward, particularist, semi-medieval, authoritarian Germany. Just because his land was so hapless and backward, because all at once and in a single leap forward she was to make up for decades of provincial stagnation and accomplish in one moment of history what in France and England had taken decades, the revolution Germany needed ought to be the most sweeping, violent, and earth-shaking in modern history. And just because all classes of German civil society were provincial, timid, and servile, a

---

[13] Published in *Vorwaerts*, August 10, 1844, dated by Marx, Paris, the 31st of July. *Werke*, Vol. I, pp. 404–05.

[14] Most of the accounts of the battle between Marx and Weitling, which ended with the purge of Weitling from the Communist Correspondence Committee in Brussels, and of his followers, workingmen also, from the Paris League of the Just, present Marx's and not Weitling's view of the affair. The best of the pro-Marx versions is in Nikolaevsky and Maenchen-Helfen, *op. cit.*, pp. 117–21, which includes a short summary of an eye-witness account from the pen of the Russian writer, Paul Anenkov. For a version highly unfavorable to Marx, see Leopold Schwarzschild, *The Red Prussian: The Life and Legend of Karl Marx*, New York, 1947, pp. 141–49. There are contemporary accounts in letters of Wilhelm Weitling and Moses Hess. The Nikolaevsky-Maenchen-Helfen book makes a mistake in the date, putting it in May 1848 (doubtless a printer's error)—it occurred in May 1846. At the same time, Marx broke with Proudhon, and on the issue of his purge of Weitling, which the gentle Moses Hess disapproved, with Hess, also. Thus the three men who had most to do with bringing Karl Marx to socialism in 1844 were excommunicated at almost the same moment, and Marx was left without his two proofs of the natural theoretical genius of the proletariat. How he managed to make good that lack provides another of the ambiguities in Marx's doctrine, on which more below.

new class had to be postulated even if it scarcely existed in germ, whose grievances must be so great, whose misery so absolute, whose reckless anger so justified and all-consuming, that it might carry the stagnant history of backward Germany forward in a great and sudden rush far beyond its middle-class limits and goals.[15]

In Germany only poets and philosophers looked beyond the narrow horizon of the local court or province. Marx's eyes, like theirs, had been fixed not on the stillness in Germany but on the swift succession of movements in France.

The German intellect was stirred, but German civil society did not move. There was lightning up in the cloud regions of thought; the earth trembled; the heavens thundered; but no one looked up and nothing moved. Political life stood still; only philosophy was in ferment. German history continued to stagnate; but philosophy engaged in a feverish activity, a tremendous to-do in the realm of pure thought where, to cite an ironic retrospective view of it by Marx, "a cataclysm" occurred, "the decomposition of the Absolute Spirit" as Hegel's disciples began their critical onslaughts on their late Master, and on each other's criticisms. But since all this took place within the University walls and the columns of abstruse journals, and since philosophy's concepts could not be given overt content—that was blocked by authority, censorship, localism, overseers of church and state, by the habitual abstruseness of the philosophers, and the indifferent passivity of the ordinary German—the revolution in thought took on an abstract form, its generalizations were algebraic formulas to whose terms no one dared supply arithmetic equivalents. Marx's break with philosophy (in which he had never really been at home) consisted precisely in his attempt to substitute his arithmetic values for their algebra.

Because everything had to be done at once to catch up in a single moment of history for what other peoples had accomplished over long periods of time, and since thought was blocked from flowing over into action, this made for greater radicalism in the theoretical sphere. It might seem a *non sequitur* that the most backward country should suddenly presume to teach and lead the others merely because it had so much to do in a hurry and all at once, just to catch up with the others. And yet, Marx asked himself, could not backwardness and accumulated energy combine to make

---

[15] Compare the reasoning of Leon Trotsky in his so-called "Law of Combined Development" for a revolution in backward Russia.

the revolution so sweeping that it could carry "the most philosophical people in Europe" to the vanguard of the historical process both in comprehension and in action? That, at least, was his hope.

In philosophy, Europe had marked time, while Germany alone had pressed forward. German thought, dammed up, had accumulated an enormous potential of energy. There, and there alone, was the ideal prolongation of German history, the reflection of the history of all the other peoples, their yesterdays, their todays, and even their tomorrows. When German philosophy would suddenly burst into historical action and be "realized" in history, then Germany would be abreast of the times. Nay more, once in motion, what could stop it from running ahead of the times? Having so long stood still, when at last German philosophy found the "material force" to realize itself in history, then Germany would make such strides that all Europe would see in her its tomorrow as now it could see its yesterday.

But for such all-at-once radicalism Marx required, and thought he had found, a force that needed to achieve everything at once, a force that aspired to be all because now it was nothing, a force that could not solve its own problems without solving all problems, an explosive revolutionary impulse springing from the very bottom of the heap, from the depths of society where, deprived of air, it had been smoldering. It was a mere pitiful detail that the German proletariat could not think. That was part of its "dehumanization." Since it had need of thought it would learn. German philosophy could set it free, therefore the proletariat would perforce seize on German philosophy. German philosophy could move all Europe forward again, hence the German proletariat would become the theoretical leader of all Europe. As yesterday all Europe had watched the French bourgeoisie, so now all Europe would watch the German proletariat. For the moment, look, there were the genius ideas and the giant children's shoes of Wilhelm Weitling. No wonder Marx seized on Weitling and overvalued him even before he took a good look at him. Philosophy needed the proletariat . . . and there was Weitling. The proletariat would need philosophy, and—unspoken assumption—philosophy was even now breaking out of the closed circle and making its own great revolutionary synthesis and leap forward in the person of Germany's first and latest and most passionately revolutionary thinker. No, he was not a proletarian, but then he was not a bourgeois either. Moreover, there are moments in history when thinkers from any class can take the standpoint of the class about to lead society forward. It was not what the proletariat thought it wanted to become, but what its condition, its very being, compelled it to do. The proletariat needed that awareness and would grasp at it, for it was the distillation of the essence of the proletariat's condition. It could free itself only by overthrowing the whole established order in Germany, its particularism, its stagnation, its authoritarianism, its theocracy, its medievalism, its pettiness, its oppression, its misery. Being at the bottom of the heap this Samson Agonistes could not rise to his full height without overthrowing the whole miserable structure. . . .

The speed with which Marx was developing his views in the highly charged atmosphere of the City of Light was nothing short of astonishing. By the time he proclaimed the genius of Weitling, his discovery of the German proletariat was nearly six months old! So far as the record shows, that discovery was made in the very midst of the preparation of the solitary double number of the *Deutsch-Franzoesische Jahrbuecher* which appeared in February 1844. The issue contained three open letters from Marx to Ruge, written during the previous year, in which Marx's arrogant temper is visible, but not a sign of his socialism. He speaks as a Democrat, but a Democrat of a special type who aims at nothing less than "to remake the consciousness of the world," and "to wake it out of its dream concerning itself by *explaining* to it its own actions."

But in the same issue, Marx made a second attempt to settle accounts with Hegel (the first being unfinished, uninteresting, and unpublished until the twentieth century). This article, too, is a fragment, labeled *Introduction to a Contribution to the Critique of the Hegelian Philosophy of Right*. Like the earlier critique it was unfinished. But in it Marx made the giant stride from critic of the consciousness of the world to "proletarian" revolutionist, and from Democrat to Socialist.

The problem he posed was: how could the "praxis" of backward Germany be brought

> . . . *à la hauteur des principes,* i.e. how could it attain to a *revolution* which would raise it not only to the *official level of the modern* nations, but to the *human height* which will be the nearest future of these nations?

Every part of German life, Marx said, was a *"partie honteuse,"* a shameful part, except her philosophy. "We are *philosophical* contemporaries of the present, without being its *historical* contemporaries."

German philosophy was a brilliant critique of German history, or lack of history, and of German institutions. But the critique left the institutions untouched in life, and the stagnation of history continuing. How break out of that vicious circle? "In one word: *You cannot abolish* *philosophy, except by realizing it. . . .* We Germans have *thought* in politics what the other nations have *done.*" Germany had been "the conscience" and "the consciousness" of the other peoples. But the time had come for action, or as Marx put it in philosophical language, for *praxis.* And for this:

The weapon of criticism can in any case not replace criticism by weapons; material force must be overthrown by material force, but theory itself can become a material force as soon as it takes possession of the masses. Theory is able to take possession of the masses as soon as it demonstrates *ad hominem,* and it demonstrates *ad hominem* as soon as it becomes radical. To be radical is to grasp the matter at the root. The root for man is however man himself. . . . It is not enough that thought presses for realization; reality must itself press for thought.

In previous revolutions, Marx explained, a single class, e.g. the bourgeoisie in 1789, had appeared to all forward-looking society as the representative of progress. But to make it appear thus, and to assure its struggle and its leadership, another class had to appear as the enemy of all progress, the incarnation of all defects of existing society.

The French bourgeoisie had found the class to make the target of its hatred in the feudal aristocracy and the clergy. But in Germany every class had showed itself:

. . . lacking in the consistency, the intelligence, the courage, the recklessness which might stamp it as the negative representative of society. . . . Where was the class bold enough to cry out the defiant challenge: *I am nought, I must become all?*

In this abstraction was born the imperative of hate for the bourgeoisie as a class, that is the inseparable polar opposite of the glorification of the proletariat, a polarity which henceforth is the dialectical core of Marxism. How large a role hate must play has been one of the problems of insoluble controversy among the con-

---

* For *abolish* Marx uses the characteristic Hegelian term *aufheben,* which means both *abolish* and *assimilate* or *transcend.*

tenders for the heritage. At the extreme end of the spectrum stands Lenin. The article continues:

In France it is enough that one be something in order that he may want to be everything. In Germany he must be nothing if he is not to renounce everything. In France partial emancipation is the foundation of universal freedom. In Germany universal emancipation is the *conditio sine qua non* of every partial freedom. In France the possibility of step-by-step emancipation must give birth to complete freedom, in Germany it is the impossibility of step-by-step emancipation that must give birth to complete freedom. In France every class of the people is *a political idealist* and feels itself directly not as a special class but as the representative of the needs of society in general. The role of *the Emancipator* therefore goes in turn in dramatic fashion to each of the different classes of the French people, until at last it reaches the class . . . which organizes all the conditions of human existence according to the postulates of social freedom. In Germany on the contrary, where practical life is as unintelligent as intellectual life is impractical, no class of civil society has the need and the capacity for general emancipation until it is forced to that by its *immediate* situation, by *material* necessity.

Where then is the positive possibility of German emancipation? *Answer:* In the formation of a class with *radical chains* a class of civil society which is no class of civil society, an estate which is the dissolution of all estates, a sphere which has a universal character through its universal suffering . . . which, in one word, represents the *complete loss* of humanity, hence only through the *complete regaining of humanity* can win its self. This dissolution of society as a special estate is the *proletariat*.

When the proletariat proclaims the *dissolution of the previous world order*, it does no more than express *the secret of its own existence*, for it is *in actuality* the dissolution of that world order. When the proletariat demands *the negation of private property*, it is only raising to *the principle of society* what society has raised to *its* principle. . . .

As philosophy finds in the proletariat its *material* weapon, so the proletariat finds in philosophy its *intellectual* weapon, and as soon as the lightning of thought has struck deeply into this naïve folk-ground, the emancipation of the *German* into the *human being* will be completed. . . .

The *emancipation of the German* is the *emancipation of man*. The *head* of this emancipation is *philosophy*, its *heart* the *proletariat*. Philosophy cannot realize itself without the abolition of the proletariat, the proletariat cannot abolish itself without the realization of philosophy.

When all these inner conditions are fulfilled, then the *German uprising* will be announced by the *crowing of the Gallic cock*.[16]

Thus, under the stimulus of the repeated crowing of the Gallic cock, in the perfervid atmosphere of a Paris in which it seemed that at any moment the cock would crow again, did a young German doctor of philosophy, his way lighted by quasi-philosophical thought, find his path to the proletariat and to socialism.

If in February 1844, Marx still left it to the Gallic cock to sound the signal for a German uprising, that is, to start the revolution, six months later, in July, his claims for the German proletariat and the explosive mixture of German political, economic, and social backwardness with advanced philosophy, became more sweeping. Perhaps because he was arguing with a fellow German, his patron of yesterday, Arnold Ruge, or because his pretensions had grown, he omitted the Gallic cock.

The German poor [Ruge had jested] *are no smarter than the poor Germans*, that is *nowhere* do they see beyond their own hearth, their own factory, their own district. . . .

To which Marx answered with the praise for the "work of genius" of the journeyman tailor, Wilhelm Weitling, which we have already quoted. Then he added this striking claim:

One must admit that the German proletariat is the *theoretician* of the European proletariat. . . . One must admit that Germany has just as much a *classical* vocation for a *social* revolution, as it has incapacity for a *political* one. . . . Only in socialism can a philosophical people find its corresponding practice. . . . Every revolution dissolves the *old society* insofar as it is social. Every revolution overthrows the *old power*, insofar as it is *political*. A *revolution* in general—the *overthrow* of the existing power and the *dissolution* of the old relationships—is a *political* act. Without *revolution*, however, *socialism* cannot be realized. It has need of this political act insofar as it has need of *destruction* and *dissolution*. [Here Marx would seem to be echoing the predilect vocabulary of Bakunin with whom he was now in contact.] But where its *organizing activity* begins, where its *real purpose*, its *soul* steps forth, there socialism throws off the *political* husk.[17]

---

[16] *Werke*, Vol. I, pp. 378–91.
[17] *Ibid.*, pp. 404–09.

"One must admit that the German proletariat is the theoretician of the European proletariat." What is admitted, says an old legal maxim, doesn't have to be proved. But was Marx really laying that large claim in the name of Weitling? Since in 1844 the German proletariat was barely coming into existence, and, except for Weitling, who had learned his socialism in France, its contributions to thought were a nullity, it seems that Marx was beginning to think of himself as destined to provide the German proletariat with its intellectual weapon, to think of classical philosophy from Kant to Hegel to Feuerbach and then to himself, as philosophy *tout court*. And to think of this as the moment when German philosophy was about to abolish, transcend, and realize itself with the aid of that material force, the German proletariat, selected by its lot and destiny to be the "theoretician of the European proletariat," and the "emancipator of man." What was needed, clearly, was a fusion or synthesis of the political economy of the English, and the political experience and élan of the French, with the theorizing genius of the German. This synthesis—the marvelous year being but half over and only these two articles published—Karl Marx, who had for the past six months been reading furiously, compulsively, from dawn to dusk and from dusk to dawn through vast mountains of books, now set himself to make.

Chapter 14

LIFE AND DEATH OF THE
FIRST INTERNATIONAL

> I was firmly determined that wherever possible not *one
> single line* of the [drafts] of Major Wolff and Lubez should
> remain. . . . My proposals all accepted by the subcom-
> mittee. Only I was obliged to accept in the Preamble of the
> Statutes two *"duty"* and *"right"* sentences, ditto *"truth,
> morality, and justice,"* which is so placed that it can do no
> harm. . . . It was hard to keep things so that our stand-
> point should appear in a form acceptable to the present labor
> movement. . . . It requires time until the reawakened move-
> ment permits the old boldness of speech. . . . Bakunin
> sends you greetings. . . . On the whole he is one of the few
> people whom I find has not gone backwards but developed
> further in the last sixteen years. . . .
>
> —Karl Marx to Friedrich Engels,
> November 4, 1864

> I am eager to see the Address to the Workingmen; from
> what you tell me, it must be a real piece of sleight-of-
> hand. . . .
>
> —Friedrich Engels to Karl Marx,
> November 7, 1864

THUS IN HIS first six months in Paris, Marx found his mission and
that of the proletariat, and in his mind they became one. The socialist ideas and revolutionary practices which constituted his doctrine
were French, but the revolutionary thought which must develop

252

them into a system was to be German, for the Germans were the most philosophical people in Europe; the German proletariat was destined to be the theoretician of the European proletariat; and Germany must surely have a "classical vocation for a *social* revolution" since it so manifestly had demonstrated its "incapacity for a *political* one." All this Marx published in German in Paris, but even if he had published it in French, we can permit ourselves to doubt that the French socialists would have been convinced.

The British, Marx thought, had something important to offer too, but, like the French, they lacked something which only the Germans could supply. They had the most developed economic theory, the most advanced industry, and the most numerous politically and economically organized industrial proletariat. As Marx would write later:

> The English have all the necessary matter for the social revolution. What they lack is the generalizing *spirit* and the revolutionary passion.[1]

How Marx strove to master French socialist theory and revolutionary practice and wed it to British economics in the bed of German philosophy; how the system-fever which possessed him caused him to force these disparate things to combine in a seeming unity of thought and feeling, and make up a doctrine worthy of the "material force" which was to become "the theoretician of Europe" and "realizer" of his doctrine; how he borrowed from, and improved upon, even as he sought to cut to pieces, all rival theories and theorists; and finally, how he labored to convince the German *and* the European proletariat that his doctrine was the substance and embodiment of their thoughts, their dreams, their conditions of existence, their historic mission—this is the real story of Marx's life.

---

[1] Letter to Kugelmann of March 28, 1870. The letters of Marx and Engels to each other are full of exasperation and self-pity that they cannot really get the British working class going in the right direction. "Every Englishman has a board nailed up somewhere in his head, and nothing gets beyond it," Engels wrote Marx on June 11, 1863. Marx began to long for the Germans who, "being Germans have heads on their shoulders capable of generalizing" and "German training in thinking." (Letters of March 6 and Sept. 26, 1868.) The foundation of the First International by the British and French workers and their acceptance of Marx as the "thinking head" of the General Council gave him some hope that at last the means had been found to shake the British out of their "political non-existence." On May 1, 1865, Marx proudly wrote Engels "Die Reform League ist our work." But by April 6, 1866 he complained that the League had been too successful in winning electoral reform and "die Reformbewegung hat uns beinahe killed."

Viewed thus, the bitter quarrels with other doctrinaires and other self-assertive and rebellious men are seen in a new light, the light no doubt in which Marx and Engels saw them. Even the nationalistic utterances we have examined take on wider meaning when they are seen, as Marx and Engels saw them, to signify such a unification and elevation of Germany in the affairs of Europe as would subserve not merely a German but also an "international socialist" purpose. Such a unification ("even under Bismarck") would "do our work for us," create a nationwide market, a nationwide economy and polity, a grander stage for the exploits of the German proletariat and the "German theory," destined to inform and transform the world. Germany's predominance would secure predominance on an international scale for the only true and scientific theory.

That predominance was anything but easy to win. In March 1844, Marx had meetings and exchanged opinions with Bakunin, Leroux, and Louis Blanc. What impression the two Frenchmen made on him or he on them we do not know, but in any case they did not warm to each other. Bakunin and Marx each felt instant admiration for a fellow titan, Bakunin admiring Marx's learning and Marx, Bakunin's revolutionary temperament. Yet even then there was the tension between two rival prima donnas in a company in which only one could be the star. In April Marx made the acquaintance of the French workingman Proudhon. There was much excited talk between them often lasting until dawn. For some time they remained friends.

When the solitary number of the *Deutsch-Franzoesische Jahrbuecher* appeared in February, Marx was much taken by one of the contributions from Friedrich Engels, a German manufacturer's son living in Birmingham, England. It was *Umrisse zu einer Kritik der Nationaloekonomie* (*Outlines of a Critique of National Economy*). It was not a long work (approximately twenty-five pages in Volume One of *Werke*) but it made a life-long impression on Marx. Engels generously ceded to his learned friend the right to the further development of the "outlines." It is noteworthy that the subtitle, *Critique of Political Economy* was to appear both in Marx's work of 1859 and in his *Das Kapital*.

He had met Engels once before and barely taken notice of him, but now they arranged to meet in Paris. In the last days of August and early September they spent ten days and nights together, talk-

ing out philosophy, politics, and economics, Hegel and the Young
Hegelians, Fourier, Saint-Simon and Robert Owen, Weitling and
Proudhon, while they imbibed copious quantities of good French
wine. They found themselves in basic agreement on everything
down to their admiration for Proudhon and their contempt for the
Young Hegelians whom yesterday Marx had been following. Engels
then was far more advanced as a socialist thinker than Marx. In the
words of Nikolaevsky and Maenchen-Helfen, Engels

> . . . brought Marx more than he received from him. . . . Engels
> had an incomparably deeper insight into the economics of bourgeois
> society. . . . He had come face to face with the real workers' move-
> ment . . . Engels helped Marx to make concrete his quite abstract
> ideas concerning the relations of state and society, and Marx helped
> Engels to understand that the dependence of politics on material
> interests . . . which Engels had only been willing to admit as apply-
> ing to England, was in reality valid for all countries alike."[2]

Young Engels had been studying British political economists,
British industry, and the British working class. More generous than
Marx and less bent on asserting his originality, he was ready to give
credit to British socialism, to Fourier and his followers in France, to
the "humane and benevolent Robert Owen." His work-in-progress,
The Condition of the Working Class in England, dedicated "To the
Working Classes of Great Britain," told them that he had forsaken

> . . . the dinner-parties, the port-wine and champaign [sic] of the
> middle-classes and devoted my leisure hours almost exclusively to the
> intercourse with plain Working Men; I am both glad and proud of
> having done so . . .[3]

Nor was he, until he subordinated his mind to Marx's, so ready
to claim priority or supremacy for German thought. As late as 1845,
in a study of Fourier which was to remain unpublished until the
twentieth century, he wrote:

> Right now the Germans have begun to spoil the Communist move-
> ment, too. As always, the late comers and the least active believe that
> they can cover up their sleepiness by contempt for their forerunners

---

[2] *Op. cit.,* pp. 94–95. This judgment is interesting chiefly because it comes from
biographers of Marx who, in general, hold him in much higher estimation than
they do Engels.

[3] The *Dedication* is printed in the German translation in *Werke,* Vol. II, pp.
232–34, and a facsimile of the first page in English is reproduced on p. 235.
The Condition of the Working Class in England in 1844, London, 1892, translated by Florence Kelley Wischnewetzky under the supervision of Friedrich
Engels, omits the *Dedication,* and adds the year studied to the title.

and philosophical bragging. . . . What the French and the English said some ten, twenty or even forty years ago—and said very well and in very beautiful language, this the Germans at long last in the past year have learned fragmentarily and Hegelized. At best they have been rediscovering and publishing in much worsened, abstract form, as a wholly new discovery, what was done by their predecessors. Nor do I exclude my own works from this stricture. . . . And what can one say of the fact that these wise theoreticians also mention with contempt the only German who has *really* done something, *Weitling*, whom many of them don't even mention at all?[4]

It is idle to speculate on what would have become of this generous, optimistic, eclectic, socialist enthusiast if he had not teamed up with Marx and instantly caught his system-fever, his high scorn for *other-thinking* socialists, his habit of "accompanying a theoretical analysis of an opponent's views with a 'demolition' of the opponent as a human being."[5]

In any case, they hit it off instantly; thenceforth the letters of Engels to Marx take on much of Marx's tone in treating rivals of every description. In fact, in the case of Lassalle, it was Engels who egged on Marx rather than vice-versa.

Doubtless, Marx increased Engels's respect for German theoretical thought, while Engels deepened Marx's incipient interest in economics and called his attention to many of the thoughts of Fourier and Saint-Simon that were to become integral to Marx's doctrine.

A study of the priorities and greater weight of emphasis in the writings of the young Engels as against those of Marx suggest that it was Engels who called Marx's attention to such propositions of the "utopians" as these:

1) Saint-Simon declares that "politics is the science of production, and foretold the complete absorption of politics by economics . . . the future conversion of the political rule over men into the administration of things, and the direction of processes of production—that is to say, the 'abolition of the state.'

2) "The present anarchy of production, which corresponds to the fact that economic relations are being developed without uniform regulation [planning], must give way to the organization of produc-

---

[4] *Werke*, Vol. II, pp. 604–05.
[5] This sentence is quoted from Werner Blumenberg's generally admiring biography of Marx, *Karl Marx in Selbstzeugnissen und Bilddokumenten*, Hamburg, 1962, p. 73.

tion. Production will not be directed by isolated *entrepreneurs* independent of each other and ignorant of the people's needs; this task will be entrusted to a specific social institution. A central committee of administration, being able to review a broad field of social economy from a higher vantage point, will regulate it in a manner useful to the whole of society, will transfer the means of production into hands appropriate for this purpose, and will be specially concerned to maintain a constant harmony between production and demand."

3) Fourier teaches that "under civilization poverty is born of superabundance itself. Fourier uses the dialectic method in the same masterful way as his contemporary, Hegel."[6]

Until those ten days and nights of feasting on the wine of thought and the wine of Paris, Engels had not had much use for Hegel. Now he contracted from Marx a determination to demolish the Young Hegelians. They planned two joint works together as the first fruits of their new partnership: *The Holy Family* and *The German Ideology*.

The first was to be a brief, biting, satirical pamphlet to heap ridicule on a philosophical journal being published by Marx's former sponsor and master, Bruno Bauer, and the latter's two brothers, Edgar and Egbert. The full title of the "brief" pamphlet was *Die Heilige Familie oder Kritik der kritischen Kritik*, the "Holy Family" being the three Bauer Brothers. Engels dashed off his part, some sixteen pages, during the ten days he spent with Marx in Paris, and left it with his co-author. To his astonishment Marx took the rest of the year and over 300 pages to do his "half." By the time it appeared in Frankfurt am Main in 1845, the journal that it was meant to satirize was dead and forgotten; the ponderous polemic dropped noiselessly into the sea. Engels observed wryly, "The sovereign contempt with which our book treated critical criticism was in sorry contradiction to its bulk."[7]

The German Ideology had an even more ignominious fate. It was supposed to settle accounts with German thought, German opinions, and German thinkers. Its two volumes in octavo, some 800 pages in all, remained in the hands of a publisher who never pub-

---

[6] All these quotations, and others like them (e.g. the changing of labor from compulsion to joy), which became constituent elements of Marx's thoughts, are from early notes and writings of Engels developed prior to his close association with Marx.

[7] Mehring, *op. cit.*, p. 126.

lished them, and we cannot blame him. Its full title, *The German Ideology, a Critique of Recent German Philosophy and Its Representatives, Feuerbach, Bruno Bauer, and Stirner, and a Critique of German Socialism and Its Various Prophets,* is enough to suggest its bulk and tone. It too waited until the present century for publication, where it served to enlighten Marx biographers and Marxicologists. Engels declared that its criticism of Stirner was no less voluminous than the book of Stirner's which it criticized. The faithful Mehring found it "a still more discursive super-polemic than *The Holy Family* even in the latter's most arid chapters, the oases in the desert still more rare, though by no means entirely absent. . . . Even when dialectical trenchancy does show itself it soon degenerates into hair-splitting and quibbling, some of it rather puerile in character."[8] Even Marx wrote:

> . . . We abandoned our manuscript to the gnawing criticism of the mice . . . with little regret because our main object had been achieved—we had come to an understanding with ourselves.[9]

Such were the first fruits of what was to be one of the most touching, devoted, and influential friendships in intellectual history.

If they treated German socialism in cavalier fashion, first excommunicating Weitling, and then Moses Hess for protesting Weitling's exclusion, Marx and Engels did seek seriously to make an alliance with the French socialists, Cabet, Louis Blanc, Blanqui (through his followers), Proudhon, the disciples of Fourier and Saint-Simon, only to quarrel with each in turn. Only old Blanqui retained their personal respect and a comparative immunity from their strictures, because of his perpetual life in prison.[10]

In *Die Heilige Familie* Marx wrote an eloquent defense of Proudhon against some critical remarks of Edgar Bauer. The defense occupies some thirty-four pages in *Werke*. In praise of Proudhon Marx wrote, much as Engels had:

---

[8] *Ibid.*, p. 137.
[9] *Ibid.*, p. 137.
[10] Gustav Mayer, *Friedrich Engels*, New York, 1936, p. 78. Engels was apparently an apt pupil of Marx's haughty attitude. Besides differences in temperament and national background and the fact of French priority, there was the spirit in which Engels, according to his biographer, approached the French socialists: "Now that Engels had worked out (with Marx) a firm theoretical basis for the revolutionization of society, he considered as enemies of communism all who thought that the proletariat could be emancipated by any other path than the one that he had discovered" (*Ibid.*, p. 73). To this even Lenin had nothing to add.

Proudhon's work, *Qu'est-ce que la propriété?* has the same significance for modern economics as Sieyès' work, *Qu'est-ce que le tiers
état?* has for modern politics. . . . Proudhon's critical examination of
private property is the first decisive, ruthless, and at the same time
scientific examination . . . which makes possible for the first time a
real science of national-economy.[11]

When, impelled by the French police, Karl Marx left Paris for
Brussels in February 1845, he carried so many bits of the mosaic of
his doctrine in his leonine head, that he felt he was moving the
center of Communist theory with him.

While he was in Brussels *The Holy Family* appeared, with his
impassioned defense of Proudhon. At the beginning of the next year,
Marx and Engels and less than two dozen German followers set up
an "international" Committee of Communist Correspondence. In
May 1846, Marx wrote to Proudhon from Brussels:

I beg you to believe me that excessive work and difficulties connected
with a change of residence, etc. are the only reasons for my silence. . . .

He explained the purpose of the Committee of Correspondence to
Proudhon as follows:

In this way differences of opinion can come to light and we will
achieve an exchange of views and an impartial criticism . . . to get
rid of *national* limitedness. . . .

Our connections with England are already established. As far as
France is concerned, we all believe that we can find no better correspondent there than you.[12]

Proudhon was tempted by the prospect of open discussion, but a
nasty postscript in Marx's letter, warning him against the German
socialist, Karl Gruen, who was translating and explaining German
texts to him, made the French printer a bit suspicious, for Marx used
against Gruen such offensive words as swindler, charlatan, parasite,
dangerous.[13]

---

11 *Werke*, Vol. II, p. 33.
12 *Werke*, Vol. XXVII, pp. 442–43. The English connection was the Chartist,
Julian Harney.
13 Franz Mehring writes that Marx and Engels in their criticism of Karl Gruen
and other German "True Socialists," "greatly exaggerated in point of fact and
[were] quite unjust as far as persons were concerned. . . . They attacked Karl
Gruen more violently than any other of its representatives not only because he
in fact offered them the greatest opportunity but because he was living in
Paris . . . and had won a disastrous influence over Proudhon." Mehring, *op. cit.*,
pp. 140–41.

Proudhon brushed aside the warning against Gruen. To the invitation to become the Paris representative of Marx's Committee of Correspondence, he replied:

My dear Mr. Marx,

Let us seek together if you wish, the laws of society, the manner in which these laws are realized, the process by which we shall succeed in discovering them. But for God's sake, after having demolished all the *a priori* dogmatisms, do not let us in our turn dream of indoctrinating the people. Let us not fall into the same contradictions as your countryman, Martin Luther, who, after having overthrown Catholic theology, began at once with the help of excommunications and anathemas to found a Protestant theology. . . .

I applaud with all my heart your thought of bringing to light all opinions; let us carry on a good and loyal polemic; let us give the world an example of a learned and far-sighted tolerance. But let us not, because we are at the head of a movement, make ourselves the leaders of a new intolerance, let us not pose as the apostles of a new religion, even if it be a religion of logic and reason. Let us gather together and encourage all protests, let us condemn all exclusiveness . . . let us never regard a question as exhausted . . .

On this condition I will gladly enter into your association. Otherwise—no![14]

No doubt Marx had overvalued Proudhon as he had Weitling, just because the tailor's apprentice and the printer were proletarians. But Proudhon's doctrines were less vague and mystical than Weitling's and his influence deeper and longer lasting. Moreover, Marx owed an intellectual debt to Proudhon as he did not to Weitling, for between them Proudhon and Engels had convinced Marx that the key to the understanding and criticism of modern industrial society

---

[14] I have used here the English translation published in *Dissent*, New York, Winter 1958. The full letter is in P. J. Proudhon, *Confessions d'un révolutionnaire*, Paris, 1929, pp. 434–35 and in *Correspondance de P. J. Proudhon*, Paris, 1875, Vol. II, pp. 198–202. To make matters worse, Proudhon added "in passing": "our proletarians have so great a thirst for science that a bad reception awaits any one who can give them nothing to drink but blood." It is hard to say which enraged Marx more, the plea for tolerance or the warning against the stressing of terror, for Marx's study of the Great French Revolution was even then leading him to fall in love with terror as an engine of progress. This "love" reached its apogee in the years 1848–50, then gradually cooled off, until in 1870 Engels could write his sharp statement against the French Terror in a letter to Marx, and in 1872 Marx would make his first public statement on the possibility of a peaceful road to socialism through universal suffrage in democratic countries.

lay in a critique of its economic foundations and of such institutions as private property and exploitation. Marx was not writing out of ignorance of Proudhon's tract, nor for purposes of flattery when he said that "it made possible for the first time a real science of political national economy." Indeed, shortly after writing those words of praise, Marx signed a contract with the German publisher, Leske, to write a two-volume *Critique of Politics and National Economy*.

Proudhon was the last remaining Frenchman over whom he had sought to win influence, and to inject German philosophical thought into his doctrine. But now Marx was in a rage. Proudhon did not have to wait long for the excommunication and anathema which he had sensed to be a part of Marx's method.

Being a printer and a proofreader, Proudhon had acquired a wide range of autodidact knowledge and information, and had the habit of putting into print many things on which he had confused, if original and generous, ideas. That same autumn he published a new book which both Marx and Engels read with censorious pencil in hand; then Marx made it the target of his accumulated wrath. *System of Economic Contradictions, or the Philosophy of Poverty*, Proudhon called it; Marx called his counterblast *The Poverty of Philosophy*. To make his attack more deadly and effective, Marx wrote it with for him unusual, even extraordinary, speed and in French—a French that was occasionally a little uncertain.

The spirit of the polemic against the man who a year before had been the "founder of the science of national economy" can be gathered from the *Avant-Propos*:

M. Proudhon has the misfortune to be singularly misknown in Europe. In France he has the right to be a bad economist because he passes for a good German philosopher. In Germany he has the right to be a bad philosopher because he passes for one of the strongest French economists. We, in our capacity of German and economist at the same time, have wanted to protest against this double error. The reader will understand that in this ungrateful task we have often had to abandon the critique of M. Proudhon to make a critique of German philosophy, and at the same time to give some *aperçus* on political economy.[15]

---

[15] *MEGA*, I/6, p. 119. *Werke* gives only a German translation of the original French work, and not always a good one. That Marx's French left something to be desired is suggested by Marx himself in his letter to Anenkov on Proudhon, and by Maximilien Rubel who permits himself when quoting to correct some *tornures vicieuses* of Marx (Rubel, *op. cit.*, p. 231 n.).

It is these positive *aperçus* that give the work its importance in the expression of Marx's thought, for added up they make the best account of his doctrine thus far published, much superior to the discursive *obiter dicta* in *Die Heilige Familie* or in the unpublished *Deutsche Ideologie*. But its "critical" side, its polemics against the workman Proudhon who has turned out to be neither a good economist nor a good philosopher, like so much of Marx's attacks on rival socialist thinkers, is tedious, prolix, elephantine, and ill-mannered to the point of embarrassing the more sensitive of his admirers. And, despite an occasional neat home-thrust, more than a little unfair.

The intended demolition does not seem to have diminished Proudhon's popularity among his countrymen. Mehring writes:

As a matter of fact Marx did not succeed, for Proudhon's influence on the French working class and on the proletariat in the Latin countries in general rose rather than fell, and for many decades Marx still had to contend with Proudhonism.

In June 1848, a year after he was "annihilated" in French by Karl Marx, Proudhon was elected by an overwhelming majority to the Constituent Assembly born of the uprising of February 1848. When Napoleon III threw him into prison, the book he wrote in his cell against the Emperor sold out six editions in its first six months. When the First International was founded, Marx was astonished to find that this self-taught "proletarian thinker" who knew neither economics nor philosophy had more influence in its congresses than he. Even when Proudhon died (in 1865) his teachings continued to flourish, leaving a lasting imprint on French socialist, syndicalist and anarchist thought, and on that of the other Latin lands and Switzerland and Holland.[16]

A decisive turning point in this struggle between French socialism and what Marx called "the German theory" seemed to come at last with the Franco-Prussian War of 1870. One day after hostilities opened, Marx wrote Engels:

The French need a thrashing. If the Prussians win, then centralization of the *state power* useful to the centralization of the German working class. Furthermore, German predominance [in Europe] would transfer the center of gravity of the West European labor movement from France to Germany, and one need only compare the

---

[16] Mehring, *op. cit.*, p. 148; Richard T. Ely, *French and German Socialism in Modern Times*, New York, 1883, pp. 130–31; Nikolaevsky and Maenchen-Helfen, op. cit., pp. 266–79.

movement from 1866 to the present in the two lands to see that the German working class is superior to the French in theory and organization. Its predominance over the French on the world stage would at the same time be the predominance of *our* theory over that of Proudhon. . . .[17]

Marx expressed the same idea in letters to German socialists including those of the Braunschweig Committee of his faction in Germany. These naïve followers thought the world should know the good news and published the letter in one of their leaflets. Marx wrote indignantly to Engels that he had not known he was dealing with "silly babies," who could not understand the difference between confidential information and instructions, and public documents, "with educated men who ought to know that the brutal language of letters is not intended for publication." He could only hope that the French members of the International were too busy with the German siege of Paris, or too unfamiliar with the German language and German political activity to take note of it.[18]

When the Paris Commune was set up, against the advice of Marx and Engels, insofar as its leaders were members of the International, they were Proudhonists and Blanquists. All that Marx could do was to annex this characteristically French *Commune* to "German theory" by his defense and legendary interpretation of it after its downfall.

The fall of the Commune did weaken the French working class for years as the German defeat of France had not. It scattered its leaders far and wide, burying some in the Grave of the Federals in Père Lachaise, sending others to penal colonies for years, driving yet others to refuge in Belgium, Switzerland, and England. Yet the followers of the dead Proudhon, reinforced by the followers of the living Bakunin (who accepted Proudhon's federalism, antistatism, and mutualism and set a new stamp upon them) gave Marx such determined battle that he had to wreck the International lest they capture it.

Thereafter, too, the spirit of Proudhon continued to be mighty still, now joined with, now separate from, the spirit of Bakunin. In the words of his biographer, Mayer, "Engels was convinced right down to the last that the doctrines of Marx and himself would eventually mold the working-class movement even in the land of

---

[17] *MEGA*, III/4, p. 340.
[18] *Ibid.*, pp. 381–83.

Proudhon." Still, in the twentieth century, the spirit of Jean Jaurès who led the French movement until 1914, and of Léon Blum who led it between the two wars, testify that Marx had not prevailed.[19]

To the day of his death, Marx never abandoned his conviction of the superiority of his "German theory" and its need and destiny to triumph over French socialism, both in France itself and in the international socialist movement. Three years before he died, he wrote to Sorge in America that with the aid of his son-in-law, Lafargue, recently converted from Proudhonism,[20] and Jules Guesde, converted from Bakuninism to Marxism, he had managed in secret to write a socialist program for one faction of the French socialists. This, he held modestly, was the "first genuine socialist program" ever to have been adopted in France. The paper they founded on its principles was "the first French workingmen's paper in the broader sense of the word." The new program and journal together had moved some hitherto recalcitrant French leaders to "profess [*sich bekennen*, basically a religious term] *le socialisme moderne scientifique*, that is to say, the *German*." The new group, Marx continued, "constitutes in my eyes . . . the *first genuine workers' group* in France." Alas for Marx's hopes, his group remained a minority and although thus sponsored by Marx in person, it gave to "the German theory" a distinct "French accent," as was to be shown by the disputes between Vaillant and Guesde as French Marxists with Bebel as a German Marxist in the councils of the Second International. When the two main currents of French socialism united in 1905, it was Jean Jaurès, anti-Marxist, who became its great spokesman, and after him the non-Marxist Léon Blum. So, too, French unionism became French syndicalism, differing profoundly from the unionism of the German labor movement. In short, the French workingman remained French, so that his parties, unions, journals, political and social and economic ideas continued to be those which Marx had considered neither worthy to be called "*socialisme moderne scientifique*" nor a "genuine workers' group."[21]

Thus, underneath the avowed internationalism of the First In-

---

[19] In 1924 the Communist Party of France described itself in its own theoretical organ, *Cahiers du Bolchevisme*, No. 2, Nov. 28, 1924, as ideologically "20 per cent Jaurèsism, 10 per cent Marxism, 20 per cent Trotskyism, and 30 per cent confusionism."

[20] Both Marx's French sons-in-law, Lafargue and Longuet, were converted by their father-in-law from Proudhonism to Marxism.

[21] Marx's letter to Sorge is in *Briefe an Sorge und andere*, Stuttgart, 1906, pp. 168–72.

ternational lay the deeper forces of disparate national character. Bakuninists, Proudhonists and Marxists reproached one another for the national stamp they each put upon their competing doctrines. Marx denounced Proudhonist internationalism as the "most Machiavellian form of French chauvinism," and he sought to "expose" Bakunin as an "agent of Russian Tsarism" trying to place the workers' movements of Europe under Russian direction in the interests of the Russian autocracy. Proudhon referred, as we have seen, to "your countryman, Martin Luther" in his warning on the authoritarian spirit of "the German doctrine." Bakunin, though he always referred to Marx's scientific studies and devotion with the greatest respect, branded Marx's views on the state, on centralism, on dictatorship, and on the supremacy and exclusive rightness of "the German theory," as the introduction of "Prussian Bismarckian authoritarianism" by this "Hebraico-Germanic sect" into a movement which should be libertarian and decentralist and should have as its main aim a series of revolutions against established authority.[22]

Indeed, it could hardly have been otherwise. These rebels and system builders were strong-willed men, each at odds with things as they were, yet bearing upon himself the stamp of the world against which he rebelled; each with a powerful belief in himself, his leadership and destiny, and the rightness of his own formulas for the salvation of mankind. Each was a selfless egoist, selfless in the sense that he was ready to forego the good things and vanities of the ordinary world, live in austere poverty, and devote himself to the cause of mankind. Yet each believed in himself with a more than ordinary belief, coveting not the pleasures of everyday life but the pleasures of authority, leadership, and a place in history.

The seeds of disunity were in the very foundations of the International Workingmen's Association, needing but a little time and the heat of battle to sprout and open great cracks in that foundation.

In the forties, fifties and sixties a platonic internationalism was growing in Europe, but, overshadowing it flourished a greatly intensified national spirit. The most diverse elements and accidents contributed to the formation of the International in 1864. One of

[22] Milorad M. Drachkovitch, *Les socialismes français et allemand et le problème de la guerre*, Geneva, 1953, pp. 308 ff; Nikolaevsky and Maenchen-Helfen, *op. cit.*, p. 288; James Guillaume, *l'Internationale, Documents et Souvenirs*, Paris, 1905, II, 269. Guillaume presents Bakunin's viewpoint, having been expelled from the First International on the insistence of Marx, at the same time as Bakunin.

them was a meeting of British Labour leaders with representatives of French workingmen who went to the London International Exposition in 1862. Part of the funds for this trip came from the Emperor, Napoleon III, and his brother, Jerome Bonaparte. The French Section of the International included not a few employers ("bourgeois") and other "middle-class" elements, doctors, journalists, even army officers, French republicans seeking to reconstitute their shattered movement against the Empire, workingmen who hoped to evade the Imperial decree against "associations of more than twenty persons" by joining a body the Emperor had seemed to sponsor, many artisans and but few industrial workers. To some extent, we do not yet know how much, Masonic lodges with their ritual liberalism and internationalism and their secret organization contributed to the International's foundation. The Swiss and Belgians greatly outnumbered the French. Among the Swiss were bodies whose main platform was "phonetic spelling." There were former rationalist societies, free-thinkers, mutualist credit movements, cooperatives, remnants of the *communeros* and Carbonari, remnants of groups descended from medieval guilds. The Italian workingmen were under the influence of Mazzini's socialistic republicanism and his struggle for the unification and independence of Italy, until Bakunin, not Marx, displaced his influence. The British members consisted of former Chartists, German emigré workingmen active in British unions, like Eccarius, who secured for Marx his entree, and trade-union leaders who hoped that an international organization might stop the importing of strikebreakers from the Continent by British employers.

The historians of the First International, Jacques Freymond and Miklos Molnar write:

> During the two years elapsing between the St. Martin's Hall [founding] meeting and the Geneva Congress, the International was able to rally under its banner over a hundred societies and groups as different from one another as the British trade unions, the French mutual-aid societies, Genevan factories, clock-makers from the Jura, Belgian free-thinkers, the first German Marxists, and republican and democratic bourgeoisie. . . . This diversity is truly decisive, since it persists in the face of the centripetal force of common aspiration and proves in the end more powerful than the momentary unity. It manifests itself in the fiercely independent attitudes of the groups. Each one jealously maintains its autonomy in relation to and against all the others. Not just the General Council in London but even the federal committees

[in the various countries] fail to impose their will on the sections.
. . . As soon as London tries to intervene and impose its policies on
the sections, the whole I.W.A. in Spain rebels, breaks away from the
General Council, and persists as before nearly indifferent to the concerns of others. This jealous independence, this spirit of autonomy
closely akin to indifference without precluding a loyal solidarity in the
case of strikes or class struggles, characterizes the whole history of the
International from its beginning to its end. . . . The First International carried from its inception the seeds of the final crisis.[23]

Thus there was little of the abstract internationalism such as
Marx envisaged in the *Communist Manifesto* (which, as we saw in
the chapter on "Nationalism or Internationalism?" did not dwell in
the breast of Marx and Engels, either). Nor much of the revolu-
tionary-socialist consciousness which Marx had postulated as part of
the existential equipment of the working class. Nor did the working
class as such have the weight which Marx attributed to it in the
Councils of the International and its local organizations.

Had it been as proletarian as he professed to believe, Marx himself might not have gotten into it any more than Mazzini and Pyat,
for of the real workingmen a great many favored the exclusion of all
who were not actually artisans or factory workers.

At the beginning Marx seemed to be aware of these things, for in
his impressive draft of the Statutes and Inaugural Address, he
avoided "the bold language" of the *Communist Manifesto,* paying
tribute instead to cooperatives, labor legislation, union organization,
democracy, and even ethical values (that *bête noire* of his "scientific
socialism"). He nourished the hope that his presence, his influence
in the General Council, his facility in preparing moderate-seeming
documents not contrary to the spirit he hoped to foster, and finally,
"the exchanges of ideas and discussion . . . will not fail to produce
gradually a common theoretical program,"[24]—that of Marx. Perhaps

---

[23] Jacques Freymond and Miklos Molnar, *The First International: Why Did It
Rise? Why Did It Fall?,* in *One Hundred Years of Revolutionary Internationals,*
Milorad Drachkovitch, Editor, Stanford University Press, 1965, Volume I.
Freymond and Molnar are also the authorities for most of the statements above
on the diverse elements forming the International Workingmen's Association.
For the role of the Free Masons see Boris Nikolaevsky's comments on the
Freymond-Molnar Paper.
[24] From the Resolution of the General Council, March 6, 1869, quoted in
Freymond, *La Première Internationale, Recueil de documents,* Geneva, 1962,
Vol. II, p. 271.

for this reason the first two documents Marx wrote for the International are among the most carefully thought out and best written programmatic documents from his hand.

But Marx's impatience grew with each year. And not only Marx's. The embattled titans each sought to provide this loose, many-colored federation of many lands, social layers, and tendencies, with his own exclusive and *alleinseligmachende* dogma of salvation. Their struggles to prevail would not let it remain a free federation of autonomous national labor movements and national bodies. From the first congress on, there contended for mastery a French theory (Proudhonist mutualism), a Russian (Bakuninist communist anarchism), and a German theory (Marx's). There was yet a fourth ideology, unnoticed as such by the other three since it was neither so noisy nor so bent on conquering. Yet it was the only ideology actually held by a genuine workingmen's mass organization: the liberal, democratic, pragmatic, Christian dissenter, Christian socialist, trade-union ideology of the great British unions. And along with these four main contending currents there were the countless vari-colored small fry of innumerable varieties in innumerable localities of the constituent countries.

There was no way in which German ideologues could be made to think like Frenchmen or Russians, or any of them like the spokesmen of the British unions. But in congress after congress, the titans fought each other, leaving little energy over to fight the "international bourgeoisie" (which was doubtless as unreal as the "international proletariat").

In 1871, perhaps because Marx thought he had prepared the ground for easy ideological and organization victory, or perhaps because in his heart he was weary of all the time this unending effort to put his stamp upon the vari-colored fabric was taking from his scientific work in the British Museum, Marx suddenly sprang the organizational trap he had been preparing and exploded the ideological bombs he had planted in the subtly worded Inaugural Address and Statutes of 1864. The General Council convened a private conference in London with a carefully prepared majority for a simultaneous offensive in the organizational, ideological and political spheres. Political action, hitherto regarded merely as one means—and a subordinate one—for economic emancipation, was now declared to be linked "indissolubly" to the economic movement, thus ruling out the Bakuninist and Proudhonist positions. The proletariat must "indispensably" be formed into a political party of the class to "assure the triumph of the social revolution." The powers of the General Council (where Marx had the upper hand) were suddenly expanded at the expense of the fiercely proud autonomous national federations and local sections. The General Council now laid claim to the right to expel even national bodies whose servant it had hitherto been. The majority of the sections revolted, including the Spanish, the Italian, the Belgian, the French Swiss, the French Emigrés in London. Some British trade-union leaders had dropped off after winning electoral reform and other labor rights, and some out of disagreement with Marx's resolution on the Paris Commune; but now the last and best of them walked out in disgust at Marx's organization methods.[25]

When at last the smoke of battle cleared, Dr. Marx stood triumphant and alone. He had prepared the private Conference of 1871 and the Hague Congress of 1872 with care (packed them to be more exact, aided by the indignant resignation of whole sections who did not send delegations). He had succeeded in transforming the once democratic, vari-colored, loosely associated, autonomous-federalist International into an autocratic-centralist instrument of the General Council; that is, of his own views and person. He captured only the hollow shell, and knew nothing better to do with it than to bury it quietly in far off America. From its hopeful beginnings in 1864 to its inglorious burial in 1876, each of the currents that had formed part of the Inter-National bore the indelible stamp of its own national origin and character. Thus the flaw had been in the foundation from the beginning.

---

[25] See Freymond and Miklos, *op. cit.*

Chapter **15**

LIFE AND DEATH OF THE
SECOND INTERNATIONAL

It must be explained to the people how great is the secrecy
with which war arises, and how helpless are the ordinary
organizations of the workers, even those calling themselves
revolutionary, in the face of a real oncoming war. . . . It
is necessary to explain to the people again and again how
matters stood in the last war, and how it cannot be otherwise. It is necessary to explain especially the significance of
those circumstances that make it inevitable that the question
of "the defense of the fatherland" will inevitably be decided by the overwhelming majority of the workers in favor
of their own bourgeoisie.

—V. I. Lenin in his confidential instructions
to his Delegation to the Hague, December 4, 1922, Lenin's last words on war.

THE DEATH of the First International cleared the ground for the
building of genuine national movements, each rooted in the soil of
its own country and shaped by that country's history and conditions.
Inevitably they were as different as the lands themselves.

The British trade unions continued as before. Alongside them
arose a powerful, well-organized German political and union movement. It had been growing for some time according to its own laws,
paying little heed to long-distance critical bombardment from Marx.
Its leaders respected Marx but felt that he was out of touch with the
realities of their land. Now at last, as Marx had foretold, "our
German movement" won a leading position in Europe, aided by the
unification and the military and industrial growth of a Greater Ger-

270

many. By its size and solidity of organization, the German labor movement should have been the main counterweight to the British in the Second International. If the debates at the congresses were between Frenchmen and Germans, rather than Englishmen and Germans, it was because the English unions were disinterested in the very terms of the controversies preoccupying the Continent.

The stormy titans all were dead: Proudhon (1865); Lassalle (1864); Mazzini (1872); Bakunin (1876); Blanqui (1881); Garibaldi (1882); Marx (1883). The heroic generation of 1848 had departed. Only Engels lingered on until the mid-nineties, a remote counselor and mellowed sage to symbolize a vanished epoch.

Even some of the generation of '48 had known that they were really national leaders of nascent national movements. Now, when those native movements began to flourish, the new leaders were less quarrelsome and more modest men, with no ambitions that sprawled across the Continent and around the world. "Our socialism is French in origin, French in inspiration, and French in character," said Jean Jaurès. And on another occasion, "A little internationalism leads away from patriotism; a great deal of it brings one back." Engels spoke in the same vein when he said, "If Russia should attack Germany, then we are as much concerned as those who rule Germany and we will resist." Still more startling were the words that Marx's old comrade-in-arms penned for the French Parti Ouvrier in 1892: "If France in alliance with Russia should declare war on Germany . . . we would have no choice but to oppose with all our strength any aggressor on Russia's side." So the co-author of the *Communist Manifesto* wrote within a year after the Second International was born. Bebel echoed his sentiments as Jaurès seemed to echo the words of Proudhon: "Patriotism may be more ardent or less in each of us; its nature is the same, its absence a monstrosity."

In the two closing decades of the nineteenth century there was a new, if milder, upsurge of international sentiment. This time it was little more than a movement for international labor legislation and the regulation of the length of the working day. Not only unions but industrialists and potentates became interested in simultaneous international labor legislation, so that no country should suffer competitively for generosity to its laboring people. Indeed, the potentates initiated the movement. As early as 1880 the German emperor, under prodding from Bismarck, called a conference for "international labor legislation," while Pope Leo XIII issued his *Rerum No-*

varum in 1891. By that time, many disparate movements and tendencies were drawing closer together: unions, labor parties or incipient labor parties, Marxists, Proudhonists, Blanquists, Anarchists, Fabians, Syndicalists, Possibilists, pacifists, and various fringe movements of reform.

There was some maneuvering for position, and several false starts. The French Possibilists, a moderate socialist movement, sent out a call for an international congress to be held in Paris in 1889. This would never do, said the German and French Marxists, so they countered with a rival international congress in the same city at the same time. One would think that the fusion of the two would get the new international off to a good start while subsequent friendly dialogue might iron out the differences. So at least the Possibilists thought. But they did not reckon with the temperament of those who were sure they had a monopoly on the truth. The Marxists, with Engels's behind-the-scenes approval, refused all truck with the other conference. Thus the principle of exclusion appeared before there existed any body from which to exclude. Though the Marxists could be snooty about the French moderates and their guests, they felt they could not do without the big English labor movement, however moderate it might be.

In the end, after several congresses and many negotiations, the new International, bearing a Marxist stamp, admitted everybody down to the Possibilists, except the Anarchists, who, on the insistence of the German movement, were excluded.[1] Thus a fairly broad International was born, under the manifest hegemony of the professedly Marxist German Social Democracy. And a new dialogue began between "the German theory" and "French Socialism," a gentler, less thunderous dialogue, for both had greatly changed in intensity, scope and passion since the disappearance of the titans. It was the muted dialogue of epigoni.

The main objective of the new organization was not an attack on capitalism as such, but on the older, unregulated capitalism of laissez faire. Though they did not then use such terms, their efforts to regulate the conditions of the employment of labor were the beginnings of a planned economy; governments began to regulate economic life as they had not done since the age of mercantilism.

---

[1] On the Anarchists and their relations to the various Internationals, including those they formed themselves, see the paper of Max Nomad, "The Anarchist Tradition," in *A Hundred Years of Revolutionary Internationals*, Ed. Milorad Drachkovitch, Stanford, 1965.

The actual occasion of the foundation of the International was neither the spreading of Marxism nor Possibilism, but the planning by labor of joint international action to promote an eight-hour day.

The national movements were more conscious now of their national differences, their diversity of organization, ideology, traditions, and problems, and more jealous for their right of autonomy, or determination of their own affairs. No general council was going to tell them now what they must believe or do, nor inform them that they were to be expelled from the labor movements of their own countries and the International they were forming.

They proclaimed their complete solidarity across frontiers and strove to employ a common language. Yet they could not agree on a common approach even to the fight for the eight-hour day. The French, who loved the words *General Strike* but did not have the requisite organization to make one, called for a one-day general strike for the eight-hour day to be proclaimed simultaneously in all lands. The Germans, who had numerous powerful, disciplined organizations but less volatile temperaments, insisted that each country must be free to decide its own action. They argued that a general strike was a leap in the dark in unknown terrain, that it was harmful to organized labor and would hurt the workingmen's families as well as those of non-workers, and that socialism and labor organization were more important than the eight-hour day. The British were for peaceful mass demonstrations in favor of new legislation. The Americans, having already won some successes by their own method, urged an industry-wide strike each first of May in a different industry, so that those on strike could be supported by workers in all other trades. Other countries, conscious of the weakness of their organizations and the tenuousness of their rights, picked the nearest Sunday for their "general strike," in place of the first of May. After arguing themselves into exhaustion, the delegates managed to attain international "unanimity" by the following resolution:

> The workers of the various countries will have to accomplish the manifestation (and the position in relation to the public authorities) under the conditions imposed on them by the particular situation in each country.[2]

The question of the general strike as a tactical or strategical one continued to be hotly debated all through the life of the International, and never finally resolved. Engels, as we have seen, was

---

[2] G. D. H. Cole, *The Second International*, Part One, London, 1956, pp. 1–11.

opposed to the very idea. The leaders of the German labor unions summarized their view in the words of their subsequent spokesman, Karl Legien, "General strike is general nonsense." Belgium and Sweden, in disproof of Engels's prophecies, succeeded in winning universal suffrage by general strikes, while similar efforts in Italy in the seventies, and in Holland in 1903, were unsuccessful. Then the startling experiences in a backward country with an unorganized labor movement—Russia in 1905 (where every industrial worker according to government statistics must have struck that year more than once)—put the General Strike back into the realm of ardent controversy, for the Tsar's Manifesto of October 1905, was obviously a result of a General Strike. This gave fresh impulse to the syndicalist notion of General Strike as the royal road to revolution, and to the demand of the more radical pacifists that war be stopped by a political mass strike, a strike in the munitions factories and strategic industries like transport, and even a "general strike" of conscripts.[3]

Despite the victory of Marx's "German theory" in the First International, that body of embattled Prometheans had had no practical ties with the nascent German movement. "Our theory" belonged to Marx, but "our party" did not. Now, in the Second International, by virtue of its rapid and solid growth, its prestige in defeating Bismarck's outlawry, its doctrinal unity, its imposing discipline, its great journals, its large and distinguished parliamentary delegation in the Reichstag, the German Social Democracy dominated the congresses. For a few years (until his death in 1895) it got encouragement, advice, and prestige from Engels. It found support, too, in Marxist minorities from other countries: the Guesdists in France, Plekhanov and his fellow Russian emigrés, a Marxist wing in hitherto exclusively Bakuninist Spain, etc. The prestige and power of the German Social Democracy, supported by the Marxist minority in France and other lands, helped to give the congresses their outward appearance of unity and agreement, ostensibly under the banner of Marxism.

The International was founded in a period of peace, after the ebbing of the storms of 1848–70 and the wars for national unification. Including the decade or so preceding its foundation, the Inter-

---

[3] On the general strike debates and their meaning, see "The Second International: 1889–1914," by Gerhart Niemeyer, in *A Hundred Years of Revolutionary Internationals.*

national was to live out its life in a period of forty-nine years when there was not one war among the great powers of Europe.

At every congress they talked of peace. Frenchmen and Germans strove to give the appearance of agreement to signify the solidity of the peace of Europe. Ritual oratory, ritual gestures, deeply felt emotions—and unanimous agreements, secured, on mere empty husks of resolutions from which all differences had first been eliminated—all contributed to the reassuring mood. During the Russo-Japanese War in 1904, the delegates at the Amsterdam Congress were profoundly moved when Plekhanov and Sen Katayama embraced and kissed each other on the platform. If it did not stop the war, it stopped the show, for the delegates were delirious with enthusiasm.

The resolutions on war and peace, militarism and colonialism, marked a steady progression at least in length from congress to congress. At the founding congress in 1889, the last order of business was *The Abolition of Standing Armies and the Arming of the People*. Actually the title was one which could easily be made to cover that "democratization of military service" (conscription) which was to transform limited war into total war. From the debate we can see that the delegates did not think of their formula—as Lenin one day would—as a cover for weakening the armed forces or arming an uprising. Vaillant, an old Blanquist, a veteran of the Commune who had gone over to Marxism, presented the resolution which was such that it could be adopted unanimously:

> *Peace* is the first and indispensable condition of any emancipation of the working class. . . . *War*, inevitable product of present economic conditions, will only *finally* disappear with the disappearance of the capitalist order . . . and the international triumph of socialism.[4]

At the Second Congress, held in Brussels in 1891, the German party played first violin and the French second. Liebknecht and Vaillant shared the platform as reporters on *Point Four: Militarism.* The delegates felt that if France and Germany could agree, there would continue to be peace at the heart of Europe. Hence "France" and "Germany" proposed a joint resolution. It was of the same tenor as last year's, but much longer:

[4] Milorad M. Drachkovitch, *Les socialismes français et allemand et le problème de la guerre*, Geneva, 1953, pp. 314–15. From here on the present chapter follows closely the selection of documents, citations, and analysis of Drachkovitch's book, which is unsurpassed in its organization of the materials dealing with socialism and war.

Only the creation of a *socialist order* [it concluded] will put an end to militarism and make peace finally secure. . . . The *international socialist party* is the true and only *party of peace*—the only means of preventing the catastrophe of a general war.

(And this in the year of the consolidation of the Franco-Russian Alliance which stirred Engels's deepest fears and wrung from him the warning to the French people that the German socialists would support their government if France and Russia attacked jointly!)

Hasten the triumph of socialism . . . protest by incessant agitation against *all traces of the will to war* and the *alliances* which favor them. . . . Before history and humanity, put upon the ruling classes responsibility for everything which might occur.

The impotence of the International showed through every threadbare phrase.

At this point a new and troubling voice was heard to upset the apparent peace, a voice that called not for mere protest and self-exculpation but for action. Domela Nieuwenhuis, thoughtful Protestant pastor turned socialist, shattered the surface harmony with which they had sought to quiet their fears. On behalf of the Dutch Party, with the support of many of the French and English delegates, he offered his proposal. "Your resolution," he told Liebknecht and Vaillant, "the Pope could accept, too, if only you changed a single word, substituting Christianity for socialism." He for his part would offer a resolution the Pope could not accept:

The socialists of all lands will reply to a proposal of war with an appeal to the people to proclaim a general strike.

Liebknecht replied on behalf of the great German Party. His reply was praised by Engels, echoed by Bebel and Plekhanov, praised by Lenin. He defended his party's orthodoxy and internationalism against the implication of "German nationalism." He attacked Nieuwenhuis's "phrase radicalism" which he said could only be entertained by the citizens of a small country, members of a small party that neither knew the weight of militarism nor possessed sufficient strength to be responsible for their country's policy and fate. But Nieuwenhuis had touched a vibrant chord in the French spirit. Of the fifty-six French delegates, thirty-two voted against the German-French resolution and for Nieuwenhuis. A majority of Englishmen, too, coming as they did from a land where dissenting Christian pacifism had combined with a habit of depending on strikes, voted for his resolution.[5] The German-French resolution won, but significantly the majority of the French delegation was not among its supporters. Two temperaments, two tactics, at the heart of Europe! Two voices on war and peace!

Of course, the debate was renewed at the Third Congress, at Zurich in 1893. Only now it was moved up to *Point Two* to give more time to settle it.

Plekhanov, Russian disciple of the German theory, speaking in impeccable French, presented the majority resolution; Nieuwenhuis, the minority. War—said the Russian voice of the German theory—is but a symptom, a symptom of the disease called capitalism. "The roots are to be found in the essence of the capitalist order. . . . When capitalism has been suppressed, war will be eliminated."

But what to do in the meantime? Certainly not a military or a general strike as proposed by Nieuwenhuis. That was mere phrase-mongering. Still worse it "would disarm in the first instance the civilized peoples [those with the most freedom and the greatest degree of socialist culture and labor organization] and deliver Western Europe as prey to the Russian cossacks."

Nieuwenhuis was not impressed. "It is you who are the phrase-mongers," he retorted, "answering rifles and cannon balls with protestations on paper. The German movement is nationalist in its heart, corroded with hatred of Russia and conciliation toward its own government. If we want to fight war, there is no way to do it except by the use of our natural weapons, a military strike, a strike of troops, reservists, conscripts, railwaymen, transport workers, women."

Again the French were stirred by the appeal to a general strike. The "German Resolution," as everyone called it despite its sponsorship by Plekhanov, carried by the affirmative votes of fourteen nations. But France, Australia, Holland, the United States, and Norway, recorded that they were abstaining.

The Belgians tried their hand at strengthening the majority resolution by adding some stipulations on the duties of socialists in parliament:

> . . . to reject all military credits . . . to protest unceasingly against *standing armies* . . . to demand *disarmament* . . . to support all *associations* aiming at *universal peace*.[6]

---

[5] *Ibid.*, pp. 315–16.
[6] *Ibid.*, pp. 317–18.

This was easier than striking, so it was accepted. But in 1914, not even this modest parliamentary action would be carried out by French and German socialists.

At the next congress, the Fourth (London, 1896), the Anarchists were expelled. Nieuwenhuis and nine members of his delegation walked out in protest, after which Nieuwenhuis joined the Anarchists. Ideological controversy in the purged International became more schoolmasterly. Still the specter of war continued to haunt the sessions. The French took up, as their temperament bade them, the opposition post which Nieuwenhuis had vacated. The resolution, German once more in its origins and backed by the usual Marxist French minority, tried added length as a substitute for added strength. Among the additional proposals were arbitration courts and a demand for a popular referendum in case the governments did not accept the verdict of the court. But in case they did not accept a referendum . . . ?

As the new century dawned, men saw in the sky a red glow. Was it the harbinger of the triumph of socialism that Engels had prophesied for the turn of the century? Or the first flicker of the flames that were to consume the ancient civilization of Europe in a "war of the races?"

The signs were disturbing: Spanish-American War; Boer War; Boxer Rebellion; Anglo-French conflict in Egypt with armed confrontation (the Fashoda Incident); Austro-Russian contention in the Balkans; Franco-German rivalry in North Africa and the Near East; rebellious Slavs in the southern provinces of Austria-Hungary; Italy and Austria each eying the Adriatic Coast; Japan and Russia thinking of advancing into Manchuria and Korea.

At the Paris Congress of the International in 1900, the war problem was expanded into two heads instead of one, Van Kol reporting on *Colonial Policy* (on which no agreement was reached or any clearly thought out proposals advanced), and Rosa Luxemburg on *International Peace, Militarism, the Abolition of Standing Armies.* Once more the resolution grew longer, and a section was added on "the education and organization of the youth"—which the German government promptly forbade, and the German Party as promptly abandoned. Once more the flood of words, when boiled down to their essence, revealed only protest, self-exculpation, and a negative parliamentary vote on war credits. Once more the general strike got a drubbing, this time not so much as a weapon against war, but rather as a weapon for bringing about the social revolution. Karl Legien, head of the German trade unions, led the attack on the very idea of the general strike. Aristide Briand—later as "bourgeois minister" to try his hand at strike-breaking himself—master in the French manner of the radical flourish, led the defense of the general strike. Once more, the incapacity to agree on anything, much less to carry it out, was concealed in a "compromise resolution" that everybody could vote for.

The 1904 Congress in Amsterdam saw Russia and Japan at war. The war was answered by the embrace of Plekhanov and Katayama, and a resolution greeting the workers of Japan and Germany "massacred by the crimes of capitalism," and urging the workers of all other lands "to oppose by all means all extension of the war." What "all means" might mean was not even touched on. Hyndman, Guesde, and Lenin, orthodox Marxists all three, favored the victory of Japan over Russia, but this did not come out at the Amsterdam Congress. It had to wait until "little Japan," the expected loser, had begun to win some victories.

The Stuttgart Congress (1907) was the high point in the life of the Second International. The stirrings of the Russian Revolution of 1905 were still felt; the general strike looked more feasible and more tempting; the arms race was becoming vertiginous; tension was mounting in the Balkans, the Near East, and at the heart of Europe; the Franco-Russian Alliance was in gingerly fashion being converted into an Anglo-French-Russian Alliance. The Congress itself was most solemn and impressive. For the first time the German Social Democracy felt strong enough to defy its government by acting as host—host to an impressive assemblage of 884 delegates and who knows how many alternates, journalists and hangers-on, from twenty-five countries. Bebel and Kautsky headed the German delegation; Jaurès, Guesde, and Vaillant the French. The Marxists under Guesde and the more moderate, indigenous and numerous wing under Jaurès, had at last united (in 1905), with Jean Jaurès as the most popular orator and undisputed tribune of the people. In Germany, the once solid orthodox Marxist left had just been torn into a "Left," led by Rosa Luxemburg, and a "Center," led by Bebel and Kautsky. The party denied Luxemburg a mandate so that she had to fall back on the Polish Party for a delegate's credential. On Jaurès's insistence (he believed in free discussion in the socialist movement as a matter of principle), the fire-eating *enfant terrible* of the general-strike and military-strike wing of the French party was given a mandate, too, although Bebel would have expelled him had he been a German. And there was Keir Hardie from England, also for a general strike against war; both Martov and Lenin from the strife-torn yet "united" Russian Social democracy; Ebert and Legien as well as Bebel and other genuine workingmen—or ex-workingmen—from Germany; Renner and Adler from Austria—no important voice, no well-known name, was missing.

This time war was put first on the order of business. For all the solemn show of international unity, there was still a French view and a German view, which only diplomatizing and *vorbeireden* could patch up into a semblance of an agreement. Bebel himself introduced the usual German resolution—longer than ever, but with only one new thought:

> In case war breaks out notwithstanding these efforts, it is their duty to intervene in favor of its early termination.

Bebel's main antagonist was Gustave Hervé (though today people have been led to believe that it was V. I. Lenin, or at least, Rosa Luxemburg). Grandson of peasants, son of a sailor, history professor, lawyer, firebrand agitator in love with the resounding phrase, founder and editor of *La Guerre Sociale* (which sounded warlike enough until you compared it with Lenin's ideas on the class war), Hervé was already famous for his opposition to the French army, the defense of his country, and French colonial wars.

> General strike against war. . . . No matter which government is the aggressor we refuse to give one drop of our blood. . . . We must respond to the order of mobilization on the first day of war by a strike of the reservists. . . . We reject bourgeois pacifism. . . . We will fight only in one cause, to install a collectivist order. . . . Either a military strike or a determination to enter the barracks, take the arms provided, make the uprising, seize the *communes* and the instruments of labor. . . .

Such was the substance of Hervé's speeches and his signed editorials in his *Guerre Sociale*. He courted arrests and they came; indictment after indictment; jail sentence after jail sentence; fresh occasion for arrest before the old charge was tried. He saw himself as a twentieth-century Blanqui, but Blanqui's conspiracies were missing. This was a war of phrases in the French radical fashion. Aristide Briand defended him in the courts with kindred French eloquence.

The French unions, dominated by syndicalism, found in him a

"political" spokesman. The socialist party was torn into factions by his stormy agitation. Given the French addiction to the stirring phrase, all factions were to some degree touched by it. Vaillant, despite his adherence to the *German theory*, led a wing that favored a general strike and a strike in the war industries, but not a strike of those in uniform or called up for service. Guesde stubbornly held to the full *German view*, opposing both kinds of strike. Jaurès found Hervé's "demagogy confused," but in line with the tolerance which Proudhon had once preached to Marx, Jaurès insisted on Hervé's right to be heard, to remain in the party, to have "proportional representation" on its leading committees. Thanks to this tolerance, here was Hervé at the Congress, attacking the venerable August Bebel and claiming to speak for France and for revolutionary socialism.

Bebel spoke wearily (he had been leading the German Social Democracy since the 1860s), but with his usual frankness. This had all been settled so many times before: the basic principle—the responsibility of capitalism for war; the sole remedy—socialism; the inadequacy, folly, and delusion of irresponsible phrase radicalism had been exposed so often. What was Hervé but Domela Nieuwenhuis *redivivus?* Those arguments had all been made and answered and voted down so many times. Besides, since Nieuwenhuis's day, the parties had grown in size and responsibility for their country's fate. They had acquired a stake in their country. It was time to revise that much misunderstood phrase in the *Communist Manifesto* which says we have no country to defend. Neither Marx nor Engels thought thus. We do not fight for the country as such; the country belongs more to us, the proletariat, than it does to the ruling classes. Hervé should be "trampled under foot" by his own comrades because of his contempt for Alsace and Lorraine and the very independence of his native land. Jaurès and Vaillant were making too many concessions to him. Surely there was a distinction between aggressive wars, which should be opposed, and defensive ones, which should be supported. In Germany general strike, desertion, refusal to serve, insurrection at the outbreak of war, were impossible. Even Germany's most extreme anti-militarist agitator, Karl Liebknecht (son of Bebel's old comrade, Wilhelm Liebknecht) was ready to recognize that much. In Germany, no one rejoiced at Hervé's agitation except the militarists. Yet, "in official circles, no one wants war since it would likely bring revolution." To that revolution the party can contribute in only one way: by "enlightening minds, making socialist propaganda, and organizing." In case war came, "each party should conserve entire freedom to do what seemed most efficacious."

Hervé was sharp in rejoinder:

You are nothing but an admirable dues-collecting machine. You have no conception of revolution. You can penetrate very deeply into the mists of thought [a crack at "German theory"], but faced by the government, you recoil. . . . You are afraid of prison.

Vandervelde, interrupting: "Bebel has been in prison!"

Hervé: Thirty years ago? Since then you have become bourgeois! Nothing left but the phraseology of revolution! . . . Your famous discipline is the discipline of a corpse. If German Social Democracy has nothing more than Bebel to offer, then I am afraid that our internationalism is only a deception of the proletariat. . . . It is your attitude that makes war possible. And if you march for the Kaiser, you should know that you will be marching against revolutionary communes that will be on their feet at the sign of war.

Vaillant, Jaurès, Vandervelde, tried to smooth things over again, but their remarks only served to make clear that, unlike Hervé, they too were ready to defend their land if it was attacked. It was hard to conceal that behind the common language and threadbare resolutions stood not disembodied international spirits but Frenchmen and Germans.

It was Rosa Luxemburg, backed in the Russian caucus by Lenin and Martov, who finally found the road to compromise. On behalf of herself and the Russians for whom she spoke as well (neither Lenin nor Martov took the floor), she offered to accept Bebel's entire resolution with the addition of three amendments. Two were not new, having been voted in other contexts at other congresses. The third was an obscure algebraic formula added to that of Bebel. Her sentence was general enough so that Bebel and the majority could accept it as not too demonstratively crackbrained, nor usable by the German police to outlaw the party "on the eve of its certain victory." At the same time, its general formulas could be given several meanings. Later Lenin would give it one meaning, Martov, and Rosa Luxemburg who presented it, yet another.

Lenin was to gloss this one sentence or rather fragment of a sentence, torn out of context, so many times since, that we are prone to forget that the context was pure Bebel, and that the amendment was drafted and presented by Rosa Luxemburg who refused to read "revolutionary defeatism" into her amendment. Bebel had written:

Should war break out none the less, it is their duty to intervene in favor of its speedy termination.

With this, Rosa Luxemburg, who detested war and the sufferings it would bring to the masses, profoundly agreed. But on behalf of the Russian and Polish delegations she proposed to add these words:

. . . and to do all in their power to utilize the economic and political crisis caused by the war in order to rouse the peoples and thereby to hasten the abolition of capitalist class rule.

Suddenly, everybody seemed satisfied.

Bebel could take it to mean: war will bring revolution (he had already said so), and the party must use the war to hasten it by "enlightening minds, making propaganda, and organizing."

Hervé thought, or professed to think, that he could read for *x* and *y* in this algebraic formula his own values. He voted for the amended resolution, the minutes record him as saying, "with both hands."

Rosa Luxemburg in 1914 would find in her half-sentence formula the warrant for her passionate struggle for peace by extra-parliamentary mass action, and the ground of her denunciation of the leaders who had failed to carry out the parliamentary action to which they were pledged. Had they done so, she thought, they might thereby have encouraged that extra-parliamentary action on which she set such store and which might bring about an early peace or even a social revolution.

Lenin, though Bebel often "looked daggers at him," admired the latter without stint or reservation as the model of the workingman become a professional socialist leader, as one who had been in personal contact with Marx and Engels, as "the most able parliamentarian in all Europe, the most talented organizer and tactician, the most influential leader of the International Social Democracy, who stood out as an enemy of reformism and opportunism." So Lenin wrote in 1913 when Bebel died. Yet, had he lived another year, Lenin would have lumped him with Kautsky as "the most dangerous enemies of all."[7] Hervé's view, Lenin found "semianarchist, naïvely proposing to 'answer' war with a strike and a revolt . . . unable to understand that war is an inevitable product of capitalism, and that

---

[7] In answer to an interviewer who asked whether to defend his country from Russia and France, he would be willing to shoot at the French Marxist, Jules Guesde, Bebel answered: "Well! Yes! I would shoot. . . . It would be a misfortune, but once again, I would be forced. . . ." (Drachkovitch, *op. cit.*, p. 353.)

there is a possibility of revolutionary wars, from which the proletariat could not abstain."

Thus Lenin was satisfied, too. He liked the solid theoretical structure of Bebel's resolution, but could not altogether withhold a covert admiration for Hervé's demon of extraparliamentary action. However, when war came, Lenin rejected the whole tenor of Bebel's resolution, even the first half of that single famous sentence which Rosa Luxemburg, with his support and Martov's, had amended. Those who, like Luxemburg and Martov worked for the "speedy termination of the war" instead of the defeat of their own government and the prolongation of the imperialist war into a civil war, he would brand as "social pacifists" and "traitors." But in the second half of that sentence he would see "lawful" warrant for the "revolutionary defeatism" which even the mover of the amendment and its other co-author would reject.[8]

The resolution was adopted unanimously, with cheers, song, waving of handkerchiefs, intense nervous relief that once more tension and discord had yielded to unanimous resolve. Side by side in the resolution one could find the duty of defending one's country against attack, the absolute rejection of war as an evil consequence of an evil system, the passivity of abstract analysis, the rejection of responsibility for the world as it was, the irresponsible separation from that world by men who thought they were already living in "the future," a hint at the possibility of revolution, a pledge of pressure to restore a speedy peace, warrant for a general strike against war, and even for working for the defeat of your own country as a royal road to revolution. Nothing made so clear as this *omnium gatherum* the tenuous and unstable nature of the internationalism that held this body together with a bond of cloudy words signifying nothing, or signifying something different to each faction, tendency, nation, even each individual who voted for it. The unanimous enthusiasm came from relief that "international solidarity" had been patched up once more as at each previous congress by a resolution which filtered out all specificity and difference.

The patch did not hold for long. At Copenhagen in 1910 the French temperament asserted itself again, and once again it met stubborn resistance from the German.

---

[8] *Ibid.*, pp. 319–32; Gankin and Fisher, *The Bolsheviks and the World War*, Stanford, 1940, pp. 50–66; Lenin, *Sochineniya*, Vol. XIII, pp. 59–77; Vol. XIV, pp. 263–68.

Vaillant, backed by Keir Hardie, attempted to introduce an "elucidation" of the Stuttgart Resolution of 1907:

Among all the means of anticipating and preventing war, the Congress regards as particularly effective a general strike, above all in the war industries. . . .

This time the German left-wing spokesman, Ledebour, led the counterattack which defeated the proposal in committee, 131 to 51. Ledebour reminded the English and French that their movements were not strong enough to carry out such strong measures, and hence they had no right to force them upon a strong and responsible party. You cannot force anything on a truly international movement "except that on which all comrades agree." The only thing on which all could agree, after a wearying, frustrating, and indecisive debate, was a unanimous resolution . . . to refer the matter to the next congress![9]

Before the matter could be taken up again, war broke out in the Balkans. The great powers readied their war machines for any eventuality. Hastily, the International called a special congress at Basel, with war as the only order of business. Lenin, who did not care about stopping war, and who thought that if Austria and Russia got involved it "would be a great trick for the revolution in Eastern Europe" but doubted that "Franz Josef and Nikolasha will give us that pleasure," did not even use his right to attend and vote.

The International put on the best demonstration of which it was capable: orations in praise of peace and against war; revolutionary songs that lifted the rafters; reminders that war might bring revolution so that the ruling classes had best avoid it; denunciation of the guilt of capitalism for war and the war danger; convocation in a church where the organ played Beethoven's *Hymn to Peace;* another kilometric resolution that achieved unanimity by avoiding explicitness; again the uneasy repression of the self-knowledge of their national loyalties and those of the workingmen in whose name they professed to speak. This time to symbolize solidarity, the spokesmen of five major parties joined in presenting a resolution: Jaurès for France, Keir Hardie for England, Plekhanov for Russia, Adler for Austria-Hungary, and Bebel for Germany—spokesmen from the great powers most likely to be involved if war became general in Europe. Again the resolution contained nothing new or specific

---

[9] Drachkovitch, *op. cit.,* pp. 333–38.

Jaurès reported for the five and for the Commission; all that he could add to the tired document was the deceptive warmth of his own eloquence. "If, because of the enormous diversity of possibilities, the resolution does not foresee a special mode of action," he said, "neither does it exclude *anything*. . . . We are ready for all sacrifices." Those who knew this man's spirit could not doubt that in his case, *all sacrifices* would willingly include his life, but not that of his country.[10]

The last word spoken in peace time came on July 29–30, 1914. The International Socialist Bureau met in Brussels in emergency session as ultimatums flew from chancery to chancery and the Austrian, Serbian, Russian, German, and French war machines were warming their engines. Again Lenin did not come, though Austria was already shelling Belgrade!

Fresh from his homeland, Victor Adler spoke with deepest gloom of the "total impotence of any proletarian action whatsoever against war" and the unexpected wildness of the enthusiasm of the masses of his country for the invasion of Serbia. Haase, fresh from Germany, could still speak of great socialist-led antiwar demonstrations in his country (but a day later they would be displaced or driven off the streets by pro-war demonstrations). Keir Hardie said that he and his socialist comrades still favored the general strike for which he had so often voted, but that the English unions—which was what counted—were against it. All that the bewildered Bureau could think of was a resolution conjuring the workers "to intensify their demonstrations for peace," and a motion moving the next congress from war-possessed Vienna where it had been scheduled to Paris and setting ahead the convocation date from the end of August to August 9th, with the idea of bringing all their forces to bear on the prevention of war. But even August 9th was as far off as eternity. On August 1st the great powers were at war. The congress never met.[11]

Across the line that divided Germany from France, the "international" working-class and socialist movement divided, and their self-appointed or duly elected spokesmen as well. Differences of history and tradition, differences of temperament and "nervous

[10] *Ibid.*, pp. 338–42; Cole, *op. cit.*, Part II, p. 976.
[11] Angelica Balabanoff, *My Life as a Rebel*, New York, 1938, pp. 113–18.

rhythm," differences of language and literature and the thoughts expressed in them, differences between the French *esprit* and the German *geist*, between the French *raison* and the German *vernunft*, between the Latin anarchic temperament and German disciplined thoroughness,[12] between great, well-organized mass organization and volatile mass demonstration, between the heritage of the Great French Revolution from below and the Bismarckian revolution from above, between the unity consolidated by revolution and the unity consolidated by *Blitzkriege* between the Jacobin oratory of Jaurès and the sober practical sense of Bebel, between—to quote Jaurès— "the people who conquered universal suffrage on the barricades and those who received it from above," between a land officially oriented to the "left," where conservative parties called themselves "radical" and the socialists, despite their fire-eating words, were constantly being invited into the government, and a land where the Social Democracy party stood alone against the rest and could neither be thought of nor think of entering into a peace-time government—all the differences subtle and gross between these two neighboring peoples in the heart of Europe had their necessary effects upon their socialisms, and made it impossible that the purely worker movements of the two countries, the German unions and the French *syndicats* should understand each other. Those who professed to speak for them might find a common language for resolutions, but as we have seen, it was only after all the real differences had been bleached out and the resolutions made colorless.

Both Bebel and Jaurès, like Engels in his late years, had openly proclaimed their love of country and their determination to defend it if it was "in danger." Both had denounced militarism, hating it with a sincere hatred. Both had proposed the abolition of standing armies in favor of a "popular militia" or an "armed people." Both rejected aggressive war and pledged themselves to support defensive war. Both had lived their lives in and for the socialist movement and deeply cherished it as the embodiment of all they considered most precious. Both were servents of "the future" and rejecters of the present, though both lived well and happily within its orbit. When they tried to give common definition to this apparent shared fund of ideas and emotions, sparks flew. Unlike most of their lesser

---

[12] Significantly, the adherents of "the German theory" in Madrid called themselves *autoritarios* while the adherents of the Proudhon-Bakunin doctrines in Barcelona called themselves *anti-autoritarios* or *libertarios*. On this see Salvador de Madariaga, *Spain: A Modern History*, New York, 1958, pp. 143–55.

followers they were too large in spirit to be insulting to each other. They had none of Lenin's love of blackening the name and the character of an opponent. On the contrary, each honored the other's *bona fides* and natural human dignity. Yet always, the same resolutions, the same formulas, the identical seeming thoughts and phrases, suffered a transformation as they passed through their two diverse temperaments in which were embodied two diverse social, psychological, and historical heritages.

Bebel died shortly before the war. Jaurès was shot on the last day of peace. His last words, pronounced only a few hours before his death, were a cry of anguish: "A kind of amazement and revolt bordering on despair invades me. What! Is it to this barbarism that the movement of humanity has come! Is it to this that they return after eighteen centuries of Christianity, the magnificent idealism of revolutionary justice, a hundred years of democracies?" His answer was an assassin's bullet. Even if these two great tribunes had lived, they would have understood each other no better than before. Perhaps they would have treated each other with more compassion, respect, and dignity than did lesser men, but that is all.

When the guns began to speak, the bright socialist birdcage called the Second International suddenly grew still. The two governments succeeded in convincing each group that their country was "in danger." Obscure, pent-up feelings burst out into delirious mass enthusiasm that would in any case have swept the "spokesmen of the masses" off their feet. Indeed, contrary to what Lenin found convenient to pretend, the leaders were more disheartened and less enthusiastic than the masses, for the cherished illusions they had lived by were swept away in the first gust of the storm. The parliamentary deputies of the two lands—"united" at least in this—voted the huge budgets that were to equip the armies into which their "followers" were streaming joyously.

Jules Guesde (who had so consistently championed the "German theory" in France); Marie-Eduard Vaillant, who had tried to "interpret" the Stuttgart Resolution to mean "general strike in the war industries"; Gustave Hervé, snorter of smoke and fire—all supported their government and the war. Guesde, who had led the classic socialist left struggle against *Ministerialism,* with Kautsky's and Bebel's support, himself became a Minister in the French wartime government. Hervé "answered" war not by a general or a military strike or a seizure of weapons and *communes,* but by changing the name of his fiery journal from *La Guerre Sociale* to *La Victoire.*

The workingmen who had been so often told that they had no enemy on the other side of the frontier and that the real enemy was within their own land, now looked across No Man's Land at the *enemy,* well armed, well uniformed, with Red Cards in their pockets.

As we examine the record of the First International, from which the German theory drove out French socialism, Russian anarchism, and British trade unionism;

And of the Second International, made up of national parties that could never agree on anything important, not even the proper tactics for winning the eight-hour day, and that kept from themselves and the world a knowledge of their disunity by bleaching out all difference in equivocal unanimous resolutions;

As we look into the ambivalent hearts of their leaders torn between their internationalist formulas and their deeply felt love of country;

Or as we look at the ambiguous, prolix and faltering words of the Stuttgart Resolution, including the ambiguous Luxemburg-Lenin-Martov amendment—

We cannot bring ourselves to agree with Lenin when he charged the entire Second International with betrayal of Marxism and of its own resolutions. But he was not wrong to say that at this moment the old Second International was dead—insofar as, as an international, it had ever lived at all.

Chapter 16

LIFE AND DEATH OF THE

THIRD INTERNATIONAL

The History of World Communism, conceived as a united movement with a common doctrine and strategy formulated from a single center, is at an end. One hundred years after the foundation of the First International and fifty years after Lenin proclaimed the need to form the Third in order to replace the Second, the doctrinal and organizational unity of the "world party" created by him has been finally broken by the rival claims to leadership of the two Communist Great Powers, and the resulting schism has opened up new possibilities of independent development to many nonruling and even some ruling Communist parties. International Communism has no longer a single worldwide organization, a single center of authority, or a single "orthodox" doctrine. But if the history of "World Communism" is at an end, the history of Communism in the world is not.

—Richard Lowenthal

WHEN LENIN founded the Third or Communist International, he claimed for it all that was good in the First and the Second. But he was determined that his new International should be kept free from the defects which had weakened the International Workingmen's Association in Marx's day, and those that had brought a tragic end to the Second International in 1914. His would be no free federation of autonomous and independent national parties, no mere "letter box," as he caustically put it, but a "single, unified world party," run from a "single center," a "world army of the revolutionary proletariat" led with "iron discipline bordering on that of the military," directed by a single, unified, authoritative "General Staff of the World Revolution" with headquarters in the Revolution's main fortress, Moscow. The parties would not be national parties in the generally accepted sense of that term at all, but "Sections" of the Communist International, which body would "give organization" uniform in character and "a clear and precise program of action." Thus his old dream of being the guardian of the purity of doctrine, the overseer of organization, strategy and tactics, the director of each fighting action, was extended from Russia to the world.[1]

As far as possible, everything was to be organized, nothing left to chance. The new world party would be as homogeneous, even homogenized, as the great sieve of the *Twenty-One Conditions of Admission* could make it. There would be no room for opportunists, centrists, phrase-revolutionists, conciliators, reformists, only for revolutionists; no room for social patriots, social chauvinists, social pacifists, nationalists, only for genuine revolutionary internationalists.

Before they would be accepted as sections of the new World Party, the several parties would have to "purge themselves of social chauvinists and social pacifists," and of tolerant people who might nourish "conciliatory" feelings toward the latter because of previous shared comradeship or shared struggles. They must purge themselves too of "all communists who might be likely to vacillate in a revolutionary situation." "The agents of imperialism" must of course be expelled, as must all those doubtful characters who "give only verbal recognition to the need of revolution." The Sections must not only purge themselves; they must wage in addition "an unswerving and ruthless war to drive out of the labor movement those opportunist leaders who earned their reputations both before the war and especially during it, in the sphere of politics . . . in the trade unions and the cooperative societies." The very notion that trade

---

[1] All the words and phrases in quotations marks in this chapter, except where otherwise noted, are taken from Lenin's early writings and speeches on the Comintern. They are to be found in Volume X of Lenin's *Selected Works*—the volume entitled *The Communist International*. The principal articles quoted are: The Tasks of the Proletariat in Our Revolution; Speech at the Opening of the First Congress; Closing Speech; The Third International and Its Place in History; Tasks of the Third International; Left-Wing Communism; Conditions of Affiliation; False Speeches about Freedom. Citations are from pages 4–13; 26; 27; 28; 34; 35; 36; 43; 44; 45; 46; 58; 60; 175–79; 200–06; 254; 256–59.

unions should be neutral as regards political parties must be recognized as "a false and despicable subterfuge."

To gain admission as sections of the Comintern, the various parties must "*everywhere* set up illegal organizations parallel with their legal ones." No matter what rights they might enjoy to work legally or strive for a majority by democratic process, they must work in their respective lands for a revolution which would and must be a violent one. The only variant Lenin would allow was

> the *possibility* that in special cases, by way of exception, for example in some little state after its great neighbor has already carried through a social revolution, there *may be* a peaceful yielding of power, if they have convinced themselves of the hopelessness of resistance, and prefer to keep their heads fastened onto their necks. It is much more probable, of course, that even in little states, socialism will not be realized without a civil war. Therefore, the *only* program . . . must be recognition of such a war, even if in our ideal there is no place for the use of force on people.[2]

In each country, the aim must be to set up not merely a "Soviet Republic" or a "Socialist nation" but to turn one's native land into a constituent part of "the international Soviet Republic" which was "impending." This he told the First Congress of the Comintern, but the thought was not new for Lenin. In 1916 more than a year before he seized power, he explained, characteristically, in a set of *Theses on the Socialist Revolution and the Right of Nations to Self-Determination:*

> The aim of socialism is the elimination of the fragmentation of humanity in petty states and the individualism of nations, not only the coming closer of nations to each other, but their merger or fusion.[3]

At the First Congress of the Comintern, which was really no Congress at all—a matter which we shall consider further below—Lenin laid down his new principles for an International as he conceived it. But he did not need to set up great obstacles to the entry of mass parties and their leaders, for none were as yet knocking at the door.

But the Second Congress of the Comintern was a genuine congress. From all over Europe delegations streamed to Moscow to find

---

[2] *Sochineniya*, Vol. XXVII, pp. 46–53. This is Lenin's sole pronouncement on the "possibility" of a "peaceful road to socialism," of which since the Twentieth Congress, Khrushchev, his lieutenants, and his successors, have made so much.
[3] *Sochineniya*, Vol. XXII, p. 135.

out what was happening there and to seek the encouragement that came from the apparent victory of their dream. The German Social Democratic Party, mainstay of the Second International, had split into three parts, and its largest antiwar section, the Independent Social Democratic Party, was debating affiliation with the Comintern. The Italian Socialists, having endorsed the Communist International immediately after its First Congress, sent a large delegation to the Second, made up of all its factions except the Right. From Britain came representatives of the Independent Labour Party, the British Socialist Party, and the British Socialist Labour Party. All three were splinters or minority groupings, but even in the British Labour Party itself there was much vague sympathy for Russia as a beleaguered fortress of workers' rule. Delegates from two American Communist Parties appeared, from Scandinavian and Balkan parties, even syndicalists and anarcho-syndicalists from the Italian and French and Spanish unions and the American I.W.W., to inquire, to see for themselves, to negotiate, to apply for admission.

It was then that Lenin set to work to raise high the barriers, to split all the great mass parties that sympathetically approached his seat of power, to name to them by name which of their leaders they *must* expel, to force them to purge themselves of those whom not they but he considered undesirable, and to accept conditions of every sort which he considered necessary to safeguard the purity of his new International. It was for the Second Congress that Lenin drafted first seventeen, then nineteen points of exclusion, later enlarged by Zinoviev in consultation with Lenin into the celebrated "Twenty-One Points" or "Conditions of Affiliation to the Communist International." The Italian leader, Serrati, said, "Lenin thinks he is inventing a *sincerometer.*" Lenin answered that Serrati was mistaken to make fun of the idea. His "Conditions of Admission" were both a proscription list and a *sincerometer* in one, stipulating in precise detail what each party must do and whom each party must cast into outer darkness, in order to make itself worthy of entering into the kingdom. Zinoviev, reporting on the "Conditions," called them "a bulwark against centrism." If he could have "thought up ten more," he told the Second Congress in his cloture address, he would have added them. "Just as it is difficult for a camel to pass through the eye of a needle, so I hope that it will not be any easier for supporters of the Center . . . to insinuate themselves into the Communist International." In the official journal, *Kommunisticheskii In-*

ternatsional, he wrote: *"It is necessary to put a reliable guard on the gate of the Communist International."*[4]

Thus Lenin provided safeguards for everything. Thanks to the persuasiveness of power and victory, he felt that everything he had done in Russia in his war with the Mensheviks, the "Economists," and the Socialist Revolutionaries, all his unending splits on matters large and small, his rigid "night watchman" organization principles (as Rosa Luxemburg had ironically called them), his extreme centralism—had been legitimatized by victory and proved correct by history. Now he prepared to enforce on every party which approached his "Holy of Holies,"* all these views and procedures, in order to banish "Menshevism" (he used the word a little gingerly in quotation marks for other parties but he was sure its essence was the same), and to banish the root evil of *nationalism,* from the ranks of the new International from the outset.

And yet, the selfsame flaw was in the foundation from the day the foundation was laid—the flaw of nationalism. It was Lenin himself who mixed it with the mortar and concrete and put it into the materials from which he built the foundations and the walls. The nationalism, unconscious but not for that less powerful, was his own Russian nationalism: his unchallengeable certitude that the Russian Revolution, or more particularly, his seizure of power, was synonymous with the beginning of an international revolution, and that the conditions he knew and the methods he had applied in the crumbling empire of the tsars, and in the overthrow of the democratic provisional government, were appropriate to, and necessary for, every country in the world.

There can be no doubt but that Lenin at this moment was completely possessed by the legends or myths within which he lived his political life. He was sure that the World War was the *"final crisis of capitalism";* that the Russian Revolution and his *coup d'état* which that Revolution had made possible were but the first act in the *"world revolution"* which must now spread swiftly through Europe and the world; that the proletariat represented the interests of the entire people; that the party was the spokesman and brain of the proletariat; that the party machine was the spokesman for the party; that its leader was the infallible interpreter of an infallible, scientific

---

[4] No. 11, June 14, 1920, column 1730.
* (The liturgical expression, *Holy of Holies,* is Stalin's, not Lenin's.)

doctrine, now being realized in life; that the Paris Commune was the "first dictatorship of the proletariat" and the seizure of power by his party in the name of the transient slogan, *All Power to the Soviets,* was the second edition of the Paris Commune, bound to be extended now throughout the world.

The overwhelmingly Russian nature of the new International seemed at first merely an unavoidable accident, one of the transient difficulties of war, blockade and *cordon sanitaire.*

Lenin had proclaimed the death of the Second International almost immediately after the war began. Wherever the "world revolution" would start, he wrote, there a new international would be born. Even as late as January 1917, he was writing: "We of the older generation may not live to see . . . this coming revolution," and he still took it for granted that it would start first in one of the more industrially advanced countries of Europe when it did begin.[5]

But in April 1917 Lenin managed to get back to Russia which he then pronounced "the freest government in the world." Taking advantage of that freedom, he declared in his *April Theses,*

It is the task of our party, acting in a country where the revolution has started earlier than in other countries, to take the initiative in creating a third international.

Once he had overthrown that "freest government in the world," he was in no hurry to take such an initiative. The Second International, he thought, was quite dead. He was busy consolidating his own power. To avoid the appearance of one-sided Russian predominance, it was necessary that at least one other great country establish a Communist Party to provide joint auspices for the issuance of a call for a Conference or Congress.

At the very end of the year 1918, two things happened which galvanized Lenin into hasty activity in the international field. The first was an attempt on the part of the various Socialist Parties to heal the deep wounds occasioned by the war by calling a conference in Berne. The second event was a break between the Spartacus League of Germany and the much more powerful Independent Social–Democratic Party of Germany. Rosa Luxemburg led the split reluctantly and with a heavy heart, but Lenin did not know this. Having split off, the Spartacus League, with a few other small frag-

---

[5] Lecture on the Revolution of 1905, delivered to young workers in Zurich, Switzerland, in January 1917. *Sochineniya,* Vol. XXIII, p. 246.

ments, proclaimed itself the Communist Party of Germany. It stumbled into these actions during the last days of December and January 1, 1919. Enchanted, Lenin wrote:

When the Spartacan League called itself "the Communist Party of Germany" then the *foundation* of a really revolutionary international, the *Communist International,* became a *fact.*[6]

But the *fact* was not a fact. Rosa Luxemburg and her associates in the leadership of the new party were opposed to the forming of a new international. It was a series of accidents and misunderstandings, and the pressure of a group of non-Spartacans under the direction of Lenin's lieutenant, Radek, that had forced a sudden and undesirable break away from the more powerful Independent Socialist Party in which there were many radical workers to be won. The Spartacan leaders felt that the situation was not ripe for splitting away from all the parties and unions of the Socialist International. The program Rosa Luxemburg wrote for the new party contained, as had all her previous writings, fundamental criticisms of Lenin's organization views and his penchant for minority dictatorship by a small élite over the great mass of the workingmen. It expressly rejected the idea of party dictatorship over the masses in the Leninist sense. Rosa Luxemburg had welcomed Lenin's revolutionary stand insofar as it seemed to her anticapitalist and antiwar. She wrote of his revolutionary withdrawal of Russia from the universal slaughter as "the most tremendous fact of the World War." But she criticized sharply his use of force against democracy and against the masses, his attempt to solve all problems by the application of terror, his dissolution of the Constituent Assembly by force of arms, his curtailment of democracy and freedom.

Dictatorship, certainly! [she said] But this dictatorship consists in *the manner of applying democracy,* not in its *elimination,* it means resolute attacks upon the well-entrenched rights and economic relations of bourgeois society without which a socialist transformation cannot be accomplished. But this dictatorship must be the work of a *class,* and not of a little leading minority in the name of the class. Freedom for the supporters of the government alone [she wrote in a truly

---

[6] *Letter to the Workers of Europe and America,* written January 12, 1919, *Sochineniya,* Vol. XXVIII, p. 408.

memorable passage of her criticism of Lenin's revolution], freedom only for the members of one party—however numerous they may be—that is no freedom at all. Freedom is always freedom for the one who thinks differently. Not because of any fanatical conception of "justice" but because all that is instructive, wholesome, and purifying in political freedom depends on this essential characteristic, and its effectiveness vanishes when "freedom" becomes a special privilege.

Examining Lenin's new régime, she foretold what would come out of it unless political democracy were restored:

. . . with the repression of political life in the land as a whole, life in the soviets must also become more and more crippled. Without general elections, without unrestricted freedom of press and assembly, without a free struggle of opinion, life dies out in every public institution, becomes a mere semblance of life, in which only the bureaucracy remains as the active element. Public life gradually falls asleep, a few dozen party leaders of inexhaustible energy . . . direct and rule . . . an élite of the working class is invited from time to time to meetings where they are to applaud the speeches of the leaders, and to approve proposed resolutions unanimously—at bottom then a clique affair . . . not the dictatorship of the proletariat but the dictatorship of a handful of politicians. . . . Such conditions must inevitably cause a brutalization of public life: attempted assassinations, shooting of hostages, etc.[7]

In the chaos attendant upon the exit of Russia from the war, the Brest-Litovsk Treaty, the fall of the Kaiser, and the unsettling two months of uncertain struggle in Germany which followed, Rosa Luxemburg was persuaded to hold up publication of her friendly yet clear-eyed critique of Lenin's régime. And in two months she was dead. But clearly the woman who wrote those lines, and who had instructed the German delegates to the Moscow Conference on a New International to vote *NO* and if necessary to walk out of the Conference, would never have passed through the great sieve of the Twenty-One Conditions of Admission to the Communist Interna-

---

[7] Rosa Luxemburg, *The Russian Revolution* and *Leninism or Marxism?* (Both in one volume). Ann Arbor, 1961, pp. 69–78. See also, Werner T. Angress, *Stillborn Revolution: The Communist Bid for Power in Germany, 1921–1923,* Princeton, 1963, pp. 9–16, Karl W. Meyer, *Karl Liebknecht,* Washington, D.C., 1957, pp. 154–56.

tional. Indeed, had she been there, she would have torn Lenin's twenty-one strand net to pieces.

The gulf between Lenin's small conspiratorial underground party of professional revolutionary intellectuals and the great, democratically (and sometimes bureaucratically) run mass parties and unions of the West was so deep that he could not understand the psychology of the West European leaders. When they had differences, a vote of their rank and file decided the controversy. But in the Russian exile colonies there was no rank and file movement to decide. Responsible to no mass organization, the little bands of dedicated, fanatical exiles fought each other endlessly in the dim light of the Russian underground. Lenin's solution to every quarrel, as he had written more than once, and as he acted always, was: "Split, split, and again split." Split, secede, expel, until the little handful who agree with you can issue a resolution you have written, in the name of some large-sounding, imaginary organization. Every matter, large and small, on which Lenin disagreed with fellow socialists somehow became to him a pundonor, a splitting point, on the basis of which those who disagreed with him had to be discredited and destroyed. He could not imagine that it mattered how large your party was or what masses had given it its guiding lines, for when you seized power, in the *troika*, in the Committee, in the Party, in the country, you would speak in the name of the masses and tell them what was what.

"A quite small party is sufficient to attract the masses," Lenin told the great Italian Party when he was naming the leaders and groups that it must expel. "In certain moments there is no need for a large organization. . . . You are in a preparatory period. The first stage of that period is a break with the Mensheviks like that we carried out in 1903." Lenin had his way with the Italian Party, splitting open the powerful workers' front in Italy; through the breach, Mussolini "marched" triumphantly on Rome, traveling all but the last few miles in a pullman sleeping car. The same pattern was repeated by Lenin's "best disciple," Josef Stalin, at the end of the twenties, enabling Hitler's storm troopers to march through the breach Stalin created between Socialists and Communists by his dogma that the main enemy was not the fascists but the "social fascists," the "Mensheviks" of the period.

But Rosa Luxemburg, Karl Liebknecht, Paul Levy, Franz Mehring, Leo Jogiches, and the other Spartacan leaders were not as blind in their pro-Russianism as the Italian leaders. They were of the generation of Lenin, and were a match for him. They had grown up in the greatest mass movement in the world, and did not share his "night-watchman's" contempt for the independent and spontaneous actions and will of the masses. They felt that they must convince and win over the masses, not merely manipulate or direct them, or arrogate the right to speak in their name. Particularly Rosa Luxemburg felt that the battle to win over the minds and hearts of the million-headed membership of the socialist and labor movements of Germany and Europe had barely begun. Had these experienced leaders lived, and entered the Comintern on their conditions, they would perhaps have cured it of its fatally one-sided Russianism.

In any case, though Lenin did not know it, there was still only one party which wanted a new international immediately, and not two. Despite his original good intentions Lenin sent out his call without the approval of the German Spartacans. Only one party signed and issued the call—the Russian—thereby sealing the fate of the Comintern.

Lenin's recklessness in splitting and denouncing those he broke with had characterized him all his life. But it was intensified now because he was living at this moment in a dream world of his own. It has been said that this loss of a sense of reality was due to the fact that for a whole year Russia had been cut off from the outside world. This of course was true, and contributed to the distortion of his image of the outside world. But the major cause lay in the blinkers of his dogmas, and in the fact that all his life, in Munich, in London, in Paris, in Zurich, in Berne, Lenin had always lived encapsuled in the same little, struggling, feuding, quarrelsome colony of Russian revolutionary exiles, whose battles with each other filled their horizon to the exclusion of their fight with the Tsar or the "ruling classes" of Russia. Lenin's letters to his disciples and Krupskaya's *Memoirs* concerning her husband are filled with accounts of his irritable absorption in these quarrels, his inability to interest himself in anything else or to find occupation each night after the local library had closed, his total lack of interest in, and his incomprehension of, the life around him, whether England or France or Germany or wherever else he lived, his completely ingrown concern with the shibboleths, the petty power mechanisms, the personal and faction feuds, of the little colony of exiles. For all the attention he had paid to the real moods of the British or German or French or Swiss workingmen among whom he lived, he might as well have been living on another planet. Now this lack of understanding, or dogmatic misunderstanding of the nature of the world around him was to take its revenge.

To the Sixth Congress of Soviets, in November 1918, when he had been in power one year, Lenin said:

When we took power, we were no more than an individual spark in Europe. . . . Now the sparks have multiplied. . . . Now the majority of the lands in the orbit of German-Austrian imperialism have been seized by the flame (Bulgaria, Austria, Hungary). . . . And from Bulgaria it has leaped to Serbia. . . .

Then, a little more vaguely, he added:

We see how England and America—lands having more possibility than others to remain democratic republics—are just as wildly burying themselves [as Germany did yesterday], and therefore also approaching just as rapidly, perhaps more rapidly, the end which German imperialism reached so quickly. . . . We have never been as near to an international proletarian revolution as we are at this moment.[8]

To Lenin this was not mere holiday rhetoric. Since the defeated régimes of Central Europe were collapsing, what could possibly take their place at this juncture in "world history" when the "world revolution had already begun?" What but more Soviets, to enlarge the "International Soviet Republic?"

In a *Letter to the Workers of Europe and America*, Lenin reviewed the dizzying progress the world revolution had made since his letter to the American workers written only five months earlier. "Five months ago the Soviets had seemed to be merely a Russian institution." Now there were "mighty Soviet movements not only in lands formerly part of the Empire of the Tsar, such as Latvia, Poland, the Ukraine, but in West European lands as well, and in the neutral countries." As lands about to go Soviet he enumerated Switzerland, Holland, Norway, Austria and Germany.

The revolution in Germany has suddenly taken on soviet forms. The

---

[8] *Sochineniya*, Vol. XXVIII, pp. 136–42.

entire march of the German revolution shows clearly that history has *put* on the order of business: "Soviet power" or a bourgeois parliament? . . .

The Soviet power is the second step in the development of the dictatorship of the proletariat on a world-historical scale. The first step was the Paris Commune.[9]

To the Communists of Russia and the world he explained that

. . . on some very important questions of the proletarian revolution, *all* countries will inevitably have to go through what Russia has gone through. . . .

He strove to be modest in his selfless egoism, so unconcerned with self in a superficial sense, so sure of his rightness in all essentials:

Of course, it would be a very great mistake to exaggerate this truth and apply it to more than some of the fundamental features of our revolution . . . after the victory of the proletarian revolution in one of the advanced countries . . . soon after that Russia will cease to be the model country and once again become a backward country (in the "Soviet" and Socialist sense).

But at the present historical moment the situation is precisely that the Russian model reveals to *all* countries something that is very essential in their near and inevitable future. . . . Herein lies the international "significance" (in the strict sense of the word) of the Soviet power, as well as the fundamentals of Bolshevik theory and tactics.

And with modest pride:

For a time—it goes without saying that it is only for a short time— hegemony in the revolutionary, proletarian International has passed to the Russians in the same way as at various periods in the nineteenth century it was enjoyed by the English, then by the French, and then by the Germans.[10]

Thus Russian Bolshevism was taking the place in the Third International which the German Social Democracy had occupied in the Second, and Lenin was naming himself the Marx of the Twentieth Century! The Paris Commune had been the first stage in the developing of a dictatorship of the proletariat on a world-historical scale, and the Petrograd and All-Russian Commune was the second stage. "As a *new type of state* it now cannot die." It could only

---

[9] *Ibid.*, pp. 407–14.
[10] Lenin *Selected Works*, Vol. X, pp. 34–35; 57–58; 68.

spread until it embraced the world. Such was the simple copy-book Marxism with which Lenin operated. This theory of three stages in the world proletarian revolution, the world proletarian dictatorship, and the world-wide republic of Soviets, was at the very core of Lenin's image of the world at that moment. This was the Marxist heritage he was claiming, and for him it had no ambiguities.

Like the extremists of the ultra-right, he had begun to see "red revolution" everywhere. He not only mistook the *Raetesystem*[11] in Germany for Communist-dominated Soviets, a plausible misunderstanding since the imperial régime had broken down and it was not yet entirely clear whether it would be replaced by constitutional democracy or dictatorship. More far-fetched, however—he confused the English shop-steward system with his Soviets also.

In Germany a council movement had sprung up spontaneously when the Kaiser fell and the old administrative machinery, local and national, suddenly broke down. The majority of the councils were of mixed composition, Social Democrats, Independent Social Democrats, a handful of Spartacans, some radical shop stewards, and representatives of the middle classes and their parties. The councils sprang up to fill a temporary vacuum caused by the collapse of the imperial régime, its officialdom and police. Their principal concern was to maintain order, take care of food rationing and the distribution of food supplies, keep transportation moving. They were temporary stopgaps to take over the functions of local government and of the demoralized imperial bureaucracy. In some of the councils radicals appeared who thought of these transitory institutions as analogues of the Russian Soviets of whose real functioning or non-functioning they had only the vaguest idea. Where there were Spartacans (in all Germany in 1918 the League's membership was no more than "several hundreds" or perhaps "several thousands") the slogan was raised: *All power to the Councils!* But the overwhelming majority, whether workingmen or soldiers or middle class delegates, considered the councils as temporary emergency bodies to function only until a new constitution and a new set of constitutional administering authorities should make them superfluous. When a "National Congress of German Workers' and Soldiers' Councils" was

---

11 The verbal identification was natural, for *soviet* is the Russian word for *council* and *Raete* the German word.

convened in Berlin on December 16 (it met from December 16–20, 1918), it debated thoroughly the issue of its role in the future of the nation, then voted by the overwhelming majority of 400 to 50 in favor of support for a National Assembly to fashion a new democratic constitution for Germany. Neither Karl Liebknecht nor Rosa Luxemburg had gotten enough votes to be elected to the Congress, so Liebknecht was reduced to the ridiculous device of invading the sessions and addressing them "unsolicited and in guerrilla fashion . . . leading invasions of supporters . . . mounting the platform . . . shouting their demands and heading for the nearest exits." Rosa Luxemburg herself was in favor of participation in the elections to the Constituent Assembly.[12]

Adjusting herself to the overwhelming verdict of the representatives chosen by the workingmen and soldiers, she urged that her own party participate in the elections to the Constituent Assembly, too. But Lenin could not get it into his head that there was no organized communist party and no disaffected garrison to seize power in the name of "Soviets" which neither wanted power, nor wanted to see the Constituent Assembly, to be elected in January 1919, dispersed by force in its name.

If Lenin's misunderstanding concerning Germany was natural since there was an actual breakdown of the old régime and hence a "revolutionary situation," his misunderstanding of the British shop-steward movement was explainable only by the false image of the world with which his mind was possessed. The demands of the Great War had rapidly transformed the industries of England into mass production industries, bringing into the factories great numbers of new, inexperienced and nonunionized war workers. The shop-steward system arose as a way of integrating all the workers in a given factory, regardless of craft divisions or union membership, into a single organized system. Sometimes the shop stewards were named by and worked through the regular union machinery, some-

---

12 Paul Froehlich in his life of Rosa Luxemburg sets the number of Spartacans as "several thousands" while Walter Rist in his *Der Weg der K.P.D.*, Berlin, 1931, sets it as "several hundreds." The exact figure is unknown. A good short account of the Council movement is in Angress, *op. cit.*, pp. 18–22. The description of Liebknecht's "guerrilla" participation in the sessions of the Congress is from Karl W. Meyer's life of Liebknecht, pp. 148–49. The most complete study of the council movement is that of Walter Tormin in Heft 4 of the *Beitraege zur Geschichte des Parliamentarismus und der politischen Parteien*, Düesseldorf, 1954.

times they by-passed it. They tended to take up shop grievances, protect needed war workers from conscription, regulate wages and piece work rates, prevent most strikes, and broaden those that were actually engaged in. They were neither "defeatist" in Lenin's sense, nor opposed to the winning of the war, nor unpatriotic, nor anxious to overthrow the government, nor did it enter their heads to set up a "shop-steward government" for England.

One of their outstanding leaders, a trade-union activist who was personally antiwar and a founder of the Communist Party of Great Britain, J. T. Murphy, has written of this movement:

> None of the strikes which took place during the war were antiwar strikes. They were frequently led by men such as myself who wanted to stop the war, but that was not the actual motive [of the strikes]. Had the question of stopping the war been put to any strikers' meetings, it would have been overwhelmingly defeated.[13]

Mr. Murphy does not venture to suggest what the shop stewards, or the workers would have done, had one of their elected spokesmen suggested that they march on Westminster Palace with rifles and cold arms to disperse the British House of Commons.

When the Birmingham City Council voted to take the shop-steward movement of Birmingham as its adviser on economic matters, and when the German National Assembly wrote the *Betriebsraete* (Works Councils) into the Weimar Constitution as an organization for the protection of the interests of the workingmen who elected them, these things were simply beyond Lenin's comprehension. He could only assume that the workingmen were infuriated by this "betrayal" on the part of their spokesmen and leaders. But Carl Landauer wrote:

> *Betriebsraete* were provided by the Weimar Constitution for the protection of employees' interests. . . . They modified the otherwise highly centralized organization of the nationwide labor movement, and acquired great popularity among the workers.[14]

It would have been natural for Lenin to believe that in the matter of soldier mutinies and general strikes of unorganized workers, the Russia of 1905 and 1917 might have something to teach Western labor. But he never recognized for a moment that in the matter of union organization and parliamentarism, Russia's experience was exiguous indeed and she had much to learn. Having been

---

[13] J. T. Murphy, *New Horizons,* London, 1941, p. 44.
[14] Carl Landauer, *European Socialism,* Berkely, 1959, Vol. Two, p. 836.

confirmed by success in seizing power, Lenin was in no mood to learn, only to teach.

When the Conference to form a new international convened in Moscow on March 2, 1919, Lenin, in his opening address, told the delegates that not only Russia now, but all of Europe, had found in the Russian-born Soviet:

> . . . the practical form which gives the proletariat the possibility of realizing its dictatorship. That form is the Soviet system. *The dictatorship of the proletariat!* Until now these words were Latin for the masses. Thanks to the spreading of the Soviet system throughout the world, this Latin has been translated into all contemporary languages.
> . . . The Soviet form has conquered not only in backward Russia but also in the most developed country in Europe—Germany, and in the oldest capitalist land—England.

The *Theses* Lenin prepared for the Congress and each of the addresses he delivered to it spoke of the victory of the Soviet form in the leading lands of Western Europe. For Germany he used the German words, *Raete-System,* for England, the words *Shop-Stewards' Committees.* Both were to him exact translations of the language and substance of the Russian word, *Soviets.* On March 12, he told the Petrograd Soviet that

> . . . there is a struggle for [Soviets] not only in Europe but also in America. . . . At present, an interesting moment is being experienced in America where Soviets are being established.

What Lenin saw as a Soviet in the case of America was the General Strike Committee formed to lead the general strike in Seattle from February 11 to February 16, 1919!

When Count Karolyi, in protest at the harsh peace terms offered Hungary, voluntarily turned over his government to the Hungarian Socialists and Communists, Lenin saw this as a Communist revolution for a Soviet Hungary. Privately he demanded of Bela Kun on March 23: "Please inform what concrete guarantees you have that the new Hungarian government is actually communist, and not only socialist, that is social traitors." But to the Eighth Congress of his own Party Lenin said on the same day:

> *We are certain that this will be our last difficult half-year.* We are especially confirmed in this conviction by the news . . . of the victory of the proletarian revolution in Hungary. If hitherto, Soviet power was achieved only among the peoples constituting the former Russian empire, if hitherto short-sighted people . . . could think

that the peculiarities of Russia alone were the cause of this unexpected turn toward Soviet proletarian democracy, that in the peculiarities of this democracy perhaps were reflected as in a distorting
mirror the ancient peculiarities of Tsarist Russia . . . such an opinion has now been destroyed at its roots . . .[15]

With variations and embroiderings Lenin repeated the same
thing to festive meetings of the Moscow and Petrograd Soviets and
in the columns of *Pravda.* "The foundation of the Third, Communist
International," Lenin wrote in *Pravda* of March 6, "is the prelude to
the International Republic of Soviets." In the last four months Germany had proved that Soviets were as appropriate to the most advanced land in Europe as to the most backward, and England, the
model land of "social peace" was "boiling with the mighty and un-
containable growth of Soviets" known there as "Shop-Stewards'
Committees."

Now that the word *soviet* has become understandable to everybody,
the victory of the communist revolution is assured [he told the Moscow Soviet]. The comrades in this hall have seen the Soviet Republic
founded; now they are seeing how the Communist International is
being founded; all of them will see how the Universal Federative
Republic of Soviets will be founded.[16]

"This July will be our last difficult July," Lenin reassured himself
and his auditors, "next July we shall greet the victory of the international Soviet Republic."

Zinoviev, selected by Lenin to become the Chairman of the
Communist International, outdid his leader in optimism. In the first
issue of *Kommunisticheskii Internatsional,* he wrote:

. . . one can say with certainty that in a year's time we will already
begin to forget that there was a struggle for communism in Europe,
for in a year's time the whole of Europe will be communist. . . . It
may be that in America capitalism can continue to exist for a couple
of years alongside of a communist Europe. It may perhaps be that
even in England capitalism can continue to exist for a year or two
alongside the communism that will have triumphed over the whole
European continent. But for any length of time, such a coexistence is
impossible.[17]

---

[15] *Sochineniya,* Vol. XXVIII, pp. 43–44; 199; also, *Sochineniya,* Third Edition,
Vol. XXIV, Note 63, pp. 768–9.
[16] Lenin, *Sochineniya,* Vol. XXVIII, p. 461; Vol. XXIX, p. 455.
[17] *Kommunisticheskii Internatsional,* No. 1, May, 1919, p. 21.

A manifesto addressed *To the Working People of the Whole World,* in the same issue informed them that:

In 1919 the great Communist International was born. In 1920, the great International Soviet Republic will come to birth. . . . Before a year has passed, the whole of Europe will be Soviet. In every country, the workers have realized that the decisive moment has come. . . .

If the Russian Revolution was really the first stage in a swiftly on-coming world revolution, if the Russian Communist Party was indeed the nucleus of a world Communist Party, and if Russian Soviets were actually appropriate to all lands and spreading every-where—a second, enlarged edition of the Paris Commune, and the nucleus of a World Commune—it did not matter if Moscow acted alone for the moment in setting up a new international. Within a year all continental Europe would be Communist, then the center could be moved from Moscow to Berlin and the whole problem of national narrowness and national backwardness would be solved. What was needed was haste in forming the general staff of the world revolution, for this would not brook delay. Without so much as ascertaining whether the new German Communist Party was or was not in favor of the immediate foundation of an international, Lenin hastened to send out his call.

The call was drafted by Leon Trotsky and gone over by Lenin and Chicherin (the Commissariat of Foreign Affairs was at this time more openly interested in overthrowing governments than in treating with them), and probably by Bukharin. It was published in *Pravda* and broadcast over the radio by the Commissariat of Foreign Affairs. It named thirty-nine parties, or groups, or followers of individual persons, whom Lenin deemed fit to be founders of the Communist International. The lack of precision and judgment in the list of invitees shows how little Lenin knew of the outside world.

The *Call* actually made the major decisions for the invited conferees before their arrival, and made them *po-russki,* that is, in Lenin's spirit:

The task of the proletariat now is to seize power immediately . . . destroy the State apparatus of the bourgeoisie and organize a new proletarian apparatus of power. . . . Its concrete form is given in the régime of Soviets. . . .

The socialist movement in each country must be divided into three categories: "social chauvinists toward whom no other attitude is possible but unrelenting struggle"; "centrists" from whom the "revolutionary elements must be split off," and whose leaders must be subjected to "unsparing criticism and exposure"; and those elements which are "left" or "moving in this direction," including "syndicalist elements" with whom "it is necessary to form a bloc," provided that "by and large they stand for the proletarian dictatorship in the form of Soviet power."

Most important to Lenin, and not subject to argument:

The Congress must assume the name of "The First Congress of the Communist International," and the individual parties shall become its Sections.[18]

The document was signed by only one genuine Communist Party, the Russian, and by some of Lenin's followers from other lands then resident in Russia, who purported to use the names of other parties, without such parties either existing or giving authorization. Thus the auspices were exclusively Russian and crypto-Russian.

The gathering itself was such as might be expected from a conference so ill prepared and carelessly called. At best it would have taken many months to split parties, set up Communist groups, elect delegates, and prepare their difficult journey through the *cordon sanitaire* surrounding Lenin's Russia. But if all Europe was to be made Soviet within a year, there was no time, and no inclination on Lenin's part, for such niceties.

Like the congresses of his own party, this conference was packed with Leninists. This did not seem objectionable to him: quite the contrary, since those who did not meet his rigorous tests were to be excluded anyhow. Most of the "delegates" were prisoners of war from various countries who had been converted to Communism while in Russia, designated as representatives from parties which did not yet exist, or had not given them a mandate. Besides Russian prisoners of war, there were a number of "delegates" from the borderlands and peoples of the old Russian Empire: Poland, Finland, the Ukraine, Armenia, Latvia, Estonia, White Russia, Lithuania, and a "united group of the Eastern peoples of Russia" who were collectively awarded a single delegate. Those who "represented" all these borderlands were in reality Bolsheviks, that is members of Lenin's

---

[18] An English translation of this *Call* or *Invitation* is in *The Communist International 1919–1943: Documents Selected and Edited by Jane Degras*, New York, 1956, Vol. I, pp. 1–5.

party and his faction, subject to Lenin's instructions, discipline and views.

All in all thirty-five delegates were recognized as entitled to full voting rights, "representing" nineteen different countries or parties. Twenty-five or twenty-six additional delegates were seated with a "consultative voice," or as our usage has it, with voice but no vote. Russian Turkestan, Azerbaijan, and Georgia had such "consultative" delegates, as did China, Korea and Persia. All these "delegates" were resident in the Russian capital and represented parties that had not sent them and did not yet exist. Christian Rakovsky purported to speak for a Balkan Revolutionary Social Democratic Federation. He had, to be sure, been active in both Bulgaria and Rumania, and had at one time been an agent of the German government, but he was a member of Lenin's party, had been a member of Lenin's Secret Police, and was at this moment nominal head of Lenin's government in the Ukraine. It was on Lenin's instruction that he appeared as representative of the Balkan Revolutionary Social Democratic Federation, which came into shadowy existence by virtue of his act of presenting his "mandate."[19]

Hungary was represented by one Rudnyansky, a Hungarian Slav resident in Moscow, but there was as yet no Hungarian Communist Party to elect him. Indeed, during the short-lived Hungarian "Soviet Republic" without Soviets, which came into existence shortly after the Congress adjourned, Bela Kun refused to follow Lenin's telegraphed suggestion that he set up a separate Hungarian Communist Party and break away from the United Socialist Party of Hungary.[20]

France was represented by two Frenchmen who happened to be in Russia, Captain Jacques Sadoul, listed in the proceedings as "a French officer in the ranks of the Red Army," and Henri Guilbeaux, an adventurous journalist-poet and pacifist who had been elected by nobody, and who broke with Communism and became anticommunist a few years later. In short, "most of the thirty-five delegates and fifteen guests," as the First Secretary of the Communist International, Angelica Balabanoff, was to write in her memoirs:

---

[19] On Rakovsky as a German agent, see *Akten des Auswaertigen Amtes, Weltkrieg, 2 Geheim,* as cited in Scharlau and Zeman, *Freibeuter der Revolution, Parvus-Helphand,* Cologne, 1964, p. 152, n. 1.
[20] Lenin's telegram and Bela Kun's negative reply were both published without editorial comment in *Kommunisticheskii Internatsional,* No. 2, 1919.

. . . had been handpicked by the Russian Central Committee from so-called "Communist Parties" in those smaller "nations" which had formerly comprised the Russian Empire . . . or they were war prisoners, or foreign radicals who happened to be in Russia at that time.

To which Franz Borkenau adds the information that many of them were "financially entirely dependent on Moscow" not merely for their intended political activities but for their very personal existence in a land of disorder and famine. But this last fact should not be taken as a primary motive nor does it necessarily imply any lack of loyalty to Lenin and his successful revolution.[21]

Poland was represented by the Polish Bolshevik, Unschlicht, an official of Lenin's *Cheka* or Secret Police; Switzerland was represented by Fritz Platten who had been Lenin's go-between with the German Government in the matter of the "sealed train" on which Lenin passed through the German lines to return to Russia.

The only delegates actually arriving from abroad for the Conference were Eberlein, from the German Spartacans; Gruber (Steinhardt), from Austria; Rutgers, a Dutch Left Socialist who had been in America and claimed to represent both the American Socialist Propaganda League and a small Dutch Communist group; and a representative each from Norway and Sweden. The delegate from England was the Russian, Fineberg, self-appointed; the delegate from America, the Russian Reinstein, who had been sent by the Socialist Labor Party to a Congress at Stockholm which never took place, and had been spending the last two years in Russia. The S.L.P. repudiated their "representative" as soon as they learned what he had done in their name.

As if to emphasize still further the overwhelmingly Russian complexion of the gathering, the representatives of the Russian Communist Party were selected from among Bolshevism's top figures: Lenin, Trotsky, Zinoviev, Bukharin, and Chicherin.

To the consternation of the Russians, the party that was supposed to co-sponsor the foundation of the Communist International and cure it of its one-sided Russian national character, having discussed Lenin's invitation, had decided against forming a new International at that time. Rosa Luxemburg, Leo Jogiches, Karl Lieb-

---

21 Angelica Balabanoff, *My Life as a Rebel*, New York, 1938, p. 213; Franz Borkenau, *World Communism*, New York, 1939, p. 181.

knecht and Paul Levi had all been against Lenin's proposal, both for its timing and because Rosa Luxemburg disapproved of so much that Lenin wanted to make mandatory, even axiomatic, in the structure and function of the International. On January 12, with an unwanted uprising on their hands, the Spartacan leaders named two delegates, Leviné, who was stopped at the German border, and Eberlein, who got through. Their instructions were categorical and binding: to oppose the formation of a new international and to refuse in the name of the German Communist Party to join it if Lenin should use his Russian machine to put it through. Three days after the instructions were voted, both Liebknecht and Luxemburg were dead, assassinated in the aftermath of a putschist uprising, an uprising which they had opposed as ill-timed and unprepared. And here was the young Eberlein, alone in Moscow and under heavy pressure from Lenin, Zinoviev and other Russians to violate his instructions. Lenin, Zinoviev, and Bukharin tried both private conversation and public pressure, but Eberlein held to his instructions, not as Rosa Luxemburg might have done, for she was a match for Lenin, but to the best of his ability. For several days he held out against the private discussions with the authoritative Lenin, the public onslaughts of the Russian delegation, the emotional impact of greetings from the Red Army. All the delegates and pseudo-delegates worked on the young man.

> We have a victorious revolution in a great country [Zinoviev told him] . . . our banner device is the International Soviet Republic, and no one can call that utopian. . . . It is a question for the immediate future. . . . In Germany you have a party . . . which in a few months will establish a proletarian government. And are we still to delay? Nobody will understand it. . . .

While Eberlein held firm, Lenin kept the very news that the Conference was meeting out of the press. But on the third day, the Austrian delegate arrived. Gruber (Steinhardt) had been traveling seventeen days, had crossed the lines of both Reds and Whites in the Russian Civil War; now he gave a highly colored and unrealistic account of what he had seen, assuring his listeners that the Austrian proletariat was but waiting for their call to establish a proletarian dictatorship. Amidst the excitement, Eberlein at last gave in to the extent of agreeing not to vote against and not to withdraw, merely to register his abstention on behalf of the German Communist Party. Thus, one-sidedly and in the womb of illusion, the Communist In-

ternational was born. There being no true representation from most
of the countries, it was decided that:

> Until the arrival of these representatives from abroad [from sup-
> posedly affiliated parties] to serve on the Executive Committee, the
> comrades of the country where the Executive Committee has its seat
> shall take over the work.

That country was Russia; the seat of the Executive was in Moscow;
Lenin and his appointees "took over the work."

The rest of the story is too recent and too well known to require
more than summary retelling here.

With his *Twenty-One Conditions* Lenin split every mass party
that approached his International, dictated the exclusion of all the
leaders of sufficient stature to oppose his dogmas with some chance
of success, and dictated the adoption of the tactics which his Russian experiences had, he believed, legitimatized for all lands.

Inevitably, the "Sections" of the Communist International became blurred carbon copies of their model, the Russian Communist
Party. More and more openly, the needs of the Dictatorship in
Russia determined the actions of the other parties. Then came their
"Bolshevization" and the growing insistence that their internal
differences whether on matters of strategy and tactics or on matters
of personnel should be settled in Moscow and not in their own
land.

Within a few years all the early leaders and founders of the
Comintern from other lands were out, either having resigned in
protest at the excessive centralization and Russianism of the tactics
dictated to them, or having been expelled and discredited. Increasingly, the controversies in the Russian Party after Lenin's death
were exported into the various sections in other lands; leaders were
picked or ousted according to how they stood not on the problems
of their own land, but according to their attitude toward Zinoviev,
or Trotsky, or Bukharin, or Stalin.

In the thirties, the test of "internationalism" was loyalty to the
only "socialist nation," the Soviet Union, and devotion to Stalin. In
the later thirties the great purge spread from land to land. To remain loyal to the Comintern one had to denounce all its Russian
founders save Lenin, who was dead, and Stalin, who was infallible.
Then the Communists of lands where Communist Parties were outlawed, who had sought safety in the land of the proletarian dictatorship, were arrested and executed. The victims included Eberlein,

who had been at the founding Congress, and many German Communist leaders who had sought refuge from Hitler in the Soviet Union; Bela Kun who had led the Hungarian "Soviet Republic"; the entire Central Committee of the Polish Communist Party; and Members of the Executive Committee of the Communist International from many lands. Stalin's purges took the lives of more Communists than all the anticommunist régimes from which they had fled, put together.

The parties became weather vanes to show which way the wind was blowing over the great Eurasian plain. When Stalin made a pact with Hitler, the Stalinist parties in France, England, and the United States became antiwar. When Hitler double-crossed his pact partner, they became pro-war, crying aloud for an immediate "Second Front." In 1943, by *ukaz*, Stalin decreed the dissolution of the Communist International, without so much as calling it into session to vote its own demise!

The dissolution was, as the leaders of England and the United States and other Western lands were to learn to their cost, only a tactical maneuver. As the Russian armies advanced over Europe they carried with them as proconsuls those Communist leaders who had somehow escaped the great purge.

It was only then that the flaw in the foundation became an ever-widening fissure. Hitherto those who objected to Russian dictation had always been expelled and discredited, but now the proconsuls became rulers of nations. Though they depended on Russian support to insure their rule, increasingly they felt the pressure of the peoples over whom they ruled, and became aware of the separate national interests of the members of the "international communist camp."

With Tito's break, and Stalin's failure to destroy him by anathema, came a fresh fury of purges, of the so-called Titoists—preventive purges to forestall the growth of relatively independent Communist national leaderships. Once more Stalin ordered the death of more Communist leaders than were ever executed by anticommunist régimes.

Somehow, Stalin held the flawed edifice together by his machine-made prestige and his wide-ranging terror, until his death. The interregnum before a more or less authoritative successor emerged in Russia, and the shocking revelations of the "destalinization" and "rehabilitation" campaigns, revealed how strong the national centrifugal forces of revolt against exclusive Russian domination had gone: uprising in Hungary, in Prague, in East Berlin, near revolt in Poland; the widening Sino-Soviet conflict where diverging national interests mingled with ideological charges of heresy, revisionism, and betrayal. When the two giants, China and Russia, Communist and Internationalist both, began to quarrel, all the lesser lands found elbow room in the crevices and interstices thus created. And as this book goes to press another interregnum has begun in Russia.

Whatever the further course of autocephalic or "polycentralist" development, the exclusive Russian domination that Lenin mixed into the mortar and concrete of the foundation of the Communist International has revealed itself as fatally flawed. In the Third International, as in the Second and the First, the name of the flaw is *nationalism*—differing national traditions, national histories, national institutions, national psychologies and national interests.

Though all these lands invoke the same Marxism, or Marxism-Leninism; though they all have at present varying degrees of totalitarian and authoritarian one-party rule and conceivably a common interest in defending it—yet the rifts widen, the differences grow, the quest for national autonomy in each *Communist-International* nation will not cease.

Indeed, precisely because they claim to share a common ideology and a quasi-religious faith, even minor differences of tactics and interests tend to be enlarged by appeals and counterappeals to the support of the infallible doctrine. Then they are no longer differences but heresies, no longer disagreements but betrayals.

At this stage it is impossible to predict the further course of the greater and lesser schisms, but as Richard Lowenthal writes in the epigraph with which this chapter began:

International Communism has no longer a single worldwide organization, a single center of authority, or a single "orthodox" doctrine. But if the history of "World Communism" is at an end, the history of Communism in the world is not.

And out of that ambiguous history, the latest chapter in the ambiguous heritage of Marxism, many surprises will yet come.

PART VI

Problems of Utopia

A map of the world that does not include Utopia is hardly worth
glancing at. . . .
        —Oscar Wilde

Power unanointed may come—
Dominion (unsought by the free)
    And the Iron Dome,
Stronger for stress and strain,
Fling her huge shadow athwart the main;
But the Founders' dream shall flee.
        —Herman Melville

Walk lightly. Things are not so simple.
        —Charles A. Beard

Chapter 17

THE WORKINGMAN REJECTS

HIS "MISSION"

We have been naught
We shall be all.
—from the words of *The International*

Those who, being naught were to become all, become something—and the whole scheme loses its tidy outlines.
—Henrik Brugmans

ALMOST A CENTURY has elapsed since Marx published his masterpiece, Volume One of *Das Kapital;* and it is more than a century
since the *Communist Manifesto,* pronounced the "downfall of the
bourgeoisie and the victory of the proletariat equally inevitable."
That century or so has not dealt kindly with Marx's predictions.

Yet, while other nineteenth-century social thinkers and critics
have become mere names in textbooks, the name of Marx remains a
banner for millions. The rulers over one-third of mankind pronounce
him the founder of the faith (or science) by which they claim to
chart their infallible course; and the guide to correcting that course
when again and again it proves to have been fallible. Though they
move by zigzags, false starts, retracings of their steps, and reintroduction of things they had abolished because Marx denounced
them, yet they claim that their trajectory is the one his science
traced for them.

Those who are free to study his writings dispassionately—as dispassionately as men can study writings so steeped in passion—are
likely to see in him a social critic, a moralist, a seminal thinker of a

bygone day, some of whose insights, and even some of whose errors, can still fructify the social disciplines (let us not fall into his mistake of calling them "sciences"): history, sociology, economics, and political philosophy.

Today these disciplines are embarrassed by their awareness that man's values form a constitutive part of his examination of his own activities. Were it not for this false shame, political philosophy would not now be so nearly in eclipse. In better health, it would be acknowledging a debt to Marx and his fellow utopians for certain insights into that branch of political philosophy which may properly be called social criticism, a branch concerning itself with the imperfections of any society-in-being as measured against its own potentialities and man's flickering yet undying vision of the good life. It is, of course, a branch of moral philosophy as well, becoming potentially dangerous only when the hubris of the social critic persuades him that it is a branch of science.

In addition to the normative side of Marx's thought, which he was reluctant to acknowledge, there was a descriptive or objective side upon which he insisted, for his family tree derived both from such utopian critics as Saint-Simon and Fourier, and from the physiocrats and classical economists from Quesnay to Adam Smith and Ricardo.

Marx was always a passionate, even a compulsive reader, working his way day and night, often forgetting sleep, through mountains of tomes and tracts on whatever subject preoccupied him. Spurred on by the young Engels's *Umrisse zu einer Kritik der Nationaloekonomie*, his notebooks for 1844 and early 1845 are filled with excerpts from economists mostly in French translation, together with his own comments on these citations.[1]

---

[1] *MEGA*, I/3, pp. 411–583 reproduces many though by no means all of these excerpts. The range of his readings is suggested by the list of works excerpted: Pierre le Pesant de Boisguillebert, *Le détail de la France, la cause de la diminution de ses biens*, etc., Paris, 1843; Eugene Buret, *De la misère des classes labourieuses en Angleterre et en France*, Paris, 1840; Destutt de Tracy, *Éléments d'idéologie*, Paris, 1826; F. Engels, *Umrisse* etc., 1844; James Lauderdale *Recherches sur la nature et l'origine de la richesse publique;* Jean Law, *Considérations sur le numéraire et la commerce*, Paris, 1843; Friedrich List, *Das nationale System der politischen Oekonomie;* John Ramsay MacCulloch, *Discours sur l'origine, les progrès, les objets particuliers et l'importance de la économie politique.* Paris, 1825; James Mill, *Eléments d'économie politique*, Paris, 1823; H. F. Osiander, *Enttaeuschung des Publikums ueber die Interessen des Handels etc., nebst einem Gebet aus Utopien*, David Ricardo, *Des principes*

All his life, Marx continued to read and make excerpts in the same insatiable fashion. To these first readings in French and German he later added endless tomes in English, read in the library of the British Museum. The notebooks of excerpts and comments thereon grew in number to such an extent that after his death Engels could quarry from them Volumes Two and Three of *Das Kapital*, in 1885 and 1894 respectively. Then Kautsky, at Engels's behest, edited further volumes of excerpts and critical commentary as *Theorien ueber den Mehrwert* (*Theories of Surplus Value*) in four volumes which together constitute the so-called Volume Four of *Das Kapital*. To these must be added the *Grundrisse der Kritik der politischen Oekonomie* (*Rohentwurf*), 1857–1858, first published in 1939 and 1941; the *Economic-Philosophical Manuscripts of 1844*; and many still unpublished notebooks. In some of these, the excerpts are long, the comments brief; in others the reverse is true. One wonders whether in the age of the photostat, Xerox, and microfilm, Marx would not have found more time to complete his *chef d'oeuvre*, or whether all this excerpting and arguing with the books he read was necessary to his mode of thought and work.

In any case, these notebooks tell us a great deal about Marx as an economic theorist and social thinker. Above all they make clear the fact that he developed his viewpoint first, and only then went through whole libraries to find "scientific verification" of that viewpoint. Marx began his reading with the preconception expressed in the *Umrisse* of Engels, that the disintegration of the existing civil or bourgeois society was imminent, and that constant sharpening of class struggles was clearing the way for an early Communist revolution.

As his studies of the French Revolution were meant to deepen his understanding of the role played by class struggles in historical development and give him a clearer "scientific" picture of the revolution he thought was approaching, his study of capitalist society and its economists was to provide a "scientific foundation" for his pre-existing critique of that society, and to confirm his view that eco-

---

de l'économie politique etc.; Jean-Baptiste Say, *Traité d'économie politique*, Brussels, 1836; Carl Wolfgang Christoph Schuez, *Grundzaetze der National-oekonomie*, Tuebingen, 1843; Frédéric Skarbek, *Théories des richesses sociales*, Paris, 1829; Adam Smith, *Recherches sur la nature et les causes de la richesse des nations*. Paris, 1802; Xenophon, various treatises concerning the Greek economy and city-state constitutions, in German translation, Stuttgart, 1828–1830.

nomic conditions must form the revolutionary class that would over-throw it.

Like Engels, he put the word *critique* at the center of his eco-nomic analysis. It formed the title or sub-title of every treatise on economics which he published, those he drafted but did not publish, and the first work he contracted to do but never wrote. His note-books, their excerpts and his commentaries thereon, all form part of that critique. It is a critique of the existing political-economic system and a critique of all the prevailing political economists. As the Marx-ist intellectual biographer of Marx and Engels, Auguste Cornu, puts it:

> It was in the first place study to master the materials; since, however, he studied the national economy from the standpoint of the class interests of the proletariat and carried on his national economic studies in the closest connection with his communistic views, like Engels he took a stand in advance against the national economy. . . . From Engels he took over the conception of the historical conditioning and limitation [*Bedingtheit*] of this system, the stimulus to a critical investigation of economic categories from the standpoint of private property and competition and the insight into the inner contradictoriness of the capitalist system in the sharpening of the class struggles which arise therefrom, and in the necessity of the abolition of bourgeois society.[2]

In short, Marx read ardently and unceasingly to find more and more scientific proofs of what he already knew before he began his study of economics. When he found anything to the contrary, he demolished it in ironical commentaries on the excerpts he copied into his notebooks. If there are, as indeed there are, great masses of descriptive and objective materials in his economic writings, it is because he thought that these confirmed and strengthened the scien-tific nature of his preconceived doctrine. Marxists who are uncom-fortable about this and want his doctrine to be scientific in some other sense are apt to lean heavily on one or two quotations which they enlarge upon by repeating and glossing endlessly. Chief of these is a remark made in a polemical note on Malthus, whom Marx accuses of adapting his economic analyses to the "class interests of the aristocracy against the bourgeoisie, and both against the prole-tariat." Of this Marx writes:

A man who tries to *accommodate* science to a standpoint derived not

---

[2] Auguste Cornu, *Karl Marx und Friedrich Engels*, Berlin, 1962, pp. 118–126.

from science itself . . . but from *outside interests* that are alien to science itself, such a man I call "cheap" (*gemein*, literally *common*).[3]

But all this tells us is that Marx thought that the interests of the propertied were "*outside* interests" from the standpoint of the science of economics, while the interests of the proletariat were immanent in the study of that science.

In fact, this was Marx's chief reason for believing that his writings on economics were "scientific." He had the comforting and reassuring notion that all true questions have single true answers, that none is unanswerable, and that the answers can be known, and even implemented, by a combination of fearless analysis and action, provided the one who analyzed and acted was not afraid to face the truth. The early classical economists like Ricardo and Adam Smith, he thought, had been scientific since the bourgeoisie was then still a rising class and in no fear of its own extinction. Hence he could use large sections of their work and many of their basic tools and concepts. But the later economists must surely be aware of the coming storm, which they, and the class whose interests they expressed and defended, were afraid to face. Hence they had become *gemein*, vulgar economists, mere apologists, falsifiers, and prevaricators. Only those could face the facts of political economy who faced the economic system critically and saw it as a system that was doomed. Only those could ask the right questions and get the right answers from the social sphinx who were not blinded by fear of the extinction of their own class or their own standpoint. Thus the workers, and those most enlightened members of other classes who were not afraid of the truth and who took the standpoint of the workers, could alone possess the truth. The class to whom the future belonged could see clearly; the classes doomed to extinction were blinded by fear or petty class interests, petty because they were antihistorical, antisocial, and opposed to the next necessary step in progress, the communist revolution. Only the socialist or communist political economist could join the army of workers on the march, find out what was now inevitable, accept and exult in it, try to hasten its coming. This was the real meaning of Marx's assumption that his economic doctrine was both critical (of existing society and social theory) and scientific (i.e. able to predict the future contained in the present, and hasten its coming). In this lay his claim to the

---

[3] Karl Marx, *Theorien ueber den Mehrwert*, edited and published by Karl Kautsky, Stuttgart, 1921, Vol. II, Part 1, pp. 312–13.

unity of theory and practice, of analysis and action. Only thus could one ask History where she wanted to go, get the right answer, then give the old lady a helpful push in the direction she indicated.

When Marx's investigations turned up facts and trends that did not fit his theory of an inevitable collapse of the existing order and an early communist revolution, despite his brave pretensions to science, he did not pursue such facts further.

The *Communist Manifesto* was written in the expectation of the imminent end of the "bourgeois" order and the inevitability of that end. The *Manifesto* declares:

> In order to exploit a class, the conditions must be assured for that class to continue to exist, at least within its slavish existence. The serf was able to work himself up to membership in the commune, as the petty bourgeois under the yoke of absolutism was able to work himself up to a bourgeois. But the modern workingman, instead of rising with the advance of industry, sinks ever more deeply below the conditions of his own class. The workingman becomes the pauper, and pauperism develops more rapidly even than does population and wealth. It is this fact that makes it clear that the bourgeoisie is no longer fit to be the ruling class in society. . . . It is unable to rule because it is unable to assure to the slave his very existence within the conditions of his slavery, because it is forced to let him sink into a condition where it must feed him instead of being fed by him. Society can no longer live under the bourgeoisie, that is, its life is no longer reconcilable with the life of society.[4]

It was then "this fact" of the increasing misery or pauperization of the workingman which proved that the bourgeoisie was no longer fit to be the ruling class. But the fact, it turned out, was no fact at all.

Though a century has elapsed since the completion of Volume One of *Das Kapital*, the poor are still with us. There are depressed groups and areas even in the richest country in the world, but there has been no evidence of Marx's anticipated declassing or pauperization of the working class. On the contrary, in England, on the Continent, and in the United States, the curve of wages has been generally, and on the whole steadily, upward. Even in Marx's day it must have become apparent to such an assiduous reader of statis-

---

[4] *MEGA*, I/6, pp. 536–37; English translation, International Publishers, New York, 1930, p. 41.

tical reports that the pauperization theory, with its corollary of imminent revolution, could not stand up to the facts. Significantly, though his study of British statistics goes up to 1866, his study of public health reports up to 1865, of the reports of the factory inspectors up to 1866, and every other such datum is as late as he can make it, Marx has not one word to say on the movement of wages in England after 1850! Indeed, there is no serious study of the movement of real wages at all. The first edition of *Das Kapital* was completed in the summer of 1867. A second German edition was issued in 1873, and Marx took advantage of the fact to make revisions and corrections, but not a word on the movement of wages. Just before his death, he prepared a third edition which Engels issued posthumously in the year of his death, 1883. On this matter, still silence. Nor did the materials he left for Volume Two and Volume Three break the silence. That silence speaks louder than words.[5]

On the eve of the Revolutions of 1848, when Marx undertook to analyze industrial society and foretell its destiny, he saw it headed for immediate crackup, a crackup not years, but only months or weeks away. It was to come with the next street skirmishes and barricade battles. Then from a general war which would break out before the year was up. When barricades disappeared from the cities and the clash of arms grew still, and when their conspirative union with the Blanquists proved barren of uprisings, Marx and Engels grew more sober in their estimates. In a review of events from May to October, 1850, signed jointly by the two of them, there is a startled hymn to the prosperity that had taken possession of England and spread to the Continent, sparked in great measure,

---

[5] The Marxist economist, Fritz Sternberg, tried to tell Trotsky of this when the latter was in exile in France in 1934. Lenin had been wrong, he said, to assert that only a tiny upper crust of the aristocracy had gotten a higher living standard and that the main problem was to separate the impoverished mass of laboring men from the aristocracy of labor. "That is why the views of Lenin on the imminence of a revolution on a world scale were illusory, and why the October Revolution remained an isolated phenomenon. . . . One characteristic of the decades preceding the war is that the wages of the whole working class had considerably risen, and that not merely for one or another year but for decades and generations." Trotsky, who was fighting desperately to preserve and demonstrate his Leninist orthodoxy, was manifestly uncomfortable about the statistics which Sternberg had on his finger tips. He excused himself from examining the question by saying that he had had no time to read current economic literature since the Revolution of 1917. Fritz Sternberg, "Entretiens avec Trotski," *Contrat Social,* Paris, July-August, 1964, pp. 203–210.

according to the two friends, by the discovery of gold in California. *"A new revolution,"* they assure their readers in italics, *"is only possible in the wake of a new crisis. It is, however, just as certain as the crisis itself."*[6]

Impatiently, Marx waited for that next crisis, which in his opinion was inordinately delayed. But the next crisis came, and went, and no revolution accompanied it. Freed by the political stillness from the urgency of day-to-day revolutionary activity, Marx set himself to study the "law of motion" of industrial society and to demonstrate the long-run inevitability of its "final crisis," in the scholarly precincts of the British Museum. Except for the interruption that came with the birth and death of the International Workingmen's Association, this study was now to be his lifework. From it was to come his major contribution to modern thought: his unfinished masterpiece consisting of three attempts at a *critique of political economy.*[7]

I cannot agree with those who find Marx's economic writings dull and unreadable, obscure or negligible. His critique of timeless, scholastic definitions of economic categories is valuable for the awareness it gives that such categories are historically evolved and subject to further historical development and transformation.[8] His concept of *fetishism* is a useful reminder of the fact that the relations between economic products and categories is but a one-sided, inhuman and blind reflection of underlying relationships between men.[9] Marx has deepened our interest in the business cycle, pre-

---

[6] *Werke*, Vol. VII, p. 440. It was characteristic of Marx to assume that the Revolutions of 1848, were "caused" by the economic crisis of 1846–47 and to ignore the accumulation of political and nationalist tensions that gave 1848 its character.

[7] The italicized words, as we have already noted, form the title or sub-title of all three of Marx's economic works: *Grundrisse der Kritik der politischen Oekonomie; Zur Kritik der politischen Oekonomie; Das Kapital, Kritik der politischen Oekonomie*. And in January, 1845, just before he was expelled from Paris, Marx had signed a contract with a German publisher then visiting Paris to do a two-volume *Critique of National Economy and Politics*. Basically they are all one never completed work.

[8] Ironically, it is precisely this further historical development of concepts and institutions which has made Marx's own economic generalizations and pronouncements obsolete.

[9] The concept of *fetishism* was not original with Marx. He borrowed it from the classical economists, but he gave it a rich and original development of his own. What he and they meant by it was a tendency to see the social relationships between men as if they were merely relationships between things, i.e. the relationship between their products when exchanged with each other, or between men and machines, or between men and money. Underneath these, and helping to explain them, are the relationships between men and men.

cisely because of the "revolutionary" importance he attached to it. Though his theory of the nature of crises is obsolete, *konjunktur-forschung*, the interest in crises, their forecasting, and their regulation or melioration, undoubtedly owes much to him. He has deepened our sense of the historically conditioned nature of institutions and social concepts, and of our (and his) theories concerning them. His shattering picture of the evils attendant on the "primitive accumulation" of capital for industrialization, where these evils are unrestrained by social legislation or countervailing political and economic power, is a dark picture, unmatched—except by the still darker picture of primitive accumulation of capital where the one-party state is the sole owner; the sole authorized accumulator of capital for unrestricted industrialization (that is for the very ruthless production for production's sake and self-expansion of capital which Marx so sharply condemned); the sole determiner of which sectors of the population should be most ruthlessly exploited for the purpose of such accumulation; the sole master of distribution of capital, labor, income and products; the sole determiner of the comparative prices of producer and consumer goods and of their mix; the sole tenant of political and economic power; and the sole authorized interpreter and critic of its own acts and decisions and of society as a whole. This was a type of "primitive accumulation" of which Marx never dreamed because he assumed that any revolution made in the name of his doctrine would be made in an advanced industrial land where the bourgeoisie, in the words of the *Communist Manifesto*, during its short reign would have:

> . . . created more powerful, more stupendous forces of production than all the preceding generations rolled into one. The subjugation of the forces of nature, the invention of machinery, the application of chemistry to industry and agriculture, the clearing of whole continents for cultivation, the making of navigable waterways, huge populations springing up as if by magic out of the earth—what earlier generations had the remotest inkling that such productive powers slumbered in the womb of associated labor?[10]

In short, the bourgeoisie was to perform the miracle of accumulation of capital and transformation of industry, and then the proletariat would take over the vast plant and build upon its foundations a yet higher social order, namely socialism, i.e. production not for production's sake but for consumption. What Marx would have said

---

[10] *MEGA*, I/6, p. 530; English translation, New York and London, 1930, pp. 31–32.

of Lenin's seizure of power and of the totalitarian régime introduced by Lenin and his successors under the banner of Marxism-Leninism, it is impossible to conjecture. But on the face of it, Marx cannot be held responsible for the primitive accumulation of capital in the name of socialism.

Das Kapital is possessed by the same contradiction between empirical investigation and foreknown "conclusion," between realistic examination and apocalyptic expectation, that is in all Marx's thought. But precisely because of its intellectual pretension to be scientific, it is in this work that the contradiction is most deeply felt.

Das Kapital contains many brilliant pages, treasures of empirical material, digests and attempts at critical appraisal and integration of all that had been thought and said in economic theory up to Marx's day, suggestive historical sketches, analyses of the stages in the technical and economic organization of industry, interesting statistical data, keen sociological observations, striking passages of irony, wrath, poetry, and prophecy.

The substantial sections of the work which derive from the British Parliamentary Blue Books testify to the awakening conscience of the whole of British industrial society. They remind us forcefully that the dark picture Marx paints of early industrialism is the picture of an age that was already ending before he began his work.

Remembering the crushing of the June uprising in Paris in 1848, Marx had assured the proletariat in 1850 that it was a "senseless utopia" to expect "the slightest improvement in its position *within* the bourgeois republic." But in *Das Kapital* he sang a paean of praise to the victory of the Ten-Hours Bill and other social legislation in England. Here (as in the Inaugural Address of the First International of 1864), we learn that the lot of the working class is improving; its power and organization and understanding growing; that it is winning support from other layers of society, or classlessly, from society as a whole. "Capital is under compulsion from society. . . . The factory magnates have resigned themselves to the inevitable." The shortening of the working day by law, and all the other factory legislation, represents "the victory of a principle in which the political economy of the bourgeoisie has capitulated to the political economy of the working class . . . as the result of a half century of civil war. . . . The power of resistance of capital has gradually weakened . . . the power of the working class has grown with the number of its allies. . . . Hence the comparatively rapid advance since 1860."

The same thing was true on the Continent. "Most of the continental countries are accepting the English factory laws in more or less altered form, and in England itself their influence is widened by parliament from year to year."[11]

Thus the curve of wages and working conditions in a direction not toward but away from pauperization forces itself into his book, despite his refusal to analyze the statistical tables or to reproduce them. The picture seems clear enough, and comforting. But suddenly, at the volume's end, we run up against what is supposed to be the end term of the "law of motion of capitalist society," the *terminus ad quem* the whole of capitalist development has all along been tending, the "conclusion" to all the empirical and historical material: the general law or general line of the volume—*"The Historical Tendency of Capitalist Accumulation."*

Capital, we learn, came into the world conceived in original sin, "a congenital bloodstain on its cheek, dripping blood and dirty from head to foot, from every pore." And now by the inexorable workings of "the immanent law of capitalist production itself" it is destined to leave the world as bloodily as it entered, in an inevitable cataclysm:

Along with the constantly diminishing number of magnates of capital . . . grows the misery, oppression, slavery, degradation, exploitation. But with this grows too the revolt of the working class. . . .

The monopoly of capitalism becomes a fetter upon the mode of production. Centralization of the means of production and socialization of labor at last reach a point where they become incompatible with their capitalist integument. This integument is burst asunder. The knell of capitalist private property sounds. The expropriators are expropriated.[12]

But was it for this that all the labor was undertaken, all the reading of every writer and report since the end of 1843, the vast researches, the piling up and organization of empirical material? This conclusion not only directly contradicts what it professes to sum up: it is the "conclusion" that Marx had reached when he was cracking the bindings on the first French books of economic theory

[11] *Capital*, Chicago, 1919, Vol. I, pp. 236, 324, 327, and *Inaugural Address*, in *Ausgewaehlte Werke*, pp. 356–57.
[12] *Das Kapital*, Stuttgart, 1922, pp. 690–91; *Capital*, pp. 836–37.

and French translations of British economists back in 1844. The "general law" was in his possession, or possessed him, before his concrete, scientific "investigation" began. It is nothing more nor less than his pre-economic prophecy of 1844: the prophecy of the imminent apocalypse.

He had not undertaken his vast work in order to deduce from the Blue Books and reports how these evils could be remedied, the lot of the workingman made better, industrial society improved. Nor had he studied commercial crises to discover their causes and how they might be controlled or mitigated. Quite the contrary. He wanted to believe that the industrial cycle, once started, was "as unalterable as the motion of the heavenly bodies."[13] "Unalterable" . . . yet bound to get faster, wilder, and deeper in its gyrations until the very system explodes.

Blue Books or no Blue Books, factory laws or no factory laws, growth of the power and organization of labor or no, there must ineluctably be a steady accumulation of wealth at one pole and of misery at the other, "the lot of the laborer, be his payment high or low, must get worse." The *General Law of Capitalist Accumulation*

> . . . establishes an accumulation of misery corresponding to the accumulation of capital. The accumulation of wealth at one pole is thus at the same time the accumulation of misery, the torment of labor, slavery, ignorance, brutalization and moral degradation at the other pole.[14]

Thus by his labor the workingman strengthens the chains which bind him "like Prometheus" to the rock where the capitalist vultures of Zeus may pick at his liver. The same process of capitalist accumulation guarantees that "one capitalist will kill many," that the whole of society will become ever more proletarianized, while the handful of magnates becomes ever smaller, until the proletariat, by virtue of its numbers, its misery, its anger, its very "ignorance, brutalization, and moral degradation" becomes the Redeemer of all Mankind.[15]

---

[13] "Just as heavenly bodies once they have been hurled into a given movement always repeat the same, so it is with social production as soon as it is once thrown into that movement of alternating expansion and contraction." *Das Kapital,* Vol. I, in *Werke,* Vol. XXIII, p. 662.

[14] *Ibid.,* 675.

[15] *Ibid.* pp. 674–75.

Whatever his revisions of his early doctrine (on the national question, war, labor legislation, use of democratic suffrage) made in the light of his continuing experience with a recalcitrant and bewilderingly changing world, at the core of Marx's thought and emotions there remained to the end this irreducible holistic and apocalyptic element.

Still he continued to think of industrial society in quasi-Hegelian terms as a "system" all the parts of which were interconnected and related to each other by a common *Zeitgeist* derived from a common economic "foundation," the laws of whose functioning, and whose future changes, he thought he knew. Still he persisted in believing that whatever defects he noted were inherent in and integral to the system, and not to be removed defect by defect, nor to be outgrown by time and change (perhaps to be replaced by defects of another order), but destined to persist and grow worse until they were ended by scrapping the system in a single devastating sweep of the iron broom of history. To the end, Marx was sure that he knew the framework of rigidities beyond which the most rapidly changing society in the whole history of man could not change, except through a shattering of the hypothetically rigid framework or system. Still he assigned to a particular class the historic mission of shattering that framework and remaking the world. Still he was sure that he could descry, and at no great distance, a day of wrath and doom. Still he insisted that continuous alteration by reform and change, changed "essentially" nothing—unless perhaps such reforms prepared the chosen class to master its mission by giving it numbers, solidarity, more leisure to study and comprehend its "mission" . . . along with more reasons for wrathful determination to carry the mission out.

In a sober moment Marx had written: "No social order ever perishes before all the productive forces for which there is room in it have developed."[16] On examination, this proves no more explicit than any other of Marx's sweeping generalizations. Nor any truer, as the Chinese and Russian Revolutions were to demonstrate. Whether the one-party totalitarian systems the Russian and Chinese Communists have put in place of their old régimes is *socialist* or not is a

---

[16] *Zur Kritik der Politischen Oekenomie,* Vorwort, January 1859, in *Werke,* Vol. XIII, p. 9.

problem in semantics for adherents of the faith to decide. Great battles have been waged over it. But certainly in both cases, most clearly in the case of Russia, the old order was overthrown precisely when its productive forces were developing rapidly. With singular perversity, history has vouchsafed revolutions invoking Marx's name in countries on the eve of industrialization or in its early stages, and denied them in the advanced societies which Marx's law specifically pronounced to be alone ripe for revolution.

The pronouncement of the continuance of a social order as long as it has room for the further development of productive forces, would seem to have been made as an *ex post facto* explanation for the failure of the socialist revolution set by Marx for 1848 and reset for two years thereafter. He made the pronouncement in 1850, when he discovered that there was still enormous room "for the further development of the productive forces" in England, on the Continent, and in America. Thus it belongs to the quiet, undeclared revisions of the Marxism of 1848 made by Marx himself. Which Marxism is the more Marxist, is a question for exegetes, who differ on which Marx to quote according to their differing estimates of their own time and situation. In general we may assume that the more experienced and older Marx was the wiser, though it never occurred to him to go so far in his use of "scientific method" as to throw doubt upon his basic premises, or to ask whether there might not be "room for further development" in directions which neither resembled his systemic capitalism nor led to his systemic socialist revolution.

The industrial revolution Marx knew had not only not reached the end of its growth in 1844 when Marx first pronounced its doom, nor in 1848 when he delivered its death sentence so stirringly, nor in 1859 when he allowed it more time to live while it exhibited room for growth, nor in 1867 when he tacked the apocalypse on to the empirical material of *Das Kapital* that so manifestly contradicted it. Actually, the industrial society Marx knew was in 1867 scarcely at the beginning of a vertiginous "development of its productive forces."

The industrial revolution that Marx studied in *Das Kapital* (the change from man, animal, wind, and waterpower to steampower, and from cottage handicraft and small tool artisanship to large factories and machinofacture) was but the first of a series of industrial revolutions. It was to be followed by a second: from the age of steam to the age of electricity. And by a third, fourth, fifth and nth: conveyor belt, combustion engine, synthetic chemistry, mechanized agriculture, electronics, automation, atomic fission, atomic fusion . . . and the end of the development of the productive forces under this "system," whose only fixed point is that it has change built into it, is not in sight. True the latest revolution of atomic fusion does make a "cataclysm" unpleasantly possible, but, in any case it is not Marx's cataclysm. If it comes it may clear the ground, but not for the construction of a higher social order.

In place of the extreme polarization Marx predicted, somewhat the opposite has occurred. Far from being pauperized, the "proletariat" has won status for itself in a society from which it is no longer as completely excluded as in Marx's day. In England it has formed labor governments and forced its policies and requirements upon the opposing Conservative Party so that it becomes harder and harder for it to make its own special labor character felt in the hustings. Sometimes it complains as Marx complained of the Reform Bill, "Success is killing us." It has won the demands of the Chartists for universal suffrage, equal and secret ballot, salaried parliamentarians, the abolition of rotten boroughs, equality before the law, the partial disestablishment of the church.[17]

Along with considerable political influence, labor has won a surprising measure of social security and economic improvement. The intermediate classes which were to have been ground down into the proletariat have greatly changed their character and functions and greatly multiplied. Far from absorbing the intermediate classes and becoming virtually the whole of society, the industrial "proletariat" has actually lost in numerical weight in the total population. The service trades, which Marx contemptuously treated as sheer economic waste, "parasitic servitors to the parasites," have increased steadily in number and variety, increasingly becoming servitors to the working class as well.

To be sure, the redistribution of wealth by graduated taxation or curbs on monopoly and government regulation is not to be exaggerated. The tendency of wealth to accumulate more wealth assumes new forms and meets new limitations but continues to persist. Thus a survey of the National Bureau of Economic Research shows that in the United States since 1949 there has once more been a

---

[17] The only demand in the Charter that has not been won, and is no longer desired, is that of automatic annual election of Parliament.

trend to more wealth in fewer hands, though the degree and speed of concentration is much lower than prior to the Depression.[18]

The state, too, has proved refractory. Supposed to be the "executive committee" of a numerically dwindling handful of the bourgeoisie, its democratization has made it ever more subject to the labor vote, the farm vote, the vote of the intermediate or "middle" classes.

Out of labor's influence on government and out of a general or quite classless state of mind of society as a whole (of which the British Parliamentary Blue Books were but a harbinger), have come state regulation of economic life, the legal limitation of the working day, minimum wage, regulation of sanitary, safety, and other working conditions, legalization of the right to organize, to assemble, to petition (or demand), institutionalizing of collective bargaining, and the whole astonishing sweep of social security legislation. In democratic countries the labor vote and the farm vote have become far more important than the banker or broker or business-man vote. None of these blocs is without influence on government, whose political decisions are the result of the pushes and pulls of the various

---

[18] The survey, based upon state tax returns, purported to show that from 1929 to 1949 there had been a more equal distribution of personal holdings, but by 1953 a reversal of this trend was evident. At that point 1.6 per cent of the country's population held 30 per cent of the nation's personal wealth. Other methods of analysis would of course give other results, and the sixties have not yet been adequately studied to show whether this trend is still continuing, and if so, at what rate. But while wealth draws unto itself more wealth, both by stock and bond investment, by inside knowledge and by managerial manipulation, it is manifest that the "owning class" is losing ground to paid managerial forces in decision making and control, and often even in money-making opportunities. In any case, all this suits ill with Marx's apocalyptic picture. Neither has "one capitalist killed many," nor, what with minimum wage, social security, inheritance, income and profit taxes, and many other devices Marx did not dream of, is there any possibility of lower income groups sinking as low or the higher income groups getting such exclusive and omnipotent power as Marx, extrapolating a real or fancied trend in *laissez faire* capitalism, predicted. Indeed, this *laissez faire* picture itself has proved the biggest illusion. With the state regulating more and more of economic life, its share is actually growing faster than the share of any nongovernmental sector of society. So on the whole is the number of its employees. This is true even if we exclude the huge military establishment and the kindred fact that more and more industry works on government orders. (One worker in four is now employed in a plant that works substantially on such orders.) Two total wars and two ages of false peace that succeeded them have added their contribution to the growth of government, as has the growth of government regulation, until the very boundaries between the private and the public sectors of a mixed economy tend to blur.

blocs, with the democratic political leader ever aware of the fact that ultimately he must win the vote of Main Street rather than Wall Street if an election is to be won.

The problem of whether to sympathize with the workingmen ("the class most numerous and poor"), help him improve his lot, and integrate him into society, has gotten separated from the problem of whether society should trust its fate and future exclusively to the class which Marx said was to be ever more "brutalized, dehumanized, degraded, and outraged." To the first question, history has already answered *yes*. To the second it has answered *no*. And the workingmen themselves, where they have been consulted and given the right to decide, have given the same answer as the rest of society.

For the workingman has never accepted the "mission" which Marx assigned to him, nor consented to becoming ever more miserable, impoverished, proletarianized, or pauperized. It is precisely in fighting this supposed inexorable law of his increasing impoverishment and degradation that he has displayed tireless courage, skill, solidarity, stubbornness, incapacity to know when he has been defeated, ability to enlist the sympathy of much of the rest of society. The workingmen have had no stomach for becoming naught in order to prepare themselves for becoming all. It is against this reduction to naught that their real "class" struggle has been steadily directed. They have striven for political rights, for social status, for rights as workingmen, and for rights as citizens and men. They have striven to become something in the real world in which they live their lives and have their being, not everything in a world which exists only in the eschatological fantasy of the utopians of whom Marx, despite his disclaimers, was the most influential.

Chapter **18**

UTOPIA OR SCIENCE?

> When a man begins with the pompous formula—"the verdict
> of history is"—suspect him at once, for he is merely dressing
> up his own opinions in big words.
>
> —G. M. Trevelyan in *Clio Rediscovered*

REPEATEDLY I have called Marx a *utopian*. He would not have liked
the label, for it was his pride to call himself a *scientist* and a useful
weapon in the technique of "Marxian annihilation by labels" to call
his precursors and his rivals *utopians*. But I do not use the term as
an unfavorable epithet. It is not the fact that he criticized the evils
of his day from a standpoint of his values, nor that he dreamed of a
better world, that has caused so many brutalities to be perpetrated
in his name. It was the *hubris* that prompted him to call his critique
and proposals *scientific* that was the source of the corruption of his
dogmas and his disciples.

In the beginning, both he and Engels thought of themselves as
disciples of the utopians. Thus in 1846 Engels published a "Fragment of Fourier on Trade" with an introduction which said:

> What the French and English said as much as ten, twenty, and even
> forty years ago—and said very well, very clearly, in a beautiful style,
> the Germans have at last in the past year learned to know fragmentar-
> ily and to Hegelianize, or, in the best case, they have discovered it
> anew in a much worse, more abstract form, and printed it as a brand
> new discovery. I do not except my own works from this.

To be sure, he said nothing of Marx's work, but the stricture was not
less applicable to what Marx was then writing. After a little fun with
some of the weirder fantasies of Fourier, Engels praised his genius,
and called his "*critique of existing society* the real foundation and

the chief task of all concern with social questions."[1] That same year, Marx wrote a description of the future communist society which is the very paradigm of a utopian dream:

> . . . as soon as labor is distributed [i.e. as soon as a division of labor develops], each man has a particular, exclusive sphere of activity which is forced upon him and from which he cannot escape. He is a hunter, a fisherman, a shepherd, or a critical critic, and must remain so if he does not want to lose his means of livelihood; while in a communist society, where nobody has one exclusive sphere of activity, but each can become skilled in any branch he desires, society regulates general production and thus makes it possible for me to do one thing today and another tomorrow; to hunt in the morning, fish in the afternoon, raise cattle in the evening, criticize after dinner, whichever I please, without ever becoming hunter, fisherman, shepherd, or critic.[2]

This may be an enchanting picture but it is hardly a scientific extrapolation of the trends observable in Marx's day. The division of labor is inherent in modern industry, and not a function as Marx imagined, of the "system" of ownership. Professional specialization has developed since then beyond what the most prophetic mind could have foretold. Perhaps one can still imagine people being at the same time hunters, cowherds, and fishermen, but it is harder to imagine a man being a brain surgeon in the morning, a nuclear physicist in the afternoon, a ballet dancer or baseball player in the evening.

Engels, too, in his draft for the *Communist Manifesto* (*Grundzaetze des Kommunismus*) suggested that the abolition of private property would bring in its train a polytechnical education in which children would be trained to pass easily from job to job and men's capacities would have a "many-sided development." This would lead to the disappearance of classes as well as of the division of labor.[3]

Marx's determination not to be "utopian" soon caused him to cease writing about the nature of the society which was to take the place of the one he was calling on men to destroy. Hence the economist Abba Lerner can say with justice, "Marxists must be described as people who concentrate on destroying what we have without considering what we will get in its place." Even the devout disciple, Lenin, would one day complain:

---

[1] *MEGA*, I/4, p. 410.
[2] *Die Deutsche Ideologie*, *MEGA*, I/5, p. 22.
[3] *MEGA*, VI/1, pp. 516–19.

It did not even occur to Marx to write a word on this subject and he died without leaving a single precise quotation or irrefutable instruction on this. That is why we must get out of the difficulty entirely by our own efforts.[4]

Yet when, pressed by his rivalry with Duehring or Lassalle, Marx found himself obliged (either directly or through Engels) to suggest some picture of his imagined society of the future, we get evidence that he had done no fresh thinking since his early utopian days so that his image of the future retained many of the same features he had described in the early 1840s. Thus in his *Critique of the Gotha Program* the "higher phase of Communist society" is portrayed as one in which "the servile subjection of individuals to the division of labor will disappear," as would the differences between rural and urban life and between intellectual and physical labor.

Actually, this many-sided man free from "the crippling consequences of the division of labor" is straight out of Fourier. In describing a day in the life of an inhabitant of the future, Fourier pictures him as participating in a "hunting group," a "fishing group," an "agricultural group," and still other groups, then working in a library, and visiting a "court of arts, ball, theater, receptions."[5]

We can trace to the "utopians" many other ideas of Marx and Engels concerning the future socialist society. It was from Saint-Simon that Marx got his "From each according to his capacity, to each according to his performance." It was from Robert Owen that the idea came of combining industry and agriculture and wiping out the differences between them. Owen, too, thought that all-round practical training for all jobs required by the community would enable all members of society to be fully integrated into it and would put an end to the division of labor. It was Fourier who suggested that daily work was to be performed with joy in beautiful edifices as a necessity of life's expression, thus yielding an unprecedented increase in productivity and veritable torrents of goods.

Of the ten transitional measures which are the immediate "practical" program of the *Communist Manifesto,* the following are indebted to the "utopians":

The third, the abolition of the right of inheritance, and the fifth, the centralization of credit in the hands of the state by means of a

---

[4] Lenin, "Report of the Central Committee to the Eleventh Congress," *Selected Works,* Vol. IX, p. 338.
[5] On the indebtedness of Marx to Fourier, see H. B. Acton, *The Illusion of the Epoch,* London, 1955, pp. 233–36.

national bank with state capital and an exclusive monopoly of banking, both come from the followers of Saint-Simon (as does Lenin's whole fantastic idea that one could take over and centrally run capitalist industry simply by taking over the banks, and making of them a single state bank).

The eighth, the organization of industrial armies for agriculture—a grim thought—comes from Fourier.

The ninth, "agriculture and industry to work hand in hand," the wiping out of the distinction between town and country, and the combining of the education of the young with their training in material production, comes from Robert Owen.

As I have said elsewhere in this book, my attempt to make clear the debt that Marx owed to French "utopian" socialism should not be taken to deny originality to Marx and his imposing construct of thought, analysis, prophecy, value-charged social criticism, and vision of utopia. The point is that Marx and Engels were at such pains to conceal their debt to the utopians, or condescendingly to attenuate it, because they wished, even though perhaps only unconsciously, to conceal the core of utopia at the heart of their doctrine.

As late as November 27, 1851, Engels was still urging Marx to paint his own vision of the future society. They had withdrawn from "the party" and from active politics. The thing for Marx to do now was to finish a "thick work" of four volumes. The first two, already long contracted for, should be a critique of political economy plus the necessary elements of economic history. The third should deal with the various socialists and their theories. The fourth should contain the "so much talked of *Positive*, that is that which you 'really' want." This should be reserved for the end, Engels added, because otherwise the curiosity of the bourgeois would not carry them through all the volumes if "the great mysterium has already been revealed to them in Volume One."[6] But Marx worked too slowly to stumble into that pitfall; by the time he finished his first partial work, *Zur Kritik der politischen Oekonomie*, the masterpiece of Darwin had appeared and the determination to widen the abyss between the *utopians* and Marx's *science* had become a settled polemical policy.

Coming out of the Hegelian milieu the young Marx began avowedly as a social critic of the German society of his own day. "*War*

---

[6] *Werke*, Vol. XXVII, pp. 373-74.

against German conditions!" he cried in his first article which may be termed socialist:

> They are *beneath the level of history*, they are beneath *all criticism*, but they remain an object of criticism just as the criminal who is beneath the level of humanity remains an object for the *executioner*. In a struggle with them, criticism is no passion of the head, it is the very head of passion. It is not an anatomical knife, it is a weapon. Its object is its *enemy*, which it does not want to negate but *destroy*. . . . Its essential pathos is its indignation, its essential task, *denunciation*.[7]

The frequent italics suggest the passion of his critique, which is at the same time a declaration of war and a determination to destroy. The critique, insofar as it remained a critique, was a part of the fashionable German philosophy of the day, hence of the hated German conditions which were to be destroyed root and branch. The critique could not "realize itself without abolishing itself" along with all other existing German conditions. Hence "the weapon of criticism" must be supplemented and fulfilled by means of "criticism by weapons," for "material force could only be overthrown by material force." To get such a material force, the philosophers (the critics) would have to act so that their ideas should take possession of the masses, for "theory becomes a material force as soon as it takes possession of the masses." This could only be done by means of the "*argumentum ad hominem*," by a radical appeal to the interests of the masses, by adopting as a "*categorical imperative, the overthrow of all conditions*, in which man is a humiliated, an enslaved, a neglected, a contemptible being. . . ."[8]

This was Marx's way of declaring himself a revolutionist, of explaining to his fellow philosophers how they might find physical weapons to give a cutting edge to their weapon of criticism, why and how they must appeal to the lowest class of German society, why they must aim to humanize and transform the world if that appeal were to be attractive to the humiliated, the enslaved and the humbled. In this there was no pretense at science, it was an activist cry for a humanist remaking of an inhuman world. This and not philosophical reasoning à la Hegel was to aid man to become whole, and reconcile his existence with his human essence. "Philosophers

---

[7] "Zur Kritik der Hegelschen Rechtsphilosophie," *MEGA*, I/1, p. 609.
[8] *Ibid.*, pp. 614–15.

have hitherto only interpreted the world differently, but the point is to make it different."

Thus in Paris in early 1844, in contact with all the visions of a new social order of the French utopians, Marx took a fresh, scornful look at German conditions and declared himself a utopian activist aiming to remake the world in ways which would redeem the humiliated, the enslaved, and the outraged, recruiting these for the war on their own condition of subjection and the inhuman condition of man in contemporary society. His demand for the "objectification" or "realization" of philosophy was but a plea for bringing the way things *are* into conformity with his philosophical picture of the way things *ought to be*. Only after the miscarriage and defeat of the revolutions of 1848 did the bright vision begin to fade. Only then did Marx begin to seek solace in the effort to prove that his future society was not so much desirable and a product of reason and ethics as inevitable and a matter of science and of history, not the way things *ought* to be, but the way things *have* to be.

Marx offered two main scientific proofs of the inevitability of the social revolution for which he longed. The first was the essential or existential nature of the working class. Quite early he had said, as the reader may remember:

> Private property in any case drives itself in its national economic movement forward to its own dissolution . . . but only because it begets the proletariat *as* proletariat whose spiritual and physical misery becomes conscious misery, its dehumanization conscious and therefore self-abolishing dehumanization. . . .

> When the socialist writers ascribe this world historical role to the proletariat, this is by no means . . . because they hold the proletarians to be *gods*. Rather quite the contrary. Because the abstraction from all humanness, even from the *appearance* of being human is in practice completed in the fully formed proletariat, because in the living conditions of the proletariat all the living conditions of contemporary society are concentrated in their inhuman extreme, because the human being in him is itself lost but at the same time has won not only the theoretical consciousness of this loss . . . but also is forced to rebellion against this dehumanization, therefore the proletariat can and must emancipate itself. . . . It cannot abolish its own conditions of life without abolishing *all* the inhuman conditions of the life of present-day society which are concentrated in its situation. It is not a matter of what this or that proletarian or even the whole proletariat

imagines at one time or another to be its goal. It is a matter of *what it* [the proletariat] *is*, and what in accordance with this *being* it will historically be forced to do.[9]

Through the *Communist Manifesto*, through political articles and pamphlets, through letters of advice to disciples, through annihilating criticism of rival socialist schools and programs, through his work in the First International and his programmatic documents written for it, Marx attempted to convince the proletariat of this its essence and its historic mission.

But as we have seen the proletariat did not content itself with its depressed status nor accept the mission. Rather it waged its own "class struggle" to improve its subhuman conditions and achieve higher status, more rights, dignity, leisure, remuneration, better housing, clothing, food, sanitation, protection in the factory and in the vicissitudes of life in the society in which it found itself.

At the Sixth Congress of the Socialist International in Hamburg in 1959, Oscar Pollak, making the main analytical talk on the present state of socialist thought, complained of "the disappointment of achievement." By this he meant that the many gains made by the workingmen in Western Europe in the past fifty years, and the—to classical Marxism—incredible improvement of their economic and social standard of living, had dimmed their enthusiasm for and faith in socialism. As Marx had put it concerning the victory of the Reform Bill in England, "Our success is killing us."

The English socialist theoretician, C. A. R. Crosland has written:

Traditional socialism was largely concerned with the evils of traditional capitalism. But today traditional capitalism has been reformed and modified almost out of existence, and it is quite a different society the socialists must now concern themselves with. . . . Marx has little or nothing to offer the contemporary socialists, either in respect of practical policy, or of the correct analysis of our society, or even of the right conceptual tools or framework. . . . One of the greatest errors of Marxism was absurdly to underrate the socio-economic consequences of political democracy.

Such is the testimony of a German and an English socialist. If we turn to a spokesman for Russian Communism, we get unexpected confirmation; Nikita Sergeevich Khrushchev, the latest Soviet spokesman to pass into the limbo of unpersons, blurted out to an

---

[9] *Die Heilige Familie, MEGA,* I/3, pp. 206–07.

audience in Iowa in September 1959: "I have seen the slaves of capitalism, and they live well!"[10]

The other road that Marx followed to prove that socialism was not so much desirable according to his system of values as inevitable according to his scientific investigation of capitalist society, was the attempt to prove that inherent in the industrial economy itself were such laws as an automatic recurrence and enlargement of the crises of the business cycle leading inevitably to a final crisis or crackup; an automatic "falling rate of profit" which must continue until the prevailing system became unworkable; an automatic polarization of a few surviving capitalist giants at one pole, and all the rest of society, totally proletarianized and pauperized, at the other; a steady and automatic enlargement of the control of economics over politics in the form of ever tighter control of government by a handful of magnates and ever more oppressive use of the instruments of government by them—and other such autonomous and automatic processes, independent of the human will or human action, that in the end must lead to the eschatological cataclysm of a social revolution.

The tension between voluntarism and fatalism remained in Marx's spirit to the end, but more and more he masked his will under the protective disguise of necessity, as he did the ethical and the esthetic values which made him so powerful a critic of the evils to which he bore witness.

At Marx's graveside, his friend and lifelong collaborator, Friedrich Engels, testified to the ambiguity of Marx's thought in these words:

As Darwin discovered the law of the development of organic nature, so Marx discovered the law of the development of human history . . . as well as the special law of motion of the present-day capitalist mode of production and the civil society engendered by it. . . .

---

[10] The testimony of Oscar Pollak is from an address at the July 1959, Congress of the Socialist International in Hamburg; that of C.A.R. Crosland from his book, *The Future of Socialism*, pp. 528 ff. As for Khrushchev's off-the-cuff testimony, reported in *The New York Times* of Sept. 24, 1959, like so many of his addresses, it was censored for "Marxist" consumption inside Russia. The famous sentence was stricken out when his address was published in *Pravda*, and when the Voice of America and Radio Liberation tried to broadcast a tape recording to Russia, the Moscow radio-jamming system put all its jamming equipment on to prevent the address of Russia's chief spokesman from being heard in his own land.

After three paragraphs dealing with Marx "the man of science," Engels continued:

Above all else, Marx was a revolutionist. His real mission in life was to contribute, in one way or another, to the overthrow of capitalist society and of the state institutions which it had brought into being, to contribute to the emancipation of the modern proletariat, which *he* was the first to make conscious of its own position and its needs, conscious of the conditions of its emancipation. Fighting was his element.[11]

If increasingly in his last years Marx was to let the "man of science" displace the "man of struggle," after Marx's death, Engels carried this displacement much further in the direction of fatalism and scientific inevitability. Engels's last years, and the continuation of this trend by his close disciples, Kautsky and Plekhanov, carried this development so far that in the end socialism was literally putting all its stakes on "scientific inevitability" and the "automatic laws of capitalist development"[12]—until Lenin returned to the extreme voluntarism of the young Marx of 1844 to the middle of 1850.

But it was precisely during Marx's last years, and still more obviously during the additional twelve years by which Engels outlived him, that a striking series of politico-economic novelties or innovations made the entire concept of autonomic economic laws obsolete. The novelties in question made the abstractions of the classical economists of the eighteenth and nineteenth centuries (Adam Smith's *Wealth of Nations* was published in 1776 and Ricardo's *Principles of Political Economy and Taxation* in 1817) both obsolete and irrelevant. This was true for Adam Smith and Ricardo, for Bastiat and Malthus, no less than for Marx who derived his doctrine from the classical economists and developed it in combat with the Bastiats and Malthuses and other more nearly contemporary theorists.

These novelties are the result of the massive intervention of the modern state into sphere after sphere of the economy. Political regulation of the economy is a form of planning and control (regulation) of the "free play" of the economic process. But it was precisely from this intervention of the state that the classical econ-

---

[11] Marx-Engels, *Ausgewaehlte Werke*, Vol. II, pp. 156–57; *Selected Works*, Vol. II, pp. 153-54. (English, Moscow, 1951; German, Berlin, 1958).
[12] For an analysis of this displacement and its significance see Lichtheim, *op. cit.*, pp. 234–44.

omists, and Marx along with his masters, deliberately abstracted. Not that such intervention had ever altogether vanished from the social scene. But from the age of elaborate mercantilist regulation to the age of so-called *laissez faire* there was a notable diminution in such state intervention. Hence to the classical economists it seemed —quite legitimately—that government regulation was on the way out, that *laissez faire, laissez passer* was a worthy and enlightened motto for the modern state, that the trend toward complete freedom for the market and other economic institutions, complete nonregulation and nonintervention of politics into economics, was enlightened, progressive, and destined to continue until the state would be no more than policeman or judge to prevent crass cheating (even in this field one could rely heavily on the maxim, *caveat emptor*), or outright robbery and piracy, and unfaithfulness in contracts. The state was to diminish its intervention until it was no more than the impartial umpire who assured fairness in the rules of the game, but otherwise did not intervene at all, whether as manager, captain, or player.

Since, when Smith and Ricardo wrote, this seemed to be the long term trend, it seemed useful to abstract from the "remnants" of mercantilist state regulation and construct a model of the economy for examination in which there was a free play of economic forces "undisturbed" by political interference and unregulated by the state.

To this methodology of his classical masters, Marx added an additional consideration of his own. He not only consciously abstracted from such political forces; he held them to be nugatory as well, because of his dogma of the primacy of economics over politics. "La legislation, tant politique que civile, ne fait que prononcer, verbaliser, le vouloir des rapports économique," he wrote. (Legislation, whether political or civil, does no more than enunciate, verbalize, the will of the economic relations.)[13] And in his theorizing, he proceeded accordingly. This viewpoint, if not in Marx's version, at least in that of Adam Smith and Ricardo, was fruitful in its day.

But in place of shrinking to the vanishing point, the trend to economic regulation began to grow again as the nineteenth century advanced toward its close. The forms of state intervention into the economy and of state regulation came in time to include: protective tariffs; government marketing and withholding from the market; government ownership and government regulation of common car-

---

[13] Karl Marx, *Misère de la philosophie, MEGA,* I/6, p. 160.

riers and public utilities and other enterprises that are either of
concern to virtually all enterprises or of potential military importance; a vast construction program of roads, dams, hydroelectric
developments, bridges, railroads, canals; subsidy and other regulation of merchant fleets and air fleets; government banking, bank
regulation, fixing of interest and rediscount rates, deposit insurance,
stock-exchange regulation; cost-plus contracts, subsidy of desirable
but at the outset unprofitable industrial innovations; insurance of
profits in certain industries whether because they are in grave
trouble, or because the government deems them essential, or because they involve great masses of the population and electorate as
in the case of the farmers; price floors and price ceilings; state-
fostered cartelization and state investment in cartels in certain countries and extractive industries, and legal maintenance of competition
in others (this last has been attempted notably only in the United
States); regulation of "legitimate" competition; currency manipulation, regulation of inflow and outflow and "flight" of capital; fixing
of exchange rates; deficit spending as a deliberate policy instead of
an occasional unavoidable misfortune; employment of tax policy as
a regulator of the business cycle; the over-all organization, mobilization, and central planning of the entire economy and the establishing of priorities in men, money, and materials for the purposes of
total war;[14] rationing and price fixing in the same context; supra-
national economies such as the Inner Six, the Outer Seven, the European Common Market, and Comecon—the Soviet Bloc Council
for Mutual Economic Assistance—(all of them restrained and modified by the durability of nationalism); world-governmental banks
and technical and financial aid systems; and—in vast areas of the
world—that absolute in governmental regulation and control—
autarky.

In addition there is the whole complex of intervention in the
labor relations of industry and agriculture already referred to in the
preceding chapter: minimum wage; maximum hours; regulation of
night work, child and woman labor; sanitary conditions; length of

---

[14] In many respects the economies of the totalitarian states are economies of
total and permanent state of war, as is the psychology they seek to foster with
their fronts (ranging from agricultural and production fronts to ideological and
literary fronts), their fear of hostile, alien intention, their spy psychology, their
morbid secrecy concerning statistical matters, their total mobilization of the
laboring population, their reintroduction of the death penalty in the twentieth
century for crimes against property.

the working week; regulation of collective bargaining and safe-guarding of the right of organization of labor; unemployment insurance; retirement insurance; sickness and accident insurance, etc., and free and compulsory public education.

Whether these features are to be welcomed or feared, or noted and analyzed and their new problems faced and new safeguards set up against their abuse, the fact remains that the *laissez faire* state and the "free market" economy have vanished insofar as they ever existed. These features dominate the economy of the twentieth century. Taken together they have produced a world which makes the projections of Marx, as it does those of his classical predecessors and his contemporaneous opponents, irrelevant to today's economic scene. Not only does economics not control politics, as Marx fancied, but it is not autonomous in its development either. Often the state may achieve quite other things than it intends by its intervention, but this merely calls forth further measures of intervention. The autonomous economic constructs of the first half of the nineteenth century, from which Marx's picture of the "law of motion" derives, are as useless for understanding contemporary society as Watt's steam engine for running an airplane or a space ship.

As Hayek and Roepke have sought to keep alive the vanished dream of the "eternal harmonies" of Bastiat, so Hilferding, Luxemburg, Lenin, Bukharin, and Sternberg have sought to keep alive and enlarge the eternal disharmonies of Marx, derived from the in essence identical vanished world of autonomous economic processes.

The epigoni of the one school and the other still continue to feel at home in this world of abstract principles and of a principle of abstraction the justification for which has vanished, for only in that world can they theorize freely according to their bent, cosily abstracting from both the historical survivals of the earlier mercantilist period and the historical novelties of the second half of the nineteenth century and all of the twentieth, abstract from all the extra-economic and non-economic factors that make the real world so complex, so criss-crossed with regulation, so doctrinally unmanageable, so resistant, and so unpredictable.

Actually, both opponent schools live in a lost world, for what the latter half of the nineteenth century with its economic nationalism and awakening social conscience began, and the twentieth century with its world wars, increasing politicalization, and widespread totalitarianism have enormously accelerated, is the total breakdown of the usefulness of the very concept of autonomous economic laws driving to an inevitable end or fulfillment. And with it, the concept of "economic man," so dear to nineteenth-century theory, has become obsolete also. These things have brought in their train the total shipwreck of all the predictions, the method of approach to the economy, and the "general law of motion" that Marx derived from the transformation of these concepts into absolutes.[15]

Many of the features which Marx identified with "capitalism" were actually features of modern industry under any *ism*. Many of the evils he pointed out have been healed or have vanished, many are evils still, some of them have even grown ranker, and evils he never dreamed of have appeared.

The dwarfing of the individual when his artisan's tool grew into the mighty machine and finally into the automated plant; the weakening of the instinct of workmanship when in place of producing an entire product one does only some partial detail process; the growing division of labor and specialization in every aspect of physical, supervising, accounting, intellectual, and scientific work; the loss of individual control over tool, productive process, pace, and final product; the subordination of the individual to the specialty, the producing team, the workings of the factory or the industry; the consequent "alienation" from control of the product (an "alienation" which is perhaps capable of compensation, and in some cases of reversal, but in any case has little to do with "alienation" as used in the philosophical and existentialist sense); the lack of a rounded, all-sided development and polytechnical omnicompetence; the growth of highly specialized and esoteric branches of knowledge and of one-sided scientific and artistic-humanist cultures—these characterize modern industry and modern science whether they are subordinated to democratic controls or put to totalitarian purposes and uses.

Indeed, nowhere are these features so aggravated and their effects so uncontrolled and unrelieved as in Soviet Russia and in the blue-clad ant-heap economy and polity of totalitarian China. For here "alienation" of control extends also to the political and cultural spheres. The one-party totalist state seeks to control the individual's private life, to narrow as much as possible the scope of his privacy, to regiment his "off" or leisure time and fill it with state designated

---

[15] For the best critique of the concept of autonomous economic laws and the Marxist use of them, see Herbert Luthy, *"L'Histoire du Monde: Une Deviation?"* in *Preuves*, Paris, May, 1958, pp. 68–78.

and regulated activities, to control his very thoughts and feelings insofar as the ruling party and its ideological-political machine can get at them. All production and distribution is owned and controlled by a single owner so that there are no interstices in which an "offbeat" individual, an innovator or a dissenter can find freedom or privacy or a way of making a living. The natural mysteries of life are aggravated by becoming state secrets access to which is allowed only to a little band of infallibles, possessing an infallible doctrine, which ultimately must be interpreted by a single infallible leader, and which becomes more demanding and ruthless in its oppressiveness the more it shows itself on examination to be remote from reality. Whatever mysteries cannot be made into state monopolies and state secrets are simply declared non-existent, or, worse still, denounced as enmity to society or treason.

To the end of their days, neither Marx nor Engels nor their orthodox disciples ever succeeded in separating in their thought "capitalism" and industrialism and considering the problems of each in its own terms. Marx never addressed his powerful intellect and deeply engaged spirit to the problem of moderating the evils of large scale industrialism as such. For he began with the dogmatic and most utopian of all his assumptions, one he did not permit himself to doubt or examine as every true scientist must his major hypotheses—namely, that a mere change in property forms would end all the evils which he imperfectly experienced and perceived. His "total solution" only added a new and graver problem, the gravest of our age; namely, the problem of the total state which has a monopoly both of political and economic ownership, control, and power.

Even the limited and pluralist state, with its retention of many of the aspects of the free market, a culture and a political system free from state control, a free press, and a party system, has become large enough in its often unavoidable functions so that in its case, too, there is a problem of whether the state shall exist for the people or the people for the state. But in the totalist state, invoking the name of Marx and his simplistic, total solution through the nationalization of everything from jobs and factories to press and party and thoughts and dreams, the very problem has been—as far as the omnipresent machine can manage it—"abolished." There *homo faber* has not only lost his bit of earth and the ownership of his tools, but he has lost as well his ownership of the state and of his own organizations, which are now the state's and the party's transmission belts to tighten control of his work and his leisure, his views, his thoughts, his dreams, the very language with which he must do his thinking, and all the means of communication by which he must speak to his fellow men.[16]

As the phenomena of state-intervention, state-regulation, the welfare state and the totalitarian state grew apace, the phenomena from which classical economics had abstracted became central to the economy and tended to fill the horizon. As reality departed further and further from the abstract models based upon the autonomous working of economic forces, all schools of theoretical economics based on these assumptions went into a decline. In the economics of the schools came the age of the epigoni, the exegetes, the dogmatists, and the fragmentalists. These last abandoned an over-all view of the economy and its problems to work with particular marginal and derivative phenomena and statistical series.

In the Marxian school which had carried both the labor theory of value and the theory of the autonomy and dominance of economics over politics to the point of absurdity, the stagnation was even greater: repetition, exposition, simplification, exegesis, dogmatic deduction from untouchable first principles, authoritarian orthodoxy and a bitter war on those who hesitantly sought to re-examine the fundamentals ("revisionism"), a war made more bitter by the vague feeling of the orthodox that the first principles would not bear re-examination nor stand up to open-minded questioning.

Marxist scholarship, when it was not merely repeating, or making popularizations, simplifications, and vulgarizations of Marx's doctrines, was chiefly concerned to reduce the new phenomena of the twentieth century to manageability in terms of the dogmas of the nineteenth. Or it was occupied with the task of explaining that, even though Marx's predictions and his timetable for their fulfillment had manifestly been disproved by a recalcitrant history, all this had but been a series of detours for all sorts of special reasons,

---

[16] For an analysis of the consequent disillusionment of the European intellectual with socialism, see Richard Pipes, "The Historical Evolution of the Russian Intelligensia," in *Daedalus*, Summer 1960, pp. 469–99. For an example of one of the directions Western thinking has taken on the problem of "alienation" of the worker in modern industry, see Daniel Bell, *Work and Its Discontents*, Boston, 1956. For the oppressive power of the totalitarian state over the spirit of man, see the present writer's *Communist Totalitarianism*, Boston, 1961, "The Second Key: The Coordination of Culture," pp. 37–142.

but the general forecast had been right all along, and the general line or law of motion was about to resume its operation now that this or that detour had been safely passed and explained away.[17]

Some sought to show that "imperialism" and "colonialism" were something new in history, as if Marx had not written after the greatest age of empire building was over, and that the "third parties"—neither capital nor labor—in the backward lands had "so far" absorbed the surplus capital and surplus goods, moderated the commercial crises, and offset the falling rate of profit. But now the "third parties" were being industrialized and would pour their goods into the world market, too, thus aggravating the death throes and deepening the final crisis. As soon as the colonies became independent, capitalism in the mother country must fall.

Belgium and Holland and England and France and Spain and the United States have lost or freed their colonies now but the great detour of history perversely continues, the rate of profit perversely continues to rise and commercial crises to be somewhat moderated or flattened out. Perversely, the British workingmen continue to live well after England has lost or liberated her colonies, while the workingmen of Portugal live in miserable poverty although Portugal stubbornly holds on to hers.

A lesser Marxist scholastic operation concerned itself with softening the firm outlines of Marx's pronouncements, as when the aging Engels began to explain that economics determines politics only "in the long run," or that "pauperization" really meant not absolute increasing misery but only *relative* poverty of the worker in a world where the rich get richer at a much faster rate than the worker improves his standard of living.

Thus orthodox Marxism got more and more deeply involved in an enormous rescue operation in which it sought to explain, or explain away, the treacherous behavior of history and of actual economic development, by treating each novelty separately as a deviation from the essential and lawful which must in "the long run" still be fulfilled. All of history's slyness, unpredictability, novelty and invention are but a series of detours on a road for which the guide book is still sound. The explanations become as complicated as the courses of the stars among those who sought to hold on to the geocentric theory of the motion of the planets and the sun after

---

[17] On this see Herbert Luthy's article, already referred to, *"L'Histoire du Monde, Une Deviation?"* (See above, note 15).

Kepler had worked out a sounder and intellectually more economical picture of the universe.

But in the years 1936 to 1939 the last and greatest of the twentieth-century Marxist economists, Rudolf Hilferding, took a fresh and courageous look at the relationship between the state and the economy. The great Austrian Marxist and one-time Austrian finance minister refused to flee from Paris before the Nazi advance, as earlier he had fled from Vienna. Within two years, he was killed by the Gestapo. But in his last years he published four painfully thought out articles, signed with the pseudonym *Richard Kern*, in which he recognized the need to drop the Marxist dogma that economics determines politics and that the state is the mere instrument of a class, to wit the propertied class. He had been feeling his way toward this fundamental re-examination for several years. His point of departure was more limited than the one we have outlined in the present chapter, for the other forms of state intervention escaped him or he missed their significance. But from 1936 to 1939, he published, in all, four articles re-examining the relationship between economics and politics as it presented itself to him in the light of a period of total wars and a "permanent war economy" (*Kriegswirtschaft*).

He still maintained that the "classic" Marxist view had been sound for the "liberal era," and he showed no recognition of the role played even in Marx's day by such political interventions as protective tariffs and welfare legislation, in altering the free play of "autonomous" economic forces. Hence he dated the "new period" from the First World War, and regarded the domination of the state over the economy as distinctly a phenomenon of imperialism, war, and totalitarianism.

In the third of these four articles, published in *Neuer Vorwaerts* for January 1, 1939, Richard Kern–Hilferding wrote:

> It is becoming increasingly difficult to describe the course of economic events in purely economic terms. The laws peculiar to the capitalist economy have been progressively modified as a result of their subordination to the requirements of politics. In Japan, Russia, Germany, and Italy, a dictatorial government apparatus has acquired control of the material and human forces of production, and has compelled them to operate for the maintenance and expansion of its own power. Politics dominates economics for its own ends. . . .
>
> In Eastern and Central Europe, and in many Latin and South

American countries, political power has achieved decisive influence on economic development. And in many areas of the so-called free economy, principally in Switzerland, Belgium, Holland, the British Empire and the United States, attempts have been made to create a controlled economy. They have had considerable influence on the course of economic development, especially in France and the United States. . . .

The power of the state made the economy the servant of war [Hilferding is speaking here of the First World War], but the recognition of the possibility of state intervention in the economy persisted. The relative autonomy and independence of the economic system which characterizes the liberal era is at an end. Politics now determines the fate of the economy, and its power is apparently great enough to modify the operation of economic laws. . . . The State has been developing into an enormous apparatus with a purpose of its own. . . .[18]

These four articles of Rudolf Hilferding bring the period of classical orthodox Marxism to a belated but noble close. Henceforth only Communist ideologists and apologists regard "revisionism," that is continued scientific questioning and re-examination, as the crime of heresy. In these neo-orthodox circles, Marxism drained alike of its humane utopian values and its scientific desire to take account of empirical phenomena and data, has become an obligatory creed. One does not think, one quotes. Yet this does not prevent these self-styled orthodox from "creatively" revising Marxism beyond all recognition as *raison d'état* or party-power needs may dictate.[19]

In recent decades the economic theory of the academy has taken on a new life, posing new problems, principally those of planning on an enterprise-wide and nation-wide basis, and using new methods in their solution. This new mainstream of economic theory, having no frozen dogmas to cope with, has swept swiftly by, leaving Marxist economics eddying in its own backwater.

The new theory springs from a fresh combination of three main sources, marginal utility economics, the study of government policy, budgetary taxation, interest rate, and currency manipulation and

---

[18] The four Hilferding articles, slightly condensed and translated into English by Morris Watnick are in *Modern Review*, New York, October, 1947.

[19] Leopold Labedz in his Introduction to *Revisionism: Essays on the History of Marxist Ideas*, New York, 1962, writes: "When revision comes from above, one dogma replaces another. It is then called 'a creative development of Marxism.' When it comes from independent thinkers, it is considered heresy."

their influence on investment, employment, consumer expenditure and the business cycle (a school of theory associated with the name of Keynes), and the use of computer mathematics for a study of input, output, linear programming, and the optimum uses of scarce resources for alternative and competing aims. But this mathematics and this economic theory are precisely the computations and the theory needed for economic planning. They are most badly needed in those lands where the free market, with its automatic regulatory devices, has been destroyed in the interests of totally centralized and totally politicalized command-planning.

Yet Soviet Marxism has a threefold prejudice against using the instruments it most needs. First, the labor theory of value is totally useless in calculating rival or competing uses of scarce raw materials, capital, capital goods, energy, and labor. The labor theory of value, that central concept of classical and Marxian economics, always of dubious theoretical and nugatory practical value in market policy (price) or in enterprise policy or in national economic policy, has simply faded out. Second, Marxism hastened to ridicule the marginal utility theory when it was still in its embryonic form and was still concerned primarily with consumer choice of alternate ways of spending a limited income. The classic work of destruction of the marginal utility theory for Marxists while it was in its infancy was performed by Nikolai Bukharin in a book the title of which tells its own story: *The Economic Theory of the Leisure Class.*[20] Third, the theories associated with the name of John Maynard Keynes[21] were rejected *a priori* because they concerned themselves with the regulation of the business cycle and commercial crises, which an *ipse dixit* of Karl Marx declared could not be regulated but must grow deeper and deeper, come faster and faster, until they ended in a crackup of the system and a revolt of the proletariat. To make matters worse, the autodidact bosses of Soviet planning have a deep-seated prejudice against cybernetics and against computer operated planning,[22] and an equally deep-seated prejudice against the idea

[20] Bukharin finished his work in 1914. It was first published in Russian in 1919 and an English translation was published in New York by International Publishers in 1927.

[21] The principal works in which Keynes developed his theories were *A Tract on Monetary Reform, The End of Laissez Faire, A Treatise on Money,* and, above all, *The General Theory of Employment, Interest and Money.* The latter was published in 1936.

[22] The classic formulation of their prejudice was put into the mouth of a nineteenth century bureaucrat by the Russian satirist, Saltykov-Shchedrin "What I do not understand is dangerous for the state."

that a factory or machine can become "morally" obsolete long before it has become physically used up.

Now that these new schools are producing a new synthesis and a new and significant way of measuring value, not so much in exchange (a derivative of merchant economics) as in applied technical use for alternative purposes (a derivative of production and planning economics), nothing is so pitiful as the attempts of a few Soviet economists to borrow, or work out independently, some of the elements of this new synthesis for the purposes of Soviet planning, without revealing that they are rejecting the Marxian theory of value, or, more simply, ignoring it as a useless abstraction from the very facts that concern them as planning economists. They have been carrying on a cautious yet courageous war for the recognition of some of these new concepts and methods, a war largely associated in the technical and popular press with such names as Kantorovich, Novozhilov, the recently deceased head of the Soviet Union's first economic-mathematical laboratory, the statistician Nemchinov, and the somewhat over-publicized Liberman. Often mathematicians have been called in instead of economic theorists, since Marxian economics is so sterile, for the practical planning of the economy of this "Marxist" society.

But the specialists in power and ideology who run the Communist Party and the Soviet Union are profoundly suspicious of the move to liberate economic theory and practical planning from the inherited dogmas of Marxism, and the burdens of their excessively centralized political control.

Yet, as the rate of growth slows up, as the paperwork of centralized dogmatic allocation, quota-fixing, price-fixing etc. threatens to drown the Soviet economy in a paper sea, the dead hand of dogmatic control is forced to relax a little.

Recently, Victor Glushkov, the head of the Soviet research program in cybernetics, warned the political planning and control bureaucracy that if there did not soon come a radical reform in planning methods, in decentralization, in the developing of objective tests of success such as are supplied by the indices of profit and loss and by the free market, the number of bureaucrats engaged in planning and its paperwork would grow thirty-six-fold by 1980, and embrace the entire projected Soviet population.

The complaint is old. The dying Lenin wrote in his last active year:

The machine refused to obey the hand that guided it. It was like an automobile that is going, not in the direction of the man who is driving it, but in the direction desired by someone else, as if it were being driven by some secret, illegal hand. God knows whose. . . . Be that as it may, the car is not going in the direction the man at the wheel imagines.

And again:

The vital work we do is sinking in a dead sea of paperwork.

But the evil has grown apace, faster than the considerable growth of the heavy industry sector of the economy, and much faster than the growth of the economy as a whole. More and more plans are published, for one year, for two years, for five years, for seven years, for fifteen years, but their precision grows less and the fanfare for each of them more feeble. Almost as swiftly as they are published, they have had to be disregarded, and the attention distracted from their failure by the announcement of yet another plan.

The signs of crisis multiply. It is a crisis in centralized command planning itself, and in the blueprint for remaking man without regard to the nature of his incentives and concerns as an individual and as a member of a family. The "anarchy of the market" that Marxism was intended to abolish is as nothing compared with the "anarchy" that has set in with this overzealous, centralized command "planning."[23]

As to agriculture, the manifest bankruptcy and chronic crisis of centralized ownership and planning has been continuous since Stalin's war on the peasant and his brutal forced collectivization drive. The only thing that saves this great nation from chronic famine is the un-Marxist private parcel on which the collectivized serf is still a free peasant working for himself. With a spade, a watering can, and a back bent over the tiny plot of soil that matters to him, he raises enormously more per capita than do the tractorized and collectivized broad acres with which he feels no sense of identity, and thus he manages tolerably to feed himself, his family, and some of the neighboring towns.

Indeed, this chronic crisis in agriculture might have been anticipated from the writings of Karl Marx himself, who expressed his

---

[23] The technical press of planners, economists, and mathematical planners is filled with muted cries of alarm and a Cassandra-like despair. For those who cannot follow this literature in Russian, the following are recommended in English: Robert W. Campbell, "Marx, Kantorovich, and Novozhilov," *Slavic Review,* October 1961; Gregory Grossmann, "Scarce Capital and Soviet Doctrine," *Quarterly Journal of Economics,* August 1953; Leon Smolinski, "What Next in Soviet Planning?," *Foreign Affairs,* July 1964.

feelings toward the peasant and the free farmer by his famous phrase, "the idiocy of rural life." As Camus reminded us:

Finally the law of concentration has proved absolutely false in agricultural economy, which was treated with considerable frivolity by Marx. . . . In one of its aspects, the history of socialism in our times can be considered as the struggle between the proletarian movement and the peasant class. [Rather, I should say, between intellectuals claiming to represent the proletariat and those claiming to represent the peasantry]. . . . Marx had, in the ideological material of his time, the elements for a study of the peasant problem. But his desire to systematize made him oversimplify everything. This particular simplification was to prove expensive for the "kulaks" who constituted more than five million historic exceptions to be brought, by death and deportation, within the Marxist pattern.[24]

Hence the crisis that is manifestly building up in the Soviet Union is a crisis in the command economy, in centralized and bureaucratic planning, in collectivized agriculture, and, by virtue of their invocation of Marx's name and their attempts to follow his theories on the market economy and the labor theory of value and on nationalized "factory farms" with "labor armies," a crisis in Marxism itself.

[24] Albert Camus, The Rebel (L'Homme Révolté), New York, 1956, p. 213. On Marx's attitude toward agriculture and the peasantry see the much neglected work of David Mitrany, Marx against the Peasant: A Study in Social Dogmatism, University of North Carolina Press, 1951. Figures published by the Soviet Government in 1961 show that a mere 3.3 per cent of all the land cultivated in the U.S.S.R. was in private parcels. Without benefit of modern implements, fertilizer, etc. the potato yield was 11.6 tons per hectare on private parcels as against 7.1 tons per hectare on state and collective farms. In tons of grapes the disparity was much greater: 3.9 tons per hectare on the "socialized" as against 7.3 tons per hectare on the private parcels. Not only do the collective farmers use the private parcels to feed themselves and their families, but even the State in 1962 obtained 26 per cent of its potatoes, 7 per cent of its vegetables, 14 per cent of its cattle and poultry, 5 per cent of its milk, 15 per cent of its wool, and 34 per cent of its eggs from private farmers. (Narodnoe khozyaistvo SSSR v 1961 godu, Moscow, 1962, p. 316, and SSSR v tsifrakh v 1962 godu, Moscow, 1963, p. 172). Because of their dogmas which do not permit them to take the obvious into account in their planning if it goes "against Marxism," the Bolshevik leaders are perpetually uncomfortable about this fact. It was not because Khrushchev became an unperson, that the new leaders of the moment have given more liberty to the private parcel. It is because agriculture went so badly during the preceding year that enormous purchases had to be made abroad. If things should pick up even slightly in a good harvest, the private parcel will no doubt be subject to harassment once more. When the Devil was sick, the Devil a Saint would be; when the Devil got well, the Devil a Saint was he!

Chapter 19

DEMONOLOGY AND UTOPIA

Revolutionary chiliasm thrives best where history is imagined as having an inherent purpose which is preordained to be realized on this earth in a single, final consummation. It is such a view of history, at once teleological and cataclysmic, that has been presupposed and invoked alike by the medieval movements described in the present study and by the great totalitarian movements of our own day.
—Norman Cohen in *The Pursuit of the Millennium*

No more good must be attempted than the nation can bear.
—Thomas Jefferson on taking office in 1801

Qui veut faire l'ange, fait la bête.
—Blaise Pascal

THE SECRET of Marxism's power to survive the shipwreck of its prophecies lies in its inherently dual character.

On the one hand it claims to be a science and to have made sciences of history, sociology, economics, political philosophy and politics. But so badly has a century of actual history dealt with these claims that in lands where one is free to question, no Marxist intellectual approaches the intelligent non-believer without a large measure of what the lawyers call *confession and avoidance*.

If one presses on details, the Western Marxist is likely to discard one by one all the major results arrived at by the Marxian scientific method, insisting only on the validity of the method itself. Thus we are confronted with a spectacle that would have astonished both sides in the great revisionist controversy of the turn of the century, Bernstein and Kautsky alike. For today, *in partibus infidelium*, all

356

orthodox Marxists are at the same time revisionists, albeit reluctant ones.

If as a science Marxism has been stripped down to a method that has yielded only invalid or unmeaningful results, its real staying power lies in the fact that it is also an *ism*, i.e. a faith. It is noteworthy that the other great social thinkers of modern times do not have an *ism* attached to their names. There is no Lockeism, Smithism, Millism, Weberism, Schumpeterism, Durkheimism, Taineism, Micheletism, Rankeism, Gibbonism.

As an *ism*, Marxism is a creed to be clung to when the intellect questions and rejects. It is a deeply emotional faith, with true believers, orthodoxy and its inevitable shadow of heresy, dedication, confession, schism, anathema, excommunication, even imprisonment and execution and erasure of one's name, where the faith and the secular arm are one. When Marx's newly formed organization in Brussels numbered no more than a dozen members, Marx expelled one who had gone off to America for a (somewhat caricatured) preaching of human love as the basis of socialism when Marx was just discovering the scientific driving force of history to be class-hatred. The man thus cut off was a bit mad—he died in an insane asylum four years later—but Marx then excommunicated Wilhelm Weitling for actively opposing the decision, and was preparing to do the same with Moses Hess when the latter forestalled him by resigning. And in that same year 1846, he cast Proudhon into outer darkness too. An *ism* does not have to possess the fearful implements of state power to cut off a deviant or heretical member.

Marxism, as Marxism-Leninism in power, has more terrible weapons at its command. Until recently, when it began to fall into schism because of the Sino-Soviet rivalry between Pope and Anti-Pope, it had a single leading center on an ecumenical scale which was to the true believer both Vatican and Heaven in one. It had a single infallible and only authorized interpreter who always spoke *ex cathedra*. His powers came from an antireligious apostolic succession: Marx-Engels-Lenin-Stalin-Khrushchev—and so on as long as faith and ideologically-based power endure.

It is a faith which demands total dedication even to the sacrifice of individual judgment and conscience, one's life, and the lives of others.

None of us can be right against the Party [Trotsky told the Stalin-rigged Thirteenth Congress in 1924, after he had just narrowly lost the apostolic succession himself]. In the last instance the Party is always right, because it is *the only historical instrument which the working class possesses for the solution of its fundamental tasks*. I know that one cannot be right against the Party. One can be right only with the Party and through the Party, because History has not created any other way for the realization of one's rightness.[1]

Marx would not have put it that way, for the faith had not yet been institutionalized in a spiritual-and-temporal power, and there was no party against which he could not feel himself right, and to which he did not feel superior, even contemptuous. But his doctrine of the ineluctable mission of the working class to which Trotsky's words refer was the primary source of Leon Trotsky's pronouncement, a pronouncement which would in the end cost him his life, and in his own land where the victors write history, his honor.

The party born of that *ism* makes its dogmas the test of truth. Truth, and all pronouncements concerning it, must be approached in the party spirit which the Russian Communists call *partiinost*. There is no possibility of objective truth, outside or against the truth which Marx has revealed to them, or any corollary they have derived from it. Where the true believers have power over society, they ignore, suppress, and deny the facts which call the faith in question. Access to possible contradiction or refutation of the established truth is cut off spiritually by contempt for "alien, bourgeois science," and physically by walls and watchtowers, border guards, guns and dogs, wastelands flood-lighted, strewn with mines, and kept fresh plowed so that no footprint will be hidden. The foreign press is excluded, foreign books embargoed, foreign broadcasts jammed, "alien" views falsified, to preserve the ever more vulnerable orthodox truth from contact with "vulgar factology," thus making "truth" a prison for body and mind.

The reverse movement of fact is also suppressed, not as superficial journalism has suggested because of the "inherent secretiveness of the Russian mind" nor primarily for military reasons, but because the abolition of private property has not yielded the miraculous results which Marx and Lenin expected. In the twenties, while the Bolshevik leaders still expected that nationalization would work an economic miracle, they published their "control figures" openly and challenged the capitalist world to abolish its "economic secrets."

Their first secrecy came not in the spheres of military production but in social welfare. In 1927 they ceased publishing industrial ac-

---

[1] Isaac Deutscher, *The Prophet Unarmed*, New York, 1959, p. 139.

cident statistics. In the course of the First Five Year Plan they suppressed the statistical data on real wages, cost-of-living index, family-budget sampling, food-consumption in rural areas, prices of agricultural products in terms of industrial prices. In 1931 as forced collectivization spread disease, starvation, death, and a lower birth-rate caused by despair in the villages, they suppressed the annual figures on vital statistics. Only in the late thirties did they begin to suppress statistical series of potential military and strategic significance.

In short, not only must the truth about the outside world be kept from filtering in, the truth about life in the workers' paradise must be kept from leaking out, from becoming known inside or outside the country. To this day, after nearly half a century of "socialism" there is less straightforward and intelligible publication of statistics in Russia than there was in the first few optimistic years of the Soviet régime, or under the last two tsars.[2]

Perhaps all this is inseparable from closed societies and state enforced doctrine. One remembers that Plato too recommended for his utopia ruled by philosophers:

First, no man under forty years shall obtain permission to go abroad to whatever place it may be. Second, nobody shall obtain permission in a private capacity; in a public capacity, permission may be granted only to heralds, ambassadors, and certain missions of inspection. . . . And these men after their return will teach the young that the political institutions of other countries are inferior to their own.[3]

Today this system of foreign travel is known as "cultural exchange."

For its adepts, the doctrine is superior to mere objective fact, or, as it is called in the Soviet Union, *vulgar factology*. All facts must be relative to it since it alone is true and scientific. What challenges it must be made to conform, explained as a deviation, or explained away. When the facts are stubborn, the doctrine-in-power does whatever is necessary to subject them to its higher truth.

From the Kronstadt Insurrection which was put down with bloody measures as the work of "White Guardists and Foreign

---

[2] For a good analysis of the suppression of these figures, see Leon Herman, "Figures Unfit to Print," in *Problems of Communism*, Washington, D.C., November-December, 1964, pp. 14–22. For the fate of the statisticians and statistical journals, see my "The Great Blackout," in *Communist Totalitarianism*, Boston, 1961, pp. 137–42.

[3] *Laws*, 950 d.

Agents" while Lenin was telling his Party Congress, "They do not want the White Guard nor do they want our rule," to the Budapest uprising of 1956 which Khrushchev disposed of with tanks and the explanation that the workingmen of Budapest, led by their own Communists, were engaged in a "fascist uprising instigated by imperialist powers,"—the line is a continuous one.

"Strikes under the dictatorship of the proletariat!" a Soviet official told Emma Goldman. "There is no such thing. Against whom indeed should the workers strike? Against themselves?"

Even so did Nikolai Bukharin explain to Hamilton Fish Armstrong in 1935: "National rivalry between Communist states is by definition an impossibility."[4]

By definition, too, it is impossible for a socialist country to be imperialist. When Communist China and Communist Russia divide between them the peoples of Asiatic Turkestan, Uighurs, Kazakhs, and Kirgiz, by definition this must be a spread of civilization (socialism) and cannot be imperialistic.

Only when they begin to quarrel with each other over their shares of these unfortunate peoples, whom the tsarist and the Chinese empires and some of whom the "socialist lands" have conquered, do they begin to call each other imperialist.

With this a new ambiguity arises. But the ambiguity is only an ambiguity for the non-believer. For the true believer, one of these two great socialist powers must have remained socialist and is therefore incapable by definition of imperialism, while the other must be relapsing into a bourgeois, imperialist power. That is what makes the differences on policy between China and Russia so much more bitter than those between France and the United States. Where both acknowledge a common, infallible (scientific) doctrine, there cannot be mere difference alone; there must also be heresy.

So by definition, the interests of the working class of a given country must be identical with the interests of the whole people. By definition, the Communist Party is the vanguard of the working class, and what it says must be the voice of the working class, otherwise voiceless. By definition, the Central Committee is the spokesman for the Party. And the Presidium, the Secretariat, the *Apparat*, and ultimately the Leader, who is the undisputed and infallible interpreter of the doctrine, must speak for the Party machine, the

---

[4] Emma Goldman, *Living My Life,* New York, 1931, p. 878; Hamilton Fish Armstrong, *Tito and Goliath,* New York, 1951.

Central Committee, the Party, the working class, and the people.

Though neither Soviet Constitution nor Party Constitution provides for such a Leader, a collective leadership is never a long-run possibility. For there cannot be two rival interpretations of any application of an infallible doctrine. One interpretation has to be truth, the other antiparty heresy, lest two interpretations reintroduce the germs of a two-party system.

In short, all truths are relativized with reference to the absolute truth of Marxism-in-power, which explains the fruitlessness of so many arguments between its representatives and the representatives of non-Marxist governments.

It may seem to the non-Communist as if the Communist is simply lying when actually for him truth itself emerges only as the result of a power struggle in which the ultimate question is: which interpretation of the facts will prevail? Nor is this to him an open question, since history is on the side of his doctrine and therefore his version must win. *Weltgeschichte ist Weltgericht.* The victor will write the history which justifies him. There is no other judge than history, and in history the losers are always wrong. At least until the next turn of the wheel of fortune. But Marxism makes no allowance for this since with its victory the vicissitudes of history cease.

Such a creed is one to live and die and deal death by. It gives meaning to the life of the true believer beyond his life. And beyond that of the generation which he sacrifices on the altar of his vision of the future. He cannot understand what the historian Ranke may mean when he says: "Every epoch is immediate to God." Nor how a rebel can say with Camus: "Real generosity toward the future lies in giving all to the present." For fifty years now, the Soviet Marxists have been sacrificing present generations to a future that still refuses to arrive.

As an *ism*, Marxism in any of its varieties is charged with the deepest feeling and maintained by rationalizations fed from the wellsprings of emotion. Hence it cannot be shaken by mere rational or factual refutation of any number of its concrete propositions, even those that are central to its logical structure.

Marx himself set the pattern of scorn toward opposing views, a scorn so intense that it prevented him from considering objections raised by men. When on occasion he did correct himself, it was because stubborn facts had forced their way into his powerful mind, not because of any objection from scholarly opponents or rival socialists. We need only recall his assaults on Moses Hess and Proudhon, his threat to "excommunicate" Bakunin, his denigrating fury toward Lassalle, Engels's ponderous annihilation of Professor Duehring on Marxism's behalf, and the verdict of Marx's biographer, Werner Blumenberg: "Usually such theoretical discussion (*Auseinandersetzung*) meant that Marx also 'dispatched' (*erledigte*) his opponent in a human sense, so that personal relations with him were no longer possible."

Yet we cannot be sure that the only difference between Marx and his heirs was that the latter's treatment of those who disagreed has been implemented by the fearful instruments of power. Despite his polemical scorns and furies, there are elements in his temperament which leave room for doubt that Marx would have disposed of his opponents as Lenin and Stalin did.

There are passages in Marx which reveal his humanist values despite his attempt to suppress them, passages which display a love for European civilization despite his determination to destroy it without having any clear idea of what to preserve of it or what to put in its place. There are passages, too, indicating a belief in freedom, democracy, and human dignity.

There are other passages—far more numerous, more explicit, more charged with passion, more central to his system of thought—which hold that the only forms of humiliation and dehumanization are those connected with property relations and that the only thing needed to end them is a mere change in the form of property. Central to Marx's creed is the expectation of an economic and social miracle to take place when property is nationalized. It is, as Karl Loewith has put it, a "story of salvation in the language of economics."

It is this simplification of the manifold and complex problems of the human condition which makes Marx into a "terrible simplifier," and makes so many of his followers into internal barbarians, and nihilists concerning any standard of values outside of history by which history (and institutions) must be judged if we are to attempt to make history, as far as we can influence it, more human.

In the *Economic-Philosophical Manuscripts of 1844*, we can watch Marx actually at work in this enormous labor of reductivism. It is in this early work that he tries hardest to reduce all the essential problems of the human condition, and of the philosophy he has learned, to problems in economics. Here he professes to know what man's "essential human nature" is—a nature which existed in the Golden Age before the Fall, before the knowledge of mine and thine was discovered, and the sin of "private property" drove man out of Paradise. And he is sure that Paradise may be regained by the mere abolition of private property.

Whatever form of "alienation" Marx touches on, his explanation is always the same, his solution always the same, too. Do the philosophers talk of an alienation of man's actual existence from his true essence? The cause, Marx declares, is the fact that the workingman has to alienate the product of his hands. Someone else takes it, owns it, disposes of it, accumulates it as capital, which then rules over the workingman. The remedy? Let "society" take the completed object and the accumulated wealth, in the name of the workingman, and the alienation will cease, the workingman will become the complete human being, his existence will correspond with his essence, he will be made whole again.

Is man fated to be born into a world already given, a world physical and social which he never made and in which he is forever alien? The cause is the same; the remedy the same.

In short, all the varieties of ontological "alienation," all the intractable problems of the human condition, are reduced to the same "alienation of the workingman's product"; he then faces it as an "alien" force. And all the problems are soluble by the same economic miracle. As soon as a single monopoly state or its rulers, professing to act in his name, take over his product and the accumulated wealth, all the crippling one-sidedness of the division of labor will vanish; all the power of those who control the product will become his own socialized power over himself. It never even occurs to Marx to ask, either then or later, whether the new men who rule in his name, monopolizing in their hands economic power, political power, and power over the means of communication, may not prove more remote, alien, omnipotent, and oppressive than the diffuse and pluralistic power in the society of his day. In the *Economic-Philosophical Manuscripts of 1844* the young Marx has just begun his terrible simplification of the problems of man's condition and has just begun to work out the outlines of his prophecy of an economic miracle that will solve all problems and make all things straight.

Marx himself never chose to publish these random notes. Within a year he outgrew this phase of his development. His reductivism having been completed, the traces of the simplification are removed.

Henceforth, he will use the term *alienation* only rarely and mockingly ("to make myself comprehensible to philosophers"). By 1846 he has come to detest all appeals to humanism, to emotionalism, to sentiment of any kind, to explicit values, truth, justice, morality, human rights.

Henceforth, he will no longer deal with the *ought*, only with the scientific and inevitable *must be*. Conveniently, his *must be* is strangely like his yesterday's *ought*, but it angers him to have this noted. He will have none of yesterday's value-judgments. He excoriates those who write in such terms. He seeks to eliminate the terms themselves from the documents he prepares for the workers' organizations, and from the very vocabulary of socialism and the working class—to eliminate the whole "litany" and "stock-in-trade" of dreamers, reformers, and revolutionists who speak of freedom, justice, and humanity.

Yet singularly, for differing reasons, neo-Marxists in the free world and young rebels in the "Marxist" Communist world, turn precisely to this unpublished and repudiated work for sustenance and solace, giving it preference over the more impressive work of the mature Marx who repudiated it. For it is from the Marxism of the mature Marx that so much obvious and shocking evil has flowed.

The *Manuscripts* may exhibit Marx as a poor philosopher who willfully misunderstands the problems of the ontology which he is simplifying. And as a poor economist who does not seem to have an inkling of the fact that a single monopoly of economics, politics, communication, information, and culture may prove a far more powerful and domineering master than any of the masters in a pluralistic society. But on these *Manuscripts* are still traces of the morning dew of Marx's humanist youth and humanist values. And Marxism, forced by the tragedies and errors which its subsequent history have revealed, goes full circle back to the young Marx, before the traces of his values, his utopianism, his indebtedness to Moses Hess and Wilhelm Weitling, to Fourier and Saint-Simon, have been removed by him in a rigorous process of self-surgery.

In the free world those who appeal to the *Manuscripts* of 1844 are retreating from the shipwreck of his prophecies and the bitter fruit of Marxism-Leninism in power. They seek to show their colleagues that Marx was really an "existentialist" in line with one of the most recent fashions in philosophy. They seek to show that Marx never did outgrow this stage and that he himself was mistaken to think he did.

But in Marxist lands, where any sentence from the sacred canon may be treated as having decisive probative value, restless and rebellious intellectuals discover this, and another of Marx's manuscripts of 1844 (his critique—unfinished—of Hegel's Philosophy of Right or Law), with a joyous sense of liberation from the rigorous "science," the "value-free" prophecies, and the "inevitable law of motion" of capitalist society.

In a dictatorship, one does not think, one quotes. Marxism can be fought only in Marx's name with quotations from "the true Marx." What echoes of humanity and liberty reverberate in the closed vault of totalitarian society when youthful rebels in quest of freedom stumble over such *ipse dixits* of 1844 as *To be radical is to go to the root of things, but the root for man is man himself*. Or when they find the *categorical imperative* that *all relationships must be overthrown in which man is humbled, enslaved, abandoned, despised*. Or find *Communism* actually defined in these sketchy, cryptic and suggestive terms:

Communism as the *positive* transcendence of *private property*, as *human self-estrangement*, and therefore as the real *appropriation of the human* essence by and for man; communism therefore as the complete return of man to himself as a *social* (i.e. human) being—a return become conscious, and accomplished within the entire wealth of previous development. This communism, as fully developed naturalism, equals humanism, and as fully developed humanism, equals naturalism; it is the *genuine* resolution of the conflict between man and nature and between man and man—the true resolution of the strife between essence and existence, between objectification and self-confirmation, between freedom and necessity, between the individual and the species. Communism is the riddle of history solved, and it knows itself to be this solution.[5]

As a creed for the masses Marxism is a chiliastic drama rather than a complicated scientific exposition, the only aspect of scientism retained being the certainty of victory and the fulfillment of the prophecies. Those who accept the creed find in it assurance of their own virtue and triumph. They acquire a new freedom, for in corporate solidarity with their movement they find the justification for

[5] The first two quotations are from *Zur Kritik der Hegelschen Rechstphilosophie;* the definition of Communism is from the *Economic-Philosophical Manuscripts* and typical of its notebook form. I have used the English translation, Moscow, 1961, p. 102.

all resentments, envy, and hatred toward those outside the body of the justified.

Thus the summons to fight for the millennium is at the same time a uniter and a divider. It unites with those in the movement, and sets up a wall against other men, a defense mechanism against the need of understanding and the impulse to sympathy or pity, a wall of contempt and hatred against entire classes of society who are "historically doomed."

Having enlisted in the army of the future, one has no obligation to interest one's self in the present and its melioration. The happiness without end of future generations justifies the sacrifice of one, then of a number, of present generations, and of any number of dissenters within one's own ranks. Total abundance in the future justifies privation in the present; total future liberation the taking of any number of present lives. The true believer can overlook the living because his eyes are fixed on the boundless happiness to which he would compel them.

Such an end sanctifies all means which may be declared to lead to it. Whatever furthers the goal is good, whatever hinders it, evil. For that sacred purpose, everything is permitted.[6] With that "everything is permitted," as Camus reminds us, "the history of contemporary nihilism begins." The words themselves are the words of the Devil speaking to Ivan Karamazov:

> Man will be lifted up with a spirit of divine, titanic pride, and the man-god will appear. . . . There is no law for God. . . . "All things are permitted," and that's the end of it.

If the victory of one's own nation over other nations becomes an absolute good, then for that victory all things are permitted. Hitler is quoted by his spokesmen as believing that "Right is whatever is good for the German people." And sometimes, more esoterically, "Right is whatever is good for the movement." History will realize this good, and everything done to realize it is part of history. There is no standard outside of the goal, or outside of history, by which

---

[6] Lenin used the word, "sacred," in connection with the ruthless means used in 1918 in his "crusade for bread"—the shooting of the "speculators," those "bagmen" who brought grain to the cities to exchange for industrial goods in bags on their backs, and the collection of grain from the peasants at gun-point by workers' detachments. (See for instance the use of "crusade" and "sacred" in *Sochineniya,* Vol. XXVII, p. 398). Later Lenin repudiated these means after they had brought a catastrophic drop in the planting of grain and a string of revolts. Instead he introduced the *NEP.* But as long as he thought that those means led toward his "sacred" goal, the means themselves were sanctified.

actions are to be judged in the struggle to achieve it. That is what Camus meant by "modern nihilism."

Marx's goal is a nobler one, not the victory of a nation over other nations but of a class over other classes, of the class who, by definition, "represents the future of humanity." But Marx too finds no standards to judge history outside of history itself and this goal which he ascribes to it. The denial of values that transcend history or class begins in obscure formulations. In *Die Deutsche Ideologie* Marx wrote:

> Dissatisfaction with one's self is either dissatisfaction with one's self within a certain environment conditioning the entire personality (e.g. dissatisfaction with one's self as a worker)—or moral dissatisfaction. In the first case it is thus simultaneously, and primarily, dissatisfaction with existing conditions. In the second case it is an ideological expression of these conditions themselves, which in no way transcends them but is a part of them.[7]

Engels, on behalf of Marx and himself, in his *Anti-Duehring* carries this relativization a step further:

> Which is then the true [morality]? None of them in the sense of an absolute finality; but surely that morality will possess the most elements promising to endure which represents in the present the revolutionizing of the present, the future, hence the proletarian morality. . . .
>
> We reject every attempt to impose on us any moral dogma whatsoever as an eternal, ultimate, and forever immutable moral law on the pretext that the moral world also has its enduring principles. . . .
> We maintain on the contrary that all moral theory up to now is the product, in the last instance, of its corresponding economic social situation. And as society until now has moved in class contradictions, the morality was always a class morality. . . .[8]

Lenin took this class morality from Marx and Engels, and carried it still further, with an intelligence trained to unmask moral forces as sloppy and hypocritical ideologies, and to interpret human affairs wholly in terms of interest, power, struggle, and historical necessity. Lenin's own morality was entirely warlike—what furthered the struggle was good, what hampered it bad. To the idealists of the Young Communist League in 1920 he said:

---

[7] *MEGA,* I/5, p. 357.
[8] Engels, *Anti-Duehring,* in *Werke,* Vol. XX, pp. 87–88.

Is there such a thing as Communist morality? Of course there is.
. . . In what sense do we repudiate morality, repudiate ethics?

All morality, taken from outside of humanity, outside of class, we
repudiate. . . . We say that our morality is completely subordinated
to the interests of the class struggle of the proletariat. Our morality is
deduced from the interests of the class struggle of the proletariat.
. . . Communist morality is that which serves this struggle. . . .
When they speak to us of morality, we say: for a Communist, morality is entirely in this firm solidary discipline and conscious mass
struggle against the exploiters.[9]

Thus Lenin left his disciples with a morality which completely
relativized all ethical values defining them only in terms of service to
the party and success in a perpetual war. But party interest, and
party right and wrong are relative, too, since they change with
changing strategic and tactical situations, with the fortunes of the
unending war, and with the wisdom of a Lenin, a Stalin, a Khrushchev, or an X, who gives the marching orders.

"Blind, total subjection to the Party thus remains the only straw
to which the practical reason [and the emotional faith] of Communists can cling."[10] This is still a religion or faith, and a moral
code of sorts, but a thin and impoverished one, not to be distinguished from immorality in the service of the same cause. Here is its
expression in the official organ of the *Cheka, Krasnyi Mech* (Red
Sword), No. 1, August 18, 1919:

Ours is a new moral code. Our humanitarianism is absolute, for it is
based on the glorious ideal of the abolition of tyranny and oppression.
All is permitted for us, for we are the first in the world to draw the
sword not in behalf of enslavement and oppression but for the sake of
freedom and emancipation from servitude.

Out of this new moral code in which "all is permitted" came the
"liquidation of the kulaks as a class," the forced collectivization, the
concentration camps, the show trials and confessions, the blood
purges, the grisly spectacle of selective rehabilitations engineered by
those who share guilt for the murders which they now repudiate,
but fail to repent. The rehabilitations are welcome, though they
cannot resurrect. But there can be no forgiveness where there is no
repentance, and where there is no attempt to devise such checks on

---

9 "Tasks of the League of Youth," *Sochineniya*, Vol. XXXI, pp. 266–68.
10 Gerhart Niemeyer, "Lenin and the Total Critique of Society," *The Review of
Politics*, Oct. 1964, p. 502.

the flow of power to the top as may make another such spectacle less likely or less possible.

In an age prepared for by nearly two thousand years of Christianity with its millennial expectations, when the faith of millions has grown dim and the altar seems vacant of its image, Marxism has arisen to offer a fresh, antireligious religion, a new faith, passionate and demanding, a new vision of the Last Things, a new Apocalypse, and a new Paradise. Like the Apocalypse of the Bible, the Revolution is a day of judgment when the mighty shall be humbled and those of low degree exalted. It is the beginning of a Millennium (the very word is the same), a new thousand-year reign of historyless history.

Things will then be subject to and fully possessed by generic man, for everything will be held in his name. Life will lose its uncertainties and cease to play unexpected tricks upon men, for everything will be planned. Who the planners will be, how they will be chosen, how removed or how perpetuate themselves, how the plan will be enforced, what be done to those who have other plans or do not joyously or willingly take their place in the over-all mechanism—to ask such questions now is to be not scientific but utopian, and even "philistine."[11]

With a single leap, men will spring from the "Kingdom of Necessity" into the "Kingdom of Freedom," thenceforth to make their own history, a history without the driving force of the class struggle or the locomotive of revolutions, a history in its essentials unchanging, totally under control, given a new meaning and a new end in time— the "end of prehistory."[12]

Marx's doctrine took possession of men's imaginations while the teachings of a Comte, a Buckle or a Taine were relegated to the scholar's study because only Marx's doctrine possessed true dramatic and epic qualities: a hero, a villain, a happy ending in the triumph of the lowly, the children of light, over the mighty, the sons of darkness. Misery and outrage themselves are what fit the hero for his role and give evidence that his victory is certain. Blessed are the

---

[11] "It is W's [Wilhelm Liebknecht's] mania," Engels wrote to Marx on May 28, 1876, "to remedy the lack in our theory, to have to answer every philistine's objection, and to have a picture of the future society, because you see even the philistine asks about it."
[12] Marx in *Zur Kritik der politischen Oekonomie, Werke*, Vol. XIII, p. 9; Engels in *Anti-Duehring, Werke*, Vol. XX, p. 264.

poor for they shall inherit the earth. The disinherited becomes the redeemer, not only of himself, but of all mankind. The roots of this vision are deep in religious faith and in folklore.

With the apotheosis of the proletarian, man will at last become as God, no longer the humble, inquiring, self-doubting student of nature and her laws which in part he adapts to his purposes, but the master of nature and his own nature, the master of history and its maker, the master, knower and maker of his own destiny, the creator of his own world, the Prometheus who dispossesses the gods and becomes as God, the Saviour of himself who makes his kingdom come on earth. For this supreme terrestrial drama, Marxism provides a Science, a Script, a Bible, a Church Militant, a prophetic certitude, a transposition into secular terms of the Apocalypse.

Thus Marxism—as Henri de Man wrote striving to explain its attraction for him—seems "as certain as science, as integral as religion." It is a "secularized sociology," a scientific faith, a "story of salvation told in the language of economics."[13]

The Hebrew-Christian Messianic expectation is fused with the worship of Science, the Faustian Devil of the Middle Ages and the fashionable deity of nineteenth-century secular worship. Thus in Marxism the Devil of Faust and the Man-God of Christianity become one.

For the better part of two centuries we have been living in an age of rapid, continuous, irregular, and unpredictable change—more rapid and unsettling than at any time in history, at least since the great changes attendant upon the domestication of plants and animals. These cumulative changes represent a mutation or revolution in the economic, social, political, cultural, spiritual, and even biological life of mankind—a radical increase in mobility and restlessness, in the means of communication and information (and the compelling power of misinformation), in population and its concentration, in the development of urban life, in the degree of automation, specialization, and division of labor, in the ways of life and thought.

Each achievement and triumph has brought with it new problems. The problem of the population explosion arises just as the problem of poverty and the precariousness of life seem close to solution. As the invention of devices and civic practices makes it

---

[13] The last two quotations are from Irving Fetscher, "Marxismusstudien," in *Soviet Survey*, July–September, 1960. He derives the first from Ernst Bloch and the second from Karl Loewith.

possible for all men to learn to read, it becomes harder for those who can read to know what to read, how to choose their reading, defend themselves against indoctrination and the tyranny of persuasive rhetoric, keep their heads above the flood of printed trash.

This great "acceleration of history" originated in the West, with its greater dynamism and openness; with its disbelief in fatalism; its creeds and social arrangements implying greater freedom of the individual to make changes in his own life, thereby contributing unwittingly to the augmentation of the flood of general social change, and its comparative absence of a rigid framework of paralyzing institutions.[14]

For this rapid acceleration of history there has been no central plan, no single directing center, no general theory, no expressed intention, at most a common mood, never a common blueprint. In each country it has proceeded according to that country's own past and traditions, the nature and accidents of its own history, the character of its history-making men, the nature of its imitations and siftings into assimilable form of what it borrows from other lands.

In those societies where adjustments to the new conditions and possibilities were made most readily and willingly, without too much time lag, even if fumblingly and incompletely, change has taken place by and large without great friction or internal strife, and without the necessity for a chiliastic myth to solace the desperate and despairing. In those lands where traditions or institutions or men in power have inhibited timely adjustments, there have been political explosions to which we attach the term *revolution* in its narrower sense, often accompanied by millenarian moods and movements, religious or secular.

In the first set of countries, among which we may instance the British lands from England to Australia and New Zealand, the United States, Belgium, Holland, Switzerland, Norway, Sweden, and Denmark, the general attitude has on the whole been unfavorable to revolutionary chiliastic moods. (The same has been true for quite other reasons in such lands as India with their built-in stability, their deeply rooted, widely accepted, and religiously sanctioned

---

[14] On the rigid institutional framework of despotism, its built-in staying powers, and its inhibiting effect upon various types of change, see the author's "The Durability of Despotism" in *Communist Totalitarianism*, Boston, 1961, pp. 270–93. The first four pages of this essay deal with "rigid institutional frameworks" in general, the rest with the durability of despotism in the Soviet system.

caste system, their fatalism, their comparative immunity to social and political and economic change—until the rude knocking on their doors of the Western invader awakened them from their "millennial slumber.")

In the "Western" lands enumerated above, not the whole West by any means, there has gradually grown up, though with great variations, an awareness that history is an immensely complex and contingent process, full of novelty, accident, the unpredictable, with no predetermined course nor settled formulas for change.

With it has come an awareness that every action turns out differently in some respects than intended; that every willed change has unwilled consequences; that every problem solved opens up new problems; that there are retrogressions as well as advances, and changes which are neither the one nor the other; that man's efforts to improve the human condition and his control of his life is a piecemeal, modest, unending labor; that many human problems remain, as before—and perhaps forever—insoluble; that man's intelligence is but a feeble torch to illuminate a vast and inscrutable universe, the very reason for the existence of which is an unanswerable mystery, unless the answer is shifted one remove to rest on the will of the Creator.

There is a greater awareness, too, of the intractable recalcitrance of life and the universe in which it finds itself; of how much wider and deeper its non-rational aspects are than its rational; of the stubborn, and probably wise refusal of life to submit itself wholly to rational planning, to a central command or a single, self-appointed draftsman's blueprint, which he cannot begin to put into execution before he has destroyed everything which already exists, has grown up, and stands in his way.

To these knowledges we must add an awareness of how small the known is of which we are so inordinately proud, and how vast the unknown, and vaster still the unknowable, an awareness of man's limitations in the midst of his achievements, and the core of life's uncertainty, spontaneity, ambiguity and mystery.

This is no absolute pessimism which despairs of action or piecemeal improvement, but a sense of limits and proportion, a proper humility before man's inability to become totally the master of his own spirit or of nature, many of whose laws he may learn to use and adapt to his requirements but of whom he can never, become "the master."

Such a view of the world and of man and his limitations has

prompted men in the lands where it prevails to work assiduously and unceasingly at the correcting of evils as they develop or are recognized as soluble, to seek to enlarge the scope of living and reduce the burden of suffering. But they have not provided the climate for revolutionary chiliasm nor encouraged megalomaniacal efforts to remake the world once and for all by force according to some one man's blueprint.[15]

It may be urged that these awarenesses and this perception of limits are of recent origin, a by-product of the terrible outcome of the totalitarian experiments in the remaking of men and nations. But this is only partly true.

No doubt, recent grim experiences have reinforced this strain in Western thought, but the strain itself is of great age and has competed in many periods with the rival strains of chiliastic expectation, of hardened opposition to all change, or denial of man's capacity to influence his history and society at all.

In many periods of its history, we find the church reminding us that man, being capable of evil, cannot be entrusted with unrestricted power. Its doctrine of natural law is a doctrine of limits and of inalienable rights, backed by an insistence on a moral judgment of the action and will even of princes, and an ultimate day of reckoning for the powerful and the lowly alike.

So too the English doctrine of a dense continuity of precedent, the inviolability of the person, the regarding of each man's home as his "castle," the prohibition of cruel and unusual punishment, the requirement of a trial by a jury of one's peers, and all the manifold protections and limitations on power extended by precedent, or written into the American Constitution, and enlarged by judicial interpretation and custom, represent restrictions on arbitrary power and gradual extensions of the rights of man.

Even classic absolutism in the West was never total but limited, limited by rival centers of power, castles, church militant, walled cities, whose consent to levies of men and money must be secured. And limited both for technological reasons and by virtue of the ruler's essential outlook, to include a recognition that there is a wide variety of spheres and levels of personal and collective endeavor which are outside the purview of politics and power.

If we go back to the ancient Greek sources of our civilization, alongside the totalist picture of a Plato, we find a Socrates urging us

---

[15] On this see Norman Cohen, *The Pursuit of the Millennium,* Fairlawn, New Jersey, 1957, pp. 307–14.

to be reasonable in the only way men can be reasonable, by questioning our preconceptions and judgments and by "having only a hesitating confidence in human reason." We find Democritus reminding us that "every man is a little world of his own." We find Nemesis, daughter of Night, who represented the righteous anger of the gods toward the proud, the insolent, the breakers of the laws: a goddess of moderation, the implacable enemy of the immoderate. On the whole, the spirit of the classic Greek civilization may be summed up in the virtue of a sense of limits and moderation, and a rejection of excess.[16] We need not pay attention to the argument whether this spirit is "Mediterranean" or "Western," or how widely it is spread. Suffice to note that there are lands and times which possess it and lands and times which do not. In any case it is a tradition of our culture on which we can build. Its spirit was admirably summed up by Charles Beard after a lifetime spent in the study of history: *Walk lightly. Things are not so simple.*

This is not to say that we must be the mere playthings of changes we can neither understand nor direct. Our social environment is, after all, man-made. Many of its institutions embody years and centuries of organic growth, of which the worthwhile and still viable elements must be jealously preserved, and the outlived sloughed off. ("Prove all things, and hold on to that which is good.") They are neither the work of God nor of an inanimate and non-human natural law, but the results—expected and unexpected—of human actions, human choices and decisions, human habits and beliefs, and the requirements of man as a human and social animal, endowed, at least potentially, with a sense of his own individual interests, aims and worth, and an awareness of past and future such as is not given to other animals, along with instincts and biological traits that are common to the animal kingdom.

Our institutions can be shaped, influenced and altered by human actions, choices, and decisions. But this does not mean that they are

---

[16] Thus Camus writes: "The idea of innocence opposed to guilt, the concept of all history as summed up in the struggle between good and evil, was foreign to the Greeks. In their universe there were more mistakes than crimes, and the only definitive crime was excess. In a world entirely dominated by history, such as ours threatens to become, there are no longer any mistakes but only crimes, of which the greatest is moderation. . . . The Greeks never made the human mind into an armed camp, and in this respect we are inferior to them." Albert Camus, *The Rebel,* New York, 1958, p. 28, a revision of his *L'Homme Révolté,* Paris, 1951.

consciously designed or rationally explicable. Even those which arise because of our conscious actions and intentions are as a rule the indirect and unintended, often the unwanted by-products of those very actions.[17]

Neither man's world, nor his society, nor his actions, nor his self, is totally penetrated by consciousness or reason or totally understood by him. All he can do is turn the light of reason upon them and hope that it will provide some illumination, remembering that we are neither perfect, nor unlimited in our powers; omniscient neither in our knowledge of ourself nor of our world. To think otherwise is to nourish delusions that border on the paranoid.

Indeed, to paraphrase Marx, such ideas, "once they take possession of the masses," and of some militant party that instructs, leads, then takes power through and rules over them, do become paranoid.

If one would arrive at an adequate interpretation whether of the outbreaks of revolutionary chiliasm which occurred during the Middle Ages or of the totalitarian movements which have arisen during the last couple of generations [writes Norman Cohen], one cannot afford to ignore the psychic content of the phantasies which have inspired them. And these phantasies are precisely such as are commonly found in individual cases of paranoia. The megalomaniac view of oneself as the Elect, wholly good, abominably persecuted, yet assured of ultimate triumph; the attribution of gigantic and demonic powers to the adversary; the refusal to accept the ineluctable limitations and imperfections of human existence, such as transience, dissension, conflict, fallibility whether intellectual or moral; the obsession with inerrable prophecies—these attitudes are symptoms which together constitute the unmistakable syndrome of paranoia. But a paranoiac delusion does not cease to be so because it is shared by many individuals, nor yet because these individuals have real and ample grounds for regarding themselves as victims of oppression. What is decisive is that objective situations of a given type are constantly interpreted in terms of psychic conflicts which themselves remain unconscious; so that the interpretations are systematized misinterpretations, always gross and often grotesque. . . . In our own time National-Socialist and Communist leaders, despite the hard-headed realism which has characterized their tactics ["There is method in their madness"], have exhibited and imparted to their followers a truly psychotic irrationality wherever the eschatological phantasy it-

---

17 *Cf.* the French proverb: *"Il n'y a que le provisoire qui dure."*

self has been involved. It is not a matter of ruthlessness, for ordinary interest groups will use ruthlessly whatever power they possess if the interests are important enough. It is a matter of ruthlessness directed toward an end which by its very nature cannot be realized—toward a total and final solution such as cannot be attained at any actual time, but only in the timeless and autistic realm of phantasy. Chilias-tically minded movements are ruthless not simply in order to safe-guard or further specific interests but also—and above all—in an effort to clear the way for the Millennium. What else can have in-duced the Nazis, in the middle of a desperate war, to allot manpower, money and materials to the wholly irrelevant enterprise of exterminat-ing millions of Jews ["the final solution"]?[18]

In the case of the Communists Mr. Cohen instances the example of their persistence in seeing ever greater misery and impoverish-ment of the working class in lands "where an *embourgeoisement* has been in progress for generations." He might well have instanced the killing by Stalin of virtually all his general staff (seventy-five per cent from the rank of colonel up) on the eve of war, and of all his leading factory-heads and technicians when he was trying to catch up with and surpass the West industrially.

It has been argued that not the chiliastic fantasy but only the personality of a single individual, Joseph Stalin or Adolph Hitler, was paranoid. But this raises the question: What is there in the nature of these two rival and in so many ways opposite totalitarian systems that makes it possible for a paranoiac to rise to the top and play so well the leading role in great societies previously distin-guished for their humanist cultures?

There is a wide range of utopias, a spectrum that goes from the aspiration to make the world a better place to live in to an aspiration to destroy all that exists and force the world into total, final, all-out, and all-at-once perfection.

Utopianism is worthy of respect, and admiration, insofar as it represents an assertion of the will to improve the world and strive toward "the good life" or "the good society." It is worthy of a ra-tional man's approval insofar as it denies that history is blindly determined and denies that human effort and human vision are

18 Norman Cohen, *The Pursuit of the Millennium,* pp. 309–10.

powerless to inform it. This utopianism, which is not bereft of a sense of limits, strictly speaking should be called meliorism.

But the line between the realistic and the paranoid, like the line between the angelic and the satanic, is an uncertain one. All who dream of making the world a better place to live in may be credited at the outset with a touch of the angelic. But at a point which cannot be clearly marked off, that touch of the angelic, so ready to become too proud and too certain of itself, may exceed its proper limits. Then it becomes demonic.

It is at that point that pity for the sufferings of one's less fortunate fellows turns into a detachment from their suffering. In its place arises the conviction that the suffering cannot be assuaged without following a particular blueprint. With that the utopia without limits becomes a defense mechanism against the impulse to pity and to help. Its place is taken by a desire for greater suffering to hasten the great day of revolt. ("It will have to get worse before it can get better.")

Thus it is that limitless utopianism may become a barrier to striving for reforms, instill a contempt for reforms, prevent genuine involvement in the present because of concern only with the future. At this point dreams of justice turn into nightmares of tyranny. Even the tyrant becomes the prisoner of his tyranny, as the fate of a Trotsky, the fate of a Stalin, and the fate of a Khrushchev, has each in its way made clear. As even a jailer or the builder of a Berlin Wall must know, when you wall in your prisoners you must needs wall yourself in with them. For freedom, like love, is something you cannot keep yourself without sharing it with others.

The history of chiliastic dreams makes it clear that with them comes nihilism as to the means, for the means are rendered sacred by the end they serve. With that the end recedes into the distance, losing its own justification, and thereby losing whatever power it may have had to justify. The means, for their part, such as power, and the violence that comes from a monopoly of the means of persuasion, become ends in themselves, leading inexorably toward ends of their own that have nothing in common with the original dream. This bitter discovery has been made many times in the past, and is being made afresh in our time. None other than Saint-Just rises from the ashes of his dream to remind us:

When all the stones are cut to build the structure of freedom—you can build a palace or a tomb of the self-same stones.

And in our own day, the voice of a Polish Communist poet admonishes us in the name of the new economy that "out of one cross, two gallows can be made."

So Isaac Rosenfeld, the American literary critic, wrote of the utopian expectations of his generation:

To us has been willed also a fortune; as yet it has no value except in our own circle. . . . But what a fortune! The whole world! Some day the whole world will actually fall into our hands! Then, where shall we hide?

In March 1850, Marx and Engels sent out a circular to the members of the Communist League in which they called for "the most decisive centralization of power in the hands of the state." When Marx wrote those lines, he was obsessed by the need for the unification of Germany into a single "indivisible German Republic." Yet, though Germany was unified within his lifetime, he never recalled the words, nor limited their scope.

Except for his discussion of the right of recall of officials and the limitation of their wage to that of skilled workers in his pages on the mythical Paris Commune, there is nothing in his writings suggesting limitations on the power of the state or its officials, but many pages both on economics and politics strongly suggesting the opposite. Nowhere has Marx or Engels written about the rights of the individual as against the state, the rights of the local community or the non-state organization, or the possible line of demarcation where political power ends and private rights and simple privacy begin. There is nothing about how state officials shall be chosen or how the state should be controlled by "the class" or by society—why bother when your blueprint assures you that the state must "wither away"? There is nothing about limitations on the dictatorship of the proletariat, nor any clear statement of what they meant by it. Neither Marx nor Engels ever asked the simple yet all-important political question, *Quis custodiet custodes?* Nowhere is there any suggestion that more important than the problem of *Who shall be the rulers?* or *How shall we select them?* is the problem *How shall we tame them?* and *What part of our lives shall be free from their scrutiny and control?*

Nowhere in the writings of the founding fathers is there so much as an inkling that the real problem of politics and economics is the problem of power, and not the nominal title to possession of property.

So sure were Marx and Engels that the power born of their blueprint must be beneficent and worthy of the most decisive centralization of might in its hands that it never occurred to them to note that power is most dangerous when it is concentrated in the hands of men who are absolutely sure of their benevolent intentions. Thus Justice Brandeis, having our own "good government" in mind, warned on occasion:

> Experience teaches us to be most on our guard to protect liberty when the government's purposes are beneficent. Men born to freedom are naturally alert to repel invasion of their liberty by evil-minded rulers. The greatest dangers to liberty lurk in insidious encroachment by men of zeal, well meaning but without understanding.

If that be so, how much more dangerous are the encroachments on freedom by rulers who are not only sure of their beneficence but of their all-knowing wisdom, nourishing as they do the magnificent presumption that they are the masters of a philosophical and scientific system based on the knowledge of the laws of history, and bent on subjecting to their infallible science all spheres of life, economic, political, social, cultural, and private. "For who can rule men if not he who holds their conscience and their bread in his hands?" How long can one compel enthusiasm for one's blueprint and one's wisdom without the aid of the police? And how can we check on our rulers or they on themselves, if their wisdom is certified in advance, or can only be checked generations hence when their ever-receding goal is attained in the fullness of time?

It was not the dream of a better world that was the mortal fault in Marx and the danger in his doctrine. This dream he shared with many generous men of every generation including his own.

The evil inhered in the suppression of the value-judgments by which he arrived at his vision, and of the very awareness of their role. The evil lay in pronouncing his dream to be science while he pronounced all other value-judgments concerning history and society to be "utopian" or contemptible.

For to pronounce his dream to be the end result of a scientific investigation of reality, not even an hypothesis of which it is science's duty and custom to doubt but a scientifically proved conclusion and system of thought—was to pronounce his vision to be inevitable, to give to those who possessed it, or were possessed by it, an illusion of their own infallibility, and of the firm support of history. Hence, also, of the predestined and unchallengeable right to enforce their blueprint upon other more ignorant, recalcitrant, reluctant men. What mercy should be shown to men who stood in the way of History and opposed her will, who rejected the tenets of science and refused to abide by them? The deadly epithet to use on them was not antihistorical or antiscientific but counterrevolutionary. And, since one's doctrine was by definition the will of the people, an "enemy of the people" as well.

Marx's merit was to ask large questions, and sociology and economics are the richer for his having asked them. His defect was to give shallow, oversimplified, dogmatic answers, to advance them, not tentatively as his own provisional answers, but categorically as the answers of History and Science to man's questions concerning his society.

This it was that gave Lenin the illusion that he could not be wrong, and that those who questioned him or differed with him on any question large or small which he made a pundonor, could not be right. Their arguments need not be answered since they were arguing against science; they need only be discredited so that they would lose their power to stand in science's or history's way.

Even to dream a slightly different dream was to sin against science, to be a heretic, a willful obstructionist in the path of history. Those who knew that they had mastered the infallible doctrine and foreknew the inevitable future felt a self-evident right, nay duty, to shove aside and "sweep into the dustbin of history" (the words are Trotsky's) whoever and whatever stood in history's way.

Those who mastered this doctrine which was the philosophy and science of the proletariat by existential definition, were by definition those who "saw farther than the rest" (*The Communist Manifesto*). They were the vanguard of the proletariat and of society, with the obligation to act as guardians of the rest.

For men thus armed, as Trotsky wrote even after he had fallen from power and been exiled, in his *Their Morals and Ours*,[19] "questions of revolutionary morality fuse with questions of revolutionary strategy and tactics."

---

[19] Published in 1938, two years before his murder at Stalin's order. It is to be found in its most accessible form in *The Basic Writings of Trotsky*, edited and introduced by Irving Howe, New York, 1963.

To those who are sure with a scientific certainty and faith that they are right and are fulfilling history's immanent will, to those sure furthermore that the sole way to fulfillment is in their custody and theirs alone, what shall not be permitted? Again to quote the eloquent Trotsky from the same work published so shortly before the Alpine pick of "history" directed by another master of its secrets shattered his powerful brain:

> A society without social contradictions will naturally be a society without lies and violence. However, there is no way of building a bridge to that society save by revolutionary, that is, violent, means. . . . Thus "lying and worse" are an inseparable part of the class struggle even in its most elementary form. It remains to add that the very conception of *truth* and *lie* was born of social contradictions.[20]

Could nihilism or moral relativism go any further?

History does not say whether the mind and hand that directed the Alpine pick was executing her will, or the crushed brain that had criticized Stalin's methods of doing things in History's name, was expressing her will. History has no answers to such questions. Man's judgments of historical acts, including Stalin's, Trotsky's, and Hitler's, all of which are part of history, have to be sought outside of history if history is to be humanized. History becomes more brutal in proportion as man abdicates his values or seeks to derive them entirely from "history's will."

The last question that remains for us to ask is: Would Marx have recognized the work of his disciples as the fulfillment of his doctrine or its precedent dream? On this question we can give no answer, for the thought and writings of Marx are ambiguous here, too. Indeed, in all the ambiguous heritage of Marxism, this is the greatest ambiguity of all.

---

[20] *Ibid.*, pp. 387 and 396.

INDEX